MANAGEMENT
Selected
Readings

Management
SELECTED
READINGS

GEORGE R. TERRY, Ph.D.

Professor of General Business Administration
College of Business
Ball State University

 1973

RICHARD D. IRWIN, INC. *Homewood, Illinois 60430*
IRWIN-DORSEY INTERNATIONAL *London, England WC2H 9NJ*
IRWIN-DORSEY LIMITED *Georgetown, Ontario L7G 4B3*

First Printing, January 1973
Second Printing, June 1974

ISBN 0-256-01438-8
Library of Congress Catalog Card No. 72–90536
Printed in the United States of America

Preface

Management literature is extensive; it covers a wide spectrum of disciplines and topics. Indeed, the availability of management material showing current trends, useful techniques, basic concepts, and research findings is so extensive that the management reader has difficulty in selecting what to read in order to be aware of significant developments and to be informed of recent management activities.

The purpose of *Management: Selected Readings* is to provide within a useful framework a satisfactory collection of selected readings of helpful management material giving useful explanations of concepts, examples of practical applications, and new thoughts and techniques of management. The book is assembled to provide a convenient, concise, and challenging one-volume panorama of contemporary managerial thought.

This book serves as a supplement to any management text. A grid, or cross reference table, suggesting what readings go with what chapter of various management texts, is included in this volume immediately following the Table of Contents. Also, this book can be used as the main text for seminars, managerial development groups, or managerial discussion meetings. In addition, it is helpful for students in independent study and for practicing managers who wish to update their understanding of current management.

Featured at the end of each reading are questions designed to incite discussion about issues raised in the article. Furthermore, these questions provide practice in extracting the most pertinent thoughts of the reading and also present the opportunity for self-testing for the reading's content.

The articles included were selected from a vast quantity of management literature. Efforts were made to include an article that effectively expresses an important managerial issue. However, materials presenting different views, concepts, and approaches are included so that the total package of readings offers an inclusive and balanced coverage of management thought. Both long and short articles, dealing with management theory, practice, continuing analysis, research, and philosophy are included. The criteria employed in deciding what material to include were articles featuring: (1) a subject of contemporary interest and importance, (2) clearly expressed ideas and readability for the management student or trainee, (3) recent publication (preferably within the last two or three years), (4) stimulation of interest in and discussion of management, and (5) maximum contribution to the reader's understanding and use of management.

The book is organized around eleven parts. At the beginning of each part is a short commentary which sets the perspective and gives guidance for the readings that follow. The eleven parts are management objectives, values and social considerations in management, dynamics of management, systems, computers, and quantitative techniques, decision making, planning, organizing, management and human behavior, actuating, controlling, and the future and management. These major parts supply a broad continuum of modern management. A total of forty-two readings make up the book.

Deep appreciation is expressed for the interest, generosity, and cooperation of the authors and publishers who granted permission to reprint their materials. They made this book a reality.

December 1972   GEORGE R. TERRY

CONTRIBUTORS

Russell L. Ackoff
Fred C. Allvine
David C. Anderson
Robert H. Becknell
V. Steven Blood
William L. Campfield
Frank S. Capon
John C. Chambers
Andrew B. Chase, Jr.
John T. Connor
Edward S. Cornish
John W. Coughlan
John Diebold
Richard A. Elnicki
John R. Emery
Gary Gemmill
Norman George
Surender N. Goel
J. Phillip Golds
William H. Gruber
Lawrence T. Harbeck
David O. Jenkins
Merritt L. Kastens
M. Jane Kay
Arlen J. Large
Baruch Lev
Robert N. McMurry
Santinder K. Mullick
Richard S. Muti
John S. Niles
Simon Ramo
Joan Riehm
Vermont Royster
William V. Santos
Robert H. Schaffer
Aba Schwartz
Robert E. Shannon
Richard D. Shell
Andrew F. Sikula
David F. Stelzer
Richard J. Tersine
Duane E. Thompson
Thomas J. Von Der Embse
Martin Weinberger
William Wong

Contents

CROSS REFERENCE TABLE

For relating these readings to Terry—*Principles of Management*, 6th ed., 1972 and other management textbooks

Parts in *Management: Selected Readings*

Selected Management Textbooks	I Management Objectives	II Values and Social Considerations of Management	III Dynamics of Management	IV Systems, Computers, and Quantitative Techniques
Terry, George R. *Principles of Management,* Homewood, Ill.: Richard D. Irwin, Inc., 1972.	3	2	4, 5	8
Albers, Henry H. *Principles of Management,* New York: John Wiley & Sons, Inc., 1969.			1, 2, 3	4
Dale, Ernest. *Management: Theory and Practice,* New York: McGraw-Hill Book Co., 1969.		5, 22	6, 7, 8, 9, 21	27, 28, 29
Donnelly, James H.; James L. Gibson; and John M. Ivancevich. *Fundamentals of Management: Functions Behavior Models,* Dallas: Business Publications Inc., 1971.			3	13, 14, 15, 16, 17, 18
Filley, Allan C. and Robert J. House. *Managerial Process and Organizational Behavior,* Glenview, Ill.: Scott, Foresman and Co., 1969.	6		2, 18	
Flippo, Edwin B. *Management: A Behavioral Approach,* Boston: Allyn and Bacon, 1970.	2		1	4
Haiman, Theo. and William G. Scott. *Management in the Modern Organization,* Boston: Houghton Mifflin Co., 1970.	6	6		
Haynes, W. Warren and Joseph L. Massie. *Management: Analysis, Concepts and Cases,* Englewood Cliffs, N.J.: Prentice-Hall, Inc., 1969.		3, 4, 29, 30	1, 2	19, 20, 25, 26

V Decision Making	VI Planning	VII Organizing	VIII Management and Human Behavior	IX Actuating	X Controlling	XI The Future and Management
6, 7, 8	10, 11, 12, 13	14, 15, 16, 17, 18	9, 19	20, 21, 22	23, 24, 25, 26	27
4	14, 15, 16, 17	5, 6, 7, 8, 9, 10, 11, 12, 13	18, 19, 20, 21, 22	23, 24, 25, 26		
23	16	10, 11, 12, 13, 14, 15, 17	19	18	20	30
14	4	5, 9, 11, 12	7, 8	10	6	19
5	7, 8	3, 4, 9, 10, 11, 12, 13, 14, 18	15	16, 17	8	19
3	5	8, 9, 10, 11, 12, 13	6, 7, 17, 18	14, 15, 16, 19	20, 21, 22, 23	
4, 5	7, 8, 9, 20	11, 12, 13, 14, 15, 16, 17, 18, 19, 28	5, 25, 26, 27	22, 23, 24	21, 29, 30, 31, 32	33
15, 16, 17, 18	11, 12	5, 6, 7, 8	9, 10		13, 14, 23, 24	29, 30

xvi   *Cross Reference Table*

Parts in *Management: Selected Readings*

Selected Management Textbooks	I Management Objectives	II Values and Social Considerations of Management	III Dynamics of Management	IV Systems, Computers, and Quantitative Techniques
Hicks, Herbert G. *The Management of Organizations: A Systems and Human Resources Approach*, New York: McGraw-Hill Book Co., 1972.	3, 4	5	6, 13, 14, 15, 24	29, 30
Hodge, Billy J. and Herbert J. Johnson. *Management and Organizational Behavior*, New York: John Wiley & Sons, Inc., 1970.		3	2	
Kast, Fremont E. and James E. Rosenzweig. *Organization and Management*, New York: McGraw-Hill Book Co., 1970.		2	4, 5	
Koontz, Harold and Cyril O'Donnell. *Principles of Management*, New York: McGraw-Hill Book Co., 1972.	7	4	1	
Longnecker, Justin G. *Principles of Management and Organizational Behavior*, Columbus, O.: Charles E. Merrill Publishing Co., 1969.	4	3	3	2
McFarland, Dalton E. *Management: Principles and Practices*, New York: The Macmillan Co., 1970.	7	3, 24	23	5, 13
Newman, William H., Charles E. Summer, and E. Kirby Warren. *The Process of Management—Concepts, Behavior, and Practice*, Englewood Cliffs, N.J.: Prentice-Hall, Inc., 1972.	8, 17		12	
Richards, Max D. and Paul S. Greenlaw. *Management Decision Making*, Homewood, Ill.: Richard D. Irwin, Inc., 1973.		2	1	4, 14, 17, 18, 19

V Decision Making	VI Planning	VII Organizing	VIII Management and Human Behavior	IX Actuating	X Controlling	XI The Future and Management
	16	1, 2, 11, 17, 25, 27	7, 8, 9, 10, 21, 22	18, 19, 20, 28	23	32
13, 14, 15	13	1, 2, 4, 5, 6, 7, 18, 20	10, 11	9, 12	16, 17	21
12, 13, 14	15	6, 7, 10	8, 9	11	16	20
9	6, 8, 10, 11	12, 13, 14, 15, 16, 17, 18, 19, 20, 21, 22	25, 26, 27	23, 24, 28	29, 30, 31, 32	
7	5, 6	8, 9, 10, 11, 12, 13, 14, 15, 16, 17, 18, 19	19, 20, 22, 23	21	24, 25, 26	27
4	6, 8, 9	14, 15, 16, 17	18, 20, 22	12, 19, 21	11	
11, 13, 14, 15	16, 18, 19, 28	2, 3, 4, 5, 6, 7, 10	9, 22, 23	20, 21	24, 25, 26, 27	
3, 15	12	8, 9, 10, 11	5, 6, 7		13, 16	

Parts in *Management: Selected Readings*

Selected Management Textbooks	I Management Objectives	II Values and Social Considerations of Management	III Dynamics of Management	IV Systems, Computers, and Quantitative Techniques
Sisk, Henry L. *Principles of Management: A Systems Approach to the Management Process*, Cincinnati: South-Western Publishing Co., 1969.	3			8
Torgersen, Paul E. and Irwin T. Weinstock. *Management: An Integrated Approach*, Englewood Cliffs, N.J.: Prentice-Hall, Inc., 1972.	6, 7, 8		1	9
Voich, Dan, Jr., and Daniel A. Wren. *Principles of Management*, New York: Ronald Press Co., 1968.	4	3		2, 6, 20

V Decision Making	VI Planning	VII Organiz-ing	VIII Manage-ment and Human Behavior	IX Actuating	X Control-ling	XI The Future and Manage-ment
9	4, 5, 6, 7	10, 11, 12, 13, 14, 15	18	16, 17, 20	21, 22, 23	
2, 3, 4	5	12, 14, 15, 16, 17, 18	10, 19	13	20, 21	
	5	7, 8	14	15, 17, 19	9, 10	

part ONE

Management Objectives

Management is or should be performed to achieve an objective or objectives. The manager uses resources to accomplish some desired goal. Objectives are the raison d'être for management. What the manager does should contribute directly or indirectly to achieving the objective.

Since the objectives are vital in management, it is logical and convenient to start our discussion of management with this major topic. Some contend that objectives are given to managers, and this may be true for broad general objectives at the top level of an organization. However, in the majority of cases, a management member must determine objectives. And, as the old saying goes, "Knowing what is trying to be achieved is an important part of the achievement."

The first reading in Part One, "Some Plain Truth about Profit" is a short but thought-provoking discussion of a subject commonly brought into discussions of management objectives. Some erroneous beliefs are exposed, and rethinking about profit in our whole economic and social order is presented with candor.

The second article deals with another aspect of objectives, namely, productivity. The author, Mr. Anderson, discusses some important factors influencing productivity and implies what might be done to turn around our current decline in productivity. The challenge to management and the tie-in of productivity to management objectives are set forth effectively.

In the next reading, "Value and Value Systems: Relationship to Personal Goals," Professor Sikula presents helpful material on the analysis and measurement of personal goals. Contemporary managers give considerable attention to personal goals, for the knowledge and use of them play a dominant role in motivational and developmental efforts by the manager in dealing with members of his work group. Further, as demonstrated in

1

Parts Eight and Nine, the relationships of personal goals to company goals have significant bearing on the calibre of management attained.

Managing by objectives that utilizes objectives as the foci around which managerial attention and effort are concentrated, is growing in usage. Sometimes referred to as results management, or goals management, its common name is management by objectives (MBO). In the reading, "How to Manage by Objectives," the techniques for successfully using this approach are spelled out. The observation is made in this article that sound objectives may or may not lead to sound decisions. And for maximum benefit, objectives must be measurable, specific, tangible, and under the effective control of those setting the goals. The requirements for effective goals, the number needed and their characteristics are also indicated in this article.

1. Some Plain Truth about Profit*

LAWRENCE T. HARBECK

Free enterprise acknowledges human selfishness and directs it to constructive ends. Partisans of free enterprise claim this as a virtue; they believe selfishness is a fact of life. Opponents express horror at this pragmatic view; they believe government can eliminate human imperfection.

Profit brings into sharpest focus the fight between free enterprise and socialism-communism. The battle lines seem to be clear, but they are not. Profit is a deceptive subject. And on no other topic are friends of free enterprise less convincing.

Practical businessmen state forthrightly that profit makes the wheels go 'round. Opponents think they already know this too well; the fact torments them. Academic proponents of free enterprise unintentionally encourage two negative inferences in their usual argument. They imply that profit exists only in a free enterprise system (and only there because of imperfections), and that the profit motive is synonymous with selfishness.

For example, many textbooks say: Profit is money left after cost is subtracted from selling price. This definition is narrowly accurate but broadly misleading. It sounds as if the seller is getting something for nothing. (If the costs are met, why should there be a remainder?) It implies by omission that profit is associated only with money and sales oriented economic systems.

Economic experts agree to disagree on profits. They describe profits variously as: high earnings from entrepreneurship; discrepancies arising from uncertainty; results of a monopoly position; return from a contrived scarcity; unnecessary surplus; implicit interest, rent, and wages; an accounting residual needed to balance earnings against the value of goods and services; a mixture of these. None of this is helpful.

---

* Source: Reprinted with permission of *The Wall Street Journal*, January 20, 1972, p. 12. Mr. Harbeck, a management consultant, lives in Ann Arbor, Michigan.

Take Robinson Crusoe

As the profit concept is widely misunderstood (or understood diversely) and an emotional issue, it must be approached with precision. A simple economic model is needed to permit discussion in basic English and short words. Tradition is helpful; it calls for economic analysis to begin with Robinson Crusoe.

Consider the lone castaway. He has drinking water but no food. At rest, his body uses material and energy equivalent to one fish per day. If he does not eat one fish per day, while resting, he will starve.

He must work to catch fish. He pays a price for each day's effort. The price is extra material and energy used by his body while fishing. His efforts, successful or not, require a second fish each day. If he catches two fish each day he will live; if his catch averages less than two, he will die.

If he catches a third fish one day, it is profit. He can afford to rest the next day and not fish at all. Or, he can keep working and save his extra fish for the day when he gets less than two. Or he can start to build a supply to allow him to stop fishing, temporarily, and make a net to improve his productivity. The extra fish, the profit, gives him the option of doing something other than fishing.

Time is a factor in measuring profit. The preceding discussion defines it over a 24-hour day. We can also define it as occurring only during production, and conclude that the castaway makes a profit of one fish every eight-hour working day that he catches two. It gives him the option of not fishing at night. The significant point is this: During a productive period, however defined, he produced more than he consumed.

Profit is the difference between production and consumption of the producing unit—while it is producing.

All living things and all organizations of living things must be profitable to exist. Bears, squirrels and trees must make a profit in the summer to survive the winter and start producing again next spring. Life survives unprofitable periods only if production exceeded consumption during an earlier period.

Profit achieved during eight hours enables the worker to not work the remaining sixteen hours of the day. The worker's profits permit his children to not work at all. Profit during good times, if not all removed, enables a business and the jobs it provides to continue during bad times.

Profit is needed to start an enterprise. A new business, a bear cub, and a plant seed owe their lives to profits generated before their birth. They could not come into existence, or continue to exist at first while still unprofitable, unless some other producer first generated a profit.

Profit should not be confused with savings. Living things must save, if only in the form of fat, to survive profitless periods. But before they can save they must profit.

The real argument between free enterprise and socialism-communism is not about profit per se; all systems must profit to exist. The contentious issues are these: Who produces it? Who gets it? How is it used? How are these decisions reached?

Opinion on these questions should be developed and evaluated in the bright light of one glaring fact: No one gets it if there isn't any. Profit must precede allocation. It is pointless to give food stamps to poor people if farmers don't produce more food than farmers eat. Persons in government can't "give" a subsidy to an unprofitable activity unless they are first able to take a profit from some other enterprise.

The total subsidy of some units of an economic system can not exceed the profits of the others. This hard fact applies equally to the castaway, families of bears, the U.S. and all other nations—no matter what their economic and political structures. (Nations living on the international dole are not exceptions; they are parts of larger economic systems.)

The finer things in life—sports, vacations, better homes, art, etc.—and the "free" things—welfare payments, low cost (to the user) government housing, foreign aid, etc.—are possible only if profits occur first. It seems reasonable, therefore, that current profits should be distributed in a manner designed to encourage the continued and increasing availability of future profits.

To achieve this objective an economic system must take into account many things, including a few facts of human nature. Such as:

1. You can not destroy incentive. You can not stop the superior individual's efforts to exceed his fellow men. With taxes, laws, and regulations you may be able to destroy his incentive to make a profit, but this forces him to express his superiority through less productive actions.

2. People expect to benefit directly and commensurately from their own productivity. Within the limits of their profitability they provide for their families. Few are willing to give a large share of their profit to strangers.

3. Saints appear from time to time, but most of us do not qualify. Organizations based on the assumption that humans are saintly, or can be taught or legislated to be saintly, do not function as planned. They change, or cease to exist. Often they become totalitarian in an effort to force people to be saintly.

4. Precisely half the people are below average in ability. As a group, they produce much less than half of total profit. They are willing but unable. These underachievers must be given a greater share of profit than they produce or, in their frustration, they will diminish or destroy total profitability. They can do this by vote or direct action. They are not

stupid. Given a chance to understand the choice, they will elect to dine on 25% of a turkey rather than 50% of a sparrow.

Free enterprise comes closest to balancing these and other items—many of them conflicting—and is the most productive economic system.

An Analogy

Idealists who confuse profits and selfishness often follow this pattern: They avoid profit-making jobs, seek profit-using careers and clamor simultaneously for government action to prevent others from generating profits. The analogy would be to destroy part of the food and water in a life boat because the rowers are getting larger shares than those who can not or will not help row the boat to safety.

If somebody wants to help the poor he should start a new enterprise, or work with an existing one, to create more jobs and profits. The extra jobs and increased production will provide more help than will militant marching and loud-mouthed sympathy. If a person hopes to use profits—as a government employee or a social worker, for example—he should be sure that his political actions do not discourage efficient producers from supplying the profits that permit him to appear altruistic. He should support the economic system that can best support him and those he wishes to help.

Free enterprise is superior to socialism and communism in many ways, including profitability. It is not superior because it *is* profitable, however, but because it is *more* profitable.

QUESTIONS FOR REVIEW AND DISCUSSION

1. Do you feel that the profit motive is synonymous with selfishness? Justify your viewpoint.
2. How does the concept of profit being the difference between production and consumption of the producing unit differ from that of profit being money left after cost is subtracted from selling price? Discuss.
3. Would you say that everybody is or should be concerned about profit? Why?
4. In your opinion, is profit economically and socially a legitimate objective of a manager? Elaborate on your answer.

2. Some Heady Ideas about Productivity[*]

DAVID C. ANDERSON

Productivity is the measurement of output of goods or services per man-hour of work. Productivity measurements are most accurate for manufacturing firms with tangible units of output. It is harder to determine for service industries and artistic or scholarly endeavor. And most discussions of productivity simply ignore the sizable chunk of the economy devoted to government.

Productivity is still a useful measure, however, and has proved to behave in predictable ways over the years in response to fluctuations of the business cycle. It declines at the peak of a boom, as managers sacrifice efficiency to expand output rapidly; it begins to level off in a slowdown, as extra workers are laid off; then it rises sharply in a recovery, since managers are slow to hire new people, and the regular labor force produces more.

Data since 1889

More remarkably, though, productivity has shown a persistent tendency to increase over the long term. Since 1889, for example, output per man-hour has grown at an average rate of 2.4% a year. And this rate has itself increased; since World War II, the productivity rate has been rising at an average annual rate of 3% or more.

This long-term growth results from increasing health and education levels of the work force as well as advances in research, engineering and management. To a certain extent it is a product of growth itself, since as companies grow in size efficiencies of scale become possible.

Current administration worries over productivity reflect its behavior in the recent period of boom, recession and recovery, as compared to longer-

---

[*] Source: Reprinted with permission of The Wall Street Journal, February 15, 1972. Mr. Anderson is a member of the Journal's editorial-page staff.

term figures. The economy has been following the normal technical pattern; in 1969 and 1970, with a boom ending and the economy turning down, productivity was low; it increased at rates of less than one percent in each year. But last year productivity growth revived, averaging a 3.6% increase for the year, although the fourth-quarter rate had fallen off from the third quarter.

What disturbs some, though, is that since 1966, productivity growth has been sluggish to an extent that can't be fully explained by changes in the business cycle.

Economist John W. Kendrick, author of major productivity studies, for example, wrote in a recent issue of "Business Economics" that though the recent recession has been relatively mild compared to the previous postwar slumps, it revealed unusually low rates of productivity increase.

And Leon Greenberg, staff director of the National Commission on Productivity, wrote recently that in the four-year period ended in 1970, output per man-hour rose at an average annual rate of only 1.7%, compared with an average annual rate of 3.1% for the previous 16 years. After studying the business cycle during those 16 years, Mr. Greenberg concluded that the 1966–70 rate of productivity increase was at least .5% lower than what it should have been according to the output rate increase. This slowdown, moreover, seemed to affect every major industry.

These figures may seem less depressing now after release of the figures showing a 3.6% average rise for 1971, but they still have raised a disturbing thought: Could it be that the noncyclical factors that fed the long-term growth of productivity—and with it the U.S. standard of living and world trade advantage—have begun to change? The thought is highly speculative, certainly, but such a seemingly uncomfortable speculation is not necessarily unsound.

Economists tend to explain the reduced recent rates of productivity increase in terms of various other strictly economic developments: the increase of service industry jobs, which don't lend themselves easily to productivity measurement; the decline of high productivity farm jobs; recent low levels of spending for productivity boosting capital equipment; the current youthfulness of the work force.

Yet for those willing to indulge in some bolder thoughts, another, more basic, factor comes to mind: the basic shifting of values and priorities in American society. This has effects both tangible and intangible.

To consider the most tangible first, there is the problem of the environment, already frustratingly concrete for some companies—auto-makers, for example. What it means in general terms, rather obviously, is that if companies will have to divert some of their resources to cleaning up after themselves where they hadn't done so before, then their output per man-hour will be reduced to that extent.

The second tangible effect of changing values has to do with the shift away from celebration of technology to mild suspicion of it. Scientific developments and management skills that enhance productivity in private enterprises are often spin-offs from high powered national undertakings—the space program, for example, and the development of sophisticated military hardware.

In fact, Mr. Kendrick, perhaps putting too fine a point on this issue, argues that productivity increase is tied closely to research and development spending, which has declined in recent years with cutbacks in government funding.

Yet the current national mood, certified in the Senate vote defeating the supersonic transport, has turned highly skeptical of technology as a way to achieve great national goals. After the initial landings, trips to the moon soon lost their glamor with the public. As for national defense, the Nixon administration has rather dramatically indicated a new belief in diplomatic accommodation as a source of security, a long-term fact that could easily outweigh provisions for increased strategic weapons spending in the recent federal budget.

The intangible effects of the current national mood, defying any quantification, but not therefore unreal, involve changing attitudes toward education and toward work itself.

To a certain extent people seem to have reached the limit of what they are willing to pay for education, leaving school districts and universities in financial straits. And the current economy has left Ph.D.s, scientists, engineers and schoolteachers out of work, while boosting union workers and skilled tradesmen into the upper middle class. These developments might suggest that the economy has reached a point where it can no longer absorb increased formal education and put it to beneficial practical use.

Changing Attitudes

Changing attitudes toward work reflect the notion that money and sense of achievement are not in themselves enough to justify sacrifices involved in doing a job. Younger workers are expressing concern with working conditions and job satisfaction, and more generally some analysts contend that the idea of hard work for material reward simply is not as universally accepted today as it was earlier in the century.

These ideas are highly impressionistic, to be sure, but they throw an unaccustomed new light on the administration's attempts to jawbone business men into improving productivity.

First, they suggest, the degree to which an individual businessman can affect productivity is distinctly limited, lying mostly in his possible power to increase capital equipment and research and development spending. He can't increase the average age of the work force, or send workers back to farms, or reduce the growth of service industries. And he can't change widespread human attitudes.

Second, though, if there is not much short-run activity that might improve productivity performance, the long-term outlook need not be viewed with such alarm. There is reason to believe managers will eventually develop new ways to measure and improve service industry productivity; the average age of the work force, current demographic trends suggest, is bound to increase.

More important, perhaps, is the observation of some economists that if it is true that changing attitudes could prove a drag on productivity growth as traditionally measured, that does not reflect on productivity itself so much as on how it is measured.

Concern for the environment, for example, may result in reduced output per man-hour, but it also will mean less pollution per man-hour; if adjusted for the benefits of clean air and water, productivity in an era of environmental concern would be the same as previously.

The same might be said for new attitudes toward work and career success. More people might opt for low pay, less pressure and more free time; they wouldn't be as productive in material terms, but they would be healthier and happier.

What all of this really implies, then, is that our economy is evolving to a point beyond productivity-fed development, as currently understood, and that no one can do much about that. It also implies, of course, that the concern of those who worry about productivity increases has merit. A post-development society could well prove to be expensive, even chronically prone to inflation, and less competitive in world trade. Our current economic troubles may be some sort of foretaste.

But such evolution wouldn't necessarily be calamitous either at home or abroad. If the long term rate of productivity increase did fall back, say, to the 2.5% range from the current 3% range, one suspects, we would feel the effects, but no doubt we would consider them worth some of the benefits to the quality of our lives at home.

A Sanguine View

Furthermore, evolution in the U.S. may well be duplicated by other countries, Germany and Japan, for example, which currently boast large productivity increase rates. "Technology can be imitated and we should expect this kind of growth from our imitators," remarks one economist, who takes a sanguine view of trade competition. Eventually such rapidly developing nations will reach a stage of post development too, he suggests, perhaps then leaving the U.S. with new advantage.

All of this remains, it should be emphasized again, in the realm of speculation, and rather heady speculation at that. "In the early '60's everyone was writing that we were in a new era too," cautions another economist. At the same time, though, a dose of such speculation can serve well to add perspective to an issue, especially when the problem is to understand what is possible and what isn't.

And it is most disturbing that such perspective is not well reflected in the words and actions of powerful people who currently read productivity figures and make policy decisions. If it were, one suspects, a lot of words and a lot of worry might be saved.

QUESTIONS FOR REVIEW AND DISCUSSION

1. According to Mr. Anderson, what are the major reasons for productivity growth in the United States?
2. Do you feel productivity is a worthy objective of American management? Why?
3. Do you believe that the current U.S. economy has reached the point where it can no longer absorb and put to beneficial use the offerings of formal education? Substantiate your answer.

3. Value and Value Systems: Relationship to Personal Goals*

ANDREW F. SIKULA

What determines individual behavior? This is a question which philosophers and theologians have debated for centuries. While various answers can be given to this question, one of the more popular responses is that personal goals determine individual behavior.

This emphasis on personal goals ties in with and is related to the dual concepts of self-determination and self-actualization. The first concept is especially popular in our society which theoretically, at least, places a premium on freedom of choice. Such freedom is repeatedly being utilized in various forms including political debates, religious confrontations, civil rights movements, campus revolutions and even women's liberation. Understandably, people want and demand to determine, direct and control their own destinies. Not only is there a growing tendency toward self-determination, there is also an increased movement toward its ultimate state, namely, self-actualization.

Self-actualization is a fancy, academic word which basically means the same thing as today's younger generation's "finding your own bag," "doing your own thing," or "getting it all together." It involves an individual knowing his own personal goals and then striving to reach these goals through the maximum development and utilization of his human capacity and potential. In this manner, personal goals can then direct and determine individual behavior.

This is not to say that personal goals are the sole determinant. Other theories emphasize such factors as "needs," "drives," "tensions," "aspirations," "expectations," et al. In addition, the influences of groups, organizations, and society in general independently and collectively affect indi-

---

* Source: Reprinted with permission of *Personnel Journal*, April 1971, pp. 310–12. Andrew F. Sikula is assistant professor of management, University of Illinois, Chicago Circle Campus.

vidual behavior. In actuality, all of these, plus other factors, almost infinite in number, are constantly interacting to ultimately determine any and all individual behavior. But the human mind is unable to grasp and understand such a complex phenomenon and accordingly, key factors are picked out of the total situation and subjected to analysis. One such common factor to date has been personal goals.

How to Analyze and Measure Personal Goals

If personal goals determine individual behavior, what determines personal goals? This question is also subject to conjecture. Hundreds of attempts have been made and techniques formulated and used in an endeavor to better analyze them. The purpose here is not to provide a review of existing procedures, but to report a new and promising approach to the analysis of personal goals.

An abundance of recent research is available which supports the contention that individual behavior is best understood as being related to and/or determined by personal values and value systems. In addition, some empirical evidence is also available which illustrates the relationship between personal values and value systems and personal goals. For example, a comprehensive and recently completed research study by Dr. James Morrison used concepts from Herzberg in attempting to measure "personal job goals" (PJGs) using a scale of six elements, namely: advancement, achievement, helping the company, broad social concern, trust, and security.[1] The research involved 1990 respondents at various job levels in six corporations (seventeen plants) in eleven communities of three midwestern states. In addition to the PJG scale, Dr. Morrison made use of the Rokeach Value Survey which consists of two scales comprised of eighteen individual values each. One scale, the "terminal" or "end-states of existence" scale, includes the following eighteen values: a comfortable life, an exciting life, a sense of accomplishment, a world at peace, a world of beauty, equality, family security, freedom, happiness, inner harmony, mature love, national security, pleasure, salvation, self respect, social recognition, true friendship, and wisdom. The "instrumental" or "means" scale consists of the following eighteen values: ambitious, broadminded, capable, cheerful, clean, courageous, forgiving, helpful, honest, imaginative, independent, intellectual, logical, loving, obedient, polite, responsible, and self controlled. The "means" are envisioned as manners

---

[1] James Clifford Morrison, "Organizational Climate, Individual Background, and Values and Personal Job Goals in a Sample of Scanlon Plan Plants" (unpublished Ph.D. dissertation, Michigan State University, 1970).

The Morrison research project was affiliated with the Division of Organizational Research, Department of Psychology, Michigan State University, said Division being under the direction of Dr. Carl Frost.

FIGURE 1. Summary of Significant Relationships between Value Rankings on the Rokeach Value Survey and Ratings of Personal Job Goals for 1990 Industrial Workers

	Those Who Score above the Mean on PJG		
	Advancement	*Achievement*	*Helping The Company*

Tend to rank *above* the median on:	A comfortable life
	Sense of
	  accomplishment
	Pleasure
	Self-respect
		An exciting life
		Sense of accom-
		  plishment
		Wisdom
			Equality
			Family security
			National security

	Ambitious Imaginative Independent	Ambitious Imaginative Independent Intellectual	Ambitious Obedient
And *below* the median on:	A world of peace Equality Inner harmony Salvation	A world of peace Inner harmony	Happiness Inner harmony Mature love
	Forgiving Honest Loving	Clean Honest Loving Polite	Cheerful Logical Loving

	Those Who Score above the Mean on PJG		
	Broad Social Concern	*Interpersonal Trust*	*Security*
Tend to rank *above* the median on:	A world of peace A world of beauty Equality Freedom	A world of peace Happiness	A world of peace Freedom National Security Pleasure
	Clean Forgiving Helpful Honest	Clean Helpful Responsible	Cheerful Clean Obedient Polite

And *below* the median on:	Sense of
	  accomplishment
	Inner harmony
			Exciting life
			Sense of accom-
			  plishment

	Salvation Self-respect Wisdom		Inner harmony Self-respect Wisdom
	Capable Logical Responsible	Capable Logical	Capable Imaginative Intellectual Logical

Source: James C. Morrison, "Organizational Climate, Individual Background, and Values and Personal Job Goals in a Sample of Scanlon Plan Plants" (unpublished Ph.D. dissertation, Michigan State University, 1970), pp. 96–97. Used by permission.

FIGURE 2. Conceptual Model for the Study of Industrial Workers

Background	*Values*	*Personal Job Goals*	*Work Experience*
Age	Characteristic		Achievement
Sex	hierarchy of		opportunities
Education	preferred		Organizational
Community	ends and means		climate
Status of parents,			Job climate
etc.			Training etc.

*Basic Orientations
Toward Work*
Alienation vs.
Satisfaction
Identification
Commitment

Source: James C. Morrison, "Organizational Climate, Individual Background, and Values and Personal Job Goals in a Sample of Scanlon Plan Plants," (unpublished Ph.D. dissertation, Michigan State University, 1970), p. 114. Used by permission.

by which to obtain the "end-states of existences." Each scale is ranked from one to eighteen respectively, indicating the most down through the least important values of the respondent.

Morrison examined personal job goals in relation to three phenomena: organization climate, individual background, and individual values. He used six factors to measure organization climate but, in general, concluded that none of them were significantly related to the six PJG factors. In regard to individual background factors, e.g., social class or education level, Morrison concluded that such factors did affect PJG rankings. In reference to individual values, he found that the Herzberg PJGs were similar and related to some of the Rokeach Values. "The relationships between the Rokeach Values and the PJGs revealed that for each PJG there was a pattern of relationships with values that was distinguishable from the pattern of relationships for other PJGs."[2] Morrison also concluded that the patterns of relationship were exceedingly complex and accordingly—he supported the "complex man" model of individual behavior. Figure 1 summarizes the significant relationships between the value rankings of the Rokeach Value Survey and the ratings of the Personal Job Goals. Figure 2 presents Morrison's conceptual model for the study of industrial workers.

In summary, personal goals direct and determine individual behavior. They, in turn, are determined by and sometimes even considered to be synonymous with individual values and value systems (ranking-ordering of values along a continuum of importance). A growing body of recent research knowledge is accumulating which indicates the importance of

---

2 Morrison, "Organizational Climate," p. 95.

values and value systems in explaining and determining not only individual but also group and organizational behavior.

QUESTIONS FOR REVIEW AND DISCUSSION

1. Do you believe that most persons have strong and well-defined personal goals? Of what significance is your answer in the study of management?
2. Are personal goals the sole determinates of individual behavior? Discuss.
3. State several significant observations from the information shown in Figure 1 of this article.

4. How to Manage
by Objectives*

Many of our "objectives" are no more than light at the end of the tunnel. Bringing "a just and lasting peace to Southeast Asia" or "cleaning up the environment" are examples of phrases that may spur activity, but do little to tell us where we want to go, how we are going to get there, and how we will know when we have arrived.

The parallel for managers is this: Most companies believe they are managing by objectives. But many objectives are platitudes, such as, "We will maximize our profits" or "We will improve our market penetration." Even quantified objectives, such as, "We will increase our return on investment from 20 to 23%," contain a vital flaw; if you don't make it, you don't know why.

"If you don't know why you failed to reach the target," says Herbert E. Geissler, management consultant in the Cleveland office of McKinsey & Co., "you don't know what to do differently next year. And, the likelihood of not making this objective is further increased, if managers have put some stretch in their goals—which they should—for objectives should always be just beyond the reach of the manager, far enough so he stretches for the objective but not so far he doesn't bother trying."

Dr. George S. Odiorne, author of the book *Management by Objectives*, describes the process as one "whereby the superior and subordinate managers of an organization jointly identify its common goals, define each individual's major areas of responsibility in terms of the results expected of him, and use these measures as guides for operating the unit and assessing the contribution of each of its members."

Contrasted with management by objectives, or ends, is management by controls, or means. Managers who practice management by objectives think and speak in terms of results. Those who practice management by controls think and speak in terms of what people are doing.

* Source: Reprinted with permission from *Industry Week,* June 8, 1970. Copyright, Penton Publishing Co., Cleveland, Ohio.

The interesting paradox of many organizations is that increasing management by control can easily result from an effort to fulfill objectives. To such managers, Charles L. Hughes, author of the award-winning book, *Goal Setting*, suggests that "if they would think not so much about the doing of a task as about the final outcome, they would be taking advantage of supervisory tactics which would allow them to profit from self-control on the part of their employees."

Mr. Hughes continues, "A goal is an end, a result, not just a task or function to be performed. The identification of meaningful goals both for the organization and the individual that will effectively influence and support each other is essential to effective performance on the part of the organization and its members alike."

Goal Characteristics

Time out for a quiz. The 20 most common errors in setting goals are shown in Figure 1, based on a study of 1,100 managers reported by Dr. Odiorne. Mr. Geissler says that most companies, in setting objectives, go through a pattern that starts with objectives so nebulous that they hamper the ability to perform, let alone to measure. Next time around, they start putting numbers on the objectives, such as increasing return on investment from 20 to 23%, but the numbers don't tell them how to get from where they are to where they want to go.

A year or two farther down the road, says Mr. Geissler, the company learns to develop subobjectives: the action steps needed to move the organization toward its objectives. Then, in the next steps, understanding and using the objectives become part of the management process in terms of exploding specific objectives into discrete steps and actions that individual managers have to execute by a specific date.

Learning to manage by objectives may be something like learning to ride a bicycle—just reading about it doesn't develop the process. "Objectives are evolved through trial and error," says Mr. Geissler. "If companies make them a meaningful part of the management process, actually set their objectives down in writing and try to monitor results along the way, they will learn what the deficiencies are, but it takes time."

Top Down or Bottom Up

Where do objectives originate, at the top or at the bottom? Mr. Hughes points out that major business objectives can be set only by people who are in a position to understand the broad, long-range implications of forecast trends and strategies to meet the company's requirements.

Dr. Odiorne describes top management measures of organizational performance as necessary to define the boundaries within which subordinates can legitimately propose goals. Once these boundaries are known, individual goals and budgets should be solicited and to the extent possible should be used to adapt to organization goals.

FIGURE 1. Where Goals Go Astray . . .

Common errors managers make in setting goals, based on a survey of 1,100 managers, are reported by Dr. George S. Odiorne:

Doesn't clarify common objectives for the whole unit.

Sets goals too low to challenge the individual subordinate.

Doesn't use prior results as a basis for using intrinsic creativity to find new and unusual combinations.

Doesn't clearly shape his unit's common objectives to fit those of the larger unit of which he is a part.

Overloads individuals with patently inappropriate or impossible goals.

Fails to cluster responsibilities in the most appropriate positions.

Allows two or more individuals to believe themselves responsible for doing exactly the same things when he knows having one man responsible is better.

Stresses methods of working rather than clarifying individual areas of responsibility.

Emphasizes tacitly that it is pleasing him rather than achieving the job objective which counts.

Makes no policies as guides to action, but waits for results and then issues ad hoc judgments in correction.

Doesn't probe to discover what program his subordinate proposes to follow to achieve his goals but accepts every goal uncritically without a plan for its successful achievement.

Is too reluctant to add his own (or higher management's) known needs to the programs of his subordinates.

Ignores the very real obstacles that are likely to hinder the subordinate in achieving his goals, including the numerous emergency or routine duties which consume time.

Ignores the new goals or ideas proposed by his subordinates and imposes only those which he deems suitable.

Doesn't think through and act upon what he must do to help his subordinates succeed.

Fails to set intermediate target dates by which to measure his subordinates' progress toward their goals.

Doesn't introduce new ideas from outside the organization, nor does he permit or encourage subordinates to do so, thereby freezing the status quo.

Fails to permit his subordinates to seize targets of opportunity in lieu of stated objectives that are less important.

Is rigid about not scrapping previously agreed-upon goals that have subsequently proved unfeasible, irrelevant or impossible.

Doesn't reinforce successful behavior when goals are achieved, or correct unsuccessful behavior when they are missed.

"The establishment of measures of organization performance should precede goal-setting meetings between managers and subordinates. These measures of organization performance delineate the areas of decision of both parties in the joint goal-setting process," says Dr. Odiorne.

Mr. Geissler agrees that "the top of the house has to determine where they want to go, how they want to get there, when they want to get there, and what resources they have available to get them there. These basic parameters have to be communicated downward so that the down-the-line managers can then outline how they think they can achieve these things."

But he suggests that this must then form the basis for a dialog over a period of time. "Without a continuing dialog rather than a series of edicts zinging back and forth, you'll never get meaningful objectives. The man at the top isn't familiar enough with the specifics to say, 'Here are the five things we have to do'—he can only provide broad directions. The manager down the line lacks the overview to choose the broad objectives but he is expert on the detail. So it takes a continuing dialog between top, middle, and line managers to make them work as a really effective team."

Mr. Geissler describes the dialog concept as relatively new in the area of planning. "In the past, it was generally thought you went through a very mechanistic procedure in which you analyzed your operating environment and isolated the opportunities that were most attractive. Once you had figured out what opportunities you wished to capitalize on, you outlined what it would take to do the job in terms of steps and resources. Then you exploded that into programs, timetables, budgets, and so forth to do it.

"Where that breaks down," says Mr. Geissler, "is in not permitting feedback of knowledge between the various levels of the operating organization."

In his view, objective-setting and action programming are a continuous process. "To do that, you have to have frequent face-to-face discussions, not dog and pony shows in which the division manager comes in and puts on a glowing presentation for one day, lays out so much detail that nobody can understand it, and gets a rubber stamp approval because he wore the president out," Mr. Geissler comments with a smile.

"Modern objectives setting involves the division manager sitting down with the president and talking through basic parameters such as what are the issues that are going to dictate the future of this piece of the business, what are the major problems that you see in the future, and why are they major to you. While you get some chaff with the seed," admits Mr. Geissler, "the process builds understanding between the two men as to what's important in that piece of the business. And once that step is taken you've isolated the issues both in terms of opportunities and of problems."

The division manager is then prepared to go back and meet with his own staff people to discuss how they can capitalize on the opportunities and solve the problems. Various alternatives can be considered together with the resource requirements for each to develop practicality and feasibility trade-offs.

"The division manager again can meet with the president in a relatively informal discussion. The division manager outlines the ways in which he can capitalize the opportunities and lick the problems in a way that permits the president to consider what resources he can apply and what resources he may wish to juggle throughout the business.

"The dialog process enhances understanding and mutual respect, and brings increased credibility both for the objectives and for the entire planning process," believes Mr. Geissler. "And, if the division manager builds his own dialogs among marketing, manufacturing, engineering, and others, he can achieve the same thing."

Kinds of Objectives

Dr. Odiorne believes that performance goals are needed in every position where performance and results directly and vitally affect the contribution of the man to the organization. He points out that almost without exception, the application of time study techniques to managerial work has failed. "If the job being studied lends itself to measurement of repetitive cycles of work performed, it probably isn't supervisory work to begin with," says Dr. Odiorne. "Increased effort doesn't necessarily produce better results; selective choices of effort are more important."

On this basis, he believes goals fall into three basic categories: regular or routine objectives, problem solving objectives, and innovative or improvement objectives.

Regular or routine objectives he characterizes as statements of ordinary requirements which are necessary for the survival of the firm. Often they are covered by the job description as the purpose and duties of the position and thus as a charter to perform certain duties attached to it. But he points out that management by objectives can enlarge the job description in two ways: first, all such duties are reviewed annually and changes noted in writing with mutual agreement on those duties as a result; second, measures are established specifying when those routine duties are well done.

Problem solving objectives most often are performed by staff department groups. Industrial engineers, cost accountants, quality control men, production planners, and other such specialists find most of their objectives in the areas of problem solving, says Dr. Odiorne. The importance of stating problems in these areas as objectives lies in the fact that they are specified with some precision, the causes of the variance from standards are determined, and a solution is developed and applied.

Innovative or improvement objectives differ from the first two in being action decisions rather than reaction decisions. The innovative category

of objectives starts with the assumption that even the perfect completion
of routine objectives isn't good enough, says Dr. Odiorne, and that problem solving is merely a necessary step in keeping that regular level of
objective at the regular level.

Objectives for Change

For that reason, innovative or improvement objectives are most essential to company growth, are of a higher order than the others, and are
rarest in occurrence. These are the objectives most vulnerable to platitudes.

"Simply having an objective doesn't lead to sound decisions," says Dr.
Odiorne. "The objective must be stated in terms which lend themselves to
measurement of results. Indeed, the reason for establishing an objective
is to permit its use in measurement later on."

Objectives must also be specific, tangible, and under the effective
control or influence of those setting the goals. "To some," he notes, "these
limits bar the establishment of objectives, for at first glance, many areas
seem to be incapable of being precisely defined." But he suggests approaches to measuring the unmeasurable in Figure 2.

Because of the measurement aspect and interfunctional familiarity with
the organization, many companies assign the planning function to accounting. "Many outstanding accountants function well in a planning
role," agrees Mr. Geissler, "but by nature most accountants are oriented
to the past rather than to the future." For that reason, he suggests that
while the quantification of performance and the monitoring and measurement of results may be carried out by accountants, marketing men are the
logical ones to handle planning.

"The marketing man is the one who has been given the staff responsibility for determining which products are best suited to the needs of the
customers and what it takes to get those products to the customer at a
price the company can make a profit on," says Mr. Geissler. "This makes
him the logical individual to spearhead the planning function, the pulling
together of information to set objectives, to lay out strategies, to build
the programs to carry out those strategies. He will act as the catalyst
between all of the functions in carrying out the planning exercise.

"Business strategy is related to a specific market line or product of most
companies. It is an extension of the overall business objectives, but it is
the next level of detail," explains Mr. Geissler. "The overall company
might wish to grow in sales and earnings per share of a given amount. The
product/marketing manager's first task is to lay out the strategy within his
business segment to support that corporate objective. He has to make
sure his product is the right product for the market, that it is focused in
the right market segments, that it is getting to the customer in the most

FIGURE 2. Setting Goals to Measure the Unmeasurable . . .

1. It is often necessary to devise measurements of present levels in order to be able to estimate or calculate change from this level.

2. The most reliable measures are the real time or raw data in which the physical objects involved comprise the measures to be used (dollars of sales, tone of output, number of home runs hit).

3. When raw data can't be used, an index or ratio is the next most accurate measure. This is a batting average, a percentage, a fraction, or a ratio.

4. If neither of the above two can be used, a scale may be constructed. Such scales may rate "from one to ten," a nominal rating against a checklist of adjectives such as "excellent, fair, poor" or one which describes "better than or worse than" some arbitrary scale. These are useful but less precise than the above.

5. Verbal scales are the least precise but can be extremely useful in identifying present levels and noting real change. Verbs such as "directs, checks, and reports" are indicative of actions to be taken.

6. General descriptions are the least useful, but still have value in establishing benchmarks for change. "A clear, cloudless fall day" is obviously not the same as a "cloudy, foggy misty day" and the two descriptions could be used to state conditions as they exist and conditions as they should be.

7. The statements of measurement should be directed more toward results than toward activity. (Much activity may prove impossible to state in specific terms, whereas results of that activity can be stated.)

8. In stating results sought or defining present levels, effort should be made to find indicative tangible levels and convert verbal or general descriptions into such tangible scales, ratios or raw measures where possible.

9. If you can't count it, measure it, or describe it, you probably don't know what you want and often can forget about it as a goal.

effective manner, that manufacturing is supporting his effort with the right quality as well as reliable delivery and competitive delivery times, that engineering is designing a product that has relatively low cost.

"Over the longer pull," says Mr. Geissler, "the product/marketing manager is responsible for new product developments, for changes in the manufacturing processes to permit economies and hence better pricing, for predicting future price levels, for determining the service to be provided to the customer, for pulling together all the actions needed to support that market segment. He has to take the broad corporate objectives and figure out what targets he must hit and the actions needed to hit those targets."

Mr. Geissler suggests that in the typical corporation there would be several of these men, each directing a specific area of the enterprise, their combined and individual efforts contributing to and supporting the corporate objectives.

How Many Objectives?

It is very hard for a man to work on more than three or four major objectives at one time, believes Mr. Geissler. But he notes that some companies have a dozen objectives on the basis that if a man hits a third of them, management will be happy. "The problem," suggests Mr. Geissler, "is that he may hit the wrong third. It is better practice to have a focused effort and move in sequence; hit the most important third this year, the next third the year after."

Another point Mr. Geissler makes is that objectives can be conflicting. "Inventory levels are a good example," he says. "The financial manager has the objective of keeping the investment in the company to a minimum so that for a given amount of profit you have a good rate of return. The sales department wants to have inventory levels up to reduce the possibility of a stock-out and a dissatisfied customer.

"Conflicts like this become a trading off situation," says Mr. Geissler, "where a price tag must be put on the merits of each of these objectives. What is the cost of a stock-out? What is the cost of holding inventory? Where they balance out is the inventory level."

Similar trade-offs are involved in setting corporate objectives, Mr. Geissler observes. "You must eventually start balancing out the merits of increasing market share against the possible threat of competitive retaliation and price cutting; or the profit value of an extra share point versus the profit value of an extra price point. This is the science of management, quantifying things that have been determined by but feel over the years.

Corporate Goals Vary

"Different businesses of necessity have different objectives. If a company is like E. I. du Pont de Nemours & Co., one of the major goals has to be return on investment because it has so much of it. If a company is interested in going the conglomerate route, it has to maximize earnings per share growth. Other companies just like to maximize volume," says Mr. Geissler.

He also notes that corporate objectives are surprisingly personal, reflecting the nature and character of the chief executive and involving the kind of business he wants to run. But he adds, "In setting corporate objectives, what you are doing through the dialog process is determining what is feasible and most desirable in terms of the capabilities and potentialities of the various areas of the corporation combined."

He illustrates with increasing return on investment. "Return on investment is specific, profits divided by assets, but highly complex," says Mr. Geissler. "Profit, for example, is a function of sales levels, cost levels, price levels, and product mix. Assets also get broken down into a number of pieces.

"To get at improving return on investment, each of these pieces should be broken down into specific objectives, both short term and long term.

The next level of management must be involved in a dialog to set objectives for the components that end up as return on investment even though they are tied together at the corporate level."

"The degree of improvement has to be cut and fit in order to meet the overall goal and often involves an iterative process in which some managers will try to set easy targets and be told they're not enough," says Mr. Geissler.

"Trade-offs again come into play," he says, "concerning such questions as: 'Should a greater effort be placed on increasing sales or on reducing costs?' Usually it is easier to reduce costs than to increase sales, but the marginal income on sales is typically two to three times that of the percentage improvement you can get in costs. The trade-off may thus depend on the point in time. If the chief executive needs profits in a hurry, he's better off with cost reduction; if he wants to build a viable business, he's better off building sales.

"And this is why," adds Mr. Geissler, "objectives of necessity change from time to time—because the environment the company operates in is always shifting."

Numerical Fairy Tales

Most budgeting and profit planning tend to be numerical fairy tales, observes Mr. Geissler, and most managers are adept at playing the numbers game. But unless the numbers are supported by discrete actions to be carried out by specific individuals by a specified time, it's unlikely that the numbers will come true.

"That's the big shortcoming, the usual pitfall. And yet you have to do that kind of planning successfully before you can do the more esoteric but more important kinds like strategic planning," concludes Mr. Geissler.

FOR FURTHER INFORMATION . . .

Dr. George S. Odiorne, *Management by Objectives,* Pitman Publishing Corp., New York.

Charles L. Hughes, *Goal Setting,* American Management Assn., New York.

Dr. George S. Odiorne, *Management Decisions by Objectives,* Prentice-Hall Inc., Englewood Cliffs, N.J.

QUESTIONS FOR REVIEW AND DISCUSSION

1. Elaborate on consultant Geissler's statement, "Without a dialog, you'll never get meaningful objectives."
2. Using your own experience from any area as a guide, select one common error in setting goals from the list shown in this article. Relate how your

experience confirms this error as resulting in a management objective going astray.

3. From this article, what is meant by "trade-offs"? Discuss their relationship to setting corporate objectives.

part TWO

Values and Social Considerations of Management

Every individual has basic beliefs that he applies as a guide for his behavior. These beliefs are a product of experience, formal education, and other influences. To the manager, they provide a framework of thought that facilitates his decision-making efforts. Commonly, we refer to these basic beliefs as values and point out that every manager must "believe in something and stand for something" if he is to succeed as a manager.

But values change—slowly for some people, quite rapidly for others. As the forces influencing values change, so the values themselves are altered. These changes take place not only within the individual, but also within the group or organization of which he is a part. Every enterprise, for example, is conditioned by the people manning it, and in turn, the enterprise must adapt itself to its environment of economical and societal changes and forces. Failure to adapt itself results in death to the enterprise.

During the past several decades we have witnessed wide and deep changes in our beliefs, thoughts, and actions. Economic, social, technological, and governmental changes have brought about "a whole new ball game." The effect of these changes upon management is the subject of Part Two. We can view values and social considerations as guidelines or constraints for both goals and operations and, in addition, prescribing within what limits the manager will manage.

"Who Shot Santa Claus" is the first reading. In it the interdependence of business, labor, and government is stressed. The author, John R. Emery, suggests sound values to be regained—the values of eliminating waste, improving productivity, and achieving competitiveness.

27

In the next reading, "The Place of Business in Society," Frank S. Capon supplies a backdrop for the entire stage of business management and its relation to society. He points out that unrestrained freedom by either management or nonmanagement members means ultimate destruction of our social institutions, structures, and way of life. Technology developments can pose complex management problems. As our demands skyrocket, the quest for new ways and methods of satisfying these demands are stimulated.

"Learning To Discipline Technology" by Arlen J. Large is the third reading. In it are discussed the efforts being made to assess technology by means of technology assessment centers in the federal and state governments. The intent is to prevent or at least to minimize bad side effects from the use of technology.

The subject of city problems and ills is dealt with in Joan Riehm's "Country, Suburban Dwellers, Beware . . . City Problems Are Catching up with You" which foretells of the future growth of cities forming huge "urban conglomerates" with 28 such regions accounting for 85 percent of the U.S. population by the year 2000. This growth will carry the current ghetto problems of the city to many present suburbs and farm land, unless the social and environmental problems are successfully managed.

"Black Business Development" by Dr. Fred C. Allvine deals with another change in society in which management will play an important part. A current thrust of the black community is business development. Blacks are interested in owning and operating a wide variety of businesses. The issues, problems, and developments are effectively presented in this reading.

Last, consideration of the pollution problem in our society is presented by John T. Connor's "What Is the Corporate Responsibility for Pollution Control?" Some of the more important difficulties, present degree of success, and possible future accomplishments in antipollution efforts are offered. In the words of the author, ". . . pollution is an American problem, not merely an industrial problem."

5. Who Shot Santa Claus?*

JOHN R. EMERY

Santa Claus is dead!

He died last year, when price and wage controls were imposed, the dollar was devalued and the whole trend of American economic policy and thought was abruptly reversed.

He died when the dreams died. The dream of something for nothing. The illusion that everything—prices, wages, profits, benefits, everything—could go forever up, without ever coming down. The fantasy of an endless and effortless expansion of output, with no increase in input. The vision of permanent, ordained U.S. domination of world markets.

What happened? Who killed Santa Claus?

A lot of things happened, all at once. But what principally happened was that the most productive economy in the history of the world became steadily less productive, and less competitive.

U.S. productivity in terms of total output declined. For over two decades, the gross national product increased at an average rate of about 4% per year. For 1970 and 1971, the rate dropped by almost three fourths —to 1.0%. The loss in output for the two years was $60 billion.

Productivity in terms of output per man-hour declined.

From an average annual increase of 3.1%, 1950–1968, to an average 1.7%, 1968–1971.

Productivity in terms of cost efficiency declined. While output per man-hour was increasing less than 2% a year, compensation per man-hour was increasing 7.4% a year.

Meanwhile, other changes were occurring.

The structure of the U.S. economy was changing. Services accounted for 30% of the GNP in 1950—37% in 1960—42% in 1970.

* Source: Reprinted with permission of McGraw-Hill Publications Co. John R. Emery is president of McGraw-Hill Publications Co. The following footnote appeared with this article in *Business Week*, May 20, 1972, pp. 80–81: "We at McGraw-Hill believe in the interdependence of American society. We believe that, particularly among the major groups—business, professions, labor and government—there is too little recognition of our mutual dependence, and of our respective contributions. And we believe that it is the responsibility of the media to improve this recognition."

Demands on the shrinking producing base were increasing. The military burden, the burden of public needs, the tax burden, all grew heavier.

Competition in the world marketplace was increasing. Our major competitors became more productive.

West Germany continued to increase GNP and output per man-hour both at an average annual rate of 6%—and to increase exports 7% a year.

Japan increased GNP by an amazing 9% a year—output per man-hour 12%—exports 15%.

The U.S., in contrast, increased exports a bare 2% in 1971, and for the first time in this century imported more than it exported, by about $2 billion.

What, or who, caused the decline in U.S. productivity?

What, and who, did not?

The measurements of output, of output per man-hour, or of cost efficiency do not measure the effectiveness of labor alone, or of management alone, or of government alone. They measure and reflect on the efficiency of labor *and* of management *and* of government—and of the system that links all three in a functioning whole.

The decline in productivity is a result of the attitudes and actions of labor, and of management, and of government, and of the American people. It is the final result of a national attitude, and of the sum total of 200 million actions and inactions.

Because the decline is, above all, the result of waste. Waste of time, waste of money, waste of materials, waste of effort, and waste of spirit. And the truth is, this is an extravagantly, almost proudly, wasteful society.

So who is to blame? Nobody. And everybody. In the immortal words of Pogo: "We have met the enemy, and he is us." Who shot Santa Claus? We did.

And it doesn't matter. What matters is that, for whatever reason, we are all in the same boat. Neither labor nor management nor government can prosper, and most assuredly the American public cannot prosper in an unproductive and noncompetitive America.

It is time to stop fixing the blame and start fixing the boat. And the place to start is with the waste.

One way or another, we have got to reduce the waste of time—on or off the job. Due to the attitudes or actions of labor, or of management, or of government.

The waste of money—squandered, misspent or lost down a multitude of ratholes by careless labor, careless management and magnificently careless government.

The waste of materials—due to heedless consumption and needless neglect—by labor, management, government and the public.

The waste of effort—in meaningless, misdirected, mismanaged work. The fault of management, and of labor, and of government.

And the waste of spirit, energy and goodwill—in endless confrontation between labor, management, government and the myriad other groupings in a contentious society.

Quite an order! To make America productive again, all we have to do is reform the attitudes and redirect the actions of a nation.

But all great endeavors begin with a single idea. And in this case the idea is simple, stark and direct—we can no longer *afford* the waste. The richest nation on earth is no longer so rich or so abundantly wealthy as to be able to ignore reality.

Santa Claus is dead!

We had best learn to live without him. Starting now.

QUESTIONS FOR REVIEW AND DISCUSSION

1. What actions do you recommend for stopping the waste of our money, materials, effort, and spirit?
2. Is the stopping of waste management's job, labor's job, government's job, the public's job, or whose? Discuss.
3. What changes in our values do you feel are necessary to help bring about correction of our problems as stated in this article? Discuss.

6. The Place of Business in Society*

FRANK S. CAPON

As the human animal developed the intellectual capacity to outsmart his fellow creatures, he appropriated this planet for his personal satisfaction, claiming ownership rights over all matter and life on earth. And stronger individuals claimed rights over weaker individuals, using war as a means to enforce such claims. But we recently passed over one of the great thresholds of change. A sudden fantastic upsurge in technology, with all its ramifications, has caused man to realize that his species can continue only if nations, tribes, families, and even individuals recognize the interdependence of all life on earth. The overpowering necessity to bring order into our seething overpopulated and overpolluted world demonstrates our absolute dependence on a visible structure, which I shall call society. Society is the total system of humanity in all its aspects. It is man on earth, with all the institutions, traditions, guidelines, taboos, and so forth that he has built painstakingly for the purpose of ordering his living and his development into eternity.

Such a definition of society is compatible with McLuhan's concept of the "global village," or Barbara Ward's concept of "spaceship earth." In the latter, the planet is a vast complex spaceship hurtling through the universe at Mach V speed, finite in size, with a waning stock of resources, but carrying an exploding population of humans and other life. Obviously, the success of the eternal voyage and the safety of the spaceship depend upon the cooperation of every passenger and upon the direction and control of the entire enterprise by those best qualified. Thus, all human individuals and groups are interdependent, each depending for his welfare, his peace, and his prosperity upon all others and upon his own cooperation in the total system. And each human passenger occupies his place on the spaceship in trust for all future generations of humanity.

* Source: Reprinted with permission of *Financial Executive*, October 1970, pp. 34–47. Mr. Frank S. Capon is vice president, DuPont of Canada, Ltd.

If estimates in Robert Ardrey's *African Genesis* are reasonable, the human animal has been developing on earth for something over 5 million years, but social structures beyond the most primitive of group or tribal arrangements have existed for only about 10,000 years. In this one fifth of 1 percent of the time he has spent on earth—and in fact in only about 5 percent of even that tiny fraction—man has developed the staggering list of macroproblems which now threaten his very existence in our lifetimes. I shall state a few of these, without either defining or explaining them:

1. Population increase at its explosive rate.
2. Speed of change—experience of the father is almost irrelevant to conditions under which the son will live.
3. Technological and social innovations at the threshold of safety; countless innovations are being introduced simultaneously affecting all aspects of life before anything is known of potential effects on human organisms, social structures, or the environment.
4. Ecological effects of chemicals and other industrialization of the food production process.
5. Wholesale destruction of forests (not by commercial users) to satisfy needs for industrialization and urbanization, changing the water cycle and disrupting ecology.
6. Moral or ethical problems of urbanization and overcrowding.
7. Rapid consumption and wanton waste or pollution of resources.
8. Medical science developments permitting interventions on a scale which can affect simultaneously and unpredictably the fate of masses of people and their descendants.

These are only a few of our very recent macroproblems, and the challenges posed to the immediate and the long-term future of man on earth are clear.

If we are to have any hope of progressing as a species, humanity must have some objectives. Lack of understandable objectives to which mankind can become rapidly committed can only bring on the utter chaos of which we see signs all around us today. As René Dubos put it, "Western man will either choose a new society or a new society will abolish him; this means in practice that we shall have to change our technical environment or it will change us." Civilization has progressed slowly, methodically to the point of this confrontation, but it is we alone, and not some future generation, who must now face up to the election of objectives, to the direction of progress, to the choice between prosperity or total disintegration.

To me, society can be likened to a bicycle wheel. Its sectors are the spokes, held together by the hub of government policy, and kept in place by the rim of essential government controls. Business is a sector, and so is education. Business is that sector charged with exploiting or managing a great proportion of our total resources so as to produce most of the real wealth that provides our living standards. Business accounts for most of the "quantity" in our way of life; other sectors concentrate more on "quality" of life. Quality of life is, of course, very poor if there is not enough wealth to provide a living standard, as is clear in the undeveloped countries.

The task of business is to make the most efficient use of the resources entrusted to it so as to produce the maximum benefit for all society. And, assuming competitive conditions, profit is the measurement of that efficiency, for the existence of profit tells us that the value to society of what we produce is greater than the value of the resources we consumed in making the product. When a businessman tells you that the first task of business is to make a profit, he is guilty of gross oversimplification, which often leads to misunderstanding of the true role of business. The task of business is to manage resources efficiently, and profit is the measure of efficiency.

On the whole, business has done an outstandingly efficient job of carrying out its duties and an inconceivably bad job of explaining its function to other sectors. It is criticized severely in all quarters for callous disregard of the interests of society, for profiteering, for polluting, for exploitation, and for countless other sins against society. And yet our historically high living standards, plus the degree to which other sectors are free to concentrate attention on the quality of life, are due entirely to the magnificently effective way in which business as a whole has performed for society.

At this point in history, we must choose between affluence and collapse. Affluence means sufficient total income, combined with a sound income distribution system, so that all Canadians can be prosperous with a satisfying quality of life. We have the resources we need for affluence, we have the technology now to provide it, even though policies that seem to be emerging are more likely to produce poverty than affluence.

The equation for national economic health has income generated on the one side equal to income distributed on the other. Affluence requires both high income generation and the broadest possible equitable distribution of that income among our households.

Business accounts for most of the wealth generation, developing and managing the capital needed to finance the structures of business, using raw materials, employing the human talents and skills, developing the technology, and distributing the product. Some other sectors generate some wealth, but other sectors are concerned mostly with the wealth distribution side of the equation.

Business is also a factor in the wealth distribution side, since it pays wages for work done, pays others for goods and services, donates money to educational and health institutions, and pays large amounts to government as taxes. Governments in Canada now take almost 40 percent of our total GNP, mostly for redistribution of wealth. Education receives money from governments, from parents or students, from sponsors of research, and pays it out mostly as wages for work done. And this is how the very complex equation of affluence is worked out. My main point here is the overpowering importance to society of the business sector, which really determines by its productivity whether we can have any significant standard, and therefore quality, of life.

Both the standard and the quality of life have risen fantastically in recent years, due essentially to exponential gains in technology. The technological revolution is only the latest stage of the industrial revolution, but it has been so great and compressed into so short a time that it appears to be a separate phenomenon. Every sector of society is shaken to its very foundations by the impact of technological change; every policy, institution, or structure is either obsoleted or threatened by it. As Dubos points out, "the experience of the father is almost irrelevant to the conditions under which his son will live, and can no longer serve as a dependable guide for judgment or action." This is a frightening thought when we realize that education is a passing on of experience from one generation to the next so that the latter can develop successfully.

It was the thrust of business for efficiency, the incentive of profit, that facilitated the technological revolution. Technological change, if allowed to proceed uncontrolled, threatens all aspects of life on earth—but technological change is also our only hope to achieve the affluence we now know to be possible. We must allow it to continue, because we cannot turn back the clock. But business, in developing and exploiting technology, has a responsibility to do its work in accordance with the interdependent needs of all sectors of society. The leisurely pace of change in the past enabled each sector to make its adjustments reasonably comfortably, but today the need to coordinate the interests of all sectors is imperative.

Technology development is designed to replace human effort by machines and systems. Its entire purpose is to increase efficiency, to reduce cost per unit of output. As the demands of workers skyrocket, so too does the incentive to replace men with machines. But this substitution raises hell with the wealth distribution side of the equation of affluence. More wealth is produced by capital, less by human effort. Yet because capital ownership is narrow, it does not serve as a good base for wealth distribution. And thus we see a sharp increase in the role of government taking wealth from capital owners who earn it to hand it over to people who did not earn it. This Robin Hood role of government may appeal to a large number of voters, but if continued and expanded through such devices as the guaranteed annual income it can assure us only of poverty rather than affluence in the long run.

If we are going to make progress, we have to develop some concrete objectives to which we can all subscribe. I am going to suggest an objective of high incomes for all citizens as first priority, because this is necessary if we are to be freed from the daily battle for food and shelter to concern ourselves with the quality of life. High incomes depend upon generating the maximum national real wealth, and this in turn depends upon a successful business sector which must generate almost all the wealth. Therefore, our number one national priority is to ensure that business prospers and grows, so that it can fulfill its function in society.

The competitive marketplace in which each individual has a choice between alternatives is at the very heart of our system, and it is an incredibly complex mechanism. We usually think of competition in terms of competitive prices of goods or services, but competition is equally vital in the allocation of capital and thus in the exploitation of resources to generate wealth. If business is to function effectively in generating our national income, it must be able to produce goods and services at competitive prices which will also yield a competitive return on investment so as to attract capital. Competition protects both the consumer and the investor, but in formulating our national fiscal and economic policies we have to be sure to keep these conflicting competitive interests in balance.

No country lives alone any more. Competition from other nations has become a determining factor for national prosperity in this modern world of efficient transportation and disappearing tariff barriers. No longer does competition operate merely to maximize a nation's internal business efficiencies—it now operates to favor international cost comparisons. And once we open up the world markets to free competition between nations, there is a confrontation between our objective of high incomes and affluence on the one hand and our abilities to compete in costs, prices, and return on capital on the other hand. We have to decide whether we want to maximize incomes of our own citizens or whether we want to achieve equality of incomes for all nations around the world. If we opt for the former, we had better realize that it requires national policies to protect our business system against excessive competition from low-wage areas.

There is a general lack of understanding on just what competition implies. For example, wage rates in Canada are seven to ten times those in such countries as Taiwan or Korea. For labor-intensive industries, such as textiles, there is no way in which a Canadian producer can pay the current wage demanded by Canadian labor and still provide a product at a price competitive with that from the underdeveloped country.

And wages are not the only cost item. Take pollution. We businessmen agree entirely that the environment must be protected, that all sectors of society must carry out their functions so as not to damage the ecology. But heavy costs may be involved in guarding against pollution or other environmental quality control. And costs must be paid for in the price of a product, allowing capital to earn a competitive return, or that capital will be invested elsewhere where costs are lower and return higher.

It is here that a nation's tax and tariff policies are so important, and so little understood. The traditional patent protection of proprietary technology is no longer significant as technology moves readily across national boundaries and patents are generally licensed at reasonable royalties. This leaves tariffs, quotas, and lower costs as the only effective ways to ensure that domestic markets will be supplied by the nation's business.

Canada has elected to dismantle its tariff barriers by international agreement, but our cost structures are high and rising faster than those of almost every country with which we must compete. This is primarily because North American wage rates are much higher than those of any other area. But if we then add other major cost items which stem from our increasing concern with the quality of life and which just do not apply in countries still concerned with trying to achieve some kind of living standard, we add to the competitive disadvantage of Canadian business. These are facts of life. There is no sense blaming business for not being competitive when the costs which affect our ability to compete are beyond our control. Our technology and efficiency match or better those of any other nation, but national wage rates and the cost of national policies are not decided by business alone.

Business fully supports sound national policies, including particularly those intended to protect our ecological environment in all its aspects. But business can carry out its task of producing the nation's real wealth in a freely competitive market only if the nation is prepared to pay the cost of its policies without damaging the competitive position of its business.

So much for the wealth generation function of business in society. Let us now look at the wealth distribution side.

The gross national wealth generated by business is distributed mainly through wages for work done, payment for materials and services, taxes to governments, donations to educational, health, and other charitable organizations, and payment of interest or dividends to those who put up the capital. For the most part, these payments are in turn passed on to cover the cost to employees or to capital owners of living expenses, education, health care, recreation, savings, and so forth. Tax payments in turn are for the most part redistributed in the form of education grants, pensions, family allowances, medicare, unemployment insurance, poverty assistance, and general services.

Our present structure is based primarily on the concept that wealth is generated by human effort and will be distributed equitably as wages for work done. The very rapid growth in wealth redistribution government is, however, an indication of the extent to which our basic structure is out of tune with reality. We would not need government social programs if in fact wealth were produced by human effort and distributed as wages; we would need only full employment.

Technological change has resulted in a spectacular increase in that part of the wealth that is produced by capital and thus belongs to the owners of capital. However, as the proportion of wealth produced by capital increases, the concentration of capital ownership results in too narrow a distribution of wealth. The present answer is to use the government as the mechanism to take from those who produce it an increasing share of the total wealth for redistribution, but this system necessarily weakens the competitive position of the wealth-generation system and thus reduces prosperity. If we were to bring about a widespread ownership of capital among our households—and this could be done by nonsocialist, nontax means—then we would not need the massive and expanding redistribution of income through the government. If we go to the alternative, and at present logical, conclusion of a negative income tax or guaranteed annual income, we necessarily doom ourselves to the mediocrity of total socialism and destruction of all the incentives for maximum generation of wealth. To me, this is the great dilemma of our time.

The concept of a negative income tax or guaranteed annual income appeals to the idealist, the humanist, the intellectual, because he is so sure that all men are like himself and will work at peak productivity for the common good. But experience shows us that this is just not so. The individual should have the right to work as hard as he cares to produce what he wants to satisfy his aspirations, and he should therefore own what he, himself, produces. No man likes to work hard to produce goods to be taken from him and handed to another who did not work as hard. If we are sufficiently productive to earn more than we need, we get a warm glow from giving of our surplus to charity, but we get only a deep sense of frustration from having that surplus taken from us arbitrarily to be handed over to someone deemed by some bureaucrat to be deserving of the handout. The negative income tax is inherently an income equalizer and therefore a frustrator of our most productive people, while at the same time it destroys whatever incentive to produce may remain in those with low incomes. It is inherently inflationary, containing within itself the need for an everincreasing minimum figure which would increasingly weaken incentives and productivity.

Like all sectors of society, the business sector is composed of human beings—in spite of the fact that most other sectors tend to label business as inhuman. The business decision process bears vitally upon national prosperity and thus on the attainment of other national goals; yet is often humanly selfish and short-sighted. That this is true of every sector is borne out in the age-old complaint of "man's inhumanity to man."

Much of the ugliness of modern industrial life is directly related to, and blamed on, business. There is no question that we have pursued technological gain often without regard to the ecological impact; we have exploited the world for economic aims with little attention to social needs; we have ignored esthetics or moral values in developing industry with its attendant urbanization. But by demanding the benefit of competitive costs and by failing to establish and enforce adequate ecological or ethical standards, society as a whole must accept the responsibility for the ugliness of life. We can be both productive and beautiful, but only at a cost, and personally I would be glad to pay that cost. But the cost is not low, and it can be borne only by society as a whole.

Business is often accused of ruthless exploitation of workers. This age-old battle cry, although it was justified at the outset of the industrial revolution, has long since ceased to have much meaning. It is true, however, that labor, through the misuse of the monopoly power of the strike, is now making society pay exorbitant prices for products and services, particularly government services for which the consumer has no competitive choice.

There are, of course, other confrontations in this area of "blue collar," "white collar," and knowledge workers. Today, so-called white-collar workers outnumber blue-collar workers, and the swing away from blue-collar jobs continues to speed up. Organized labor sees its power base diminishing and reacts understandably, but by the same token society will surely become progressively more frustrated if its total wealth generation system and its services keep being shut down to enforce unrealistic demands by a shrinking minority making a rapidly decreasing contribution to the generation of wealth. Then, also, the education sector must meet a new challenge from the fact that the blue-collar job could usually be done effectively with a grade school education, whereas the white-collar job needs a minimum of high school graduation, and the rapidly expanding knowledge job demands at least college graduation and often postgraduate education. We have not yet adjusted our ways of life to the fact that there are now more leisure hours than work hours, and the trend continues to increase. We are only beginning to understand that unemployment is now permanent in underprivileged classes, and that this situation will worsen rapidly as job demands become increasingly exacting. And all of these immensely complex challenges to our total social system can be traced to the performance of business in bringing about technological change.

There is probably no more universal complaint against business than that which arises from a total misunderstanding of profit. I have already explained what profit is, and how misleading is the statement heard so often from businessmen that the primary purpose of business is to earn a profit. Certainly, profit is a vitally important incentive to that human animal, the capitalist, just as salary is an important incentive to an educator or other professional. Only when we eliminate "human-ness" from all sectors of society can we scrap the incentives based on human nature. In the meantime, let us recognize their benefits in helping us to achieve our goals.

It is only fairly recently that our biologists and ethologists have been explaining the total social system of humanity in layman's terms. Man is only one of many species which inhabit this planet, along with all other forms of life and matter. It is clear that over the long run we must live in harmony with all other forms of life in order to protect our ecology for all future generations. In the past, we have made short-term decisions without regard for their ultimate implications. But as we multiply in the confines of spaceship earth, the luxury of short-term selfish decisions becomes rapidly less acceptable. There are fundamental dichotomies which cannot long be ignored—one of which is a developing dichotomy between man and business.

Industry requires urbanization. Man, the animal, requires wilderness. Total urbanization would result in total destruction of mankind as a species. We have already seen the violence, intemperance, and immorality which stem from the frustrations and fears inherent in overcrowding, even though this very recent phenomenon has only begun to manifest itself. And yet it is a problem related most intimately with business as a main sector of society.

In the long run, and possibly in the short run, we shall have to restore some balance between man and nature, between urbanization and wilderness, between industrial development and all forms of pollution or ecological disturbance. The cost of restoring such balances will have to be borne, if for no other reason than that the alternative of refusing to pay the cost will prove to be inconceivable.

Restraint is essential to civilization. Unrestrained freedom has to mean destruction of our institutions, structures, and ways of life. Civilization was built up laboriously through the development of standards, ethics, and laws, and without them it ceases to exist. Controls are essential if progress is to be made. And in this sense, control is an essential democratic system, whereas license or unrestrained freedom is undemocratic demagoguery.

Which gets me back full circle to society as a whole. As the population of spaceship earth increases, the limitation or progressive exhaustion of total resources will inevitably require that its economy be based strictly on ecological principles. We must arrange all our actions, our plans, our programs according to the most meticulous, long-term principles; we must have objectives that stretch into infinity and then husband our resources and systems so as to attain infinite objectives. And because of what has already happened to our population, both absolute and projected, we must accept in our lifetimes new kinds of controls or plans for society as a whole.

The professional students of the human animal point out that biological and social change has been minimal in relation to technological and environmental change. The resulting imbalance means that technicized societies, such as the U.S. and Canada, are close to the threshold beyond which we cannot evaluate—let alone control—the innumerable effects on humanity of further change. And these effects are not limited to those nations which have led the process of technological development. As technology flows freely across boundaries, the technization of underdeveloped countries can proceed with lightning rapidity, and with crushing impact on their social structures and therefore on the human creature.

The place of business in our society, its impact and its interrelationships with other sectors, is very clearly put by Dubos when he says: "Most of man's problems in the modern world arise from the constant and unavoidable exposure to the stimuli of urban and industrial civilization, the varied aspects of environmental pollution, the physiological disturbances associated with sudden changes in ways of life, the estrangement from the conditions and natural cycles under which human evolution took place, the emotional trauma and the paradoxical solitude in congested cities, the monotony and boredom of compulsory leisure—in brief, all the environmental conditions that undisciplined technology creates."

The action word in this quotation is, of course, "undisciplined." We are already far into the technological revolution, and we cannot turn back. We have tasted high living standards, travel, educational and health services of unparalleled quality, and we know that far more can be made readily available. These can come only from increasing reliance upon technology. But technological change cannot continue to surge uncontrolled up its exponential curve; its effects are too devastating.

We in business are so confident of our great ability to generate the nation's wealth, to improve its technology, to raise its real living standards, that we have little patience with the controls placed on us by other sectors of society, with their complaints and incomprehension. We are so sure of the efficacy of free market competition and the profit system that we want to rely upon them exclusively as the controls on business. If we were honest, we would recognize that these controls have proven themselves hopelessly inadequate, that all sectors of society must have a voice in the management of spaceship earth.

But if businessmen cannot be left in sole control of business, still less can any other sector, especially that predator, the politician. In fact, of course, if there is to be balance in our total system, each sector must make its contribution and must be listened to. Our frightening imbalance is due largely to the fact that every sector, like business, has been doing its thing selfishly, avoiding genuine participation in government, contenting itself with criticizing on a "we-they" basis. And government has been comprised largely of those individuals who enjoy authority and power, who have too frequently no great skill in the sectors other than law, and no real understanding of how our total system functions. It is not surprising that spaceship earth is off course, heading for trouble at breakneck speed. Like Apollo 13, we need some delicate and crucial readjustments.

That there should be widespread criticism of business from other sectors is not surprising, and much of it is justified. However, since the business sector is also primarily responsible for most of mankind's progress toward the number one objective of prosperity and improving quality of life, there is far more to be said in its favor than against it. Probably our greatest difficulties stem from the inevitable imbalance resulting from the fact that the business sector has moved much faster, much more efficiently, than have other sectors, so that we are all out of step. All mankind's experience to date confirms that the private enterprise business system is by far the most effective method of exploiting our total resources so as to assure maximum generation of wealth; even if, left with inadequate control mechanisms, it has created some vast problems. We can rightly blame the business system for much of the ugliness of modern life, but let us not underestimate the cost of achieving our prosperity objectives by beautiful routes. Man may be happy to pay such costs to improve the quality of life, but I cannot imagine a businessman devising and recommending such a program, not because businessmen like ugliness, but because their primary yardstick is money rather than beauty. Only society as a whole can formulate this type of policy and undertake to meet the cost.

The ugliness of modern industrial life, the urbanization of our populations, the destruction or pollution of wilderness, the social and moral breakdowns which result all have to do primarily with the wealth generation side of the equation of prosperity. But our greatest challenges may well be in the wealth distribution side, because our total system can collapse as readily from attack by socialist theories as from emotional outbursts against technology and its side effects. The business system generates the wealth, but society as a whole becomes deeply involved with its distribution. In Canada, for example, the excessive proportion of our total national wealth now syphoned off by governments for state purposes and redistribution in fact reduces the effectiveness with which the nation and its business system exploits our total resources. An imaginative and concentrated effort will have to be made by all sectors working together to devise improved wealth distribution structures if we are to preserve our carefully devised incentive system and avoid the pitfalls which would set us back into mediocrity.

And let us never forget that in this fast-moving technological world, no nation stands alone. Spaceship earth contains many diverse peoples, all interdependent; and technological gain has increased that interdependence many times. We, in Canada, share this continent with the greatest power on earth, and it is foolish to believe that we can design and achieve our destiny without considering that of the U.S. Our business sector is probably more intertwined with that of the U.S. than is any other sector, but all walks of life in Canada are increasingly dependent for success upon constant intimate interchange with the U.S. While we may talk emotionally of independence, and while in many ways we can still make our own decisions, the scope of common interest between our two countries is now so broad, and is increasing so rapidly, that I see no way of either country achieving its objectives unless we follow fundamentally parallel or common paths. I do see successions of joint programs and activities as we take our place in the world of the future; I see us getting ever closer together for mutual benefit, and I would not consider it unlikely that we shall devise some new type of political structure to enable us to unite—possibly for economic and technical purposes at first, but ultimately on a much broader plane.

Such concepts do not scare me. But they make it clear that we must decide upon objectives if we are to progress in a world of sudden and total change. We have to choose between such alternatives as maximum prosperity and national independence if, as I believe, the two are incompatible. North Americans will have to choose finally between capitalism and communism if these are the extremes visualized by our youth. It is only when we face up to such issues that we can establish objectives for our whole society.

And such choices must be made by society as a whole, with each sector bringing its special advice to the conference table, then each carrying out its task effectively toward achieving national goals. If affluence and the quality of life are top priorities, then the business sector is absolutely critical. But it remains a sector which must work in harmony with all other sectors in the definition and achievement of objectives for society as a whole.

I have tried to say to you that business is good per se. It has faults, just as has education or any other sector; and optimum progress depends upon each sector overcoming its faults or weaknesses and working in harmony with other sectors to achieve the objectives of total society. But let us all agree that business, by its nature, is good—that it is a constructive sector of society, one in which your graduates can be proud to participate as they seek to make their greatest contribution to the welfare and progress of humanity.

QUESTIONS FOR REVIEW AND DISCUSSION

1. Discuss either your agreement or disagreement with the following quotation, "The task of business is to manage resources efficiently, and profit is the measure of efficiency."

2. Discuss what specific actions you feel business might take to explain successfully its function to other sectors of society.

3. Explain the meaning of the wealth generation and the wealth distribution sides of business as discussed in this reading. Of what significance are these concepts in modern management?

4. Do you agree with Mr. Capon's viewpoint on air and water pollution? Why? On technology? Why? On participation in government? Why?

5. Select one concept presented by Mr. Capon in this reading. Relate its importance to the subject of business values and society.

7. Learning to Discipline Technology*

ARLEN J. LARGE

Nearly three years ago, the National Academy of Sciences made a rather remarkable statement on the future coexistence of man and his machines: "Our visions and capacities have so broadened and deepened that we can now, for the first time in human history, realistically aspire to have it both ways: to maximize our gains while minimizing our losses. The challenge is to discipline technological progress in order to make the most of this vast new opportunity."

A chance to have it both ways is so unusual that it ought not to be neglected. What follows is a progress report on the academy's call for "technology assessment," a formalized attempt to forecast—and thus prevent—bad side effects from good machines. The academy proposed the establishment of new technology assessment centers in the federal government, both in the Executive Branch and Congress.

This plan is quite far along. What's more, technology assessors are busily organizing themselves in the academic-industrial complexes around the government's fringes. You can even join a club. What can't be assessed yet, however, is the fear of some businessmen that government-instigated technology assessment will impede the marketing of new products. Technology assessment is still in the organizing stage, but some notion of its actual impact may come soon.

An initial experiment will come here on Capitol Hill. Congress is creating its own Office of Technology Assessment. Under legislation already passed by the House and pending without serious opposition in the Senate, congressional committees would take their technological problems to the office director, who would farm them out for study by in-

---

* Source: Reprinted with permission of *The Wall Street Journal*, May 2, 1972, p. 14. Mr. Arlen J. Large is a member of the *Journal's* Washington bureau.

dustrial or academic contractors. As specified by the House-passed bill, the Office of Technology Assessment wouldn't make specific recommendations on what Congress should do. It supposedly would be an impartial source of information on the effects of new machines on society.

The SST Example

Everybody cites the bruising SST fights of 1970–71 as an example of how badly Congress needs this kind of advice. Amid fierce political and economic pressures, lawmakers were only confused by the platoons of scientists each side wheeled up to give expert opinions on sonic booms, ultra-violet rays and skin cancer.

How would the Office of Technology Assessment function in the middle of scientific controversy? Arthur Kantrowitz, an Avco Corp. research executive, made this suggestion during Senate hearings last month on the House-passed bill. When scientists disagree, he said, turn the Office of Technology Assessment into a sort of court. Let the disputants argue their cases and cross-examine each other before "a group of scientific judges." The panel then presumably would hand down a verdict, which Congressmen could heed or ignore when they vote.

Even before Congress sets up its own technology assessment machinery, this kind of activity is spreading elsewhere through the federal government. Most of it seeks to avert damage to the physical environment. Pending in the House is a Senate-passed bill establishing six "national environmental laboratories" to do basic research on the impact of future technology on the planet's air and water. The House version of a new water pollution control bill assigns a big technology assessment job to the National Academy of Sciences; the quasi-governmental organization would make a two-year study of the economic, social and environmental consequences of banning the discharge of all contaminants by 1985.

The academy is already trying to predict whether the auto industry can devise exhaust control technology in time to meet congressional clean-air deadlines later in this decade. Agencies throughout the government must comply with a 1969 law requiring them to account for the environmental impact of the work they do. The Atomic Energy Commission, for example, analyzes the heat and radiation hazards of proposed nuclear power reactors it issues licenses for; the Interior Department has done one of the most elaborate technology assessments so far on what to expect from a pipeline spanning Alaska.

State governments, too, are putting "technology assessment" signs on office doors. Hawaii has a new Center for Science Policy and Technology Assessment. A Georgia Center for Technology Forecasting and Assessment has studied how to cope with a natural gas shortage. In New York, the consequences of weather modification are being examined by a state agency; in California, the topic is potential invasion-of-privacy problems due to increased police use of computers.

Governmental and private technology assessors have even formed an international club, and outsiders are invited to join. The just-organized International Society for Technology Assessment plans to publish a quarterly journal, and is calling a "congress" for next March in The Hague.

The society's president, Walter Hahn, a senior science specialist at the Library of Congress, hopes the group will have a nucleus of "practitioners" —scientists and engineers who perform technology assessments. Also invited are Congressmen, corporate executives, mayors and other power-structure types. "A third group," says Mr. Hahn, "will be made up of just anybody—students, Mrs. Murphy down the street, a guy in the Sanitation Department in Rochester. I call them the 'affected parties,' because they not only have to pay for technology but also have to live with the consequences of what these other people do."

And technology assessment (now shortened by jargonists to T.A., naturally) is hitting the seminar circuit. Assessors will swap ideas at a two-day session later this month here at the National Graduate University. A reservation application gives an example of the kind of troubleshooting these people want to do: "Zero population growth may be a worthwhile goal, but in practice it will cause the average age to increase, a phenomenon of profound sociological, political and economic consequences, since older populations do not vote or follow the same life style as younger ones."

All this law-passing and sign-painting and dues-collecting is evidence that something definitely is afoot. So far, however, there has been more organizing than assessing. Practitioners can't point to many new machines that were changed before introduction because of a forecast of bad side effects. "Everybody is just moving in and staking out claims," says a National Academy of Sciences official.

One actual candidate for a preventive assessment job was suggested in the February issue of *Scientific American* magazine. Authors Raymond Bowers and Jeffrey Frey outlined problems that could arise because of a proliferation of microwave transmitters.

This costly, complex equipment is currently used for aircraft radar and hilltop-to-hilltop telecommunications. New ways of making microwave transmitters simple and cheap open the prospect of a radar set and radio-telephone in every car and private boat. It's a potential problem of "scale," in T.A. lingo, in which sheer volume of increased microwave transmissions flooding the landscape brings the threat of mutual interference and damage to the human body.

Messrs. Bowers and Frey urged more research on methods to avert this threat while allowing people to enjoy the use of the new microwave technology, adding: "If this research is not done, public controversy will surely develop once the devices proliferate, just as controversy has arisen over low-level radiation emitted from nuclear reactors."

The NSF Study

The National Science Foundation wants to know how much of this kind of thinking is going on now in governments, universities and private industry. It has commissioned a nearly finished survey being conducted by the big auditing firm of Peat, Marwick, Mitchell & Co. Very few companies acknowledged doing technology assessment as such, reports Frederick Giggey in the firm's Washington office, "but a great many of them were conducting what was really T.A. without being aware of that term." (Like many other technology assessment fans, Mr. Giggey wishes they could think of a less stuffy name for it.)

Significantly, the survey found that "industry is not doing any voluntary T.A.," he says; it comes mostly in response to enforcement of federal regulations. For years the drug industry has tried to anticipate unwanted side effects of medicines lest they run afoul of the Food and Drug Administration. More recently, federal laws on safety and pollution are making the auto industry jump through T.A. hoops.

It's Mr. Giggey's view that more businessmen should undertake voluntary assessment of what their new machines will do to people, in line with a growing demand for social accountability by business. If business leaves T.A. initiatives entirely to the government, he says, "it runs the distinct danger of waking up one day soon to the realization that the capitalistic, free-enterprise structure with its reasonably free competitive options might be gone for good."

If Washington remains the prime mover in technology assessment, that will make the new congressional office more important than it might seem at first glance. Congressmen who feel ill-equipped to judge scientific matters will look to the director and his staff for impartial guidance. That office in turn will be tugged by businessmen trying to protect their old technologies or get subsidies for new ones and by environmentalists who reflect the recent disenchantment with technology itself.

A desire to overcome this disenchantment and keep the technology subsidies flowing appears to be a major motive of the sponsors of the congressional office. The real instigator was former Rep. Emilio Daddario, who left Congress in 1970 to run unsuccessfully for governor of Connecticut. Mr. Daddario was that relatively rare kind of politician who can talk with scientists, and he usually was their champion on Capitol Hill. Testifying at Senate hearings in March, he said Congress shouldn't try to block technological progress in response to "the pressures of society." Another key backer, Rep. Charles Mosher of Ohio, said he doesn't want the new assessment office to be "anything which would enshrine negative thinking."

The Judgment 'Mix'

Scientific judgments, no matter how "impartial," are of course just one element of a major legislative scrap like the SST decision. A technological subsidy means jobs, a real trophy for Congressmen to brag about at home. Conversely, someone like Sen. William Proxmire acquires a personal stake in fighting a subsidy year after year, then bolstering his prestige by winning. The White House tends to see technological whiz-bangs in terms of national prestige, of being "first."

Any outsider who wanders into this heavy political slugging can get bloodied, as scientists on both sides of the 1969 ABM battle soon found out. Just lately Philip Handler, president of the National Academy of Sciences, found out what happens if "impartial" technological fact-finders appear to side with polluters. Carrying out its congressional assignment to monitor Detroit's progress in suppressing auto exhaust fumes, an academy team suggested giving the industry an extra year to work on it. Mr. Handler was roasted at the witness table by Sen. Thomas Eagleton of Missouri, who complained that "too large a portion of the scientific community lines up with industry."

To Mr. Hahn at the Library of Congress, the formal structure of the new Office of Technology Assessment will make it safer for scientists who enter the political snakepits. "It will offer a slightly more sheltered framework for the scientist to give his advice," he says. "We'll have a way of talking about the technology of something like the SST in advance, before everybody runs out like Roman legions into a big clash. We'll have a much more open and participating process. If we make it open enough, I think the good guys can win."

QUESTIONS FOR REVIEW AND DISCUSSION

1. As a management member either of private enterprise, government, armed forces, or trade union, what suggestions would you offer to assist the Office of Technology Assessment to function efficiently?
2. In your opinion should business administrators undertake voluntary assessment of what their new machines and products will do to people? Why?
3. Have we reached the point where managers should seriously concern themselves with technological development? Elaborate.

8. Country, Suburban Dwellers, Beware ... City Problems Are Catching Up with You*

JOAN RIEHM

If you live in the suburbs, or out in the county, and you don't think you need worry about problems of "the city," think again.

Check the growth of crime and delinquency in the suburbs—these problems aren't confined to ghettos; watch county farmland converted to apartment communities and shopping centers; see a rural area used for a municipal airport.

If that doesn't convince you, two news items that appeared in the press recently may do the job.

One news story, written by Lynn Langway of The Chicago Daily News, quotes Sen. Philip A. Hart, D-Mich., as saying, "If you want to find out where the air and noise pollution are worst, look for where the poor are living—and remember that the middle class is next."

Sen. Hart's environmental subcommittee is holding a series of hearings on the health threats of urbanization, and witnesses so far have warned that the environmental problems now plaguing inner-city areas will spread into "even the most bucolic suburbs" in the next decade, if not stringently controlled.

Then there was the recent release of a study of U.S. urbanization trends, made for a federal-level commission by Jerome P. Pickard, a recognized authority on metropolitan growth.

Pickard predicted that, in the next 30 years, 85 per cent of the nation's people will feel the effect of city life, living in 28 huge "urban regions" covering numerous counties and smaller cities.

* Source: Reprinted with permission of *The Courier-Journal & Times*, Louisville, February 20, 1972, Section H, p. 1. Miss Riehm is a staff writer for *The Courier-Journal & Times*.

One of these urban agglomerations is called the "Bluegrass" region, and Pickard predicts it will spread over 18 counties—16 in Kentucky and two in Southern Indiana.

The region would stretch from the Louisville area at its western end to Mount Sterling in the east, Danville to the south and the Lexington area to the north. It would include such cities as Shelbyville, Georgetown, Paris, Harrodsburg, Versailles, Richmond and Winchester.

An urban region, in Pickard's definition, isn't one totally built-up area filled with streets, houses and shopping centers. It can include a variety of environments, ranging from suburbs to small farms. But it has at least a million people and a fairly high population density. And all of the people in the urban region are living in a new kind of "city," though they may persist in calling it a suburb or a small town.

Jerome Pickard is a staff consultant to the Appalachian Regional Commission. He prepared his report for the Commission on Population Growth and the American Future, a presidential-appointed group charged with formulating national policies for channeling population growth. Its full report is expected next month.

Population growth isn't the main reason for the spread of huge urban regions, Pickard says. In fact, the well-publicized population "explosion" has momentarily waned. But another kind of explosion—in land use—is booming.

Highways, especially interstate highways, have increased the scale of the city, he says, so that more and more people are living in "a huge web of urbanization linked by highways and roads, with patches of cities in the countryside and patches of countryside between cities."

As the land-use explosion continues, Pickard predicts that a majority of Americans will be facing problems once concentrated mainly in self-contained cities: pollution, congestion, housing shortages, chaotic street layouts, inadequate government services.

His gloomy prognosis is being supported in congressional hearings on the health effects of urbanization now being held by Sen. Hart, referred to earlier. One of the witnesses before Hart's environmental subcommittee was Dr. James Sullivan, a meteorologist from the Massachusetts Institute of Technology, who talked about air pollution.

"There really isn't any running away," Dr. Sullivan said. "What the poor are breathing now in the inner city, we will all be breathing in under 15 years."

What the poor are breathing, the hearings revealed, is air with carbon monoxide levels 30 percent higher than those in the suburbs; with five times the load of grit and 50 times the amount of lead. Most of this pollution is dumped on the inner city by automobiles, whose drivers usually don't live there. But pollution and other "city" problems will catch up to them before long, witnesses before the committee said.

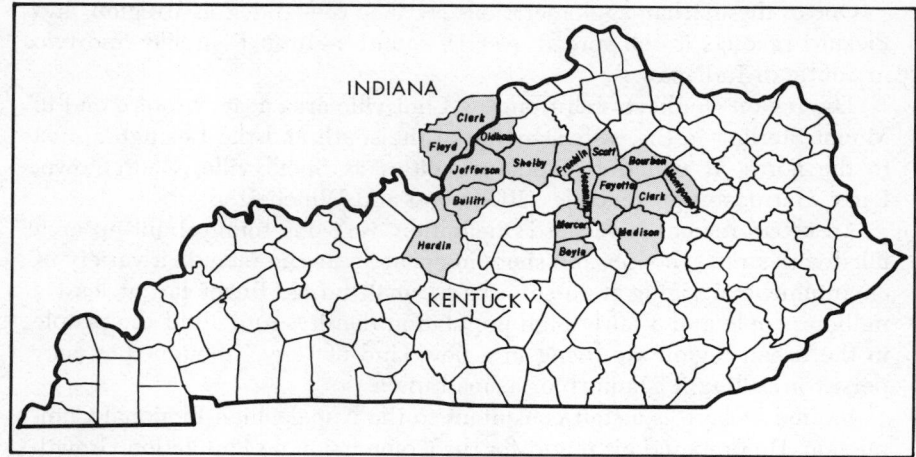

"Bluegrass" Urban Region, Year 2000

Source: Staff map by Bill Donovan. The "Bluegrass" urban region expected to develop in Kentucky encompasses 18 counties and includes Louisville and Lexington.

Regional Growth Pains

An example of the problems that will plague the nation's urban regions is now worrying officials in Southeast Florida, which Pickard says will have the most rapid urban growth of any U.S. region in the next 30 years.

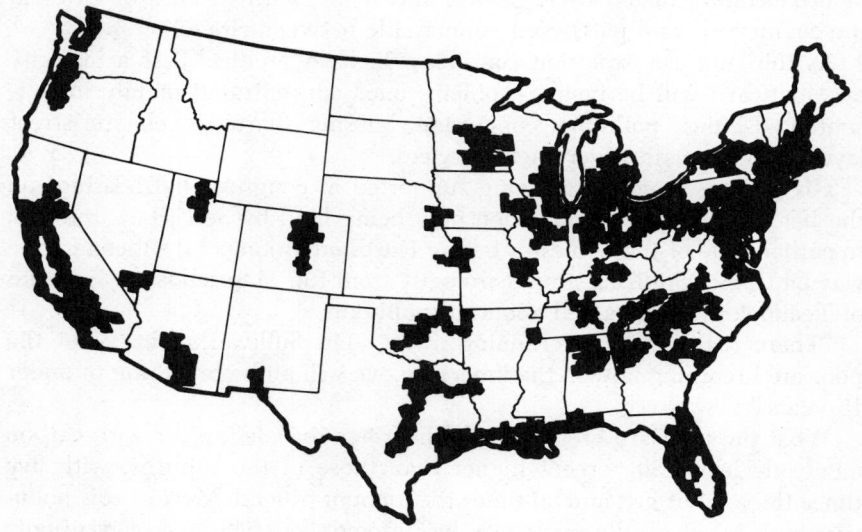

Urban Regions, Year 2000

Source: Staff map by Bill Donovan. A federal-level study predicts that 85 percent of Americans will be living in "urban regions" of one million population or more by the century's end. The 28 regions include one in Kentucky.

Even now officials there are saying that if growth goes unchecked, water shortages in Florida's dry months may become so acute that water use will have to be restricted. Even Gov. Reubin Askew has embraced the notion that development for development's sake is no longer the ideal.

Similar growth pains can be expected to plague other fast-growing urban areas, especially in the South and West, where Pickard says much of the next 30-years' growth will occur.

The Louisville metropolitan area, says Pickard, should grow near the national average and have about 1.4 million residents in 30 years, an increase of about one half million.

The Bluegrass urban region covering North and East-Central Kentucky will have a population of about 2 million in the year 2000, Pickard predicts.

Need for Regional Controls

After projecting America's urban future, Pickard made some suggestions in his report about how the country should cope with its new kinds of "cities."

"This rampant pattern of urbanization bespeaks an urgent need for some type of coordination and land-use management, environmental management (and) regional planning," he said. "By the time we have achieved metropolitan government (involving only one city and its suburbs or a city and county), we will long since have . . . needed regional governmental bodies to deal with the structure and development of urban regions."

Questions for Review and Discussion

1. In your opinion what effect will the development of the 28 urban regions have upon the values and social considerations of management?
2. Elaborate on the statement, "Urbanization of the future points out the need for coordination of land-use management, environmental management, and regional planning."
3. As Mr. Pickard defines it, what is an urban region?

9. Black Business Development*

FRED C. ALLVINE

The demands and objectives of Afro-Americans have continually changed during the last 15 years. When signs indicated conditions relating to one problem were improving, new objectives were formulated. Gradually social problems, such as the right to vote, poor and restricted housing, and substandard education, were supplemented with economic programs. More jobs and improved advancement opportunities were the central economic objectives.

The economic goals of the blacks have been enlarged within the last two years. A new objective was presented at the meeting of the Urban Coalition in Washington, D.C., during the summer of 1968. Employment was no longer the number one priority issue. It was displaced with the need to create opportunities for blacks to *own* and *manage their own businesses*. This attitude was also expressed during the Senate Small Business Committee Hearing in Newark and Harlem.[1] Furthermore, Richard Nixon sensed this development when he was campaigning for the presidency and made black entrepreneurship a central point in his program for dealing with the racial problem.

The growing black interest in business represents a new environmental condition that has affected, and will continue to affect, the operations of many businesses. Those nonblack companies feeling threatened, or those already adversely affected, tend to believe that the blacks are following high-handed techniques and are turning to extortion. Yet, the blacks believe that their cause is just and that they have been patient too long.

Looking beyond the emotional aspects of these contrasting points of view, the nonblack companies involved should be searching for the most effective way to adapt to the new environmental challenge. To make

* Source: Reprinted from *Journal of Marketing*, published by the American Marketing Association, Vol. 34, April 1970, pp. 1–7. Dr. Fred C. Allvine is assistant professor of marketing, Graduate School of Management, Northwestern University.

[1] "Enterprise," *City* (July–August 1968), p. 3.

appropriate adjustments, the affected companies will find it helpful to understand the black point of view, the direction of black business development, and the factors limiting the emergence of the black economic community.

THE BLACK BUSINESS VOID

Black businessmen have had so many obstacles in their way that relatively few of them have succeeded in the more important types of businesses. For example, as of 1968 surveys indicated that

1. Blacks held only seven of the 17,500 authorized automobile dealerships.
2. The total assets of all black-owned insurance companies was 0.2% of the industry.
3. Of the 6,000 radio stations, only eight were owned by blacks, while 108 were directly beamed at the black community.
4. Blacks operated 20 of the 13,762 commercial banks with 0.2% of the industry's assets.

There were exceptions such as John H. Johnson who heads three businesses—one each in publishing, insurance, and cosmetics; Henry G. Parks, a sausage manufacturer selling $7.5 million a year; and the Reverend Leon Sullivan who has established a business conglomerate in Philadelphia. However, such examples are few in number.[2]

Blacks primarily operate those segregated businesses which would be difficult or unattractive for nonblacks to operate. Typically, these businesses are either too small, or involve too frequent or personal contact with blacks, to be run by nonblacks. Even in the case of the marginal type of black business, the property and building are normally owned by nonblacks.

The types of businesses operated by blacks are illustrated by a 1969 survey of businesses located in the predominantly black Kenwood-Oakland community on the south side of Chicago. Kenwood-Oakland is representative of many black communities; it is neither among the poorest nor among the most well-to-do. It is a densely populated area engulfing 52,000 people in 1.1 square miles. Within the territorial confines of this community there are 244 businesses of which 142, or 58%, are black-owned. However, the numbers do not reveal the characteristics of those businesses being operated by blacks. As shown in Table 1, the vast majority of the black-operated businesses are small, service-oriented types of establishments including barber shops and beauty parlors, repair services, service stations, lounges and eating establishments, and funeral homes.

---

2 Milton Moskowitz, *Business and Society* (December 17, 1968), p. 1, and I.C.B.O., the Interracial Council for Business Opportunity with headquarters in New York City.

TABLE 1. All Businesses in the Kenwood-Oakland Area in Chicago—1969*

Black	Category	White
	Black-Dominated Businesses	
30	Barber Shop and Beauty Parlor	
19	Eating Establishment	2
14	Lounge and Tavern	2
14	Repair Shop	
6	Service Station	
4	Store Front Church	
4	Funeral Home	
2	Clothing	1
2	Record Shop	
2	Pool Hall	
13	Miscellaneous	
110		5
	Black- and White-Shared Businesses	
15	Dry Cleaning and Laundry	11
7	Small Grocery	6
22		17
	White-Dominated Businesses	
	Laundromat	9
1	Liquor Store	8
	Currency Exchange	8
3	Drug Store	6
	Construction	6
2	Furniture	4
1	Real Estate	4
	Supermarkets	4
	Light Manufacturing	4
	New and Used Cars	3
	Supply Company	3
1	Hardware	2
1	Meat Market	2
1	Shoe Repair	2
	Optometrist	2
	Insurance Agency	2
	Storage Warehouse	2
	Medical Center	1
	Bank	1
	Wholesaler	1
	Miscellaneous	6
10		80
	Total Businesses	
142	244	102

* Survey conducted by the Kenwood-Oakland Community Organization in Chicago.

In contrast, the nonblack businesses are generally less service-oriented with a lower labor to sales ratio. They are the relatively big businesses with a large sales volume and are the ones which tend to siphon black dollars directly out of the community. These businesses also require larger capital investment and much more sophisticated business skills. In essence, whites control the mainstream businesses, e.g., supermarkets, automobile agencies, supply companies, financial institutions, light manufacturing, contracting, and warehousing. What is left for the blacks is small and insignificant.

Associated Problems

The business void has created several problems for the black community. Leadership is not broadly based, and is primarily in the hands of the church. While the clergy has provided spiritual leadership, it has not been particularly skilled in providing the guidance required to reduce the acute economic and business problems of the black community. Business leaders are needed to complement the efforts of the religious spokesmen and to lead the way in the economic community as they do in the white society.

A second problem related to the dearth of substantial black businesses is that few businesses are successful enough to serve as models of what might be accomplished through intelligent and diligent effort. The black businesses that do exist are typically the small service types of businesses and marginal product retailing establishments which have little to offer the capable and ambitious black. As a result, those blacks with the capabilities to run businesses are skirting business opportunities in the black community in favor of going into government service, teaching, or working for nonblacks.[3]

A third problem linked to the restricted nature of black-business development is the lack of respect for private property in the black community. The rioting, burning, and looting of business operations in the black ghetto, which started in the summer of 1964, are evidence of this problem. Most of the businesses destroyed have been white-owned. While this problem is recognizably distasteful to the larger society, the message appears to be clear; the violent elements of the black society will strike out with the slightest excuse at the private property owned by those who to them represent their oppressors.

Finally, social and political progress will be severely constrained unless blacks develop a large number of reasonably secure and independent businesses. The resulting middle class generated by such developments would be politically active and would develop and support independent political machinery.

BLACK CAPITALISM

The approach generally being advanced for creating black businessmen and correcting the imbalance that exists is *black capitalism*. The concept of *black capitalism* was so designed that it is even endorsed by conserva-

---

[3] "Enterprise," *City* (July–August 1968), p. 3.

tive whites and militant blacks. It appeals to blacks for there is growing recognition that without black capital there will be little black power. Similarly, black capitalism is acceptable to most white businessmen because they live by the capitalistic system and understand the orderly process with which change will come.

While there seems to be general support for *black capitalism,* there are still black and white leaders who are anxious over the prospects for this new program. Some fear it will lead to further exaggeration in the number of supposedly successful businesses in the black community. Others believe *black capitalism* will be directed to developing small businesses that will be swept away in the movement toward giant businesses. There is also concern it will lead to a black nationalistic spirit which will discourage outside businesses from making needed investment in the community. Finally, there are those who believe *black capitalism* will lead to apartheid resulting in two separate economies in this country—the prosperous white and the desperate black economy.

Those blacks who advocate apartheid are very much in the minority and probably do not understand the consequences of what they are encouraging. Even many of the so-called militant blacks do not call for apartheid. What they are demanding is control over their own economic communities as other ethnic groups have, but not at the exclusion of all goods produced by blacks and whites in the giant enterprises of the U.S. They want to become the storekeepers in their own communities as are the Jewish, Italians, and Poles, and also want to engage in light manufacturing and distributing which does not require massive capital investment.

The growing black consciousness, pride, and self-respect made it possible for a number of organizations to meaningfully assist blacks in developing businesses. Some of these organizations, such as the National Business League, Interracial Council for Business Opportunity, and Operation Breadbasket, operate in the major black ghettos throughout the country. Others are much more local in scope, such as the economic development and investment corporations that have sprung up in major metropolitan areas with large black populations. Many new businesses have been started and existing businesses have been strengthened through the efforts of these organizations.

BUSINESS PLANNING ANALYZED

Black capitalism has received support from blacks and nonblacks with diverse points of view because of individual interpretations of the concept. However, differences of opinion exist as to how *black capitalism* should be implemented. Nonblacks believe the thrust of *black capitalism* will be the building of new businesses by black entrepreneurs. These new businesses would probably include small retail and service businesses, distributing operations, and light manufacturers that would sell to the ghetto; also some light manufacturers selling to nonsegregated markets.

Some black leaders are skeptical about *black capitalism* if its programs primarily involve new businesses. They reason that, first, only a very small fraction of new businesses succeed and that the rate of failure is probably even higher for black businesses. As a result, the cost of starting a few successful black businesses will be high in relation to the gains by the black community. Second, much of the money is being poured into small businesses such as restaurants, haberdasheries, service stations, painting and decorating services, which, even if they do succeed, will not amount to more than a small portion of the ghetto business. Third, they question the viability of "white capitalism" or "entrepreneurship" today. In the early formation of our economic system "white capitalism" and "entrepreneurship" played a major role. However, conditions have changed and today big business, large chain operations, and multimillion-dollar companies control the thrust of most industries.

Transfer Ownership of Ghetto Businesses

Those blacks who are not enthusiastic about the prospects of starting a number of viable black businesses recommend another program. They would prefer to have a large portion of the monies being appropriated for black capitalism channeled into financing buy-outs of existing businesses. These might include major U.S. corporations or ghetto businesses run by nonblacks. For example, Richard America, Jr., proposes that a cross section of major corporations be gradually transferred from primarily white to black ownership and control.[4] There are many serious economic, technical, and political problems associated with this program which make it unworkable. However, the essence of America's proposal could be applied in the gradual and smooth transfer of ghetto businesses owned by nonblacks to blacks.

Most of the retail businesses run by blacks have been the smaller, highly service-oriented types of businesses (see Table 1). While this type of retailing will continue to present limited opportunities in entrepreneurship, it will serve as an apprentice-type experience for black businessmen. However, blacks are increasingly interested in the more substantial types of retail and service businesses that are traditionally run by nonblacks. Some of the more coveted businesses include automobile agencies, appliance stores, supermarkets, restaurant franchises, furniture stores, liquor stores, laundromats, and loan companies.

---

[4] Richard F. America, Jr., "What Do You People Want?" *Harvard Business Review,* Vol. 47 (March–April 1969), pp. 103–7.

The aspirations of blacks to run the larger retail and service businesses are being fed by the successes of some of the first blacks who replaced nonblacks as owners of ghetto businesses. During the last three years, for example, five black automobile agencies have been established in the ghettos of Chicago. The first replacement of a nonblack by a black businessman involved a southside Oldsmobile agency. The black business community and general public responded to this black-owned Oldsmobile agency, and sales appreciably increased. This success was followed by the transfer of four additional automobile agencies to black ownership.

Another example is the Purity-Supreme Stores in Boston. They decided to sell two of their ghetto stores to black-owned Freedom Foods, Inc. Since Purity wants to recover its investment, it is anxious to see Freedom Foods succeed. As a result, Purity makes available free management consultation and has agreed to remain a source of low-cost merchandise supply as long as Freedom Foods finds the arrangement advantageous.

Large-Scale Manufacturing and Black Businesses

It is practically impossible for blacks to engage in a large number of manufacturing businesses that require large capital investment and a high level of sales. Nevertheless, because of growing black awareness and increasing control of their community, blacks do have opportunities to run marketing-distributive types of businesses. Instead of blacks engaging directly in manufacturing, they contract to purchase merchandise under their own brand from large-scale manufacturing businesses.

For example, a newly formed organization is making plans to penetrate the high-volume milk markets in the black ghettos throughout the country. The principals involved have experience in the dairy industry and distribution business. They have investigated the costs associated with the processing, marketing, and distribution of milk. In addition, they have studied the reasonably successful black-owned "Joe Louis" brand milk company in Chicago that purchases its products from a large dairy processing company. From the findings, the milk syndicate was able to negotiate a good contract with a large processor for products it wanted packaged under its own label.

The plans of another group of blacks is analogous to the previous example, but instead of a perishable product, it involves small household appliances. This group of black businessmen has some expertise in the small appliance business. It intends to develop a line of products under a brand name which, like the milk product, will be symbolic to the black community, but not detrimental to sales to potential white customers. Their target markets are the appliance stores, drug stores, and supermarkets in the black ghettos of Chicago, Detroit, Cleveland, New York City, Boston, Baltimore, and Washington.

A final example involves a black marketer of soft goods. The entrepreneur in this case resigned his job as a salesman for a hosiery company after negotiating a contract with a mill house to produce quality hosiery for him under his label. Currently he is employing four salesmen who are earning from $150 to $200 per week. He hopes to be able to branch out into new markets in the near future.

These examples illustrate how actual and planned black businesses can associate with large-scale, capital-intensive manufacturing enterprises. Without the problems of production, these companies are relatively free to concentrate on a wide range of marketing activities, including variety and quality of product line, packaging and labeling, pricing, promotion, selling, and distributing.

In contrast to the private branding approach, a group of influential blacks are proposing a rather unorthodox arrangement with large-scale manufacturers. Their plans do not include the wide range of marketing activities that were involved in the cases cited. With one exception, they want manufacturers to market their products as always. The difference is that they intend to distribute the products of selected manufacturers to established retail outlets.

This planned distribution business would be tied to a black distribution center which would control the flow of certain types of products into the ghetto. Of particular interest to the blacks are the high-volume, frequently purchased products such as milk, bread, beer, cola, and newspapers. It is anticipated that many of these products would be received in trailer or boxcar loads. Similar types of products would be combined for distribution by black-owned delivery trucks to stores. The blacks believe their proposition is not unusual; in fact, they liken it to the general merchandise delivery operations existing in many cities. The primary difference is that retail operators, rather than ultimate consumers, would be the units receiving shipment.

The planned black distribution system is noteworthy because of its sponsor—the West Side Development Corporation of Chicago. This nonprofit organization was formed by five groups and is located on Chicago's predominantly black west side. These five organizations have rejected old rivalries and have banded together to present a united front to Chicago's business and economic community. While such a program may be unacceptable to white manufacturers, it is indicative of the growing black determination to become involved in businesses selling to the black community.

Small-Scale Manufacturing Businesses

The previous discussion was concerned with those businesses where actual black manufacturing of products would be particularly difficult because of capital requirement, complex technical skills, or large-scale production. However, there are light manufacturing and processing businesses where these barriers do not represent too much of an obstacle. In such industries long hours, imagination, good business practices, and hard selling are the keys of business success. Examples would include industrial product firms doing aluminum and wood fabricating, electroplating, and chemical mixing. In the consumer products field there are opportunities in food processing (sauces, bread, soft drinks, and sausage), blending of chemicals for household use (wax, bleach, and detergent), and cosmetic manufacturing (skin lotions, deodorants, and hair care products).

The plans of manufacturers in each of the three consumer products categories are illustrated by the cooperative effort of five black manufacturers having operations in Chicago. The primary products of the five manufacturers are a lemon juice, floor wax, drain opener, pine oil, and a hand lotion. Initially, these products were sold only through the ghetto stores, but gradually distribution was increased to generally include most stores of the major chains in the greater Chicago area.

The strategy of the black manufacturers is different from most white companies with which they compete. Since the black companies cannot afford the long-run payback from advertising their products, they follow the "more for your money" approach as contrasted to the "premium product" approach. Furthermore, advertising these products does not seem to be advisable because they cannot overcome the noise level of the advertising campaigns supporting the major competitive products. What promotional dollars they have to spend are directed primarily to the trade to encourage in-store display and reduced consumer prices.

The companies producing the five products banded together during the first part of 1969 hoping to solve some of the problems they were facing. One of their objectives was a higher level of sales than could be obtained in Chicago. Individually, the companies had tried to sell their products to grocery chains outside of the Chicago market. However, for a variety of reasons their individual efforts had been rather unsuccessful.

Together they formed an organization called United Distributors, Inc. This organization was designed to be the vehicle by which the black companies could economically sell their products in large markets within a five-hundred-mile radius of Chicago. For a fee, United Distributors was to (1) sell the products to the major chains in the outlying markets; (2) handle the paper work associated with billing customers and receiving payment; (3) schedule pool shipments for lower shipping costs and better service of customers; and (4) arrange for a person to call periodically upon the stores to straighten and clean merchandise, to attempt to obtain more shelf space, and to encourage the store managers to reorder.

The five companies decided not to use the leverage approach in selling to chains in outlying markets as had been the technique employed in

Chicago. However, they did not initially want to call on the buyers because of their poor experience with this level of management. As a result, an advance group was established to talk with the chief executive officers of the supermarket chains. This group explained the need for selling their products in new markets, described the characteristics and benefits of dealing with United Distributors, asked for any helpful suggestions, and encouraged questions. The meeting was concluded with a request that the executive officer encourage middle management to support and promote their products and to give them a chance to succeed. Following the liaison contact appointments were made with buyers to sell their merchandise to the chains.

During the second quarter of 1969, the four major chains in both Detroit and Cleveland were contacted. All of the chains placed sizable orders for from three to five of the products. By the end of the year an effort will be made to sell to the four largest chains in the major markets within a five-hundred-mile radius of Chicago.

DETERMINANTS OF BLACK BUSINESS DEVELOPMENT

Blacks are generally enthusiastic about the newborn opportunities to enter the capitalistic system. As a result, there has been a great deal of planning by blacks. However, the extent to which plans are converted into reality depends upon the response of the larger society in three areas.

1. For blacks to become capitalists, large pools of funds must be made available under realistic conditions.
2. The business and technical skills of blacks must be developed and strengthened.
3. Larger numbers of white companies will have to support the efforts of black businesses if they are ever to develop markets for their products.

Capital Needs

The low level of per capita income in the black community means there is very little discretionary income that can be converted into savings. As a result, blacks do not have adequate funds to invest as risk capital in black businesses. This means blacks are unable to obtain the debt financing they need because they do not have the equity cushions which act as insurance for loans. These conditions cause a "business capital trap" that has and will continue to seriously constrain black business development unless creative programs can be found to significantly increase the capital flow into the ghetto.

The Small Business Administration is the primary government agency that is helping minority businesses obtain financing. However, for a variety of reasons, the S.B.A. is probably only an interim agency to assist black businesses. The S.B.A. record of making loans to black businesses has been very poor in an absolute and relative sense. This is due, in part, because the charter of the S.B.A. requires reasonable assurance of loan repayment. Since most blacks do not have a credit record, their loan applications are generally looked upon unfavorably. Furthermore, loans made or guaranteed by the S.B.A. require that the applicant raise 15% (the risk capital cushion) of the amount needed, which represents an insurmountable hurdle for a large number of promising black businesses. An applicant must also have adequate working capital which increases the personal investment required to start a business. An excessive amount of "red tape" and long time delay in making loans has also reduced the effectiveness of the S.B.A. assistance. Finally, S.B.A. regulations state that loans are not ordinarily eligible for transfer of assets from one owner to another, for which there is growing need.[5]

As a result of these problems, proposals have been made that would bring badly needed capital into the black community. One bill introduced in the U.S. Senate last summer was the Community Self-Determination Act which would create a series of Community Development Banks. These banks would make available funds for federally chartered Community Development Corporations that would be owned by no less than 500 residents of impoverished minority communities. The community organization would act as a conglomerate-type business that could create, acquire, and manage all businesses in its community.[6] Implicit in the bill is the assumption that the economic development of the black community cannot be effectively attacked by adaptations of conventional capitalistic machinery. While the bill at one time had the support of 25 U.S. senators, it seems to be too radical a program to be enacted into law.

The Community Credit Expansion Act was introduced in the U.S. Senate in May of this year. One of the basic differences in this bill and the Community Self-Determination Act is the source of funds that would be channeled into the ghetto. Instead of public funds, private funds would be directed into the urban ghettos and depressed rural areas. A new type of financial institution, National Development Banks, would be established for this purpose. These banks would be profit-making businesses operated as independent subsidiaries of existing banks or by independent stockholders of the Development Bank. The lending powers of the new banks would include all those of national banks, plus a number of others, including second mortgages and equity investment in business enterprises. For concentrating 80% of their loans in the ghetto, the National Develop-

---

[5] Theodore Cross, *Black Capitalism Strategy for Business in the Ghetto* (New York: Atheneum Publishers, 1969), pp. 97–102.
[6] Senate Bill 3876.

ment Banks would have special authorities including liberalized entry privileges, lower reserve requirements, and longer term advances.[7] The National Development Banks closely parallel what Theodore Cross advocates in his new book, *Black Capitalism Strategy for Business in the Ghetto*.[8]

A financial assistance program, analogous to that proposed by the Credit Expansion Act, would seem to have a fairly good chance of being adopted. It appears to be consistent with the political temperament of the times in that it would (1) be a program implemented by private businesses rather than government agencies; (2) involve private rather than public funds; and (3) be predicated on the belief that capitalism and not socialism can be made to work in the ghetto.

Developing Business Skills

Directing a capital flow into poverty areas to assist businesses is only a first step toward developing the black business potential in the ghetto. It must be supplemented by carefully thought out programs for imparting technical and managerial skills to existing and prospective black businessmen. There seems to be two types of needs:

1. Direct problem-solving assistance for the individual businessman; and
2. Educational programs to increase general business skills in the black community.

Programs by which black businessmen can call on the advice of consultants are very much needed to help young businesses overcome some basic problems and hurdles. Throughout the country volunteers from businesses, consulting companies, and schools of business have made available free assistance. The contributions of such volunteers have been very important in such areas as incorporating businesses to developing marketing programs. In addition, there has been some experience with paid consultants through programs financed by the OEO. While the cost of such programs seems high (the Chicago Economic Development Corporation budget for 1968 was $250,000 and it consulted with business projected to do $1,000,000 in sales), evidence indicates that the paid consultants have been able to work more closely with black businessmen than the volunteers. Regardless of whether the consultants are volunteers or paid, their efforts are invaluable in the building of black businesses.

While man-to-man or team consulting is important for dealing with the particular problems of individual businesses, a more formalized ap-

---

[7] Senate Bill 2146, May 13, 1969.
[8] Cross, *Black Capitalism Strategy*.

proach to developing basic business knowledge is also needed. One of the pioneering efforts in this area is the Free School of Business Management. The Cosmopolitan Chamber of Commerce of Chicago has primary responsibility for the program. Its cosponsor is the Small Business Administration. Their program consists of 16 two-hour class sessions taught by businessmen on a wide range of subject matters. More than 800 students have attended and completed the course. Now, specially designed courses in fundamentals of business are needed, including accounting and finance, production, marketing, and personnel. One might hope that the academic community will step forward with some creative programs.

Buy Black Products

The efforts put into financial assistance programs and the building of business skills will not produce maximum results unless white businesses help black businesses get started. If black businesses are restricted in their opportunities of dealing with white businesses, which control the mainstream of business in both the white and black community, many will fail. To launch a large number of black businesses, white companies will have to buy black products. In essence, they will be holding an umbrella over these infant businesses until they are strong enough to stand on their own.

The efforts of the major supermarket chains in Chicago to help black companies in producing grocery products are particularly noteworthy. For a variety of reasons the supermarket chains found that black products were not being given a real chance to succeed. As a result, each chain created a position of a black liaison man to work with the producers to help them get their products moving in the chain stores. Similarly, Ford Motor Company worked with a black company to develop a new carwash product, which they are now purchasing in thousand-case quantity. There is no doubt that Ford could have purchased a comparable product for the same price, or less, from an existing supplier with much less effort. Many more companies are needed who are willing to purchase black products and give assistance to black businesses.

CONCLUSION

The blacks can either be shut out or brought into the capitalistic system. Currently, the desire of blacks to participate in the free enterprise system is high. If concrete and adequate steps are taken now, the black economic community can be launched and ultimately developed to where it strengthens the overall economy. However, if white America turns its back on the ghetto or tries to prescribe unacceptable programs, the black community will continue to depress the total economic system.

QUESTIONS FOR REVIEW AND DISCUSSION

1. Do you view black business development as an important social consideration of modern management? Why?

2. According to Dr. Allvine, what are the major problems associated with the
so-called business void in the black community?

3. As set forth in this reading, from black capitalism what types of business
would appear to have the best chances for success? Elaborate on your answer.

4. Evaluate the purposes and efforts of the West Side Development Corporation
of Chicago, the United Distributors, Inc., and the Free School of Business
Management.

10. What Is the Corporate Responsibility for Pollution Control?*

JOHN T. CONNOR

No one has to spell out the obvious fact that the pollution problem in our society is immense. The 300 million tons of waste matter disgorged into our nation's atmosphere each year cost us an estimated $20 billion in property damage alone.

Nearly a quarter of a million tons of dirt fall on the New York area each year, and the invisible noxious gasses—sulphur dioxide, carbon monoxide, benzopyrene, to name a few—can stain, burn, corrode ordinary materials, and can even eat away stone and marble buildings. The average citizen pays an estimated $550 a year over and above normal expenses to have this pollution washed out of his clothes, or painted off his house and his public buildings.

Water pollution has destroyed fish and plant life in thousands of our rivers and streams and has wreaked almost equal havoc in the Great Lakes and along our seacoasts. Precious recreational facilities have been endangered and destroyed, and the health of millions threatened by this deterioration of our water supply.

At least as alarming are the staggering mountains of solid wastes we are accumulating. The National Center for Urban and Industrial Health recently issued a report which estimated that Americans were piling up 500,000 tons of solid wastes *each day*. Those statistics will harden the brain of the most soft-headed optimist.

Most of you are familiar with these figures. So is a growing percentage of the reading and television-watching public. Pollution has become an important target for those who think our American society is sick and getting sicker. Although I think that publicity about all our problems

* Source: Reprinted from *Industrial Development*, May/June 1970, pp. 17–19, by permission of the publisher, Conway Research, Inc., Atlanta. John T. Connor is chairman of the board, Allied Chemical Corporation.

can be constructive and help point the way to solution, as a businessman I must express my counterconcern about the way so many of the pollution exposes have made the American corporation pollution's No. 1 whipping boy, and sometimes the *only* one. This has in turn produced some rather novel proposals from the ranks of our professional idealists.

"Inalienable Right"

Chemical Week magazine took note of Norman Mailer's put-on, that the best solution to New York's air pollution problem would be an armed assault on New Jersey, to burn the offending factories to the ground. Women wearing gas masks have picketed a Philadelphia coke foundry. The Environmental Defense Fund, an organization of scientists and engineers, filed a suit against a paper mill in Missoula, Montana, charging that the factory's pollution violated their "inalienable rights" to a clean environment.

Unproductive Tactics

These tactics strike me as unproductive for several reasons. If we shut down industries guilty of pollution, we may soon end up confronting a problem that is (at least some of us consider) equally serious—namely, widespread unemployment. More important, this focus on industrial offenders is diverting the public's attention from the *total* problem of pollution, in which industry is by no means the major villain.

Water pollution from treated and untreated municipal sewage is currently equivalent to the disposal of raw sewage from a population of 50 million people. Los Angeles is a prime example of a metropolitan center that fought pollution by placing strict controls on all the usual suspects—refineries, utilities, factories. These sources were controlled by changing fuels, even changing manufacturing processes, and by removing pollutants through filtering and other devices. But the smog not only persisted, it even got worse. Next, backyard burning of trash was outlawed. Finally, there is a concentrated effort on the internal combusion engine, particularly in automobiles, with some measure of success to date.

Infamous Incinerator

Then there is the infamous incinerator. There are 14,000 of them in New York's office buildings, hotels, and apartment houses, plus eleven huge municipal installations, with their 47 furnaces to burn garbage.

I was reminded of the "living in a glass house" story when I read about the plight of Chicago's Metropolitan Sanitary District which operates a number of big incinerators. The District is prosecuting a number of companies as water polluters. It was assailed by the Cook County Air Pollution Control Board as itself one of the worst polluters in the state of Illinois. The District's defense sounded vaguely familiar: They were against pollution, but they need more money, they need better technology, they need more time.

When you get down to the nitty gritty, as the saying goes, everyone who drives a car, cooks a hamburger, flies in a jet airplane, turns up the thermostat, lights an autumn bonfire—yes, even smokes a cigarette—is polluting the air we breathe, just as surely as is the nearest factory or municipal incinerator.

An American Problem

Does this mean we should pronounce a kind of environmental absolution on American industry? No. But I do think this is an ideal opportunity to point out that pollution is an *American* problem, not merely an industrial problem.

At the same time it is also an opportunity to affirm my own deep personal conviction and the stated policy of my company—a clean environment is a right that does rightfully belong to every American. Every corporation has an inescapable responsibility to join in the national struggle to achieve this goal. To put it in somewhat broader terms, enlightened business leadership necessitates involvement in all of today's problems. No corporation can afford to ignore the condition of our cities, the health of our people, and the quality of life in America. Why? Because the whole society is the corporation's environment.

Spelling out this statement of principle in detail is the problem. The obvious self-interest of the industrial often differs from the self-interest of the community.

"Let George Do It"

In the early days of antipollution warfare, when the style was simply to inveigh against offenders, too many corporations pursued the let-George-or-Joe-do-it philosophy of the Los Angeles motorists. Only gradually did all of us—businessmen and government officials and university professors—realize that we needed, not condemnation, but a central framework of definition and control, in which the community's self-interest was spelled out. Only recently has this effective framework begun to emerge in the form of standards for air and water—standards that, in effect, define the interests of the community by democratic processes.

I think every intelligent businessman welcomes this development and supports it. At Allied Chemical we have pledged ourselves in our corporate policy statement to "contribute to the development of sound, equitable, and realistic standards, laws, and ordinances regarding pollution." In pursuit of these standards, Allied Chemical has spent more than $65 million on facilities to control air and water pollution. We are now spending over $6 million a year on pollution control equipment—both air and water.

Big Budgets

But I am not here just to tell you about my own company. Several years ago I was able to speak for the nation's businessmen as Secretary of Commerce about the start being made on the pollution problem. Now I feel an even deeper satisfaction in being able to report to you that American industry is increasing its efforts month by month, and now is spending more than $400 million a year on pollution control. In my own chemical industry, for example, about $675 million has been invested in air and water pollution control facilities. Furthermore, to support and maintain these facilities, the chemical industry is now spending over $100 million a year.

Substantial Results

Moreover, this massive effort is achieving results. A recent survey of 9,000 chemical manufacturing processes revealed that in 80 percent of them controls have been installed which reduced emissions of inorganic chemicals by 68 percent and organic chemicals by 56 percent. On the water pollution front, 83 percent of the 1.9 billion gallons of process waste water used daily in these 9,000 plants fully satisfied all control requirements, and of the remainder, half—153 million gallons daily—was receiving some degree of treatment. Only 2.8 percent of the total water discharge volume was in unsatisfactory condition—a one-third improvement in five years time.

Several automobile companies and several oil companies have joined forces, or are proceeding separately and independently, in research programs costing millions of dollars annually to provide the American motorist an almost pollution free automobile. To this has been added a $10 million industry-wide research effort under the sponsorship of the American Petroleum Institute and the Automobile Manufacturers Association. The prediction is that by 1978 cars will be less of a smog problem than they were in 1928 when the streets, roads and tunnels were much less crowded than they are today. That might sound like going backwards, but in matters of pollution that's real progress.

The Positive Approach

Businessmen have a right to be proud of these programs, and I think they ought to tell the public about them more often and more eloquently than they do at present. They have a real opportunity to help correct the negative image of businessmen, which is so prevalent among our young college students and graduates today and some business leaders recognize the opportunity. Standard Oil of New Jersey, for example, has been spending $1.4 million a year on an advertising program along this line. One ad told of the 88 species of birds and 12 kinds of butterflies found at one Esso refinery. Another described how new ocean-going tankers had oil-water separators so there was no longer any need to discharge any oil or oil polluted ballast at sea. The ads have drawn swarms of positive letters from mayors, state and federal government officials, conservationists, executives of foundations. Because they are not mere puffery, but are crammed with hard honest facts, the ads have built a bridge between industry and people who are most prone to condemn business as the No. 1 polluter. They have also reportedly helped the company recruit young scientists, who are sensitive about pollution as a moral issue.

So we see one more in the striking array of opportunities which the challenge of pollution presents to American corporations. But I have not yet mentioned what I consider the biggest and the most positive opportunity—the fight against pollution itself. By the year 2000, this will gencreate a market totalling at least hundreds of billions of dollars. Municipal and state governments must turn to industry for the know-how and equipment to solve their staggering garbage and sewage problems. More and more private companies will be set up to give expert advice to smaller cities and towns on setting local standards for water and air quality.

Profit from Pollution

For many years, the fight against pollution has inspired new processes which have turned out to be not only pollution free, but profitable. At Allied Chemical plants in New Jersey and California, for instance, we long ago developed a process which almost entirely eliminates the escape of sulphur dioxide into the atmosphere. The process reduces the gas to elemental sulphur instead. We are recovering one and a quarter million tons of sulphur a year this way—literally removing from the air what we formerly shipped in from Texas, and saving a lot of money in the bargain.

More and more, we will see the development of industry-government cooperation in the treatment and use of our water resources. The negotiations between the Ohio Water Development Authority and three steel companies in Cleveland are definitely a herald of the future. The project is the result of intense study by scientists and public administrators. The plan calls for recycling 100 million gallons a day between the three big industrial users and local sewage treatment plants. This involved analysis of the impact of steel mill wastes on the effluents from the sewage treatment plants, which proved that they were compatible. All concerned—but especially the public—stand to gain as one kind of waste helps process the other, with the same water used for both and then returned, thrice-treated and clean, to Cleveland's Cuyahoga River.

Blue-Sky Potential

Beyond this immediate opportunity, there are some blue-sky possibilities, which are certain to intrigue the imagination of our inventors, our researchers, and our designers in the years to come. More and more, our goal within industry must be manufacturing processes which do not put stresses on the environment through their wastes. A plant that produces no waste is a far more effective social instrument than one grappling with a multiplicity of treatment processes after waste is produced, particularly since waste treatment can never be 100 percent successful. I am even daring—or foolish—enough to predict that someday we will come to look on plants that require enormous air and water treatment facilities as monuments to technical failures.

Immediate Outlook Melancholy

Although I can sing the praises of the long-range financial opportunities in the pollution market, realism forces me to sound a more melancholy note about immediate financial prospects and problems. Pollution control has cost and is costing American industry staggering amounts of money. Moreover, the tendency to make business the main target of the antipollution crusade has made the initial brunt of enforcement fall far more heavily on industrial polluters than on municipalities.

Because of the financial squeeze in Washington, the federal legislation, calling for government funding of $2.4 billion for water pollution programs has fallen far behind schedule, and most states and municipalities have been loath to accept fiscal responsibility, at least in the absence of promised federal appropriations.

Many, many industries which had hoped to participate in joint treatment facilities with their municipalities now find themselves stalled by this financing bind, and yet over their shoulders they see local and state enforcement officials growing more and more aggressive. Three pollution fines in New Jersey and Texas recently totalled $37,500, and one was accompanied by a shutdown order, pending a state ruling.

With respect to the financing situation, I believe that the Congress should, with all possible speed, make tax credits available for pollution control expenditures. Some state governments have already done this, but the federal tax incentive would be far more meaningful and productive. In supporting the federal tax credit proposal, American industry is not begging for a handout. On the contrary, since there already is a national effort in which thousands of businessmen are participating, it seems only fair to ask government to share the financial burden of the partnership, in view of the fact that the pollution problem was ignored for so many years in the national effort for economic development.

In taking this position, I fully realize that this is far from the best of times to be advocating programs which cost federal dollars. The pressures to help stop both inflation and inflation psychology are enormous, and in my estimation some of the budget cuts these pressures have caused were right, necessary and even overdue. Obviously, it comes down to a matter of priorities. Defense, the terrible problems of our cities, the poverty programs, highways, agriculture, education—where should pollution control rank on this list? To me, it should rank very high.

I need hardly add that it would be helpful if other members of this team effort—the conservationists, the ecologists and other members of the intellectual and foundation community—would join us in this call for a partnership with government.

Perhaps, in the long run, this partnership itself will come to be regarded as the most valuable of the many opportunities the challenge of pollution presents to contemporary Americans. Out of it, I hope, will grow a new understanding of businessmen's needs and new respect for the role they can and must play in our society.

QUESTIONS FOR REVIEW AND DISCUSSION

1. Of what importance is the statement, "Pollution is an American problem, not merely an industrial problem"?
2. How should the financing of air and water pollution control be handled? Specifically, should (a) industry meet the cost by increasing its prices, (b) state and federal government make tax credits available to industrial plants for their pollution control expenditures, (c) government funding for pollution programs, or (d) some other means (decided by you) be followed? Substantiate your answer.
3. From the viewpoint of management, where on the list of social considerations including highways, education, urban crisis, poverty programs, and pollution control, should pollution control rank on this list? Why?

part THREE
Dynamics of Management

Change constantly challenges the manager. Goals are changed, methods of achieving them are shifted, new problems arise, and the urge to improve and to contribute more to human progress confront the typical manager. There is no permanent managerial condition that can be described as one of "no change." Management is highly dynamic.

There is no better illustration of this characteristic than that of the numerous ideas of what management is and how it should be implemented. The history of management is saturated with a myriad of theories, concepts, definitions, analytical frameworks, and research results. Since about 1940 the pace of management development has greatly accelerated and its vital contribution to man has become more fully recognized. The manager of today must chart his course carefully if he is to operate successfully in this sea of dynamicism.

In the first reading, William H. Gruber and John S. Niles set forth the belief that knowledge is replacing experience as an essential ingredient of successful management. In their opinion, we will see far greater uses of econometrics, systems analysis, information processing, and the behavioral sciences. Their "Changing Structures for Changing Times" brings out these beliefs and suggests that managers must adapt their organization structures to reflect these changes.

Creativity is essential for effective management. One interesting facet of this area in the modern organization is research and development. The reading, "Top Research Managers Speak Out on Innovation" provides insight on what research and development personnel think about innovation, what innovators are like, what motivates them, and how they should be managed. The reading is based on contributions of over 100 research managers from a variety of industries and a wide range of company sizes. This report gives an authoritative picture of current innovative activities.

In "Six Ways to Generate New Product Ideas," Martin Weinberger makes a difficult and complex subject readily comprehensible.

11. Changing Structures for Changing Times*

WILLIAM H. GRUBER and JOHN S. NILES

Corporate management enters the 1970s with new problems and constraints. Despite a rate of real growth in GNP which was twice the long-run rate achieved prior to the 1960s, the decade ended with gloom on Wall Street and concern in corporate offices about the prospect of lower profits in 1970. The following are some of the disturbing factors in the new environment of business:

The highest rate of inflation since 1950.

A volatile stock market much more demanding of corporate profits and sales growth performance.

Questioning of previously accepted national activity. For example, are private automobiles really better than mass transit?

Pollution and other environmental problems.

Consumerism (higher standards of consumer protection in a wide range of products and services).

A significant decline in the international competitive position of many United States industries.

Younger, better-educated managerial talent from an academic environment increasingly critical of business.

Computers, quantitative methods, and a revolution in new management technology.

Clearly, the businessman has greater worries today than the rigors of competition. He is now confronted with problems never before imagined. Traditionally, experience has been a vital component in successful cor-

* Source: Reprinted with permission of *Financial Executive*, April 1971, pp. 31–4. Dr. William H. Gruber is associate professor of accounting, Northeastern University and director of the University's Research Program on the Management of Science and Technology. John S. Niles is a consultant with Research and Planning Institute, Inc.

The authors acknowledge the assistance of Richard A. Akemann and Mark K. Rosenfeld of the Research and Planning Institute staff in the preparation of this article.

porate management, but management will be challenged in the 1970s by an environment in which experience provides little guidance in the design of corporate strategy.

BUSINESS UNDER PRESSURE

History suggests that business leaders will change the organizational structures of the companies they manage in order to meet the challenge. The form of management is related to the organizational framework in which it is practiced, and organization has always evolved from the pressures of changing markets and technologies.

Alfred D. Chandler in *Strategy and Structure* (Doubleday, Anchor Books ed., 1966) surveys the growth of American enterprise and describes the evolution of business through stages of its development. He traces three stages in the development of corporate structure which resulted from business' confrontation of new problems during the growth of the American economy. A review of Chandler's three stages of corporate structure will provide a basis for understanding a fourth stage which now appears to be emerging. This fourth stage provides for the synthesis of experience and knowledge needed for management in "an age of discontinuity."

STAGES OF ORGANIZATION

1. Entrepreneurial Activity

The first stage in business organization was that of the entrepreneur, which met a market demand with the aid of a small, informal organization. Practically all businesses before 1850 were organized in this fashion; large, stable, well-organized firms did not exist.

2. Centralized Formal Organizations

The second stage involved creation of an organization to administer the business that had become too large for informal control. After the Civil War, large railroads developed administrative structures consisting of functional departments linked to the central office, which monitored the enterprise as a whole. In the last half of the 19th century, industrial empire builders became increasingly concerned with management structure, but Chandler found that failure to adapt organization structures to the new economic environment was the cause of poor performance in 14 unsuccessful combinations and consolidations formed around 1900. In these 14 companies, overreliance on personal contact and individual ability was the major cause of business failure.

In this second stage—the creation of managing organizations—a separation of personnel into line and staff was developed to distinguish between those who made decisions about basic operations and those who provided staff support. The Pennsylvania Railroad pioneered this form of organizational hierarchy before the 1880s.

As firms became larger and moved into different product lines and different geographical territories, even the second-stage structure became inadequate.

3. Decentralization

The third stage was the decentralized, divisional structure, an organizational innovation which began to appear around 1920. Introduced in such firms as General Motors and DuPont, the divisionalized structure, now widely employed by large firms, permits line managers to concentrate on the problems associated with a particular market segment or product, while corporate officers coordinate the activities of the enterprise as a whole. Decentralization moved the point of decision making lower in the hierarchy.

An organization structure in harmony with the economic environment and the objectives of the corporation is a major determinant of successful performance. Thus, when product lines are narrowly defined and markets are regional, centralized management is sufficient for meeting the firm's objectives. As companies increase the number of products they produce and widen the geographic scope of their markets, decentralization permits greater flexibility by giving authority for decision making to managers in closer contact with the economic environment. And, in a study by Fouraker and Stopford published in *Administrative Science Quarterly,* June 1968, the authors found that firms with a decentralized organization structure were more successful in establishing multinational operations. Thus organization structure first developed to cope with domestic problems facilitated corporate expansion in international markets.

Chandler's third stage of organization structure was sufficient for the business environment of the 1950s, but it is now apparent that a fourth stage is necessary to meet current changes in the environment. We suggest that the development of organizational arrangements to utilize corporate staffs which rely on knowledge rather than on experience can meet most effectively the challenge offered by today's environment. Thus the historic process of adapting the corporate structure to environmental forces includes a fourth stage, which we will call knowledge-responsive management.

KNOWLEDGE-RESPONSIVE MANAGEMENT

In this "age of discontinuity," as Peter Drucker has observed (*The Age of Discontinuity,* Harper & Row, 1968), experience has become less useful. The decline in the usefulness of experience has resulted from the recognition that the primary resource in the modern economy is knowledge: systematically organized information and concepts.

In order to cope with the change from experience to knowledge, business can hire more professionals who have been trained to solve problems by drawing on their knowledge rather than on their experience. Econometricians, social psychologists, system analysts, and other such professionals rely upon knowledge rather than on operating experience to solve problems. The training of a knowledge-based professional allows him to determine what facts are needed in order to find a solution to a given problem. He understands the process of problem finding which he then links to problem solving through the use of new managerial skills such as econometrics, systems analysis, behavioral science, and information processing. Expertise in structuring procedures for the search effort and for processing information enables the professional to create relevance out of unanalyzed data.

MANAGEMENT INNOVATION AND STAFF

Management has responded to the availability of professionals trained in the new problem-solving skills by rapidly expanding corporate staffs to include them. But this influx of knowledge-based professionals into corporations has so far yielded unimpressive results because management has not created the organization structure that permits application of new management technology.

The organizational form that we think best utilizes the talents of knowledge-based people exactly parallels the product development structure. Innovation in management is similar to innovation in R&D. Just as corporations have established R&D functions to create new products and processes, they should establish a managerial innovation staff which would be responsible for the on-going task of applying new knowledge to management practice. In recognition of the fact that today science and technology are as much a part of management as they are of product R&D, the managerial innovation unit should include:

1. *Management Sciences Research Group,* which monitors the development of new management science in the academic world and conducts research in areas of potential usefulness to the management of the firm it serves;
2. *Management Technology Development Group,* which surveys the activity of the management sciences research group for useful new knowledge, monitors the internal environment of the firm for knowledge-application opportunities, and develops directly applicable cost-effective management tools for the firm it serves;
3. *Management Services Group,* which implements the work of the man-

agement technology development group through joint effort with the line managers who will use the new management tools.

The management innovation staff thus generates the entire process of applying knowledge to management. Each division within the group participates in one stage of the process of applying knowledge to management from science to technology to utilization. This is a tremendous assignment, and the challenge is equal to that of product innovation.

ANTICIPATION VERSUS REACTION

After a firm enters the fourth stage of corporate organization by establishing a management innovation staff, the process of reaction to the environment can be quickened considerably. This occurs in two ways. First, knowledge-based personnel, who understand the forces shaping the environment, can increase the speed with which trends and new events are recognized. This recognition is the key to forecasting the environment accurately, which further opens the way to anticipative action rather than reaction to events that have already occurred.

Second, knowledge is becoming a key input in the process of operations management. Knowledge-based techniques promise to give executives much tighter control of the firms they manage, which should allow a faster and more complete response to significant environmental factors.

Crisis management, the alternative to knowledge-responsiveness, is inefficient. When a "surprise" occurs in the environment, it is often impossible for a firm to recover fully. For example, a firm that allows competition from new sources to gain a share of its market will find difficulty in recovering the original market position it lost through a failure to anticipate. Government regulation is another problem: once the government begins to regulate industrial activity because firms have failed to recognize public interest, no amount of corrective action will be sufficient to satisfy the regulatory agency.

UNDERUTILIZED TECHNOLOGY

The failure of top management to develop a knowledge-responsive organization has resulted in a vast inventory of underutilized management technology. Despite the fact that a changed economic environment has rudely disciplined the managers who are attempting to work on yesterday's problems with traditional tools, a gap exists between available knowledge and knowledge utilized in management applications. The gap exists because fusion of experience and knowledge has not been attempted and, thus, the process is not understood.

Top management is willing to spend millions for computers. Knowledge-based professionals are hired at very high salaries or are employed at even higher per diem consulting rates. But the top management involvement required to achieve a knowledge-responsive management team has been missing. The willingness to spend money on development of new technology without an equal willingness to invest in the effort needed to use it was noted in the concluding chapter of *Factors in the Transfer of Technology* (Gruber and Marquis, M.I.T. Press, 1969, p. 280):

"A comparison of the amounts of money allocated to advance technical knowledge . . . with the amounts allocated for research on the process through which new technology is utilized indicates a disparity that would be corrected if a cost/benefit analysis were to be applied, and the results of this analysis implemented."

Even after top management agrees that knowledge-based professionals will be needed in the management of firms confronting new problems for which there is little experience, it will not utilize these professionals at levels adequate to handle the problems they encounter. One is reminded of Lenin's comment during a famine after the Russian revolution: "The peasants are starving. Therefore they cannot work. Therefore they are starving." At a time when business needs the professionals trained in economics, management science, computer technology, and behavioral science, top management does not know how to work with these younger professionals.

It is important that high-level management bring the special skills of the new professionals into the firm. Organizational synthesis of knowledge and experience will be the critical factor in the success of business in the new environment. The individual manager can decide if the disturbing factors listed at the beginning of this article adequately describe a crisis in business. If, as we believe, a significant new challenge is present, then the required strategy will result in more rapid progress toward knowledge-responsiveness in the organization of business firms. This adaptation of business to its economic environment will contribute significantly to national goals and needs in a way similar to that achieved by progress through the three earlier stages of business structure.

QUESTIONS FOR REVIEW AND DISCUSSION

1. Would you say that the gist of this article is that experience as an essential ingredient of successful management is declining and is being replaced by knowledge, and that this change is reflected by the organization structure used by the manager? Justify your viewpoint.
2. Describe the fourth stage of organization as set forth in this article.
3. Will a knowledge-responsive organization better utilize technology than a centralized formal organization? Explain your answer.

12. Top Research Managers Speak Out on Innovation*

Innovation—What It Is Isn't

Innovation is the process of carrying an idea—perhaps an old, well-known idea—through the laboratory, development, production and then on to successful marketing of a product. The key to innovation is successful marketing of the product. Profitability is an important aspect of innovation.

Innovation is composed of two parts: (1) the generation of an idea or invention, and (2) the conversion of that invention into a business or other useful application. The inventor (Part 1) and the entrepreneur (Part 2) are frequently not the same man. There are two kinds of innovation: (1) that which significantly changes an existing business, and (2) that which creates a business. The recipe for success might not be the same in these two kinds of innovation.

The process of innovation must be carried on all the way to the customer—who has the ultimate decision upon which success or failure of the new venture will depend.

In some areas, particularly pharmaceuticals, innovation rests heavily on a research base. The principal innovator is the research scientist who makes the breakthroughs upon which new developments are based. But, using the generally accepted (broad) definition of innovation—all of the stages from the technical invention to final commercialization—the technical contribution does not have a dominant position.

Innovation covers not only the original discovery or invention, but also its subsequent development and commercialization. Frequently innovation is really imitation—a route which management may select because it is cheaper to be a fast second or third, rather than the pioneer.

* Source: Reprinted with permission of *Research Management*, November 1970, pp. 435–43. Copyright 1970, Industrial Research Institute, Inc. New York: John Wiley & Sons, Inc. This article is based on a summary account of thoughts expressed by over 100 research managers.

The Innovators—What They Are Like and What Makes Them Tick

An innovator can be defined as someone who is sensitive to a need, responds to a need, and accepts responsibility for a solution to the need.

An innovator is one who can visualize something everyone else discounts and is willing to champion a project regardless of personal risk. This is in contrast to the majority who merely extrapolate the state of the art. An innovator does not have to be an inventor but does have to have the resourcefulness and drive to get something done.

There are three kinds of innovators:

1. Those who know what to do and why. They define the problem. They have got to know the business and the trends and be timely. They must select within the capabilities of the organization.
2. Problem solvers. They need to be good scientists but do not have to know much about the industry involved.
3. Innovator seller. They bridge the gap between research and the business community.

Innovators have the following characteristics, but not exclusively:

Provocative Description	Positive Synonym
not likeable	is different
courageous	courageous
paranoid	has character
bright	bright
secretive	values independence
conceited	self assured
has a demon	has drive
difficult to manage	a challenge

Innovators have a wide range of interests, are well read in a variety of fields, are innately curious, enthusiastic and persistent, are frequently good starters and poor finishers, are generally poor as supervisors, and have a high degree of drive for their own activities. The educational level varies considerably and is not in itself a measure of whether the man is likely or unlikely to be an innovator. They are almost always capable of identification, creation or synthesis of a need, and these are true marks of an innovator. He uses a process of inductive thinking as opposed to that often used in the solution of assigned problems, which frequently is a deductive process.

Innovators usually have a broad range of interests and experiences, they tend to be nonconformists, are self-starters, don't give up after initial failures, perform a relatively large volume of work, are sensitive to their environment, may or may not react favorably under pressure, and are generally dissatisfied with the status quo.

The Innovators—How To Care For and Feed Them

We should show our appreciation with money (spot awards up to two months salary) and verbally. We ought to treat them differently and not insist they conform. Innovators can be challenged to new heights by competitive groups. We need a system which allows the innovator to participate in the potential profits if coupled with a sharing of the risks. In short, we shouldn't be afraid of making him a rich man.

It is important to identify one's innovators and give them full recognition by financial remuneration and other rewards. When a project fails, the worker should not be punished by the stigma of failure, since future innovation would then be discouraged.

In the area of rewards, the most permanent are the promise of money, recognition, and publicity when the man succeeds. Avoid making them administrators after their first success. Encourage them to change their fields or to seek greater heights in the same field. Another aspect of the reward situation is to continue to give them recognition and to develop a top management tolerance for these types of individuals and their frequently unconventional behavior and demands.

There is often reluctance to recognize abrasive innovators. This lack of recognition dampens innovation. Thus it takes considerable skill in planning a reward system. Salary is important but that alone doesn't do it. An appreciation from management and respect from one's peers are important.

Idea men or inventors can be stimulated by temporarily relieving them of all other responsibilities than by idea generation and by working in pairs; exposing them to marketing or other business functions and people; firing noncreative types; but transfer of creative people to noninnovative organizations causes them to become less creative. These people frequently generate ideas by asking themselves "is there a better way to accomplish the function of this product?" rather than, "how do I improve this product?" The most productive of them usually have one foot in the laboratory and the other in the marketplace. Entrepreneurs (who make inventions into commercial realities) should have a high energy level (usually young), a complete dedication to success, a large degree of self confidence and initiative, preferably a "through the pores" feel for all aspects of the business and should not be smothered by administrative controls appropriate to a mature business.

Dollars, always a necessary part of reward, are not sufficient. Expanding the scope of research problems (job enrichment) for men known to be talented in innovation is equally important. The German system of rewarding inventors on the basis of patents for processes or products has disadvantages that outweigh the advantages. For the true inventor, the *job* is the thing.

An innovator comes already "turned on." The question is how to keep from turning him off for he will move if conditions aren't right. He should be in an environment where the penalty for failure is light. We need to protect the right of an innovator to make a damn fool of himself.

A double standard should be set for innovators organizationally over the rest of the organization, but it is most important that the innovators must earn the right to receive the different treatment. Other don'ts are to avoid a "not invented here" attitude developing in the rest of the organization and to avoid forcing major innovators to cooperate but rather let them run parallel to one another. In effect, they are or will become "prima donnas" and should be organizationally separate if possible.

Some companies enforce strict working hours and no work outside of these hours. Other companies give meritorious consideration to people who work longer than the 40-hour week. The real innovator "burns the midnight oil" and in some cases to the detriment of his marriage.

Education—What It Doesn't Do

Observing such outstanding innovators as Shockley, Carlson, Land, Pierce and others, we can say that the educational process does not help some innovators, but that they tend to survive in spite of it. Modern education in its demand for specialization tends not to encourage true innovators, because they are frequently those who perform best when they bridge technologies.

Extent of formal education has nothing to do with the degree of inventiveness. In fact, the educational process generally dampens the natural curiosity and imagination of the young. High levels of formal education in an individual are not required for him to be innovative. Certain aspects of formality and conformity in our higher education programs may actually discourage development of innovative characteristics. Perhaps everyone is born with a certain amount of innovative ability, but the necessity to conform to a fairly rigid curriculum may discourage the tendency to be "different." Further constraints after a person enters industry may also cause a person to tread paths with surer returns and decrease the probability of achieving substantial innovation.

The highest level of education (Ph.D.) is not a prerequisite for innovation. Some individuals with B.S. degrees from second-rate colleges have proven to be excellent innovators. However, in the present technological age a good grounding in fundamental science and engineering is necessary. It is further agreed that prolonged exposure to "academia" stifles innovation.

Universities do not teach scientists and engineers how to sell their ideas. Correction of this serious lack is needed more than further teaching on how to make undercreative people more creative.

Corporate Management—How It Can Encourage
or Discourage Innovation

Management must make goals and guidelines known in understandable terms to the innovators, and establish a good rapport with them. This is essential for successful invention and innovation, and a correlation seems to exist between the innovativeness of an industry and the perceived rapport between research and top management therein. Management must also establish an atmosphere of receptivity to innovation in the company and be prepared to back it when it occurs, even if it represents a threat to the established ways of operating.

Management should state clearly and simply the areas of interest. The individual must thoroughly understand what the objective is. Once this is established in his mind he can devote thought to the solution of the problem. Hence, communication from top management to the men at the bench, through the various levels of supervision, is an extremely important factor in innovation.

Both top management and research management must be strongly in favor of innovation and communicate their enthusiasm for it to their research people. It helps even more if the chief executive is an innovator.

Management has to be concerned with the whole sequence of innovation—not only innovation of a technical nature but all other types of innovation as well. Everything has to be put together in a coherent way, and it should be understood that no one step or contribution is more important than the others. Management should recognize the multiplicity of factors (technical, economic, marketing, etc.) needed to contribute to successful innovation—it is truly an interdisciplinary program.

Management must develop patience for the disruptive, creative innovator. Management must also teach the disruptive, innovative person to be patient with management. This can be achieved through explanation of business procedures, construction problems, consumer acceptance, and other intangibles.

The process of innovation is stimulated by an appropriate level of stress imposed by management—evidence of need and interest in a solution. However, management must protect the innovator from discouragement and frustration. Explanations must be given as to why good ideas are not pursued. Management must be ready and willing to take the risks involved in testing and using the innovative concept or innovation will be stifled.

Organization and Operation—How To Do It for Best Results

Research is generally structured along functional lines, whereas development is generally structured on a project basis. Coordination within and across these different structures requires considerable skill. A coordinator must deal with people at levels both below and above him. Success of an innovative group depends on the coordinator. He must not only be a manager of technology, he must also know how to coordinate people with different backgrounds—science, engineering, production, and sales. A coordinator must know how to use innovative talent, although he, himself, does not have to be an innovator.

It is unwise to be wedded to an inflexible organizational structure. Even after a venture group is organized, management should feel free to make changes when necessary. Innovation is less likely to occur in large, well organized groups. Formal organization, policies and control can inhibit or stifle innovation.

Too much formal organization in departments and between departments stifles innovation. Some companies are experimenting on having a temporary research project leader during the duration of each project rather than having permanent group leaders cover indefinitely broad fields of interest. This use of temporary project leaders gives management an opportunity to test more men for their leadership strengths and avoids anyone becoming overconfident or stale as a manager.

Most companies have some type of task force for innovation, new product ideas, ventures, etc. These groups vary from distinct full-time venture groups to brain-storming or similar ad hoc part-time interdisciplinary groups. Everyone has problems in trying to guide and particularly in stopping such groups when management deems it necessary.

Create a new project team for each new project, with members from research, marketing, often manufacturing and any other pertinent departments such as engineering, patent, etc. Apparently most companies create a new project team after the general manager or total division has already been committed to the success of a particular project. Some companies use this project team to sell the new project to the general manager. The higher the risk of the new project, the more important the official commitment by the general manager. Frequently the research man must prepare the first market estimate and frequently he is the chairman of the project team.

It is generally considered desirable to allocate a substantial (20–30%) amount of effort for exploratory work. It is better to have such effort dispersed throughout the entire organization, rather than earmark such a group.

A "new venture" or "new enterprise" division can handle commercial innovation combining marketing factors with technical factors in an innovative business background, allowing for early losses and starting costs, and avoiding the inhibitions of established short-term profit standards and noninnovative market concepts.

Exploratory projects require definitions stressing containment of scope to prevent diffusion and a warning that timing and the position of the company must be considered. The participation of marketing research in exploratory or central research is absolutely essential in defining desirable limits for innovation. The integration of marketing into research planning and evaluation of research results appears to require new techniques of organization. Put scientists into marketing research or have a specific marketing research function in the R&D organization.

Feedback to the laboratory of how a new development is progressing (i.e., beyond the discovery) is a significant morale factor, but implies outdated thinking. If we consider the overall innovative scheme, the laboratory must participate not only in the technical innovation step at the beginning, but should continue to contribute innovatively until final success is achieved. This represents an advance from the notion of "keeping them informed," to one of "keeping them involved."

Many divisions and corporations are beginning to periodically record for internal use the "needs in the marketplace" and then encourage their R&D men to choose which new project each would like to work on. Often several competitive approaches are permitted during the early stages of a key project. Many companies have no specific budget for each project; they merely have a total divisional R&D budget. In some companies the relative sales and profits to be expected from the successful conclusion of each new research project are told to the men after they have chosen which project they want to work on. One company apparently tells its R&D men the relative priority list of all their major research projects.

Outside Resources—When and How to Use Them

The need for outside resources depends on (1) type of project, and (2) type of company. Oftentimes, a promising project fails to achieve innovation owing to insufficient financial support. In these cases, support can be obtained from the financial community or by establishment of a joint venture with another company. Some R&D organizations depend on the federal government for financial support.

Many companies rely on outside consultants for scientific input into the innovative process. There are examples where either professors or independent laboratories have played important roles in such innovation; however, the key role must be played by the company's R&D personnel. Companies refuse to consider proposals by individual inventors except for college professors. In one case, of 400 ideas evaluated over the period of a year, 72 were by individual inventors and one was accepted compared to about 10% of the ideas from college professors or labs. For this and other reasons, most companies are not looking for innovation from out-siders except to buy established companies with innovative products.

The following individuals, who served as discussion leaders or secre-taries of the round tables, provided the reports from which this summary account was compiled.

P. W. Crane, Round-Table Chairman, Cincinnati Milling Machine Co.

D. M. McQueen, E. I. du Pont de Nemours & Co.

J. D. D'Ianni, The Goodyear Tire & Rubber Co.

L. H. Sarett, Merck Sharp & Dohme Co., Inc.

G. Brown, St. Joseph Lead Co.

L. C. Krogh, 3M Co.

R. J. Schatz, Monsanto Co.

K. J. Brunings, Geigy Pharmaceuticals

R. R. Burns, Nalco Chemical Co.

H. R. Boyd, Raytheon Co.

M. Senkus, R. J. Reynolds Tobacco Co.

D. W. Collier, Borg-Warner Corp.

L. L. Davenport, General Telephone and Electronics Lab., Inc.

D. P. Krotz, Chevron Research Co.

R. S. Crog, Union Oil Company of California

E. C. Galloway, Stauffer Chemical Co.

R. Cairns, Hercules, Inc.

QUESTIONS FOR REVIEW AND DISCUSSION

1. According to this reading, there are three kinds of innovators. Name each of these and tell what each does.

2. Briefly discuss five suggestions from the many the reading gives for success-fully managing innovators.

3. By means of an illustration, show the difference between "keeping them informed" and "keeping them involved" with reference to feedback to the laboratory on how a new development is progressing.

4. Expand on the following statement, "Success of an innovative group de-pends on the coordinator."

13. Six Ways to Generate New Product Ideas*

MARTIN WEINBERGER

Much of what has been written about generating new product ideas sounds very impressive, very mysterious and very complicated.

Trying to reverse the trend, I have tried to say something about the subject in terms that don't require a Ph.D. to understand or enjoy—categorized as "six ways to generate new product ideas."

1. Listen to Gripes

A lot of researchers say that consumers can't tell what they want. Don't believe them. Consumers often can tell you in no uncertain terms precisely what they *don't* want. Which is their way of saying what they *do* want.

In several studies we have done, consumer dissatisfaction with currently available products was so strong and so pervasive that new product concepts could be developed instantly simply by listening to what the consumer had to say. Of course, there was a subsequent need to find out if the concepts were technically feasible, to screen for the most promising concepts, and to determine the size and character of the prospective market for each concept. But the concept generation itself was based squarely on consumer gripes.

We can't reveal the specific findings we uncovered, but, by way of example, we can present some hypothetical gripes that could easily have led to new products, new forms, new packages, or new services. What would *you* do if you heard these gripes?

"It's annoying to have to look for a can opener every time you want a beer."

"I hate to pay a service charge when I haven't written any checks."

"The last few slices of bread are always stale before I get to eat them."

* Source: Reprinted with permission of *Advertising Age*, December 6, 1971, p. 41. Copyright 1971 by Crain Communications, Inc. Martin Weinberger is vice president, director of research, Oxtoby-Smith, Inc., New York.

"Sometimes my deodorant smells stronger than my perfume."

"Every so often, I lock my car keys in the car."

"There's nothing more irritating than being on a long flight when they're showing a movie you've already seen."

Maybe you would have developed self-opening beer cans, charged only for checks written, put wrappers within wrappers on bread, created an odorless deodorant, solved the car key problem, or offered more than one movie on a flight. Or maybe you would have thought of different solutions to the same problems. In any event, it should be evident that gripes can be a pregnant source of new product ideas.

2. Marry Satisfactions

Okay, suppose in your product category there are no real dissatisfactions. Everybody loves the products they use. In that case, build a new product based on those satisfactions—by marrying a pair of satisfactions. For example:

If people drink coffee in the morning to help them wake up, and drink orange juice to give them nutrition, then why not develop:

1. A coffee with nutrition; or . . .
2. An orange juice that wakes you up; or . . .
3. A new product that both wakes you up and gives you nutrition.

Furthermore, if we were to learn that people like to drink hot coffee to warm themselves on a winter day, the new beverage could be served hot.

Or, if people object to the inconvenience of preparing hot coffee, the new beverage might be served cold.

Or, to satisfy both segments of the market, the new beverage could be served *either* hot or cold, thus providing warmth when needed, convenience when demanded.

Of course, this is somewhat oversimplified—some combinations are technically not feasible, or simply not wanted (a good tasting medicine may be thought of as ineffective; ditto, a good smelling ammonia). That doesn't obviate the fact that combining satisfactions is frequently a productive, useful and lucrative way to develop new product ideas.

3. Steal

One of the problems people have when they work within a product category for a long time is that they develop tunnel vision. They've combed out all of the dissatisfactions and combined all of the satisfactions—and they don't see that there are other satisfactions around, satisfactions not necessarily provided by their own product category.

For example:

If Marlboros made men out of smokers, and Eve makes women feel feminine, can the same be done by a coffee? A beer? A soft drink?

If soft drinks make you feel young, can a fragrance? Can an airline? Can a bank?

If you can find a friend in a bank, can you find one at a gas station? At a car dealer? At a supermarket?

If Avon can sell cosmetics door-to-door, can gasoline be sold (private) garage-to-garage? Need any auto accessories, sir?

What I'm saying is that one way to get fresh ideas is to take a good look at the advertising and marketing for other product categories. Those ideas seem to be making money for others. Perhaps they can make money for you. Maybe you should steal one.

4. Borrow

Do you think consumers are using your product the way you designed it to be used? Maybe so. But very often the consumer will think of new uses for your product you never dreamed of. You can "borrow" those uses and sell them to others. For example:

Some consumers use flour to bake Christmas decorations;

Some teen-agers use iodine and baby oil for suntan lotion;

Some people shower with a liquid medicated cleanser;

Some women use Q-Tips for cleaning the stove;

Some men use marshmallows for bait when fishing.

In other words, a lot of old products are being used in new ways. Consumers themselves are making "new" products every day. If you find out what they're doing, you can "borrow" their ideas.

5. Stand on Your Head

Sometimes a new idea can be produced by turning a current product upside down.

For example, if coffee is widely consumed to help people wake up, why is there no beverage widely used to help people sleep?

Or, taking another whack: If consumers add milk to coffee to improve the taste of coffee, could they be persuaded to add coffee to milk to improve the taste of milk?

The world looks a little different when you stand on your head—and, if you don't lose your balance, you may find some new product ideas by looking at the world that way.

6. Try Harder

Your product may be No. 2 to another product. Maybe you can make it No. 1. Here is what you do:

1. First you ask consumers what brands or products they would use if they couldn't get their regular brand or product. (Suppose there *were* no cigarets, would you smoke cigars?)

2. Then you find out why they don't use that substitute product more often (cigars are too messy after you've had them in your mouth for a while).

3. Then you develop a product which improves on the current substitute (cigars with tips), and maybe you can get the consumer to use that improved product *primarily,* instead of as a substitute.

To do this properly, you would not only find out what the substitute *lacks* that the usual brand has, you would also find out if the substitute product has some *benefits* that the usual brand lacks. Then you ac-cen-tu-ate the positive and e-lim-i-nate the negative.

There they are, six easy ways to develop new product ideas. Not mysterious. Not complicated. No graduate training required. Is it possible that good, useful, and even profitable ideas can be generated in so "simple" a manner? I believe they can.

What role does research play in all of this? I believe research can and should be used as both an input to help generate the new product ideas, and as a screening device to help identify the most promising ideas, once they have been developed.

Indeed, each of the "tricks" described in this article is made easier by research. Research can:

Help to uncover gripes and dissatisfactions which new products can remedy.

Help to identify prospective satisfactions, and serve as a broker for arranging "marriages" of satisfactions.

Help lift the blindfold that restrains "stealing" gratifications from another product category.

Uncover new uses for existing products which can then be "borrowed."

Provide a portrait of gratifications to be turned upside down (an alternate to standing on your head).

Tell you *why* you're not number one, and help point out the avenues you need to pursue to catch up and move ahead of number one.

Finally, once the new ideas have been generated, research can help to identify those with the most promising market potential.

QUESTIONS FOR REVIEW AND DISCUSSION

1. Give an example to illustrate a new product idea developed from "listening to gripes."

2. Indicate four ways research can help a manager generate new product ideas.

3. Select a food product of your choice and relate how you would generate new ideas about it in order to improve its consumer satisfaction and sales.

part FOUR

Systems, Computers, and Quantitative Techniques

Attention is directed in this part to the use of computers in management, systems analysis of problems, and mathematical models. Essentially, these are aids to the manager. They help him reach the best decision and take the actions most effective in achieving the stated goals. For the most part, the systematic interrelatedness and interaction among components, the utilization of data and variables having measurable values, and a comparison of various feasible alternatives are featured by these aids. Four readings make up this part of management systems and quantitative techniques.

Professor Russell L. Ackoff's "Towards A System Of Systems Concepts" clarifies the meaning of system and suggests possible answers to questions concerning the scope, content, and taxonomy of systems.

The next reading, "Who Should Boss the Computer," stresses the need for the improved of the computer to assist management to get its job done. It is brought out that computerization of existing practices and systems commonly results in failure to gain maximum benefits that the computer is capable of providing. Interesting suggestions including what some companies are doing to improve their computer operation are offered.

"Linear Programming" by Dr. John W. Coughlan provides a specific and informative example of how a popular quantitative technique, linear programming, may be employed by a manager. It describes the use in management of measurable data, graphic models, algebra, matrix models, and the concept of optimizing—all presented in a readily understood and comprehensive manner.

The last reading "Simulation Cuts Inventory Center Costs" is by V. Steven Blood and William V. Santos. It offers an application of simulation to a common problem, namely, that of reducing the time required to order a part and await its delivery.

Simulation is fast becoming a popular quantitative means employed by management to test suggested corrective action without risking large expenditures and interfering with current operations.

14. Toward a System of Systems Concepts*

RUSSELL L. ACKOFF

INTRODUCTION

The concept *system* has come to play a critical role in contemporary science.[1] This preoccupation of scientists in general is reflected among Management Scientists in particular for whom the *systems approach* to problems is fundamental and for whom *organizations*, a special type of system, are the principal subject of study.

The systems approach to problems focuses on systems taken as a whole, not on their parts taken separately. Such an approach is concerned with total-system performance even when a change in only one or a few of its parts is contemplated because there are some properties of systems that can only be treated adequately from a holistic point of view. These properties derive from the *relationships* between parts of systems: how the parts interact and fit together. In an imperfectly organized system even if every part performs as well as possible relative to its own objectives, the total system will often not perform as well as possible relative to its objectives.

Despite the importance of systems concepts and the attention that they have received and are receiving, we do not yet have a unified or integrated set (i.e., a system) of such concepts. Different terms are used to refer to the same thing and the same term is used to refer to different things. This state is aggravated by the fact that the literature of systems research is widely dispersed and is therefore difficult to track. Researchers in a wide variety of disciplines and interdisciplines are contributing to the conceptual development of the systems sciences but these contributions

* Source: Reprinted with permission of *Management Science*, July 1971, pp. 661–71. Dr. Russell L. Ackoff is professor of operations research, University of Pennsylvania, Philadelphia.
[1] For excellent extensive and intensive discussions of "systems thinking," see F. E. Emery [3] and C. W. Churchman [2].

are not as interactive and additive as they might be. Fred Emery [3] has warned against too hasty an effort to remedy this situation:

It is almost as if the pioneers [of systems thinking], while respectfully noting each other's existence, have felt it incumbent upon themselves to work out their intuitions in their own language, for fear of what might be lost in trying to work through the language of another. Whatever the reason, the results seem to justify the standoffishness. In a short space of time there has been a considerable accumulation of insights into system dynamics that are readily translatable into different languages and with, as yet, little sign of divisive schools of thought that for instance marred psychology during the 1920s and 1930s. Perhaps this might happen if some influential group of scholars prematurely decide that the time has come for a common conceptual framework (p. 12).

Although I sympathize with Emery's fear, a fear that is rooted in a research perspective, as a teacher I feel a great need to provide my students with a conceptual framework that will assist them in absorbing and synthesizing this large accumulation of insights to which Emery refers. My intent is not to preclude further conceptual exploration, but rather to encourage it and make it more interactive and additive. Despite Emery's warning I feel benefits will accrue to systems research from an evolutionary convergence of concepts into a generally accepted framework. At any rate, little harm is likely to come from my effort to provide the beginnings of such a framework since I can hardly claim to be, or to speak for, "an influential group of scholars."

The framework that follows does not include all concepts relevant to the systems sciences. I have made an effort, however, to include enough of the key concepts so that building on this framework will not be as difficult as construction of the framework itself has been.

One final word of introduction. I have not tried to identify the origin or trace the history of each conceptual idea that is presented in what follows. Hence few credits are provided. I can only compensate for this lack of bibliographic bird-dogging by claiming no credit for any of the elements in what follows, only for the resulting system into which they have been organized. I must, of course, accept responsibility for deficiencies in either the parts or the whole.

SYSTEMS

1. A *system* is a set of interrelated elements. Thus a system is an entity which is composed of at least two elements and a relation that holds between each of its elements and at least one other element in the set. Each of a system's elements is connected to every other element, directly or indirectly. Furthermore, no subset of elements is unrelated to any other subset.

2. An *abstract system* is one all of whose elements are concepts. Languages, philosophic systems, and number systems are examples. *Numbers* are concepts but the symbols that represent them, *numerals*, are physical things. Numerals, however, are not the elements of a number system. The use of different numerals to represent the same numbers does not change the nature of the system.

In an abstract system the elements are created by defining and the relationships between them are created by assumptions (e.g., axioms and postulates). Such systems, therefore, are the subject of study of the so-called "formal sciences."

3. A *concrete system* is one at least two of whose elements are objects. It is only with such systems that we are concerned here. Unless otherwise noted, "system" will always be used to mean "concrete system."

In concrete systems establishment of the existence and properties of elements and the nature of the relationships between them requires research with an empirical component in it. Such systems, therefore, are the subject of study of the so-called "nonformal sciences."

4. The *state of a system* at a moment of time is the set of relevant properties which that system has at that time. Any system has an unlimited number of properties. Only some of these are relevant to any particular research. Hence those which are relevant may change with changes in the purpose of the research. The values of the relevant properties constitute the state of the system. In some cases we may be interested in only two possible states (e.g., off and on, or awake and asleep). In other cases we may be interested in a large or unlimited number of possible states (e.g., a system's velocity or weight).

5. The *environment of a system* is a set of elements and their relevant properties, which elements are not part of the system but a change in any of which can produce[2] a change in the state of the system. Thus a system's environment consists of all variables which can affect its state. External elements which affect irrelevant properties of a system are not part of its environment.

6. The *state of a system's environment* at a moment of time is the set of its relevant properties at that time. The state of an element or subset of elements of a system or its environment may be similarly defined.

Although concrete systems and their environments are *objective* things, they are also *subjective* insofar as the particular configuration of elements that form both is dictated by the interests of the researcher. Different

---

[2] One thing (x) can be said to produce another (y) in a specified environment and time interval if x is a necessary but not a sufficient condition for y in that environment and time period. Thus a producer is a "probabilistic cause" of its product. Every producer, since it is not sufficient for its product, has a coproducer of that product (e.g., the producer's environment).

observers of the same phenomena may conceptualize them into different systems and environments. For example, an architect may consider a house together with its electrical, heating, and water systems as one large system. But a mechanical engineer may consider the heating system as a system and the house as its environment. To a social psychologist a house may be an environment of a family, the system with which he is concerned. To him the relationship between the heating and electrical systems may be irrelevant, but to the architect it may be very relevant.

The elements that form the environment of a system and the environment itself may be conceptualized as systems when they become the focus of attention. Every system can be conceptualized as part of another and larger system.

Even an abstract system can have an environment. For example, the metalanguage in which we describe a formal system is the environment of that formal system. Therefore, logic is the environment of mathematics.

7. A *closed system* is one that has no environment. An *open system* is one that does. Thus a closed system is one which is conceptualized so that it has no interaction with any element not contained within it; it is completely self-contained. Because systems researchers have found such conceptualizations of relatively restricted use, their attention has increasingly focused on more complex and "realistic" open systems. "Openness" and "closedness" are simultaneously properties of systems and our conceptualizations of them.

Systems may or may not change over time.

8. A system (or environmental) *event* is a change in one or more structural properties of the system (or its environment) over a period of time of specified duration; that is, a change in the structural state of the system (or environment). For example, an event occurs to a house's lighting system when a fuse blows, and to its environment when night falls.

9. A *static (one-state) system* is one to which no events occur. A table, for example, can be conceptualized as a static concrete system consisting of four legs, top, screws, glue, and so on. Relative to most research purposes it displays no change of structural properties, no change of state. A compass may also be conceptualized as a static system because it virtually always points to the magnetic North Pole.

10. A *dynamic (multistate) system* is one to which events occur, whose state changes over time. An automobile which can move forward or backward and at different speeds is such a system, or a motor which can be either off or on. Such systems can be conceptualized as either open or closed; closed if its elements react or respond only to each other.

11. A *homeostatic system* is a static system whose elements and environment are dynamic. Thus a homeostatic system is one that retains its state in a changing environment by internal adjustments. A house that

maintains a constant temperature during changing external temperatures is homeostatic. The behavior of its heating subsystem makes this possible.

Note that the same object may be conceptualized as either a static or dynamic system. For most of us a building would be thought of as static, but it might be taken as dynamic by a civil engineer who is interested in structural deformation.

System Changes

12. A *reaction* of a system is a system event for which another event that occurs to the same system or its environment is sufficient. Thus a reaction is a system event that is deterministically caused by another event. For example, if an operator's moving a motor's switch is sufficient to turn that motor off or on, then the change of state of the motor is a reaction to the movement of its switch. In this case, the turning of the switch may be necessary as well as sufficient for the state of the motor. But an event that is sufficient to bring about a change in a system's state may not be necessary for it. For example, sleep may be brought about by drugs administered to a person or it may be self-induced. Thus sleep may be determined by drugs but need not be.

13. A *response* of a system is a system event for which another event that occurs to the same system or to its environment is necessary but not sufficient; that is, a system event produced by another system or environmental event (the *stimulus*). Thus a response is an event of which the system itself is a coproducer. A system does not have to respond to a stimulus, but it does have to react to its cause. Therefore, a person's turning on a light when it gets dark is a response to darkness, but the light's going on when the switch is turned is a reaction.

14. An *act* of a system is a system event for the occurrence of which no change in the system's environment is either necessary or sufficient. Acts, therefore, are self-determined events, autonomous changes. Internal changes—in the states of the system's elements—are both necessary and sufficient to bring about action. Much of the behavior of human beings is of this type, but such behavior is not restricted to humans. A computer, for example, may have its state changed or change the state of its environment because of its own program.

Systems all of whose changes are reactive, responsive, or autonomous (active) can be called reactive, responsive, or autonomous (active), respectively. Most systems, however, display some combination of these types of change.

The classification of systems into reactive, responsive, and autonomous is based on consideration of what brings about changes in them. Now let us consider systems with respect to what kind of changes in themselves and their environments their reactions, responses, and actions bring about.

15. A system's *behavior* is a system event(s) which is either necessary or sufficient for another event in that system or its environment. Thus behavior is a system change which initiates other events. Note that reactions, responses, and actions may themselves constitute behavior. Reactions, responses, and actions are system events *whose antecedents are of interest.* Behavior consists of system events *whose consequences are of interest.* We may, of course, be interested in both the antecedents and consequences of system events.

Behavioral Classification of Systems

Understanding the nature of the classification that follows may be aided by Table 1 in which the basis for the classification is revealed.

16. A *state-maintaining system* is one that (1) can react in only one way to any one external or internal event but (2) it reacts differently to different external or internal events, and (3) these different reactions produce the same external or internal state (outcome). Such a system only reacts to changes; it cannot respond because what it does is completely determined by the causing event. Nevertheless it can be said to have the *function* of maintaining the state it produces because it can produce this state in different ways under different conditions.

Thus a heating system whose internal controller turns it on when the room temperature is below a desired level, and turns it off when the temperature is above this level, is state-maintaining. The state it maintains is a room temperature that falls within a small range around its setting. Note that the temperature of the room which affects the system's behavior can be conceptualized as either part of the system or part of its environment. Hence a state-maintaining system may react to either internal or external changes.

In general, most systems with 'stats' (e.g., thermostats and humidistats) are state-maintaining. Any system with a regulated output (e.g., the voltage of the output of a generator) is also state-maintaining.

A compass is also state-maintaining because in many different environments it points to the magnetic North Pole.

A state-maintaining system must be able to *discriminate* between different internal or external states to changes in which it reacts. Furthermore, as we shall see below, such systems are necessarily *adaptive*, but unlike goal-seeking systems they are not capable of learning because they cannot choose their behavior. They cannot improve with experience.

17. A *goal-seeking system* is one that can respond differently to one or more different external or internal events in one or more different

external or internal states and that can respond differently to a particular event in an unchanging environment until it produces a particular state (outcome). Production of this state is its goal. Thus such a system has a *choice* of behavior. A goal-seeking system's behavior is responsive, but not reactive. A state which is sufficient and thus deterministically causes a reaction cannot cause different reactions in the same environment.

Under constant conditions a goal-seeking system may be able to accomplish the same thing in different ways and it may be able to do so under different conditions. If it has *memory*, it can increase its efficiency over time in producing the outcome that is its goal.

TABLE 1. Behavioral Classification of Systems

Type of System	Behavior of System	Outcome of Behavior
State-maintaining	Variable but determined (reactive)	Fixed
Goal-seeking	Variable and chosen (responsive)	Fixed
Multigoal-seeking and purposive	Variable and chosen	Variable but determined
Purposeful	Variable and chosen	Variable and chosen

For example, an electronic maze-solving rat is a goal-seeking system which, when it runs into a wall of a maze, turns right and if stopped again, goes in the opposite direction, and if stopped again, returns in the direction from which it came. In this way it can eventually solve any solvable maze. If, in addition, it has memory, it can take a 'solution path' on subsequent trials in a familiar maze.

Systems with automatic 'pilots' are goal-seeking. These and other goal-seeking systems may, of course, fail to attain their goals in some situations.

The sequence of behavior which a goal-seeking system carries out in quest of its goal is an example of a process.

18. A *process* is a sequence of behavior that constitutes a system and has a goal-producing function. In some well-definable sense each unit of behavior in the process brings the actor closer to the goal which it seeks. The sequence of behavior that is performed by the electronic rat constitutes a maze-solving process. After each move the rat is closer (i.e., has reduced the number of moves required) to solve the maze. The metabolic process in living things is a similar type of sequence the goal of which is acquisition of energy or, more generally, survival. Production processes are a similar type of sequence whose goal is a particular type of product.

Process behavior displayed by a system may be either reactive, responsive, or active.

19. A *multigoal-seeking* system is one that is goal-seeking in each of two or more different (initial) external or internal states, and which seeks different goals in at least two different states, the goal being determined by the initial state.

20. A *purposive system* is a multigoal-seeking system the different goals of which have a common property. Production of that common property is the system's purpose. These types of system can pursue different goals but they do not select the goal to be pursued. The goal is determined by the initiating event. But such a system does choose the means by which to pursue its goals.

A computer which is programmed to play more than one game (e.g., tic-tac-toe and checkers) is multigoal-seeking. What game it plays is not a matter of its choice, however; it is usually determined by an instruction from an external source. Such a system is also purposive because "game winning" is a common property of the different goals which it seeks.

21. A *purposeful system* is one which can produce the same outcome in different ways in the same (internal or external) state and can produce different outcomes in the same and different states. Thus a purposeful system is one which can change its goals under constant conditions; it selects ends as well as means and thus displays *will*. Human beings are the most familiar examples of such systems.

Ideal-seeking systems form an important subclass of purposeful systems. Before making their nature explicit we must consider the differences between goals, objectives, and ideals and some concepts related to them. The differences to be considered have relevance only to purposeful systems because only they can choose ends.

A system which can choose between different outcomes can place different values on different outcomes.

22. The *relative value of an outcome* that is a member of an exclusive and exhaustive set of outcomes, to a purposeful system, is the probability that the system will produce that outcome when each of the set of outcomes can be obtained with certainty. The relative value of an outcome can range from 0 to 1.0. That outcome with the highest relative value in a set can be said to be *preferred*.

23. The *goal* of a purposeful system in a particular situation is a preferred outcome that can be obtained within a specified time period.

24. The *objective* of a purposeful system in a particular situation is a preferred outcome that cannot be obtained within a specified period but which can be obtained over a longer time period. Consider a set of possible outcomes ordered along one or more scales (e.g., increasing speeds of travel). Then each outcome is closer to the final one than those which precede it. Each of these outcomes can be a goal in some time period after the "preceding" goal has been obtained, leading eventually to attain-

ment of the last outcome, the objective. For example, a high-school fresh-man's goal in his first year is to be promoted to his second (sophomore) year. Passing his second year is a subsequent goal. And so on to gradua-tion, which is his objective.

Pursuit of an objective requires an ability to change goals once a goal has been obtained. This is why such pursuit is possible only for a pur-poseful system.

25. An *ideal* is an objective which cannot be obtained in any time period but which can be approached without limit. Just as goals can be ordered with respect to objectives, objectives can be ordered with respect to ideals. But an ideal is an outcome which is unobtainable in practice, if not in principle. For example, an ideal of science is errorless observa-tions. The amount of observer error can be reduced without limit but can never be reduced to zero. Omniscience is another such ideal.

26. An *ideal-seeking system* is a purposeful system which, on attain-ment of any of its goals or objectives, then seeks another goal and objec-tive which more closely approximates its ideal. An ideal-seeking system is thus one which has a concept of "perfection" or the "ultimately desir-able" and pursues it systematically; that is, in interrelated steps.

From the point of view of their output, six types of system have been identified: state-maintaining, goal-seeking, multigoal-seeking, purposive, purposeful, and ideal-seeking. The elements of systems can be similarly classified. The relationship between (1) the behavior and type of a system and (2) the behavior and type of its elements is not apparent. We con-sider it next.

RELATIONSHIPS BETWEEN SYSTEMS AND THEIR ELEMENTS

Some systems can display a greater variety and higher level of behavior than can any of their elements. These can be called *variety increasing*. For example, consider two state-maintaining elements, A and B. Say A reacts to a decrease in room temperature by closing any open windows. If a short time after A has reacted the room temperature is still below a specified level, B reacts to this by turning on the furnace. Then the system consisting of A and B is goal-seeking.

Clearly, by combining two or more goal-seeking elements we can construct a multigoal-seeking (and hence a purposive) system. It is less apparent that such elements can also be combined to form a purposeful system. Suppose one element A can pursue goal G_1 in environment E_1 and goal G_2 in another environment E_2; and the other element B can pursue G_2 in E_1 and G_1 in E_2. Then the system would be capable of pur-suing G_1 and G_2 in both E_1 and E_2 if it could select between the elements in these environments. Suppose we add a third (controlling) element which responds to E_1 by "turning on" either A or B, but not both. Suppose further that it turns on A with probability P_A where $0 < P_A < 1.0$ and turns on B with probability P_B where $0 < P_B < 1.0$. (The controller could be a computer that employs random numbers for this purpose.) The resulting system could choose both ends and means in two environments and hence would be purposeful.

A system can also show less variety of behavior and operate at a lower level than at least some of its elements. Such a system is *variety reducing*. For example, consider a simple system with two elements one of which turns lights on in a room whenever the illumination in that room drops below a certain level. The other element turns the lights off whenever the illumination exceeds a level that is lower than that provided by the lights in the room. Then the lights will go off and on continuously. The system would not be state-maintaining even though its elements are.

A more familiar example of a variety-reducing system can be found in those groups of purposeful people (e.g., committees) which are incapable of reaching agreement and hence of taking any collective action.

A system must be either variety-increasing or variety-decreasing. A set of elements which collectively neither increase nor decrease variety would have to consist of identical elements either only one of which can act at a time or in which similar action by multiple units is equivalent to action by only one. In the latter case the behavior is nonadditive and the behavior is redundant. The relationships between the elements would therefore be irrelevant. For example, a set of similar automobiles owned by one person do not constitute a system because he can drive only one at a time and which he drives makes no difference. On the other hand a radio with two speakers can provide stereo sound; the speakers each do a different thing and together they do something that neither can do alone.

ADAPTATION AND LEARNING

In order to deal with the concepts "adaptation" and "learning" it is necessary first to consider the concepts "function" and "efficiency."

27. The *function(s)* of a system is production of the outcomes that define its goal(s) and objective(s). Put another way, suppose a system can display at least two structurally different types of behavior in the same or different environments and that these types of behavior produce the same kind of outcome. Then the system can be said to have the function of producing that outcome. To function, therefore, is to be able to produce the same outcome in different ways.

Let C_i $(1 \leq i \leq m)$ represent the different actions available to a system in a specific environment. Let P_i represent the probabilities that the system will select these courses of action in that environment. If the courses of action are exclusive and exhaustive, then $\Sigma_{i=1}^{m} P_i = 1.0$. Let E_{ij} represent the probability that course of action C_i will produce a particular outcome O_j in that environment. Then:

28. The *efficiency* of the system with respect to an outcome O_j which it has the function of producing is $\Sigma_{i=1}^{m} P_i E_{ij}$.

Now we can turn to "adaptation."

29. A system is *adaptive* if, when there is a change in its environmental and/or internal state which reduces its efficiency in pursuing one or more of its goals which define its function(s), it reacts or responds by changing its own state and/or that of its environment so as to increase its efficiency with respect to that goal or goals. Thus adaptiveness is the ability of a system to modify itself or its environment when either has changed to the system's disadvantage so as to regain at least some of its lost efficiency.

The definition of "adaptive" implies four types of adaptation:

29.1. *Other-other adaptation:* A system's reacting or responding to an external change by modifying the environment (e.g., when a person turns on an air conditioner in a room in which it has become too warm for him to continue to work).

29.2. *Other-self adaptation:* A system's reacting or responding to an external change by modifying itself (e.g., when the person moves to another and cooler room).

29.3. *Self-other adaptation:* A system's reacting or responding to an internal change by modifying the environment (e.g., when a person who has chills due to a cold turns up the heat).

29.4. *Self-self adaptation:* A system's reacting or responding to an internal change by modifying itself (e.g., when that person takes medication to suppress the chills). Other-self adaptation is most commonly considered because it was this type with which Darwin was concerned in his studies of biological species as systems.

It should now be apparent why state-maintaining and higher systems are necessarily adaptive. Now let us consider why nothing lower than a goal-seeking system is capable of learning.

30. To *learn* is to increase one's efficiency in the pursuit of a goal under unchanging conditions. Thus if a person increases his ability to hit a target (his goal) with repeated shooting at it, he learns how to shoot better. Note that to do so requires an ability to modify one's behavior (i.e., to display choice) and memory.

Since learning can take place only when a system has a choice among alternative courses of action, only systems that are goal-seeking or higher can learn.

If a system is repeatedly subjected to the same environmental or internal change and increases its ability to maintain its efficiency under this type of change, then it *learns how to adapt.* Thus adaptation itself can be learned.

ORGANIZATIONS

Management scientists are most concerned with that type of system called "organizations." Cyberneticians, on the other hand, are more concerned with that type of system called "organisms," but they frequently treat organizations as though they were organisms. Although these two types of system have much in common, there is an important difference between them. This difference can be identified once "organization" has been defined. I will work up to its definition by considering separately each of what I consider to be its four essential characteristics.

(1) An organization is a purposeful system that contains at least two purposeful elements which have a common purpose.

We sometimes characterize a purely mechanical system as being well organized, but we would not refer to it as an "organization." This results from the fact that we use "organize" to mean, "to make a system of," or, as one dictionary puts it, "to get into proper working order," and "to arrange or dispose systematically." Wires, poles, transformers, switchboards, and telephones may constitute a communication system, but they do not constitute an organization. The employees of a telephone company make up the organization that operates the telephone system. Organization of a system is an activity that can be carried out only by purposeful entities; to be an organization a system must contain such entities.

An aggregation of purposeful entities does not constitute an organization unless they have at least one common purpose: that is, unless there is some one or more things that they all want. An organization is always organized around this common purpose. It is the relationships between what the purposeful elements do and the pursuit of their common purpose that give unity and identity to their organization.

Without a common purpose the elements would not work together unless compelled to do so. A group of unwilling prisoners or slaves can be organized and forced to do something that they do not want to do, but if so they do not constitute an organization even though they may form a system. An organization consists of elements that have and can exercise their own wills.

(2) An organization has a functional division of labor in pursuit of the common purpose(s) of its elements that define it.

Each of two or more subsets of elements, each containing one or more purposeful elements, is responsible for choosing from among different courses of action. A choice from each subset is necessary for obtaining the common purpose. For example, if an automobile carrying two people stalls on a highway and one gets out and pushes while the other sits in the driver's seat trying to start it when it is in motion, then there is a functional division of labor and they constitute an organization. The car cannot be started (their common purpose) unless both functions are performed.

The classes of courses of action and (hence) the subsets of elements may be differentiated by a variety of types of characteristics; for example:

(a) by *function* (e.g., production, marketing, research, finance, and personnel, in the industrial context),

(b) by *space* (e.g., geography, as territories of sales offices), and

(c) by *time* (e.g., waves of an invading force).

The classes of action may, of course, also be defined by combinations of these and other characteristics.

It should be noted that individuals or groups in an organization that *make* choices need not *take* them; that is, carry them out. The actions may be carried out by other persons, groups, or even machines that are controlled by the decision makers.

(3) The functionally distinct subsets (parts of the system) can respond to each other's behavior through observation or communication.[3]

In some laboratory experiments subjects are given interrelated tasks to perform but they are not permitted to observe or communicate with each other even though they are rewarded on the basis of an outcome determined by their collective choices. In such cases the subjects are *unorganized*. If they were allowed to observe each other or to communicate with each other they could become an organization. The choices made by elements or subsets of an organization must be capable of influencing each other, otherwise they would not even constitute a system.

(4) At least one subset of the system has a system-control function.

This subset (or subsystem) compares achieved outcomes with desired outcomes and makes adjustments in the behavior of the system which are directed toward reducing the observed deficiencies. It also determines what the desired outcomes are. The control function is normally exercised by an executive body which operates on a feedback principle. "Control" requires elucidation.

31. An element or a system *controls* another element or system (or itself) if its behavior is either necessary or sufficient for subsequent behavior of the other element or system (or itself), and the subsequent behavior is necessary or sufficient for the attainment of one or more of its goals. Summarizing, then, an "organization" can be defined as follows:

---

[3] In another place, Ackoff [1], I have given operational definitions of "observation" and "communication" that fit this conceptual system. Reproduction of these treatments would require more space than is available here.

32. An *organization* is a purposeful system that contains at least two purposeful elements which have a common purpose relative to which the system has a functional division of labor; its functionally distinct subsets can respond to each other's behavior through observation or communication; and at least one subset has a system-control function.

Now the critical difference between organisms and organizations can be made explicit. Whereas both are purposeful systems, organisms do not contain purposeful elements. The elements of an organism may be state-maintaining, goal-seeking, multigoal-seeking, or purposive, but not purposeful. Thus an organism must be variety increasing. An organization, on the other hand, may be either variety increasing or decreasing (e.g., the ineffective committee). In an organism only the whole can display will; none of the parts can.

Because an organism is a system that has a functional division of labor it is also said to be "organized." Its functionally distinct parts are called "organs." Their functioning is necessary but not sufficient for accomplishment of the organism's purpose(s).

CONCLUSION

Defining concepts is frequently treated by scientists as an annoying necessity to be completed as quickly and thoughtlessly as possible. A consequence of this disinclination to define is often research carried out like surgery performed with dull instruments. The surgeon has to work harder, the patient has to suffer more, and the chances for success are decreased.

Like surgical instruments, definitions become dull with use and require frequent sharpening and, eventually, replacement. Those I have offered here are no exceptions.

Research can seldom be played with a single concept; a matched set is usually required. Matching different researches requires matching the sets of concepts used in them. A scientific field can arise only on the base of a system of concepts. Systems science is not an exception. Systems thinking, if anything, should be carried out systematically.

REFERENCES

1. Ackoff, R. L., *Choice, Communication, and Conflict,* a report to the National Science Foundation under Grant GN-389, Management Science Center, University of Pennsylvania, Philadelphia, 1967.
2. Churchman, C. W., *The Systems Approach,* Delacorte Press, New York, 1968.
3. Emery, F. E., *Systems Thinking,* Penguin Books Ltd., Harmondsworth, Middlesex, England, 1969.

QUESTIONS FOR REVIEW AND DISCUSSION

1. Give an example of a homeostatic system.
2. Do you agree with the definition of organization given in this article? Why? Discuss.
3. Give a brief comparison between a purposeful system and a purposive system.
4. What are the significant differences between a goal-seeking system and a state-maintaining system? Of what importance are these differences to a manager?

15. Who Should Boss the Computer?*

Managers, long suspicious that the computer might have a major impact on corporate profits when it grew up, are now finding another suspicion confirmed: you can't develop a prodigy by spoiling it rotten.

"Management information systems have been designed more to make the computer run efficiently than to make the company run efficiently," believes Dr. David B. Hertz, director, McKinsey & Co. Inc., New York. "Now we can see that information systems must be shaped to fit management systems."

In terms of helping management to get its job done, he believes that the computer was either 20 years too early or 20 years too late. "The computer arrived in about 1952 just in time to handle a growing avalanche of paper. So it stepped into a role of superclerk just at a time when the whole managerial process was moving from a simple hierarchy structure into entirely new kinds of managerial and decision-making relationships. Information structures, as a result, were designed to outmoded organizational concepts."

The first attempt to put the computer to work for management was the integrated systems concept. But tying everything together so that all the pieces were controlled by one master integrated program proved too rigorous and too constraining. A manager who really needed to know something found himself in a box, recalls Dr. Hertz.

Total information systems were the next to come along. "But the concept that everything is in the computer and we can get it out was found technologically infeasible and uneconomic," he says. "And, finally, the corporate data base concept, although still in its infancy, already appears to be headed down the same road of technological and managerial infeasibility."

---

* Source: Reprinted with permission from *Industry Week*, September 13, 1971, pp. 36, 38, 39, 41, and 45. Copyright, Penton Publishing Co., Cleveland, Ohio.

112

The Computer and You

"Information structures that meet the needs of *individual* managers are implicit in new developments in decision analysis," continues Dr. Hertz. "The opportunities now are between developments in computer technology and the changes in organization structures required for high flexibility in multinational, multiproduct corporations.

"What management has failed to understand about the computer is not the capabilities but the limitations. Information systems have been designed around the computer, rather than determining what was needed to serve individual management systems and fitting the computer into that.

"In the early 1950s, General Motors Corp. was a large company by any standard. It ran very well without the computer, achieving in one year the highest profit recorded before or since. It had an information system designed not to bring together every piece of information in one central room with 100,000 clerks but rather to make the information needed by managers to run the business available at the right place at the right time.

"That," he believes, "is the way the information systems using the computer must be put together in the future to run complex corporations effectively."

James B. Farley, vice president, Booz, Allen & Hamilton Inc., agrees. "The smart managers today are using the systems approach and computers in day to day operations: pricing decisions, inventory levels, and the other answers they need to operate their part of the business. The dynamics of today's world will force operating managers to use computers." But a basic problem arises in many companies, the two agree, because the men who are developing the information structures are not the same men who are developing the management structures.

"How" rather than "Who"

"A joint team of operating people and systems people should develop the system with strong participation by top management," urges Mr. Farley. "I don't get hung up on where the computer reports. But if it performs only transaction activities and reports to the controller or financial vice president, then the relationship should be changed. On the other hand, we've seen very successful computer programs where the computer reports to finance. Involvement with management needs is more important than who locks the door at night."

Mayford L. Roark, systems office director, finance staff, Ford Motor Co., concurs that "if the contribution you've been making with your computer systems has been mostly associated with accounting systems and personnel matters like payroll, you are dealing with small pieces. The computer is a resource like electricity and is pretty deeply involved in everything we do in our company today."

Because elaborate systems were built to handle transaction data, particularly among companies that got into the computer early, there is a disposition toward maintaining those old systems, warns Milton Allen, managing partner, Mandate Corp., Cleveland. "Yet among the managers of every company you find men with problems for which they lack solutions, while in every computer installation you find men with more solutions than problems to solve. That is the gap which must be bridged.

"It is more important," adds Mr. Allen, "to be able to take a poor sales forecast, run it into a poor manufacturing plan, run that into a poor requirements plan, and do a poor job of updating costs—all in a dynamic sense—than it is to do any one thing well, like manufacturing. Business has simply grown so fast that there are very few people at the top of major corporations today who can understand the total operation of their company and the proper relationship of the parts to achieve the best results for the whole."

Network Systems

"We are now more clearly able to distinguish between the transaction systems which are necessary in a business, and the total management systems," observes Dr. Hertz. "For management, such transaction systems have been almost useless or even disruptive by burying the manager in too much information. So the first thing management has to do is to recognize that traditional scorecard systems are inadequate. The next step is to replace hierarchical receipt and transmission of information with network systems designed to allow individual managers to ask questions and obtain answers.

"For the computer to be really useful it should let a manager ask a question important to a decision he's about to make. If he has to decide on next month's inventory, for example, he has to know something about the factory's capacity for next month's schedules, something about the economic situation and the marketplace, something about current pricing structures and his competitive situation," says Dr. Hertz. "And he probably will have to ask these kinds of questions across a wide range of functional locations; not just up and down, but across the organization.

"This means management must design an information system that will permit data points not predetermined and provide managers with the computer capability to ask questions and to do analysis that is nonroutine," he adds.

"The system we visualize should be future-oriented, allow the manager to ask 'what if' questions, analyze the answers, and go through successive iterations, making changes. We think computer technology has placed us at that threshold, permitting information system design appropriate to a business."

"The computer provides more information, correlates it faster, and brings it into focus more accurately. It is not a solution but a means to an end," explains Mr. Allen. "So the key to the potential of the computer is top managers who can structure their decision making and that of the people under them in such a way that the important information stands out. A clear form of organization is imperative; the computer will simply bring confusion without it."

"If the management system makes sense, then you can design the computer system to support it. So management," agrees Dr. Hertz, "must begin with reaching conclusions not about what they want the computer to do, but rather what they want people to do."

Too Many Cooks

Back in the 1960's there was a great deal of research and development as management sought to unlock the potential of the computer, recalls Dr. Hertz. But one problem was that there were too many people in the act: manufacturers' representatives, data processing managers, assorted operating managers and, from time to time, top management, all urging what should be done. The first step toward increased effectiveness in the use of the computer is to resolve this conflict, advises Dr. Hertz.

"To head up the computer staff and assume responsibility for the implementation of development plans, outstanding companies have in all cases been careful to pick a manager who will command respect and confidence throughout the organization," he says. "The appointment of the right man to this position is the first key contribution top management can make to a more effective computer effort."

Mr. Farley adds that the steering committee approach can be a useful supplement. "What's really required is a blending, a smart computer group working closely with top managers sufficiently objective and profit-minded to learn about and use computer systems. The information system and the management system must not only mesh; they must be identified by the managers who must use them as projects of management rather than as systems projects. If there has been any change in the corporate position of the computer, it is in the committee approach monitored and supported by top management," believes Mr. Farley.

The point both emphasize is that many otherwise effective top managers have failed to achieve greater computer effectiveness because they abdicated control to staff specialists—excellent as technicians but lacking the operational experience to know the jobs that need doing and the authority to get them done right.

Look at the Long Term

"Having determined the responsibility for research and development of computer applications, top management must decide what it will seek to achieve as a long term process, and fit that to long term corporate objectives, both strategic and organizational," continues Dr. Hertz.

"Then, to make sure that the plan fits the goal that it has in mind, management must see to it that a determination is made as to who controls what data, who controls what formats, how much data has to be moved where and how fast, and what kinds of questions people are expected to answer through the computer.

"This means that some individual concerned with the management process has to take action at each step along the way and give directions as to what needs to be done," says Dr. Hertz. "He must be intermediary between the computer people and the operations people. And he really must have the operational management perspective; he has to understand primarily not what the computer does but what top management wants done.

"Clearly this is a formidable undertaking," admits Dr. Hertz. "It will not be the kind of thing you complete and flip a switch. It has to be handled from the top, carefully designed and thought through. And it will have to be continuously revised and improved—as were corporate information systems long before there was a computer."

And Give Heed to These Points

As an approach to building the most effective management information system, Dr. Hertz offers two further bits of advice: Begin by deciding where the leverage on profits will be increased most through availability of better information; and do not embark on any management information program, major or minor, except to meet a well-defined need.

"We believe the computer is finally ready to move out of the mystical and into the everyday practical," says Dr. Hertz. "And we now find substantial agreement that only managers can manage the computer in the best interests of the business."

Computers at Ford Motor Company

Computers, for example, have moved into boardroom and plant alike at Ford Motor Co. "They're as broad as the company," explains Mayford L. Roark, director of the Ford systems office, finance staff.

But from top to bottom the computer is a resource rather than a decision maker.

"We do not come trotting into the boardroom and offer solutions," says Mr. Roark, "nor does the computer occupy a special chair at the end of the table. In dealing with problems and issues of interest to our top management, we try to provide insights and perspectives unobtainable otherwise.

"For example, we have done a great deal of analytical work dealing with the long range trend of car and truck sales and the impact on markets of changes in our society, changes in modes of transportation, government regulations, and many other factors.

"One of the things we use a great deal is risk analysis through which we try to identify not only the most probable outcome but what will occur if the best of all possible things happen or the worst. We try to provide a broader perspective of possibilities and, when you try to project what's going to happen in five or ten years, it's almost essential to have some kind of computer model.

"But the issues our top management faces are the kinds of things that require and will continue to require management judgment. I just don't think it's possible to structure top management problems into cold computer terms, for they involve cultural and political situations that defy quantification.

"Until recent times logistical systems have been the major area of heavy computer involvement at Ford. The payout in terms of material control is particularly attractive; you have lower levels of inventory, more efficient inventory, and the ability to handle much greater complexity and volumes. Yet a lot of companies haven't yet put in a good basic material control system.

"The other side of the material control system is sales forecasting, for you really don't have much material control without it. We work at Ford in terms of a build program for the next month, with plans extending out over the next five or six months. This is a long formalized process in which the computer plays a major role in gathering and processing all the current sales statistics, sorting out the specific forecasts that come through, and preparing and analyzing them in such a way that the final program can be reviewed and approved.

"The computer then breaks that program down into tens of thousands of items—brackets, bolts, and the like—that get down to the level of every individual component that goes into the system. One of our analysts here has calculated that just for our North American assembly plant system alone some 2 million individual forecasts are required each month.

"But the action today is the industrial control systems, smaller kinds of computers controlling industrial processes, facilities or tools in the plants. The thing that is so exciting to us is that the minicomputer has been so reduced in size, cost, and complexity that it's possible to use it in a variety of ways today we could never have considered just five years ago. There are whole realms of opportunity for special purpose kinds of applications with very important savings potentials.

"I expect to see monumental growth in the controls area in a least five major categories: process control systems (glass production), discrete process control (high bay warehouses), numerical control (machine tools), automated testing (transmission control valves), and plant monitoring (production count, identification of downtime).

"This trend hit a plateau about the mid sixties but now it is becoming exciting again because of minicomputers. They make possible greater flexibility than was possible with former types of control systems. In the challenge of improving profitability, this is the most exciting possibility that we have over the next decade."

QUESTIONS FOR REVIEW AND DISCUSSION

1. Comment fully on the statement: "Information systems have been designed around the computer rather than determining what was needed to serve industrial management systems."

2. As you see it, is there anything basically wrong in following the practice of using computers to automate paperwork existing at the time the computer is installed? Why? Elaborate on your answer.

3. As set forth in this article is the present challenge of management to decide what the computer is to do, or what employees are to do? Discuss.

4. What types of management problems do you feel are best suited to receive assistance from the computer? What types the least suited? Justify your answer.

16. Linear Programming*

JOHN W. COUGHLAN

Linear programming (LR) (or the broader field of mathematical programming of which linear programming is a part) is a tool, technique or method of analyzing certain highly complex problems in which the analyst hopes to determine the optimum course of action. Perhaps to optimize some characteristic or "figure of merit" of a system he is analyzing. He may be trying to "maximize" profits or attempting to "minimize" costs or attempting to come "as close as possible" to a particular goal. But this optimization must generally respect certain restrictions or constraints.

As a simple illustration of linear programming, consider the RUR factory which makes two principal products, Adams and Eves. The factory manager desires to maximize profits and an Adam makes a contribution toward profit (excess of sales price over variable expenses) of $100,000, whereas an Eve makes a profit contribution of $80,000 per unit. If no further restrictions were given, of course, the manager, Mr. Lord, could generate an infinite profit by producing an infinite number of both products. However, the two products require processing in three departments, and these departments have certain capacities.

For example, the flesh department consists of two DNA machines which operate about 50 hours per week each (the factory works a six-day week) for a total processing time of 100 hours per week. Production of one Adam will tie up or make use of 8 hours of that capacity and production of an Eve requires 1 hour of processing time. Each product requires 1 hour of processing time in the bone department which operates one machine for a 50-hour week.

There are two assembly lines which each operate 50 hours per week for a total capacity of 100 hours of assembly time which time can be devoted to either or both products in any combinations. (That is, either assembly line can be used for Eves and either can be used for Adams).

* Source: Reprinted with permission of *Data Management* (published by Data Processing Management Association), March 1970, pp. 30–34. Dr. John W. Coughlan is president of the CPA School of Washington.

An Adam, however, ties up the assembly line only one hour as it need not travel the full length of the assembly line and comes out in a rough and ready fashion. The Eve, being a superior styling, requires four hours of assembly time. The information given in this paragraph is summarized in Figure 1.

It is often argued that an intuitive approach to production problems of this sort is quite satisfactory in that it gives a solution which, while not an exact optimum, is sufficiently close to the optimum to make it unnecessary to adopt a more formal approach. Readers can readily check the power of their intuition by making and recording a guess about the best profit mix and computing the resulting profit and then comparing this result with the optimum or maximum figure that will be reported in a few paragraphs.

FIGURE 1. Constraints and Profit Contributions (processing times in hours)

Department	Products Adams	Eves	Departmental Capacity
Flesh	8 hours	1 hour	100 hours
Bones	1 hour	1 hour	50 hours
Assembly	1 hour	4 hours	100 hours
Profit contributions per unit of output	$100,000	$80,000	

In other words, guess the program (the number of Adams and Eves to be produced per week) which is within the capacity of the present facilities and which maximizes profit contribution. The profit contribution can be determined by multiplying the number of Adams by the profit contribution of $100,000 per Adam and adding to that figure the product of the number of Eves multiplied by $80,000.

At first guess, it might seem that since the profit contribution of an Adam is greater than that of an Eve, production should concentrate on Adams. The greatest number of Adams that can be produced is 12½ per week since, at 8 hours of processing time in the flesh department, 12½ Adams will completely tie up the capacity of that department. These 12½ Adams will produce a $1,250,000 profit contribution per week. Is this the most profit that can be had? A little reflection suggests it is not. These 12½ Adams will leave 37½ hours of unused processing time in the bone department and 87½ hours of processing time in the assembly department.

Fallacy of Intuitive Planning

If the unused or idle time in the bone and assembly departments was devoted to the production of Eves, then the factory could make a profit contribution of $80,000 per Eve provided that it made some time available for the processing of Eves in the flesh department. In fact, if one less Adam is produced, eight hours will be made available in the flesh department for production of Eves which can be processed in that department in one hour per unit at a profit contribution of $80,000 per unit.

This line of thinking and subsequent analysis shows that our initial and intuitive belief in the advisability of emphasizing production of Adams is incorrect.

For a second intuitive approach, let's set as a goal a profit of $3,400,000 to be achieved through a "program" of 10 Adams and 30 Eves as follows:

10 Adams at $100,000 each	$1,000,000
30 Eves at $80,000 each	2,400,000
Profit contribution	$3,400,000

Unlike our first program which concentrated on Adams and left some unused capacity in two departments and the Eves would require a further 30 hours for a total processing time of 110 hours which exceeds the 100-hour capacity of the flesh department.

For example, processing of 10 Adams would require 80 hours of processing time in the flesh department and the Eves would require 30 hours for a total processing time of 110 hours which exceeds the 100-hour capacity of the flesh department.

The situation may be depicted by means of the graph in Figure 2 where the horizontal axis represents the number of Adams produced and the vertical axis represents the number of Eves. The point K depicts the program 10 Adams and 30 Eves. The straight line labelled $8A + 1E = 100$ is the locus of all points which represent programs which fully utilize the capacity of the flesh department.

FIGURE 2. An Infeasible Schedule (Point K)

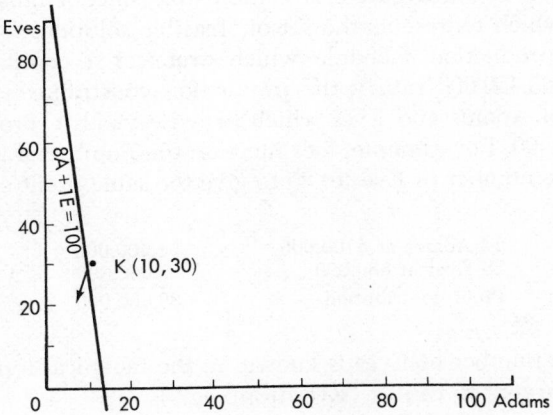

So far as the flesh department is concerned, any program represented by a point on this line or below it (note arrow pointing downward) is a "feasible solution." The fact that the program represented by the point K is infeasible (that it exceeds the capacity of the department) is represented by the fact that K lies above the line.

The capacities of the three departments set upper limits on the quantities that can be produced and these capacity constraints are represented by the three straight lines in the graph in Figure 3. The line labelled $8A + 1E = 100$ is, of course, the same one that appeared in Figure 2 as the flesh department constraint. The line labelled $1A + 1E = 50$ represents the constraint imposed by the bones department—the only admissible solutions are those represented by points below this line (note downward pointing arrow).

Similarly, the "half space" described algebraically by $1A + 4E \leqslant 100$ and geometrically represented in Figure 3 as the area below the straight line similarly labelled relates to the constraint imposed by the capacity of the assembly department.

Note that our program or production schedule must respect all three constraints so that the shaded area in Figure 3, which lies below all three bounding lines, represents the set of feasible solutions, the solutions which respect all three constraints. (Note in passing that the axes serve as lower bounds or limitations on the amount of production; despite murder and suicide, we adopt the usual "nonnegativity requirement" of linear programming in accordance with which a negative rate of production is never desirable.) The only feasible or admissible solutions are those represented by points falling within the shaded area of Figure 3.

The shaded area of Figure 3 is reproduced in Figure 4 where the search for a program which maximizes profit contribution but lives within the constraints imposed by the three departmental capacities is further pursued. Note again that the production schedule of 10 Adams and 30 Eves depicted by point K in Figure 4 is inadmissible since it falls outside the shaded area which represents the set of "feasible solutions."

Does any production schedule which promises a comparable profit contribution—$3,400,000 satisfy the production constraints? Try another combination of Adams and Eves which likewise yields a profit contribution of $3,400,000. For example, let's increase the number of Adams to 14 and reduce the number of Eves to 25 to give the same profit contribution:

14 Adams at $100,000	$1,400,000
25 Eves at $80,000	2,000,000
Profit contribution	$3,400,000

(Reducing the number of Eves is known, in the technical terminology of the complex jargon of LP, as "Evesdropping.")

This production schedule is represented in Figure 4 by the point L.

FIGURE 3. Constraints (lines) and the Feasible Set
(shaded)

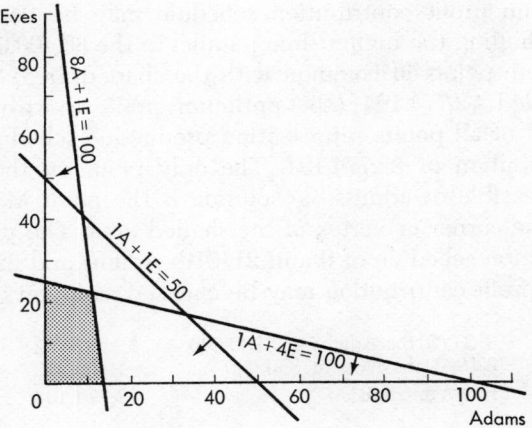

It will be noted that L falls outside the feasible set and is therefore not an admissible solution. Furthermore, the straight line on which the points K and L lie is the locus of all points which represent production schedules leading to a profit contribution of $3,400,000 and it will be further noted that no point on the straight line falls within the feasible set designated by the shaded area; a profit contribution of $3,400,000 is not possible within the capacity constraints imposed by the various departments.

FIGURE 4. Feasibility (shaded) and Optimality
(point M)

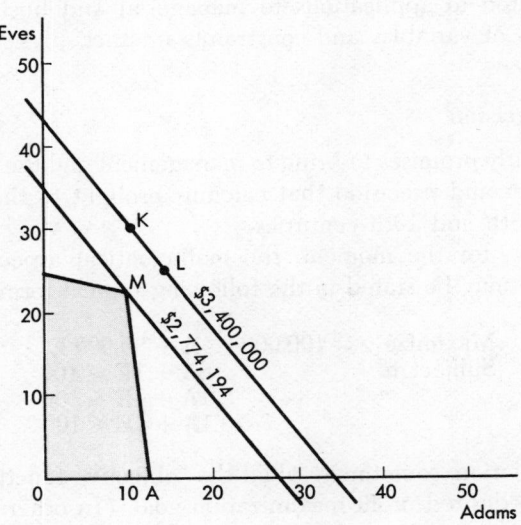

An Optimizing Technique

The optimum profit contribution schedule may be determined geometrically by finding the highest line parallel to the $3,400,000 line which has one or more points in common with the shaded area. Such a line is the line labelled $2,774,194 (the optimum profit contribution) which gives the locus of all points representing production schedules that yield a profit contribution of $2,774,194. The only point on that line which represents a feasible or admissible solution is the point M at which the line touches the corner or vertex of the shaded area. The point M represents a production schedule of 9 and 21/31th Adams and 22 and 18/31th Eves and the profit contribution may be checked as follows:

9 21/31ths Adams at $100,000	$ 967,742
22 18/31ths Eves at $80,000	1,806,452
Profit contribution	$2,774,194

While linear programming may be regarded as managerial tool, its significance is best appreciated if LP is regarded instead as an important mathematical development, which it is. From a mathematical standpoint, linear programming can be regarded as an optimizing technique or approach comparable to the calculus. There are, however, a number of significant differences.

Applications of calculus generally involve a single equation or small system of equations whereas LP deals with vast systems of inequations or inequalities. Calculus usually relates to a single variable or to a small number of variables whereas LP deals with large numbers of variables.

Calculus is accordingly well suited to mechanical and engineering applications where the number of variables is either small or controllable. LP is well suited to applications to managerial and business problems where myriads of variables and constraints interact.

Promise of Precision

LP accordingly promises to bring to management and the social sciences the same power and precision that calculus brought to the physical sciences in the 18th and 19th centuries.

Emphasizing, for the moment, the mathematical aspects of LP, the above problem may be stated in the following typical format:

$$
\begin{aligned}
\text{Maximize } z = 100,000 \quad & A + 80,000\, E \\
\text{Subject to} \quad & 8A + 1E \leq 100 \\
& 1A + 1E \leq 50 \\
& 1A + 4E \leq 100 \qquad (1)
\end{aligned}
$$

The first equation, sometimes called the "objective function," expresses in this case the desired profit maximization goal. (In other problems, the purpose is minimization as in the case of minimization of costs or operating times or length of bombing runs, etc. Sometimes "optimizing" refers neither to a maximizing nor minimizing purpose but rather to attainment of specific goals; in these cases, if properly set up, the problem can usually be adapted to the usual linear programming approach of maximizing or minimizing by requiring that the deviations from the desired goal be minimized.) The three inequalities express the constraints within which the objective function is optimized.

Duality Aspect of LP

An interesting mathematical aspect of linear programming, and one with important managerial implications, is duality. It has been demonstrated that for every linear program there is a dual or alternative problem. Thus for (1) above, the dual would be as follows:

$$\text{Minimize} \quad g = 100w_1 + 50w_2 + 100w_3$$
$$\text{Subject to}$$
$$8w_1 + w_2 + w_3 \geqslant 100,000$$
$$w_1 + w_2 + 4w_3 \geqslant 80,000 \tag{2}$$

Where the "direct" or "primal" problem deals with maximization, as here, then its dual deals with minimization. Where the constraints of the direct problem are inequalities of the "less than" variety, those of the dual problem are of the "greater than" variety.

Readers interested in the mathematical aspects of duality should compare (1) and (2) and note, among other things, that the constants in the constraints in the direct problem become the coefficients of the variables in the objective function of the dual problem; that the coefficients of the variables in the objective function in the direct problem become the constants in the constraints of the dual; that the direct problem has two variables whereas the dual has two constraints; that the direct problem has three constraints whereas the dual has three variables, and the coefficients of the variables in the constraints of the direct problem form the following matrix:

$$\begin{bmatrix} 8 & 1 \\ 1 & 1 \\ 1 & 4 \end{bmatrix}.$$

Whereas the coefficients of the variables in the constraints of the dual problem form the transpose of that matrix:

$$\begin{bmatrix} 8 & 1 & 1 \\ 1 & 1 & 4 \end{bmatrix}.$$

Geometrically, the direct problem may be visualized (Figure 3) as involving three constraining lines in two dimensions whereas the dual problem (not drawn) involves two restraining planes in three dimensions.

Perhaps the most astonishing aspect of duality is that the optimum "figure of merit" for the direct problem agrees with the optimum "figure of merit" for the dual. More specifically, for the above illustration, the maximum equals the minimum, that is, the maximum profit contribution of $2,774,194 agrees with the minimum of $2,774,194 for the dual system. Nature knows no Siamese twins more inextricably twined than the primal and its dual.

Before dismissing duality as a mere mathematical manipulation devoid of managerial meaning, the administrator must give some thought to the usual interpretation of the variables in the dual problem. In our problem these variables w^1, w^2, and w^3, may be viewed as the cost per hour of time in the flesh, bones and assembly departments. Note that in the dual problem, the cost per hour of the scarce time in various departments is evaluated as follows:

$$w^1 = \text{cost per hour of processing time}$$
$$\text{in flesh dept.} = \$10,323$$
$$w^2 = \text{cost per hour of processing time}$$
$$\text{in bone dept.} = \$0$$
$$w^3 = \text{cost per hour of processing time}$$
$$\text{in assembly dept.} = \$17,419$$

These costs are sometimes described as "opportunity costs" or "shadow prices" or "dual evaluators" and some insight into such terms may be had by comparing the above figures with Figure 3. Note from Figure 3 that the straight line representing the upper capacity of the bones department (the line labelled $1A + 1E = 50$) is a "redundant" constraint, a constraint which does not limit the set of feasible solutions any more than that set is already limited by the capacity of the flesh and assembly departments.

In other words, the bones department does not impose any limitation on the production possibilities that is not already imposed by the flesh and assembly departments. Accordingly, w^2, the cost per hour of processing time, is valued at $0. If a salesman turns up at the RUR plant to sell another bone processing machine, the purchasing agent will not be in.

In contrast, both the flesh and assembly departments impose limitations on the production possibilities, limitations which are not already implied by any other "tighter" constraints.

An hour of processing time in these departments is a scarce and valuable commodity, and the values, w^1 and w^3, assigned to an hour of processing time in the flesh and assembly departments respectively, are positive. Consider w^3, the "value" or "opportunity cost" of an hour of processing time in the assembly department. This w^3 of $17,419 per hour represents the most it would be worth paying to increase the capacity of the assembly department.

Suppose a salesman appears at the RUR factory with a device that will increase the capacity of the assembly department. If this device costs, say, $20,000 per hour of increased capacity, the purchasing agent should not consider it. But if its cost is less than $17,419 per hour, say $15,000 per hour, then it is worth investigating.

If, for example, the device can increase capacity by 50 hours, then the potential profit contribution at $17,419 is $870,950 and its cost at $15,000 per hour of increased capacity for 50 hours is only $750,000, permitting a net increase in profit contribution of $120,950. To verify the potential increase in profit contribution the reader need only crank into his original formulation an altered assembly constraint $(A + 4E = 150)$ and determine the new optimum program (8 and 2/31th Adams and 35 and 15/31th Eves). Which when priced at the original profit contributions ($100,000 and $80,000 respectively) yields a new profit contribution of $3,645,150 that exceeds the profit contribution of $2,774,200 under the program which was optimal with the original constraints by $870,950 or more than enough increase in profit contribution to pay for the additional cost per hour of the new assembly device.

The duality concept, providing as it does a means for discovering and evaluating bottlenecks, offers powerful insight into managerial problems.

QUESTIONS FOR REVIEW AND DISCUSSION

1. If the RUR factory increased the capacity of the assembly department by 50 hours, where would the straight line representing the constraints of the new assembly intersect the vertical or Eves axis and the horizontal or Adams axis?

2. Discuss the meaning and importance of the duality aspect of linear programming.

3. Why is the cost per hour of the scarce time in the bone department equal to zero? Justify the sums of the cost per hour of scarce time for processing in the flesh department and in the assembly department being equal to $27,742.

17. Simulation Cuts Inventory Center Costs*

V. STEVEN BLOOD and WILLIAM V. SANTOS

An important consideration in any parts supply system is the amount of time it takes to order a part and await its delivery. If delivery takes a long time, high costs can develop due to idle employees and work delays. Another important consideration is the inventory records for the system. If any items have a critical lead time, poor inventory records can increase costs due to out-of-stock conditions. Such conditions existed in a repair branch at Hill Air Force Base.

Originally, inventory records were maintained on a computerized batch processing system. This involved grouping similar input items for processing during the same machine run. Part delivery time averaged 10 minutes per part, but out-of-stock conditions frequently occurred. In an effort to eliminate these problems, an on-line system using an IBM 360/40 computer with a 1050 remote terminal was installed. Input data was entered into the computer before each part was issued so that the inventory records were always up-to-date. To facilitate the on-line system, all part supply centers were consolidated into one center. The result was that out-of-stock conditions decreased, but average delivery time increased from 10 minutes to 1.5 hours.

Production control management felt that the excessive turn-around time was being caused by the capacity of the remote terminal. But they insisted that inventory records were always updated prior to removal of parts from the supply center.

A study was undertaken to: (1) determine whether or not a 10 minute part delivery time was a realistic objective with present personnel and system constraints; (2) develop a part delivery system that would optimize equipment and personnel, updating all inventory records before the physical movement of parts from the supply center.

* Source: Reprinted with permission of *Industrial Engineering*, June, 1971, pp. 25–27. Mr. V. Steven Blood and Mr. William V. Santos are with the Hill Air Force Base.

It was assumed that:

1. The results of a study of day-shift operations are valid for night-shift operations.
2. Mechanics are idle after waiting 10 minutes for delivery of parts. Cost calculations for loss of productivity are based on this assumption.
3. If an additional IBM 1050 remote terminal was acquired, it would only be used to update inventory records before the movement of parts.

The present system was first documented and analyzed. Improvements to the system could then be evaluated by simulation on a computer. This approach was repeated until the optimum delivery system was found.

As a study approach, flow process charts were used to document the present system. This required actual observation and timing of each step in the request and delivery of a part. Figure 1 is a diagram of the study area.

In order to reduce the delivery mean time until the simulation study was completed, production control management agreed to have mechanics assigned from each bay to pick up and deliver parts. This resulted in a

FIGURE 1. Consolidated Supply Center—to Simplify the On-Line System

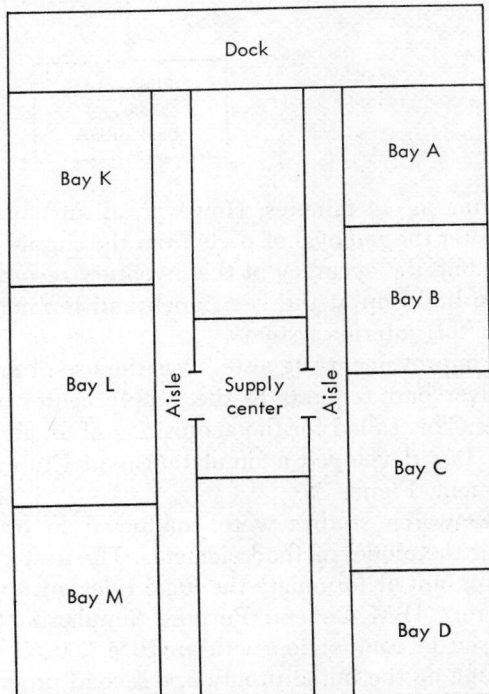

FIGURE 2. System Flow Diagram Using Mechanics to
Pick Up Their Own Parts

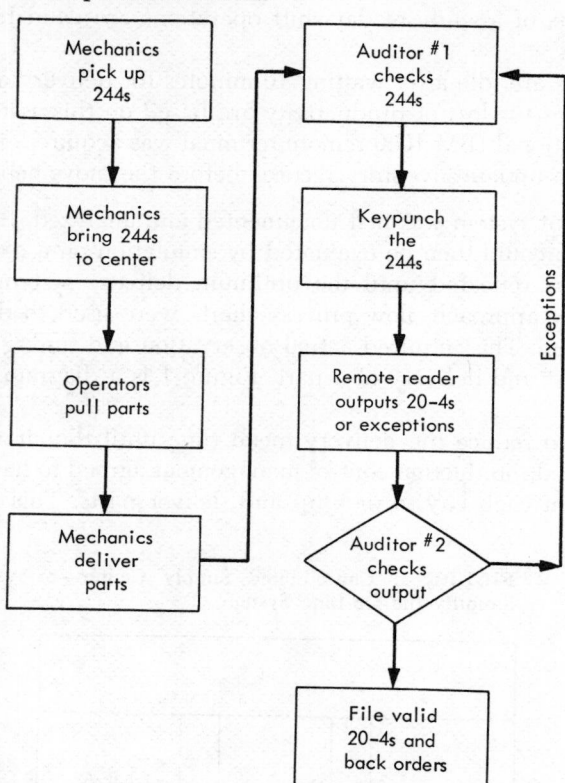

mean delivery time of 14 minutes. However, all inventory records were
being updated after the removal of parts from the supply center. This was
gradually degrading the accuracy of the inventory records, because large
queues began to build up at the key punch and terminal. Figure 2 is a
flow diagram of this interim system.

One possible improvement suggested was the use of material handlers,
who would deliver part requests to the supply center and return parts
to the mechanics. This called for the acquisition of an additional terminal
and key punch. IE's developed a simulation model to evaluate the suggested improvement, Figure 3.

Additional stopwatch studies were conducted in order to establish
realistic times for the model method elements. The next step was to write
the computer program or formulate the logic rules governing the system.
To accomplish this, IBM General Purpose Simulation System (GPSS)
language was used in conjunction with an IBM 360/65 computer. After
testing and debugging the initial program, a second program was written

FIGURE 3. Proposed System Flow Diagram Using Material Handlers to Pick Up and Deliver Parts

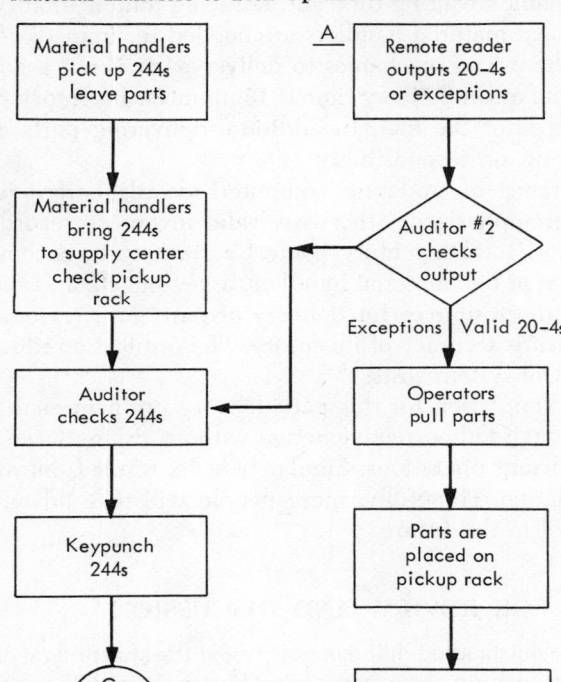

that was more specific and realistic. It contained three parts. One to simulate the flow of the parts and materials request; one to simulate the material handlers; and one to simulate the coffee and lunch breaks. This approach was necessary in order to facilitate the programming of the model.

By using time functions from the stopwatch studies to set switches on and off, all three parts of the model interacted just as in the real-life system. Several runs, each with different material demand rates, were made to determine the optimum number of material handlers in relation to the system constraints. The results showed that five material handlers are optimum for present and projected material-demand requirements. Bays A, B, C, and D need one material handler each; while bays K, L, and M need only one material handler among them. The mean delivery time in this optimum system is 21 minutes; cost savings for the expected life of the system is $568,988.

The utilization of the additional key punch is 30 percent, and the utilization of the additional terminal is 60 percent. Even though utilization is low for this equipment, justification is based on the objectives of minimizing a mechanic's waiting time and reducing total inventory cost.

The additional material handlers are needed for immediate system improvement. The use of mechanics to deliver parts is not a good practice, even though the mean delivery time is 15 minutes. Inventory records were being updated after the fact. In addition, delivering parts is not a mechanic's function or responsibility.

The importance of updating computer records before issuing parts cannot be overemphasized; otherwise, valid inventory records cannot be maintained, and total inventory control system costs become excessive.

The addition of five material handlers, a key punch, and remote equipment provide the resources for delivery of parts in a reasonable amount of time and insure accuracy of inventory. The result is a reduction of total inventory control system costs.

The use of simulation for this part delivery problem enabled management to test suggested corrective action without risking large investments or delaying current operations. Similar benefits result from most applications of simulation. Hopefully, more people will take advantage of this managerial tool in the future.

QUESTIONS FOR REVIEW AND DISCUSSION

1. Point out the outstanding differences between the system flow diagram using mechanics to pick up their own parts (Figure 2) and the diagram having material handlers pick up and deliver the parts (Figure 3).
2. Why should computer inventory records be updated before issuing parts?
3. Explain how simulation was used in assisting the company management to determine the optimum delivery system.

part FIVE

Decision Making

A vital part of management is decision making. It filters through the entire process of management. In many ways a manager is known by the decisions he makes and keeps. Managerial success or failure depends upon the decision-making skill and implementation demonstrated in solving problems and in utilizing discreetly the available fundamental resources.

In our first reading, Dr. Richard J. Tersine's "Organization Decision Theory—A Synthesis," reviews contemporary thinking about decision making in management. Rational, behavioral, and quantitative contributions to decision making are included. Normative and descriptive models are discussed as well as decision making under certainty, conflict, risk, and uncertainty. This article merits close study.

Richard L. Shell and David F. Stelzer explain and justify the systems analysis approach to decision making in their reading "Systems Analysis: Aid to Decision Making." The basic steps to follow are set forth and discussed. The general environment affecting decision making today and the handling of alternatives by the modern manager are emphasized and put out into proper perspective. Better managerial decision making can result by following the key points of this well written article.

In the next reading, "Investment Decision Making in a Multinational Enterprise," John C. Chambers and Satinder K. Mullick present the basic methodology used to decide whether a multinational company, Corning Glass Works, should add a manufacturing facility to its operations. The approach featured an impartial coordinator on the project evaluation team to reduce emotional biases in the inputs. By use of the Delphi technique, alternatives were defined. Quantified data were used with return on investment as the criteria measuring the effectiveness of various alternatives. This article provides an insight into decision making by expert application of modern decision making techniques.

18. Organization Decision Theory—A Synthesis*

RICHARD J. TERSINE

INTRODUCTION

While every rational being is an individual decision making mechanism, very little is known about what initiates this mechanism into action and how it operates. Decision making has been an integral part of the management literature for more than three decades. However, because of the emphasis on decision making as a hierarchical right, explorations of the behavioral aspects of the decision process were at a minimum for much of the time. It was not until the early 1950's that developments in decision theory gained a noticeable momentum. During this period, there emerged more powerful and sophisticated tools of mathematics and statistics as well as increased interest in the behavioral sciences. These influences have set the intellectual base for many of the current contributions on the subject.

The most significant aspect of the literature on decision making is what it does not contain. There are few, if any, systematic empirically based longitudinal studies on the decision process. There are relatively few articles classified as research although the literature abounds with limited and partial theories. Many of the theories have been developed by mathematicians and they are modifications of a completely rational man. Such theories in general ignore the psychological characteristics of men or the social environment in which they live.

Organizations per se do not make decisions, people and groups do. In many instances, the decisions made are compromise decisions. The decision maker as an individual, a member of the formal organization, and a member of an informal organization with his own philosophy and perception of the organization, selects solutions for optimizing value

* Source: Reprinted with permission of *Managerial Planning*, July-August 1972, pp. 18–26, 40. Dr. Richard J. Tersine is associate professor of business management, Old Dominion University.

within organizational constraints. The organization has objectives, policies, and standards which must be balanced with technology, attitudes, and resources.

Professor Ansoff (2, pp. 5, 6)† cuts organizational decisions into three categories:

1. Strategic Decisions—are primarily concerned with external rather than internal problems of the firm and specifically with the selection of the product mix which the firm will produce and the markets to which it will sell.
2. Administrative Decisions—are concerned with structuring the firm's resources to create maximum performance potential. This can be subdivided into:
   a) Organization Structure—involves structuring of authority and responsibility relationships, work flows, information flow, distribution channels, and location of facilities.
   b) Resource Acquisition and Development—involves the development of raw-material sources, personnel training, personnel development, financing, acquisition of facilities, and equipment.
3. Operating Decisions—are primarily concerned with the maximizing profitability of current operations. The key decisions involve pricing, establishing market strategy, setting production schedules and inventory levels, and deciding on the relative expenditures in support of R & D, marketing, and operations.

The process of management is fundamentally a process of decision making. The functions of management (planning, organizing, motivating, and controlling) all involve the process of evaluating, selecting, and initiating courses of action.

Decision making is at the center of the functions comprising the management process. The manager makes decisions in establishing objectives; he makes planning decisions, organizing decisions, motivating decisions, and control decisions. In this sense modern decision theory is a logical extension of the management process school. In addition, decision theory enters both the quantitative and behavioral domains.

Alexis and Wilson (1, p. 4) have specified three major approaches to organizational analysis which are:

1. Structural Approaches—traced to early writings of Frederick Taylor, Henri Fayol, and Max Weber. (Line/staff, division of labor, coordination, scalar authority, span of control, unity of command, etc.)
2. Behavioral Approaches—stress human variables. (Hawthorne studies and later behavioral research.)
3. Decision-Making Approaches—stress human variables and technology. It views the organization from the locations of the actual decision makers.

One acting in the capacity of a manager or executive must make choices among various plans, policies, and strategies. These choices are

---

† Numbers in parentheses refer to references at end of reading.

made with varying degrees of information. Decision theory gives structure to the different conditions under which decisions are made. The decision making process used by management is becoming more organized and systematic than the intuitive process of the past.

Dahl and Lindblom (4) have suggested four broad influencing factors on the decision making processes in organizations:

1. Hierarchical—leaders are influenced by the structure of the hierarchy itself.
2. Democratic—leaders are influenced by nonleaders through such devices as nomination and election.
3. Bargaining—leaders are to some degree independent of each other and exercise reciprocal controls over each other. (labor vs. management)
4. Pricing System—leaders are influenced by the market place.

Basically, a decision must be made when the organization faces a problem, when it is dissatisfied with existing conditions, or when it is given a choice. A considerable amount of managerial activity precedes the actual decision. In large organizations these activities may be carried on by people other than the decision maker. Staff people and others in the line organization discover problems, define them, and prepare the alternatives for decision. The actual decision is only the conclusion of a process. The process in a broad sense includes (1) the activities of discovering and defining things to decide, (2) determining the objective of the organization, and (3) the enumeration and preparation of the alternative ways of making the decision (3, p. 269).

There is no unified agreed upon structure for decision theory. This paper will add some structure to decision theory and also explore some of its dimensions.

FEATURES OF ORGANIZATIONAL DECISION MAKING

Setting of Objectives

The establishment and definition of the broad organizational goals of the firm is the basic requirement to all subsequent decisions to be made on a lesser level. From these broad objectives, strategies and departmental goals can be set to provide the framework for decision making at lower managerial levels. Even after organizational goals are set, other problems still exist such as:

1. Multiple Objectives—decision making is complicated by the existence of many diversified objectives. A number of objectives may be difficult to characterize quantitatively. These goals reflect subjective values rather than objective values. Typical objectives involve growth, diversification, industry position, profit maximization, sales maximization, social responsibility, personnel development, employee attitudes, etc.
2. Conflicting Objectives—any comprehensive list of organizational objec-

tives will have areas of conflict. Social responsibility such as pollution control projects may adversely affect profit margins. Product diversification may initially stultify the return on investment during the introductory period.

3. Hierarchy of Objectives—objectives of organizational units must be consistent with the objectives of higher organizational units. This means there are objectives within objectives, within objectives. If the cascade of organization objectives is not consistent, it results in suboptimization. Suboptimization occurs where a departmental level maximizes its own objectives, but in doing so it subverts the overall objectives of the firm. (Sales manager—large inventories; production manager—large production runs; warehouse manager—minimum inventory; purchasing agent—large lot purchases; etc.)

Planning Horizons

Decision making at various levels of management is concerned with varying degrees of futurity. Top management decisions involve longer time periods than lower level management decisions. Planning horizons precipitate the problem of temporal suboptimization.

Sequential/Interrelated Decision Making

Sequential decision making is the process of successively solving interrelated subproblems comprising a large complex problem. Because many managerial problems are extremely complex, organizations resort to specialization of labor or breaking the problem into many subproblems. Consider the problem of production where it is broken down into separate departments: procurement, scheduling, operations, quality control, shipping, etc.

Dynamic Decision Making

Dynamic decision making emphasizes that management decisions are not usually a one-time event, but are successive over a time frame. Future management decisions are to some degree influenced by past decisions.

Programmed/Nonprogrammed Decision Making

Programmed decisions are those that are repetitive and routine. Organizations usually establish definite procedures for making them. In contrast, the nonprogrammed decisions are unstructured and novel; there is no set pattern for handling them. Higher levels of management are associated with the unstructured, nonprogrammed decisions.

Cost of Decision Making

Decision making has a cost, particularly the search process, that precedes the decision. Management must determine if the cost of the search process is worth the reduced uncertainty. The cost of the search process should not exceed the benefits of improving the decision.

DECISION MODELS

One of the primary functions of management is to make decisions that determine the future course of action for the organization over the short and long term. There are two general types of broad decision models now in use; they can be classified as normative or descriptive. The normative framework describes the classical situation where a decision maker faces a known set of alternatives and selects a course of action by a rational selection process. The descriptive framework incorporates adaptive or learning features and the act of choice spans many dimensions of behavior, rational as well as nonrational.

There are at least six elements common to all decisions:

1. The decision maker—refers to the individual or group making a choice from the available strategies.
2. Goals or ends to be served—are objectives the decision maker seeks to obtain by his actions.
3. The preference or value system—refers to the criteria that the decision maker uses in making his choice. It could include maximization of income, utility, minimum cost, etc.
4. Strategies of the decision maker—are the different alternative courses of action from which the decision maker can choose. Strategies are based on resources under the control of the decision maker.
5. States of nature—are factors that are not under the control of the decision maker. They are aspects of the decision maker's environment affecting his choice of strategy.
6. The outcome—represents the resultant from a given strategy and a given state of nature. When the outcome is expressed in numerical terms, it is called a payoff. (The prediction of payoffs in a matrix is usually assumed to be perfect.)

Normative Decision Models

At the center of this framework is the concept of rationality. The normative models show how a consistent decision maker should act to be successful. Decision procedures are followed that will optimize something, usually output, income, revenue, costs, utility, etc. The ideal rational man makes a choice on the basis of: (1, p. 150)

1. A known set of relevant alternatives with corresponding outcomes.
2. An established rule or set of relations that produces a preference ordering or the alternatives.
3. The maximization of something such as money, goods, or some form of utility.

The major features of a typical decision structure are the strategies of the decision maker, the states of nature, and the outcomes. A typical decision matrix is as follows:

Strategies	States of Nature				
	N_1	N_2	.	.	N_m
S_1	O_{11}	O_{12}	.	.	O_m
S_2	O_{21}	O_{22}	.	.	O_{2m}
.	.	.	.	.	.
.	.	.	.	.	.
.	.	.	.	.	.
S_n	O_{n1}	O_{n2}	.	.	O_{nm}

The matrix formulation of a decision problem permits recognition and identification of four distinct kinds of decision situations. The classification is based on what the decision maker knows about occurrence of the various states of nature. They are decision making under certainty, under conflict, under risk, and under uncertainty. Figure 1 illustrates a rational decision theory continuum.

FIGURE 1. Rational Decision Theory Continuum

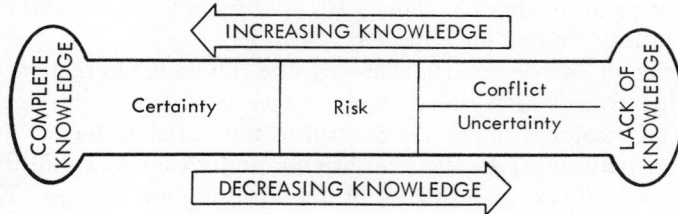

Decision Making under Certainty

Decision making under certainty is the simplest form of decision making. The outcome resulting from the selection of a particular strategy is known. There is just one state of nature for each strategy. Prediction is involved, but prediction is assumed to be perfect. There is complete and accurate knowledge of the consequence of each choice. The decision maker has perfect knowledge of the future and outcome. Certainly, implies a state of awareness on the part of the decision maker that seldom exists. The probability that a certain state of nature exists is assumed to be one. The decision maker simply selects the strategy whose payoff is the best.

Examples of decision making under certainty are the simplex method of linear programming, the transportation method of linear programming, basic inventory models, breakeven analysis, etc.

Decision Making under Conflict or Competition

The states of nature are subject to the control of an adverse intellect such as might be the case in competitive situations, bargaining, or war. The techniques for handling this type of a situation constitute the subject matter of game theory (13). The states of nature of the decision maker are the strategies of the opponent. The decision maker is in conflict with intelligent rational opponents whose interests are opposed to his own.

Games are usually classified according to the degree of conflict of interest, the relationship between opponents, and the number of opponents. When one opponent gains at the loss of the other, it is called zero-sum games. A zero-sum game involves a complete conflict of interest. Games with less than complete conflict of interest are termed nonzero-sum games. In nonzero-sum games, the gains of one competitor are not completely at the expense of the other competitors. The majority of business competitive actions involve nonzero-sum games. The simplest type of game is the two-person zero-sum game.

The Two-person Zero-sum Game. The players, X and Y, are equal in intelligence and ability. Each has a choice of two strategies. Each knows the outcome for every possible combination of strategies. The term "zero sum" is used because the sum of gains exactly equals the sum of losses. The four individual payoff possibilities are expressed as numbers; a positive number indicates a payoff to the player who plays the rows (X) and a negative number indicates a payoff to the player who plays the columns (Y). Each player desires to win or to minimize his losses, if he cannot win. An example matrix is as follows:

	Player Y	
	Strategy Q	*Strategy R*
Player X	q_1	q_2
p_1 Strategy M	X wins 2	X wins 3
p_2 Strategy N	X wins 4	Y wins 2

$$\text{or } X \begin{pmatrix} & Y & \\ 2 & & 3 \\ 4 & & -2 \end{pmatrix}$$

A *pure strategy* exists if there is one strategy for player X and one strategy for player Y that will be played each time. The payoff which is obtained when each player plays his pure strategy is called a saddle point. The saddle point is the value of the game in which each player has a pure strategy. The saddle point represents an equilibrium condition that is optimum for both competitors. The Wald criterion, which is a variant of decision making under uncertainty, is a useful technique to determine if a pure strategy exists. A saddle point can be recognized because it is both the smallest numerical value in its row and largest numerical value in its column. Not all two-person zero-sum games have a saddle point. When a saddle point is present, complex calculations to determine optimum strategies and game value are unnecessary. The following two examples illustrate how to determine if a saddle point exists:

Example 1:

		row min.	
(2	3)	2	Strategies: X,1;Y,1
(1	−2)	−2	Game Value: +2
Column Max. 2	3		Saddle Point

Example 2:

			row min.	
(−7	7	8)	−7	Strategies: X,2;Y,1
(−4	−3	−2)	−4	Game Value: −4
Column Max. −4	7	8		Saddle Point

When a pure strategy does not exist, a fundamental theorem of game theory states that the optimum can be found by using a mixed strategy. In a mixed strategy, each competitor randomly selects the strategy to employ according to previously determined probability of usage for each strategy. Using a mixed strategy involves making a selection each time period by tossing a coin, selecting a number from a table of random numbers, or by using some probabilistic process.

By referring to the originally stated matrix we will determine its mixed strategy. If p_1 and p_2 are the probabilities for Player X strategies, and q_1 and q_2 are the probabilities for Player Y strategies, we can find their values in the following manner:

$$\text{Expected Value if Q occurs} = 2p_1 + 4p_2$$
$$\text{Expected Value if R occurs} = 3p_1 - 2p_2$$

These two expected values must be equal. Therefore:

$$2p_1 + 4p_2 = 3p_1 - 2p_2$$
$$p_1 = +6p_2$$

since

$$p_1 + p_2 = 1$$

substituting

$$6p_2 + p_2 = 1$$

then

$$p_2 = 1/7; \; p_1 = 6/7$$

Under these conditions Player X would play strategy M six sevenths of the time and strategy N one seventh of the time. In a similar manner, it can be shown that Player Y will play strategy Q five sevenths of the time and strategy R two sevenths of the time. If Player X uses a chance process with the derived probabilities, his expected benefit will be the same regardless of Player Y's strategy.

If strategy Q: expected value $= 6/7(2) + 1/7(4) = 16/7$

If strategy R: expected value $= 6/7(3) + 1/7(-2) = 16/7$

If Player Y uses a chance process with the desired probabilities, his expected benefit will also be the same regardless of Player X's strategy. (Note signs of values in the matrix change when player Y's choices are considered.)

If strategy M: expected value $= 5/7(-2) + 2/7(-3) = -16/7$

If strategy N: expected value $= 5/7(-4) + 2/7(2) = -16/7$

As is always the case in the zero-sum game, Player X's gain is Player Y's loss and vice versa. The same procedure can be followed when a greater than two-by-two matrix exists, but it is usually easier to obtain the probabilities by using the simplex method of linear programming. When more than two competitors exist, various kinds of coalitions, treaties, and agreements can develop. The best example of zero-sum games are in problems of the military and various types of athletic competition (football, basketball, hockey, etc.)

The Nonzero-sum Game. The nonzero-sum games are closer to the actual problems that arise in everyday life and do not lend themselves to straightforward solutions. In most complex games there is no universally accepted solution for there is no single strategy that is clearly preferable to the others. Games with cooperative and competitive elements are usually more complex. Nonzero-sum games require that the payoffs be given for each player since the payoff of one player can no longer be deduced from the payoff of the other, as in zero-sum games. It is no longer true that a player can only benefit from the loss of his opponent. The outcome of the game is influenced by communication, the order of play, imperfect information, threats, agreements, side payments, personalities of the players, behavioral patterns, etc.

Although game models are not of particular value in their present form, they do provide a significant conceptional framework for analysis. They offer a meaningful guide for better decision making by focusing on pertinent problems that are prevalent in our everyday lives. They have found application in product development, product pricing, collective bargaining, athletic competition, war strategy, arbitration, foreign policy decisions, voting block coalitions, contract bidding, oligopolistic and monopolistic market conditions.

Decision Making under Risk

Under this form the various states of nature can be enumerated and the long-run relative frequency of their occurrence is assumed to be known. The information about the states of nature is probabilistic. Knowing the probability distribution of the states of nature, the best decision is to select the strategy which has the highest expected value.

The following is an illustrative example of decision making under risk.

An organization is determining what size plant to build to produce a new product. Three different size plants are under consideration—small (S_1), large (S_2), and very large (S_3). The best plant size is dependent on the level of product demand—low (N_1), medium (N_2), and high (N_3). The possible payoffs and the probabilities of each state of nature obtained from market research are listed on the following matrix:

	States of Nature		
	N_1	N_2	N_3
Strategy	½	¼	¼
S_1	50	−8	0
S_2	−10	64	12
S_3	−20	12	80

S_1 expected value = ½ (50) + ¼ (−8) + ¼ (0) = 23
S_2 expected value = ½ (−10) + ¼ (64) + ¼ (12) = 14
S_3 expected value = ½ (−20) + ¼ (12) + ¼ (80) = 13

The best strategy with the highest expected value is S_1. Using this approach, a small plant would be built to manufacture the new product.

Examples of decision making under risk can be found in queuing theory, statistical quality control, acceptance sampling, program evaluation and review technique (PERT), etc.

Decision Making under Uncertainty

In this case, you either don't know the probabilities associated with the states of nature or you don't know the states of nature. If you do not know the states of nature, additional research must be conducted before the problem can be approached. If you do not know the probabilities associated with the states of nature, you can use numerous techniques in arriving at a strategy. There is no one best criterion for selecting a strategy for a number of different criteria exist. The choice among the criteria depends upon the decision maker and the attitude or value system that he embraces (9, pp. 85–92). Examples of the applications of decision making under uncertainty are similar to those listed under decision making under conflict. (See Figure 2.)

FIGURE 2

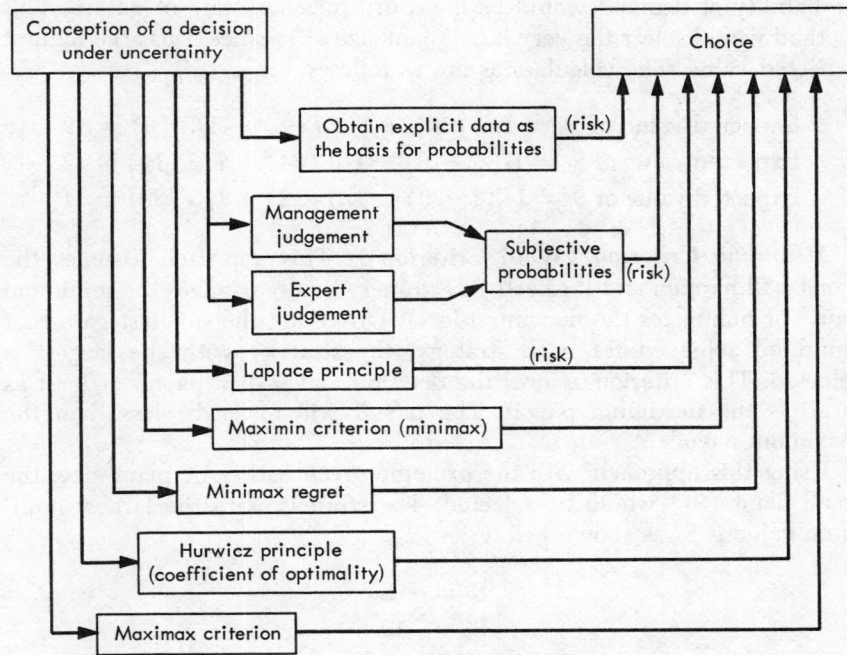

Subjective Probabilities. This approach assigns probabilities to the states of nature and reduces the problem to decision making under risk. Objective probability flows from the law of large numbers which asserts that the probability of any specified departure from the expected relative frequency of an event becomes smaller and smaller as the number of events considered becomes larger and larger. Objective or *a priori* probability of an event can be defined as the relative frequency with which an event would take place, given a large but finite number of observations. Unlike objective probability, subjective probability is heavily behavioral in its approach and it interprets likelihoods in terms of personal perception. A decision maker's experience about a situation is, in reality, his probability distribution, and his objectives and values constitute his objective function about a given situation. Objective probability does become suspect on one of a kind or nonrecurring decisions. Bayes' theorem enables a decision maker to start with prior probabilities (which can be subjective) and by taking into account additional observational information to emerge with posterior probabilities, i.e., the revised probabilities as modified by the additional information.

***Principle of Insufficient Reason* (Laplace Criterion).** This approach assigns equal probabilities to each state of nature and treats it as decision making under risk. This method selects the strategy with the highest expected value.

Using this approach with the example given earlier of plant size, the probability of demand would be one third for each state of nature. This method would select the very large plant size (S_3) since it has the highest expected value. The calculations are as follows:

Expected value of $S_1 = 1/3\ (50) + 1/3\ (-8) + 1/3\ (0) = 12$
Expected value of $S_2 = 1/3\ (-10) + 1/3\ (64) + 1/3\ (12) = 22$
Expected value of $S_3 = 1/3\ (-20) + 1/3\ (12) + 1/3\ (80) = 24$

Maximum Criterion (**Wald Criterion**). This approach assumes the worst will happen and it selects the strategy that maximizes the minimum gain (or minimizes the maximum loss). Observing the smallest gain that could be achieved for each strategy, the strategy with the largest is selected. This criterion assures the decision maker of a payoff at least as large as the maximum payoff. The payoff will never be less than the maximum payoff.

Using this approach with the example given earlier of plant size, the small plant (S_1) would be selected. The strategy with the largest minimum value is S_1 as shown below:

$$S_1 = -8$$
$$S_2 = -10$$
$$S_3 = -20$$

Minimax Regret (**Savage Criterion**) (**10**). An opportunity cost payoff matrix (regret matrix) is established. The decision maker attempts to minimize the regret he may experience. Regret is measured as the difference between the actual and possible payoff he could have received if he knew what state of nature was going to occur. The largest number in each column is subtracted from each other number in the same column. The strategy that minimizes the maximum regret is chosen.

Using this approach with the example given earlier of plant size, the large plant (S_2) would be selected as shown in the regret matrix below:

	N_1	N_2	N_3	Maximum Regret
S_1	0	72	80	80
S_2	60	0	68	68
S_3	70	52	0	70

Coefficient of Optimality (**Hurwicz Criterion**). The coefficient of optimality is a means by which the decision maker can consider both the largest and smallest payoff, and weight their importance in the decision by his feeling of optimism. A probability is assigned to the largest payoff and also to the smallest payoff; the sum of these two probabilities equals one. The payoffs other than the maximum and minimum are neglected. The probabilities assigned tend to be subjective in nature and reflect how optimistic the decision maker is about the situation. The calculations are straightforward and the selection is determined by the strategy with the largest expected value. If the coefficient of optimality is one, the decision is the same as in the maximax criterion. If the coefficient is zero, the decision is the same as in maximin criterion.

Using this approach with the example given earlier of plant size with the coefficient of optimality equal to .6, the very large plant (S_3) would be selected as shown below:

$$S_1 \text{ expected value} = .6\,(50) + .4\,(-8) = 26.8$$
$$S_2 \text{ expected value} = .6\,(64) + .4\,(-10) = 34.4$$
$$S_3 \text{ expected value} = .6\,(80) + .4\,(-20) = 40$$

Maximax Criteria. This approach is one of complete optimism. The decision maker assumes the very best outcome will occur, and he selects the strategy with the most optimum outcome, largest payoff.

Using this approach with the example given earlier of plant size, the very large plant (S_3) would be selected. The large plant had the largest payoff (80) of all the strategies.

Descriptive Decision Models

In the normative decision model, a few dimensions of the decision environment were admitted into the decision process and the decision maker was assumed to be a logical, methodical optimizer. The descriptive decision model is continually influenced by its total environment and it also influences the environment. It is concerned with how decisions are actually made. The decision maker is influenced by his personal values, the time available for decision, uncertainty, the importance of the decision, bounded rationality, satisfying behavior, etc.

The descriptive decision model is based on behavioral foundations and the decision maker is considered a complex mixture of many elements, including his culture, his personality, and his aspirations. The decision maker's behavior reflects his perceptions of people, roles, and organizations in addition to his own values and emotions. The whole collection of experiences and expectations, developed from recurring and nonrecurring situations, forms the premises for individual decisions.

An organization has the task of channeling person-centered behavior toward group-defined ends. Organizational structures provide status systems with defined roles. These become premises for individual decisions and hence behavior. The organization provides experiences and information through training and communication. These also are premises for decisions and can become powerful means of influencing individuals toward organizational goals (11, pp. 123–5). March and Simon offered a satisficing model in contrast to the classical economic rationality model. Their principle of bounded rationality stated that human beings seldom make any effort to find the optimum strategy in a decision problem. Instead, they select a number of possible outcomes of their available strategies which would be good enough (7). Then they select a strategy that is likely to achieve one of the good-enough outcomes.

In the descriptive model, the decision maker can be characterized as passing through three time periods as shown in Figure 3 (1, p. 16) (6, pp. 333–78).

Period 1: The individual starts out with an idealized goal structure. He defines one or more action goals as a first approximation to the "ideal goal" in the structure. The action goals may be considered as representative of the decision maker's "aspiration level."

Period 2: The individual engages in search activity and defines a limited number of outcomes and alternatives. He does not attempt to establish the relations rigorously. His analysis proceeds from loosely defined rules of approximation. The alternatives discovered establish a starting point for further search toward a solution.

Period 3: Search among the limited alternatives is undertaken to find a satisfactory solution, as contrasted with an optimal one. "Satisfactory" is defined in terms of the aspiration level or action goals.

Differences between normative and descriptive decision models are: (1, p. 161)

1. Predetermined goals are replaced by some unidentified structure which is approximated by an aspiration level.
2. All alternatives and outcomes are not predetermined; neither are the relationships between specific alternatives and outcomes always defined.
3. The ordering of all alternatives is replaced by a search routine which considers fewer than all alternatives.
4. The individual does not maximize but seeks to find a solution to "satisfy" an aspiration level.

Descriptive decision models add realism to the decision making framework. The human capacities of the decision maker are given some measure of recognition. They bring to bear the totality of forces—external and internal to the decision maker—influencing a decision. The normative decision models are the most valuable on recurring decisions which have a historical background; the descriptive decision models are the most significant on one-time, nonrecurring decisions. Figure 4 outlines basic approaches to decision making that can be used by organizational members in problem solving situations. The specific approach selected for problem solving will depend upon the given conditions, temporal rela-

FIGURE 3. Open Decision Model

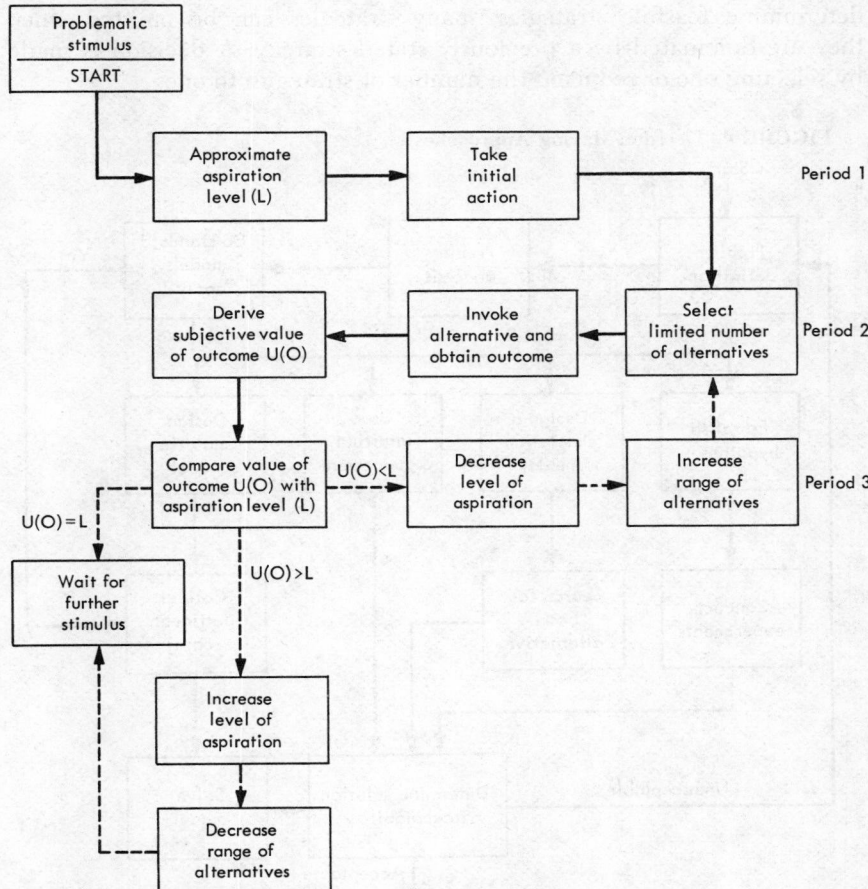

tionships, and value system of the decision maker as modified by environmental restraints.

CONCLUSION

A framework for organizational decision theory has been outlined which includes normative and descriptive models as well as other pertinent dimensions. Decisions are made with varying degrees of information, and decision theory gives structural and rationale to the different possible environmental conditions.

The manager selects one strategy over others based on some criteria such as utility, maximum sales, minimum cost, or rate of return. The specific criterion or combination of goals is not entirely the managers, for the value system is usually modified by groups with special interests such as stockholders, creditors, employers, unions, government, etc. In determining feasible strategies, many strategies can be omitted when they are dominated by a previously stated strategy. A decision is made by selecting one or reducing the number of strategies to one.

FIGURE 4. Decision-Making Approaches

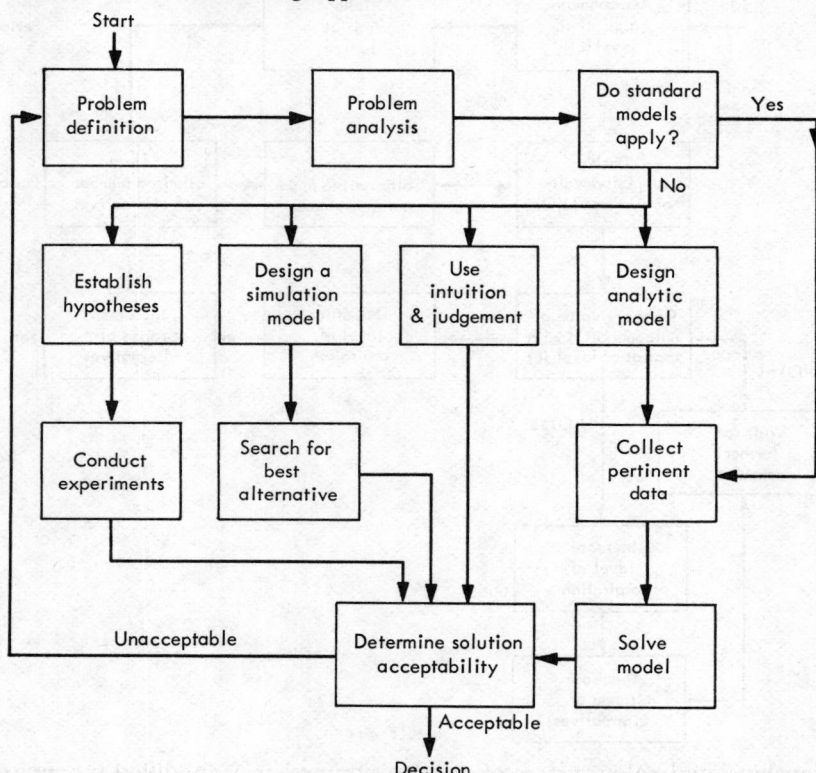

Frequently, the best strategy is that with the minimum disutility or the maximum expected utility. Utility tends to be consistent for a given individual, but for groups of individuals there tends to be inconsistence. The relationship between money and utility is complex and a doubling of profits usually does not double utility. Indifference curves are often used to forgo the utility measurement in risk problems. The decision maker chooses a strategy that provides an acceptable combination of expected payoff and risk which is usually measured as the variance of return (8). Indifference curves usually only consider two dimensions of the decision problem and they really have utility built into them. The development of indifference curves exhibit some of the same difficulties as utility indexes.

It is essential to an organization that its management develop rational decision making procedures and strive to improve their decision making capabilities. This can best be accomplished by analyzing their decisions and obtaining a better understanding of decision theory. An aim of decision theory is to better understand the decision process. Decisions are influenced by internal and external environmental factors; these factors have temporal variations which emphasize the dynamic nature of the decision process.

REFERENCES

1. Alexis, Marcus and Charles Z. Wilson. *Organization Decision Making.* Englewood Cliffs, New Jersey: Prentice-Hall, Inc. 1967.
2. Ansoff, H. Igor. *Corporate Strategy.* New York: McGraw-Hill Book Co., Inc., 1965.
3. Archer, Stephen H. "The Structure of Management Decision Theory," *Academy of Management* Journal, Vol. 7; (December 1964) pp. 269–286.
4. Dahl, Robert A. & Charles E. Lindblom. *Politics, Economics, and Welfare.* New York: Harper & Row, 1953.
5. Hurwicz, Leonid, *Optimality, Criteria for Decision Making Under Ignorance,* Cowles Commission mimeographed discussion paper, Statistics No. 370, 1951.
6. Levin, Kurt *et al.,* "Level of Aspiration," *Personality Disorders.* J. McV. Hunt, ed. New York: The Ronald Press, 1944, pp. 333–78.
7. March, J. G. and Herbert A. Simon. *Organizations,* New York: John Wiley & Sons, Inc., 1958.
8. Markowitz, Harry M. *Portfolio Selection.* New York: John Wiley & Sons, Inc., 1959.
9. Miller, David W. and Martin K. Starr, *Executive Decisions and Operations Research.* Englewood Cliffs, New Jersey: Prentice-Hall, Inc. 1960.
10. Savage, Leonard J. *The Foundation of Statistics.* New York: John Wiley and Sons, Inc., 1954.
11. Simon, Herbert A. *Administrative Behavior.* New York: The MacMillian Co., 1957.
12. Simon, Herbert A. *The New Science of Management Decision.* New York: Harper and Bros., 1960.
13. Von Neumann, John and Oskar Morgenstern. *Theory of Games and Economic Behavior.* Princeton, New Jersey: Princeton University Press, 1953.

QUESTIONS FOR REVIEW AND DISCUSSION

1. What are the six elements common to all decisions?
2. Distinguish between decision making under certainty and decision making under risk.

3. Explain Figure 4 in your own words.

4. For decision making under uncertainty, what is meant by the following and how is each used: minimax regret, coefficient of optimality, and Laplace Criterion?

19. Systems Analysis: Aid to Decision Making*

RICHARD L. SHELL and DAVID F. STELZER

Alain C. Enthoven, Assistant Secretary of Defense, systems analysis, once told the special subcommittee on the Utilization of Scientific Manpower that "systems analysis is nothing more than quantified or enlightened common sense." A simple statement at first glance, but if scrutinized, this definition turns out to be complete.

Enthoven was constantly criticized by congressmen, military strategists, and the general public for trying to run the Pentagon with a computer. The most vicious attack came from the military. General Thomas D. White, former Air Force Chief of Staff, described the systems analysts as "often overconfident, sometimes arrogant, young professors, mathematicians, and other theorists who might not have enough worldliness or motivation to stand up to the kind of enemy we face." Vice Admiral Hyman G. Rickover remarked that the systems analysis studies "read more like rules of a game of classroom logic than like a prognosis of real events in a real world."[1]

How could common sense cause such an uproar? Possibly, documenting and quantifying our human decision-making process only manifests how often we do not make decisions rationally. This is only conjecture, but let us look at systems analysis and see exactly what it is and why it is needed.

WHAT IS SYSTEMS ANALYSIS?

The systems analysis approach describes many means by which problems are analyzed to find the most effective and efficient solution within

* Source: Copyright, 1972 by the Foundation for the School of Business at Indiana University. Reprinted by permission. Dr. Richard L. Shell is associate professor of management at the University of Cincinnati. David F. Stelzer is industrial hygienist in the National Institute of Occupational Safety and Health.

[1] Herbert Chesire, "The Whiz Kids at the War Council," *Business Week* (January 30, 1971), p. 6.

certain constraints. Although there are many variations, the analysis is composed of nine basic steps:

Define the problem
Define the objectives
Define the alternatives
Make assumptions concerning the system
Define the constraints
Define the criteria
Collect the data
Build the model
Evaluate the alternatives.

The Basic Acts

Defining the problem may appear to be a needless step since this is the basic reason the analysis is being undertaken, but it is probably the most important step in the procedure. In the problem definition, there must be an accurate description of the present situation showing some sort of disparity that must be eliminated. The process of determining exactly "what is wrong" can be the most consuming part of the entire analysis and the most critical, for the most perfect solution to the wrong problem does nothing to solve the real problem.

Objectives must be defined to provide a structural framework and overall goals for the systems analysis. Clearly stated objectives are also useful for establishing limits and guidelines for the remaining basic steps.

The *definition of alternatives* should be exhaustive even though some alternatives are obviously inferior. The reasoning behind this is that some new constraints might arise, making the superior alternatives impossible to implement. These alternatives represent the competing "systems" for accomplishing the objectives. They present opposing strategies, policies, or specific actions, including the required fiscal and physical resources. "They need not be obvious substitutes for each other because the objectives should be general enough to be accomplished by many different strategies."[2]

Assumptions must be made about the larger system within which the alternatives will work. This system should include anything that affects the problem situation or the alternatives. Of course, facts are much more desirable than assumptions, but it is not always possible to know or predict precisely how things will be in the future. The statistical sensitivity of these assumptions will have to be tested when the model is built. This

---

[2] Barry G. King, "Cost Effectiveness Analysis: Implications for Accounting," *Journal of Accounting* (March 1970), p. 41.

can be accomplished by modifying different assumptions and observing the effect on the desired output.

It is difficult to *identify all constraints*. However, more information about problem restrictions will improve the presentation of analysis and will prevent inappropriate evaluations. The first and most obvious constraint in most cases is money; after this, the list becomes hazy. Constraints do not have to be physical or even measurable, but they do have to be recognized.

One constraint that must be considered early in the analysis is top management's philosophy towards scientific management. The perfect solution of an important problem could be arrived at through systems analysis and yet never be implemented because of top management's distrust (or fear) of scientific management. Other constraints are psychological, sociological, technical, traditional, administrative, political (both office and national), and, of course, physical (men and equipment).

The *definition of criteria* is important to the analyst, for these are the rules or standards by which he ranks the alternatives in order of desirability. They must be relevant to the problem area, include consideration of all major effects relative to the objectives, and, ideally, be adaptable to meaningful quantification. It is important to remember that, in some cases, the mere mention that analysis is being undertaken or action is under consideration may be enough impetus to significantly alter the problem situation.

The *collection of data* is somewhat mundane and even boring, but is obviously as important as any other part of the analysis. It is mandatory that all pertinent data of each alternative be collected in a usable format, and through a method that will not bias the solution.

Building a model is not always necessary in every analysis, but in complex problems for which a vast amount of data exists for each alternative, it is desirable to have one. A model is generally needed because experimenting with the real system is either impossible, economically infeasible, or quite dangerous, as in some defense projects. A model can also serve as an aid to thought and communication, a tool for production, and an aid for control purposes and for training and instruction.

The *evaluation of the alternatives* is the "putting-everything-together" step. This can be done through many analytical tools, using the predetermined criterion as a measuring stick. Two of the most publicized evaluation methods are cost-benefit analysis and cost-effectiveness analysis. In cost-benefit analysis, the cost of implementing each alternative is compared with the dollar value of the benefits accrued from implementation. Cost-effectiveness analysis compares the cost of implementation of each alternative with its real benefit (not in dollar terms).

Most systems analyses have these steps incorporated within their approach. Of course, some authors will have different terminology or explicit documentation, but the above nine steps are fairly basic to any analysis.

The Tenth Step

One additional step must be included. It should be understood that it is not necessarily the choice of the best alternative. As E. S. Quade puts it:

> Unfortunately, things are seldom tidy: too often the objectives are multiple, conflicting, and obscure; alternatives are not adequate to attain the objectives; the measures of effectiveness do not really measure the extent to which the objectives are attained; the predictions from the model are full of uncertainty; and other criterion that look almost as plausible as the ones chosen may lead to a different order of preference.[3]

Thus, an iterative process begins with reexamining objectives, finding new alternatives to a slightly different problem definition, and testing the statistical sensitivity of new assumptions. This is desirable for laboratory research or philosophical thought, but in practical cases the decision maker has to come up with a solution for implementation. The constraints he has defined, specifically time and money, normally will not allow him to follow the well-known theoretical problem-solving model to the perfect solution with no uncertainty as shown in Figure 1, the spiral model of problem solving.

FIGURE 1. The Spiral Model of Problem Solving

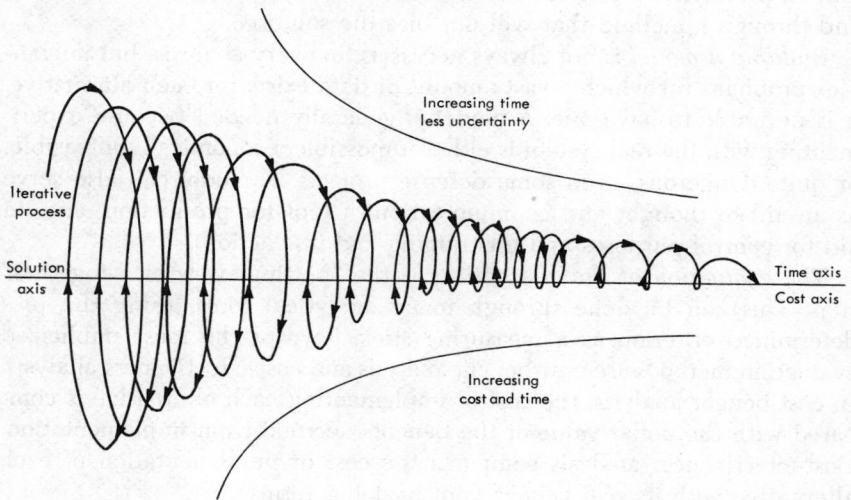

---

[3] E. S. Quade, "Systems Analysis Techniques for Planning-Programming-Budgeting," The Rand Corporation, 1966, p. 8.

After the analyst has evaluated the alternatives, the decision maker must identify the best solution by considering facts, assumptions, and uncertainties for his problem. In certain situations, the systems analyst and the decision maker are the same person, but usually the analysis is performed by someone on the staff of the decision maker.

If the alternative identified is considered acceptable by the decision maker, the plan is implemented; if not acceptable, the decision maker must evaluate his constraints in order to determine if he has the time and/or money to continue in the iterative model as shown in Figure 2. In many cases, he may be forced to implement a less than optimal plan. As implied earlier, the constraints placed on the analyst are frequently so restrictive that often his solution is nothing better than an "intelligent guess."

Something should be said about what systems analysis is not. It is not a panacea for every decision maker. It does not tell the decision maker which alternative to choose. It is a method of investigating, not solving, problems. All of the various components of the analysis are defined by man and often based on many untested assumptions. A correct decision cannot be assured even if the analysis is carried out to perfection.

Systems analysis is a tool of the decision maker, and it is not a bad tool in and of itself. Some of the general criticism of the systems analysis approach alluded to earlier seems unfounded, or as James R. Schlesinger said, "It would be a mistake to turn over a new proverbial leaf—and generally find fault with the tools rather than the craftsmen."[4]

WHY IS SYSTEMS ANALYSIS NEEDED?

New Constraints

The constraints imposed upon the decision maker are often subtle and troublesome. Although there were many constraints imposed upon the decision makers of the early 1900's, they are not comparable with the ones that have been added during recent years.

As labor unions grew in strength, management found that it could no longer assume that its employees were just another resource to be utilized in the production process. Any decision involving the labor force has to be scrutinized to ensure that a contract has not been broken. There have been many examples in which an entire factory has been closed down by a strike called because one man was fired. Legislation has recently been passed (the Occupational Safety and Health Act of 1970) that requires an employer to assure that his employees have safe and healthy work environments, and legislation has been introduced that would require the employer to pay the major part of a general health insurance

---

[4] James R. Schlesinger, "Uses and Abuses of Analysis," a memorandum prepared for the Subcommittee on National Security and International Operations, 1968.

FIGURE 2. The Iterative Cycle

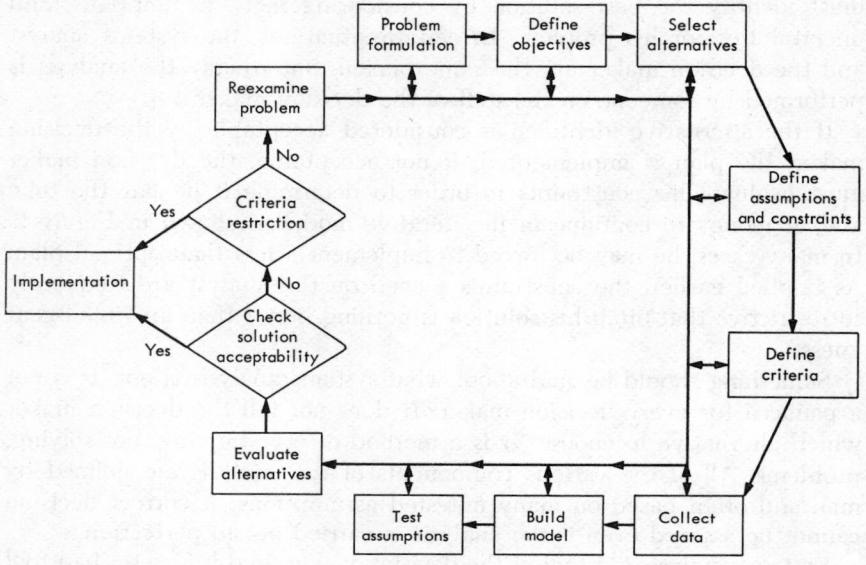

premium for all of his employees. The spiralling cost of labor in itself is enough to warrant the careful analysis of all alternatives.

"Consumerism" has come to light in the past few years, obliging industry to recognize its responsibility to its customers. Regulatory agencies, formerly puppets of the industries they regulated, have found new strength and courage in the public outcry for better and safer products. Many states have recently revised product liability laws to favor the consumer. Ronald A. Anderson, professor of law and government at Drexel University, predicts that there is "reason to believe that eventually liability will be imposed upon the producer or merchant seller of a product without regard to whether there is any defect."[5]

Since the end of World War II and the introduction of television, the vastness of the federal government has become more and more evident to the general public. The defense department can no longer give out lavish contracts to researchers to develop weapon systems that possibly will never be used. An agency or bureau can no longer hide major mistakes from the public. It is known in governmental circles that the public will view an area of government more critically if it discovers a major mistake within it. This is a great constraint placed on many governmental heads today.

---

[5] Ronald A. Anderson, "Product Liability—What Is the End of the Road?" *Case and Comment*, LXXVI (January-February, 1971), pp. 50–55.

The increasing concern about ecology has prompted many manufacturing industries to add pollution control equipment. However, the public wants ecology improvements without price increases. The systems analysis approach will aid in the development of lower cost antipollution manufacturing operations.

These are some of the recent constraints placed upon the decision maker, and more will probably develop. Decisions cannot be made without knowing their full impact on the public as well as on the various markets.

Increased Number of Alternatives

Another area that has changed for the decision maker and complicated his decision process is the number of alternatives available to him to attain a certain objective. Recently, technology has moved so rapidly that no man could possibly remain completely up-to-date even in his own field. Of course, if the best alternative is not known, the decision maker can only make an inferior decision.

The other extreme (considering too many alternatives) is demonstrated by the fact that a new breed of professional has entered the scene —the consultant salesman. In many cases, these people could be called "alternative creators." Without a systematic method to evaluate all of the various alternatives presented to him, the decision maker may choose an alternative which fulfills the consultant's objectives, but not his. Things are complicated even further when a computer is a possible component of some or all of the alternatives.

It is difficult to imagine a complex systems analysis today which does not involve the services of a computer either as part of an alternative or in the analysis of the alternatives. To a decision maker not knowledgeable in the computer field, the various design alternatives incorporating computer technology can boggle the mind. But this should not cause him to reject the computer, because it can both improve some alternatives and expedite the analysis.

The basic factor to remember is that the computer is just another tool by which the analyst or decision maker obtains his desired objectives. Also, a computer salesman who begins to describe the various characteristics of his hard and software systems is talking about means and not ends. The computer specialist who begins the conversation by asking what output is needed or what objectives are sought is the man who is going to help.

Time is a constraint in most decisions. In a market place where fad products may have a life cycle of six months, or in a world where total destruction could be complete within a day, a decision maker can ill afford not to take advantage of any tool which will speed up his decision without adding uncertainty.

Systems analysis is a technique for structuring common sense in problem evaluation. Problems confronting decision makers have become more complex by the addition of new constraints such as pollution control, more stringent product liability laws, and a more observant public. In summary, the use of systems analysis will improve the decision maker's problem-solving capability. The following points should be remembered:

Systems analysis is (or should be) the documentation of a method for analyzing problems.

Systems analysis can be applied to many business areas outside the scientific-technological field.

Systems analysis is not a panacea; the decision maker must ultimately select and implement the best alternative.

QUESTIONS FOR REVIEW AND DISCUSSION

1. What is meant by a constraint to decision making? Name some examples of such constraints.
2. Do you agree with this statement: "Systems analysis is a method of investigating, not solving, problems"? Discuss.
3. Explain Figures 1 and 2 in your own words.
4. Does the manager of today have more or less alternatives in decision making than his predecessor had? Discuss the importance of your answer in modern management.

20. Investment Decision Making in a Multinational Enterprise*

JOHN C. CHAMBERS and SATINDER K. MULLICK

This article describes an approach that has been taken by the writers to overcome the problems of suboptimization and lack of objectivity normally associated with investment decision making in multinational enterprises. The approach basically involves the participation of an impartial coordinator on the evaluation team, and the use of a detailed simulation model for evaluation purposes which also leads to the identification of additional alternatives. A brief description of the basic characteristics of the methodology is presented, followed by a detailed case study that shows how the basic approach is applied.

An Impartial Coordinator

The persons normally assigned to a project evaluation team are primarily or entirely from the areas that will be affected by the potential capital expenditures, so that they have a vested interest in the outcome. The result is that, because their future within the company depends upon the growth in profit achieved by their functional group, they seldom are able to provide objective estimates and will frequently use evaluation criteria that will maximize returns within their functional area. This means that there should preferably be someone on the project team who can act in an impartial way. This can be best achieved if the person, who we shall refer to as an impartial coordinator, is either from a corporate staff group or organizationally located so that he will not directly benefit from the success of the project. His role is to ascertain that the criteria,

*Source: Reprinted with permission of *Management Accounting*, August 1971, pp. 13–20. Dr. John C. Chambers is director of operations research, Corning Glass Works, Corning, N.Y. Dr. Satinder K. Mullick is project manager, operations research department, Corning Glass Works, Corning, N.Y.

the estimates, and all relevant factors are based on the best possible information, so that an unbiased evaluation can be made.[1]

A Simulation Model

The use of a simulation model, also, has been found to be especially valuable in a number of studies. It is a detailed computational technique that incorporates the accounting procedures, evaluation criteria, and relationships of the significant factors. It is basically a mathematical model that includes all of the computations that would be done manually if time permitted. Generally, because of the complexity of the simulation model, solutions or model computations are performed on a computer. Once the model has been programmed, the economic implications of variations in the estimates can be readily obtained. The sensitivity of the payoffs to values of the factors can be quickly determined, and new alternatives are frequently suggested by this approach.

The Case Study

One of the major product lines at Corning Glass Works is sold in the United States, Europe, Japan, Australia, Canada, Latin America, and South Africa. The manufacturing for this product involves melting, forming and finishing operations. The melting and forming operations require major capital expenditures, while the finishing process needs considerably less capital. The product demand in the United States was estimated to be greater than the total demand for all other countries and, based on the principle of dominance and economies of scale, the first forming and finishing facility to be built was located in the United States.

After the product had been successfully marketed domestically, it was then sold to international markets through the International Sales Division. As foreign sales increased, finishing facilities were built in several of the larger marketing areas. The further expansion of international sales raised the question of whether a forming facility should be built, and if so, where. The determination of whether there should be additional forming and/or finishing facilities, and if so, where they should be located, was a rather difficult problem and one for which the solution was not immediately obvious. Some of the factors that had to be considered were marketing effort, sales, manufacturing costs, duties, freights, local taxes, availability of capital for financing investments, risks of losses due to devaluation, and political and trade relations between various countries.

---

[1] The qualifications of the impartial coordinator are described in more detail in an article written by the authors. See J. C. Chambers, S. K. Mullick, and D. A. Goodman, "Catalytic Agent for Effective Planning," *Harvard Business Review,* January/February 1971.

A task force, consisting primarily of persons from the International Division, Facilities Department and the Domestic Division manufacturing the product, was formed to perform the evaluation. During this study, in which computations were done manually, it was determined that the return on investment (ROI) and other profitability measures were significantly affected by the various estimates such as manufacturing costs, sales, and assumptions relating to duties, freight, etc. The computations required considerable effort so that it was not possible to compute the effects of more than a few sets of estimates, and the economic implications of only two alternatives were performed. One alternative involved what appeared to be the most desirable domestic location, while the other alternative was one where a local government subsidy could be obtained in Europe, given that the plant was built there within a given time interval.

Based on this study, a decision was made to proceed with the engineering, with construction to begin at the European location in the following year. However, it appeared that possibly too much emphasis was being given to the local subsidy. Also, there was some concern about the accuracy of the sales estimates for various countries and when demand for the semifinished product would exceed the United States production capacity. Because of these concerns and the desire to challenge other estimates as well, the authors were requested to help re-examine the problem, working as part of a team with personnel from the International Division, Domestic Division and Facilities Dept. The request for this second study also included the right to challenge the estimates and to use any available techniques to increase their accuracy.

Defining the Alternatives

Since the earlier analysis had been somewhat restrictive in that only two alternative locations for forming capacity were considered, the problem scope was expanded to include an exhaustive investigation of other feasible alternatives. The evaluation of only a few alternative strategies, as well as personal bias, occurs frequently where the analysts have some vested interest in the result of the analysis. In this particular project, through the use of the Delphi Technique,[2] the authors were able to identify other feasible alternatives during interviews with various members of the team and other experts. The alternatives defined were (1) a new facility in Europe; (2) expansion of the existing facility in the U.S.A.

---

[2] The Delphi Method, developed by the Rand Corporation, has been used primarily to gain a consensus of a group of experts, by questioning them several times on an individual basis and using feedback information until there is a convergence of the estimates or opinions of the group. It eliminates committee activity almost entirely, thus reducing the influence of certain psychological factors such as specious persuasion, the unwillingness to abandon publicly expressed opinion, and the bandwagon effect of majority opinion.

with a relatively small investment; (3) modification of another existing domestic facility; (4) a new facility in Canada and (5) expansion of an existing facility in Europe.

For each of the alternatives a product flowchart was developed indicating which manufacturing facilities would supply each market. Examples of two of the product flowcharts, for the existing situation and alternative (1), are shown in Exhibit 1. While it would have been possible to use comprehensive analytical tools to determine which markets should be serviced by which facility, it was found that most of the decisions could be handled by relatively simple incremental cost analysis using standard costs and other accounting information, and the "allocation" was therefore performed in that way. The increased number of alternatives led to the decision to construct a simulation model to evaluate each of the alternatives.

The Payoff Criteria

Frequently, when sequential investment decisions are made (i.e., where several investments are to be made over time, such as building an assembly facility initially and then a fabrication facility at a later date), the computation of paybacks and return-on-investment will consider the overall effect of all facilities in that sequence, rather than just the payoff for the investment currently being considered. This had been done in the initial, manual analysis, where the total payback of a forming and finishing facility was computed, since the recommended forming facility was to be an extension of the European-located finishing facility.

While this may be an acceptable approach at the beginning of the expansion program, the authors felt that only the incremental profits and capital requirements for the investment being examined (and possibly later investments) should be considered. Accordingly, the first step was to get an agreement on the objective function, i.e., what type of costs and payoff criteria should be used. It was determined that the payoff criteria would be incremental ROI, rather than cumulative ROI, since ROI considered the total present and future value added at that location rather than the incremental value added by the investment currently being considered. (The ROI is defined as that return which makes the sum of discounted cash flows equal to zero.)

A related problem was whether the payoff function would be computed for the subsidiary where the facility would be located, or whether the cash flows would be obtained from a corporate point of view, since there are, for some nondomestic alternatives, restrictions on how much money can be returned to the corporation during any period of time and also associated taxes if money is returned. It was decided the model should be developed so that it could provide payoffs for both the subsidiary and the total corporation.

Another choice presented was whether total standard manufacturing costs or incremental (variable) manufacturing costs should be used for computing the manufacturing cost for the amount shipped out of the

EXHIBIT 1. Product Flow Charts for Servicing Marketing Areas

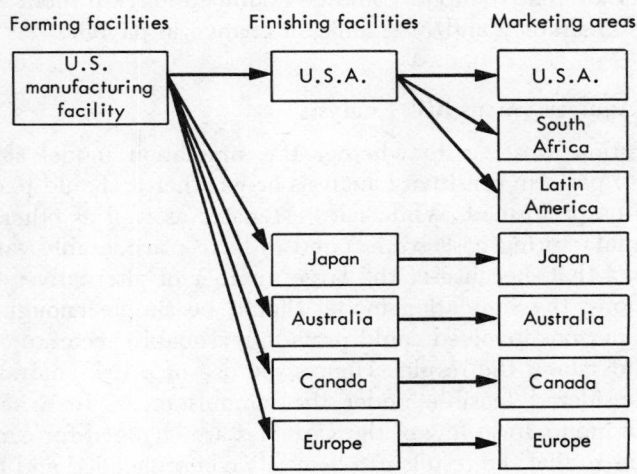

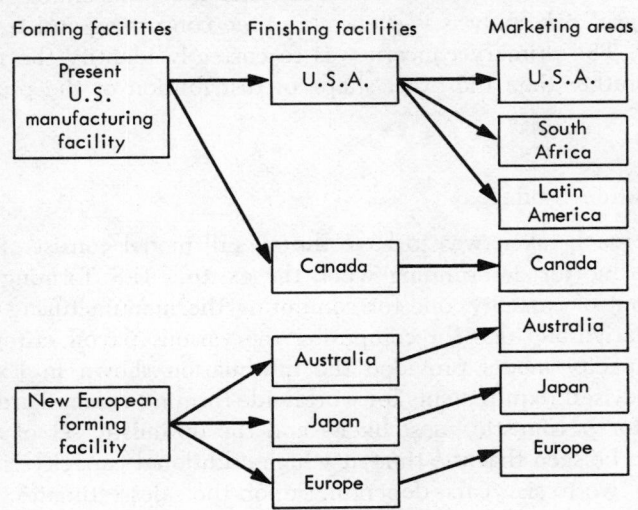

domestic forming facility. The standard cost includes both factory over-
heads and prorated set-up costs, based on average production quantities.
A similar problem involved the rate at which manufacturing costs were
increasing at the domestic facility. Again, because these questions could
not be completely resolved, it was determined that the simulation model
would be set up so that both standard and incremental manufacturing
costs and different manufacturing cost increase rates could be used as
inputs. Problems of this nature existed for some of the other parameters
as well and it was necessary to construct the model so that the effects
on payoffs of alternative inputs could be examined to see if there would be
any change in strategy and/or significant change in payoffs.

Sensitivity Analysis versus Risk Analysis

The question arose as to whether the simulation model should be
developed to perform sensitivity analysis or whether it should permit risk
analyses to be performed. While sales estimates as well as other factors,
such as manufacturing cost, were found to have considerable variability,
it was agreed that, because of the large number of alternatives and sets
of assumptions, the simulation model should be simple enough so that
the various persons involved could provide reasonably accurate estimates
and also understand the results. Hence, the use of a risk analysis model
was not considered feasible under the circumstances. In a sensitivity
analysis, the inputs for a few of the variables are changed for each set of
computations so that the results can be easily comprehended and the logic
followed. Also, while obtaining data for pessimistic, most likely and
optimistic estimates is sometimes difficult and time consuming, the data
for meaningful risk analysis is even more time consuming and frequently
very costly. The primary concern was to correctly identify the range of
variability rather than the exact shape or distribution of the probability
function.

The Simulation Model

The approach taken was to have the overall model consist of several
submodels, one for determining when the existing U.S. forming facility
would be out of capacity, one for computing the manufacturing cost for
each alternative and one for computing the various payoff criteria. The
forming capacity model provided the information shown in Exhibit 2,
where the revised requirements for worldwide forming demand are plotted
over time for pessimistic, most likely, and the optimistic set of assumptions. It can be seen that the time at which additional capacity is needed
varies from two to six years, depending upon the sales estimates.

EXHIBIT 2. Domestic Capacity versus Requirements Chart Based on Revised Estimates of Demand

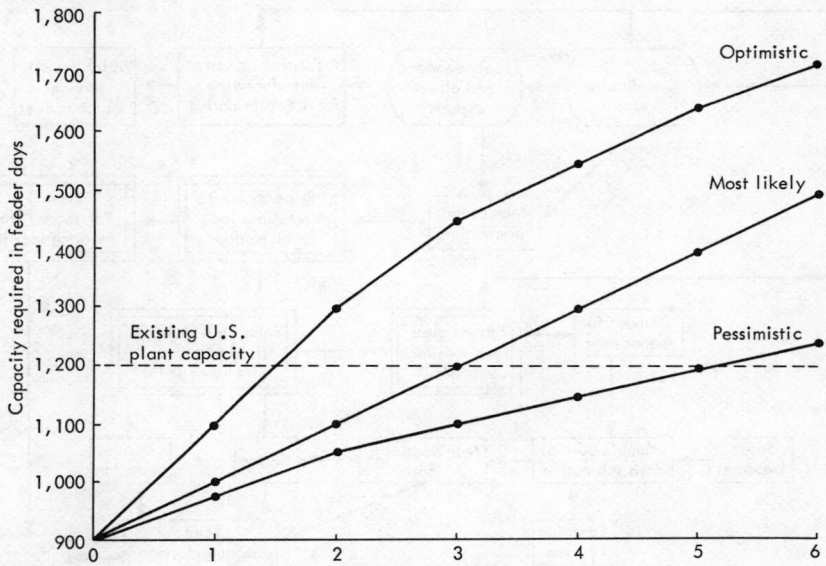

All of the considerations discussed earlier were taken into account in constructing the simulation model. The flowchart for the simulation model is given in Exhibit 3, where the people interactions, data elements, and computations are illustrated. As can be seen, the cost model contains considerable detail, arising in part from the inclusion of learning curves for new operations. Also, since incremental costs were used as well as standard costs, the manufacturing cost model had to incorporate a number of factors rather than to have the input in the form of a cost-demand functional relationship.

While subroutines could have been incorporated into the model for statistically forecasting sales, prices, etc., it was decided that these input factors would be computed by various techniques in an exogenous manner (e.g., manual computations to generate inputs). However, statistical models were used to estimate sales and manufacturing costs and they were compared with inputs provided by other groups within the company. It was possible to obtain reasonably good consensus of virtually all estimates and, as has been experienced in other studies, the sensitivity analysis approach forced more realism into the inputs and permitted decision-makers at various levels to see what the implications were for varying inputs. It also enabled each decision maker to see what the implications were for the set of inputs that he believed were most probable.

EXHIBIT 3. Flow Chart for Multinational Investment Model

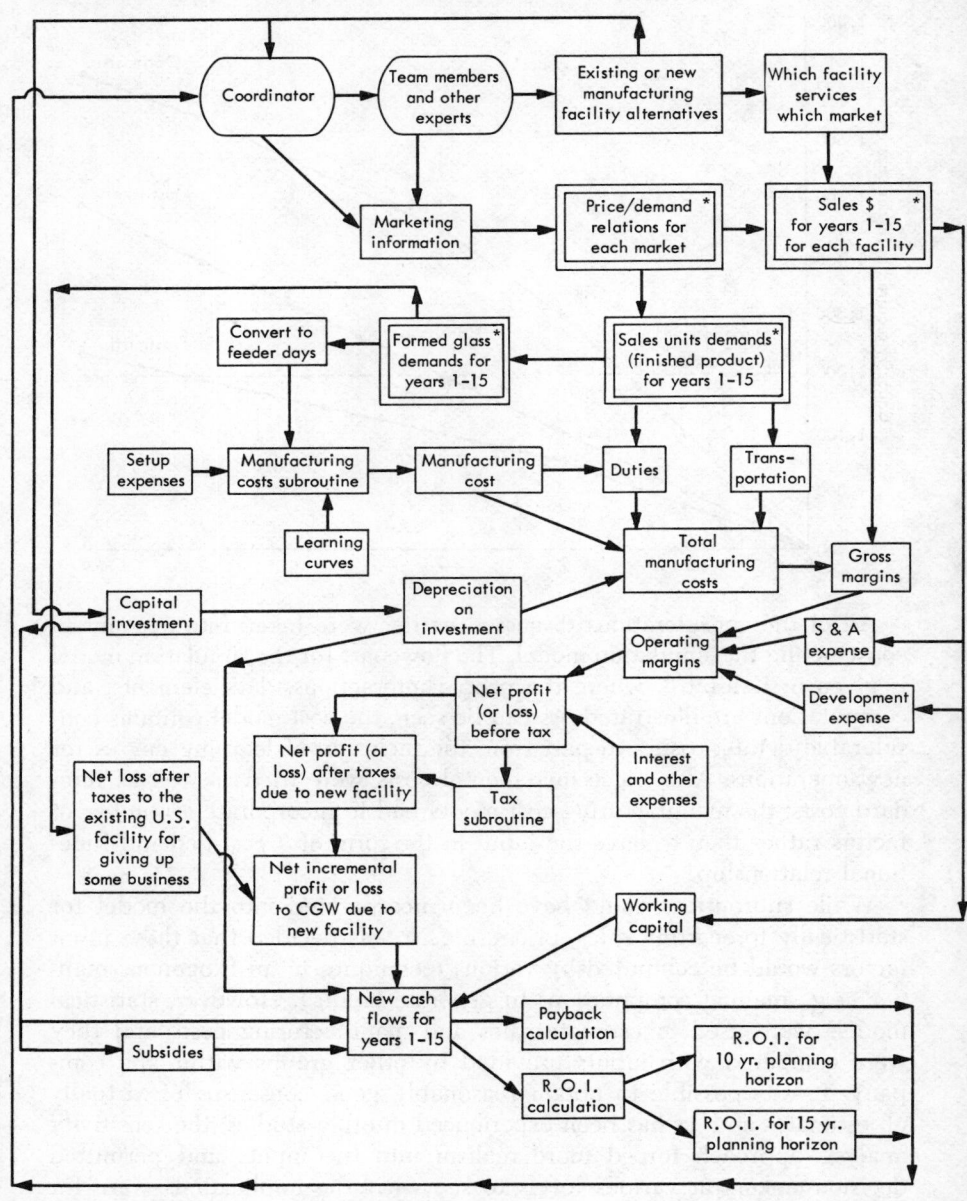

* Boxes with double lines are where pessimistic, most likely, and optimistic estimates are used for sensitivity analysis.

The manufacturing costs included such factors as hourly labor costs, salaried labor costs, batch materials, packing materials, gas (fixed and variable), oxygen, water (fixed and variable), power (fixed and variable), machinery repairs, mold repairs, mold replacement, furnace accrual, technical assistance, departmental expense, property and other taxes, other insurance, building and service maintenance, building rental, finishing costs, freight, duties, depreciation, etc. The model was designed for maximum flexibility and the authors were able to vary any estimate that was questionable or uncertain. Detailed sales (units and prices), manufacturing costs, selling and administrative costs, developmental expenses, gross margins, operating margins, net income, etc., were included in the printouts for pessimistic, most likely and optimistic assumptions for management review.

The computer model also had different income tax computing rules for each country and was able to handle the possibility of subsidies in one country versus the possibility of no subsidy in others.

Computational Results

There were a number of inputs for each set of assumptions and each alternative. These inputs included the manufacturing cost for the semifinished product, standard and variable costs for the existing facilities, ocean freight, duties, average retail price for each product type, the price paid by the international subsidiaries for the semifinished product, sales forecasts by product type by marketing area, and the finishing cost for each product by operation.

Several types of information were provided in computer outputs for each given alternative or strategy. This detail permitted the decision makers to understand not only the overall implication of the strategy but how individual segments of the business were affected. The computer output included gross margin in dollars, gross margin as a percent of sales, development expense, operating expense, set-up cost, operating margin, operating margin for other operations, total operating margin, other expenses, net profit before tax, losses carried forward, net profit after tax (make), net profit after tax (buy), net income-incremental, depreciation-incremental, investment-incremental, working capital-incremental, cash flow-incremental, assumptions relating to working capital as a percent of change of sales dollars, ROI for 5, 10 and 15 years cash flows, and payback period. The variation in the planning horizon (years of cash flows) was due to political uncertainties in the foreign markets. Where appropriate, the cost and profits and other cash flows were listed by year for the total planning horizon.

The computations for ROI were summarized in the form shown in Exhibits 4 and 5. A total of 2,160 ROI computations were performed for

EXHIBIT 4. True Incremental Profits to the Corporation: Computational Results for Cases I and II (C.G.W. incremental ROI in percent)

Computational results for Case I—Existing plant costs increase at 8 percent per year

Comparison	Pessimistic sales		Most likely sales		Optimistic sales	
	10 years cash flows	15 years cash flows	10 years cash flows	15 years cash flows	10 years cash flows	15 years cash flows
Europe make vs. buy from U.S.A., no expansion in U.S. facility	Negative	Negative	Negative	1.6	3.2	6.1
Europe make vs. buy from U.S.A., U.S. facility expansion in 1971– low investment	Negative	Negative	Negative	4.0	7.0	11.0
Europe make vs. buy from U.S.A., U.S. facility expansion in 1971– high investment	Negative	Negative	Negative	6.1	9.8	14.2
Europe make vs. buy from U.S.A., U.S. facility expansion in 1973– low investment	Negative	Negative	Negative	2.9	4.9	8.6
Europe make vs. buy from U.S.A., U.S. facility expansion in 1973– high investment	Negative	Negative	Negative	4.8	7.7	11.7

Computational results for Case II–Existing plant costs increase at 4 percent per year

Comparison	Pessimistic sales		Most likely sales		Optimistic sales	
	10 years cash flows	15 years cash flows	10 years cash flows	15 years cash flows	10 years cash flows	15 years cash flows
Europe make vs. buy from U.S.A., no expansion in U.S. facility	Negative	Negative	Negative	Negative	Negative	Negative
Europe make vs. buy from U.S.A., U.S. facility expansion in 1971–low investment	Negative	Negative	Negative	Negative	Negative	2.0
Europe make vs. buy from U.S.A., U.S. facility expansion in 1971–high investment	Negative	Negative	Negative	Negative	0.6	4.9
Europe make vs. buy from U.S.A., U.S. facility expansion in 1973–low investment	Negative	Negative	Negative	Negative	Negative	Negative
Europe make vs. buy from U.S.A., U.S. facility expansion in 1973–high investment	Negative	Negative	Negative	Negative	Negative	2.6

Main Assumptions
1. If make in Europe, Europe tank manufacturers European, Japanese, and Australian sales load.
2. a) If buy in Europe from U.S. plants, selling prices to Europe represent existing plants variable costs including third party costs (freight and duty).
   b) Buy situation considers the European sales load only.
3. Net profit after tax fixed cost loss to the existing facility due to loss of Japanese and Australian business deducted from Europe's profit.

EXHIBIT 5. Incremental Profits to the European Subsidiary: Computational Results for Cases III and IV (European subsidiary incremental ROI in percent)

Computational results for Case III—Existing plant costs increase at 8 percent per year

Comparison	Pessimistic sales		Most likely sales		Optimistic sales	
	10 years cash flows	15 years cash flows	10 years cash flows	15 years cash flows	10 years cash flows	15 years cash flows
Europe make vs. buy from U.S.A., no expansion in U.S. facility	Negative	3.8	11.3	14.5	18.1	20.9
Europe make vs. buy from U.S.A., U.S. facility expansion in 1971–low investment	2.3	8.9	15.5	20.7	24.2	29.1
Europe make vs. buy from U.S.A., U.S. facility expansion in 1971–high investment	6.1	12.1	19.4	24.9	28.9	34.3
Europe make vs. buy from U.S.A., U.S. facility expansion in 1973–low investment	0.1	6.3	12.6	16.3	20.1	24.1
Europe make vs. buy from U.S.A., U.S. facility expansion in 1973–high investment	3.8	9.2	17.1	20.2	24.7	29.2

Computational results for Case IV–Existing plant costs increase at 4 percent per year

Comparison	Pessimistic sales		Most likely sales		Optimistic sales	
	10 years cash flows	15 years cash flows	10 years cash flows	15 years cash flows	10 years cash flows	15 years cash flows
Europe make vs. buy from U.S.A., no expansion in U.S. facility	Negative	Negative	2.2	5.2	9.1	12.0
Europe make vs. buy from U.S.A., U.S. facility expansion in 1971– low investment	Negative	Negative	6.3	11.6	15.3	20.3
Europe make vs. buy from U.S.A., U.S. facility expansion in 1971– high investment	Negative	3.0	10.4	15.8	20.0	25.2
Europe make vs. buy from U.S.A., U.S. facility expansion in 1973– low investment	Negative	Negative	3.7	7.3	11.2	15.1
Europe make vs. buy from U.S.A., U.S. facility expansion in 1973– high investment	Negative	0.2	8.3	11.3	15.8	20.1

Main Assumptions
1. If make in Europe, Europe tank manufacturers European, Japanese, and Australian sales load.
2. a) If buy in Europe from U.S. plants, selling prices to Europe represent existing plants variable costs including third party costs (freight and duty).
   b) Buy situation considers the European sales load only.
3. Net profit after tax fixed cost loss to the existing facility due to loss of Japanese and Australian business deducted from Europe's profit.

various assumptions and alternatives. Whenever incremental margins were considered, as in this exhibit, comparisons between alternatives were made. (As stated earlier, ROI is defined as that return which makes the sum of discounted cash flows equal to zero.) Exhibit 4 provides a comparison of the effects of the domestic variable cost increasing at annual rates of 8 percent and 4 percent, respectively. It provides an indication of how the European alternative, with its investment subsidy, becomes less attractive as true incremental profits are considered and the U.S. facility improves productivity. The reader should consider these *only* as recognition of the problem and not as predictions. For 8 percent annual cost increase, as was found in some of the other comparisons that were made, it is necessary to use the longer planning horizon of 15 years to get even a positive ROI for the most likely estimates. For a 4 percent annual cost increase, only the optimistic sales estimates yield a positive ROI.

A comparison of Exhibits 4 and 5 shows what the ROI will be to the total CGW corporation compared with the total ROI to the European subsidiary, for its subsidized new plant versus expansion of an existing facility in the U.S. From the European subsidiary viewpoint, the ROI looked reasonable for the most likely and optimistic cases, whereas from the corporation viewpoint, the ROI is unacceptable even under optimistic conditions. Exhibit 5 demonstrates the effects of rising costs in the U.S. plant as shown in Exhibit 4 but for other sets of assumptions.

A number of comparisons of the type given above were also made for variable costs versus standard costs, for plant locations in various countries with or without tax subsidies, for varying sizes of facility, and the use of excess capacity of alternative domestic locations. These analyses showed that the fixed cost in existing plants and the low initial utilization of a new plant would be too much to be offset by savings in duties and freight cost. Hence, unless it would be possible to combine the manufacturing operations for the product being considered with other similar products which would increase the utilization of the new plant, a new facility in Europe with its attractive subsidies could not be justified.

Various investment figures were inserted into the model to determine at what investment cost the payoffs would be favorable to a European location. It was found that with a reasonable investment cost, the capital required for a new plant, even if there was a subsidy, would be such that the returns would not meet corporate criteria. Foreign expansion became economical only when the existing domestic facilities could not be expanded further or this product could be made at an existing European plant with extremely small investment for comparable U.S. manufacturing costs. Yearly operating costs were found to be more significant than the investment subsidy. The importance and value of improving productivity at the domestic facility was highlighted by the analysis.

Conclusion

The inclusion of an impartial coordinator on the evaluation team and his use of a simulation model for performing evaluations was found to provide a better quantitative base for decision making, having led to more realistic estimates and having permitted the identification and evaluation of alternatives that would not have normally been considered if the computations were performed manually. In addition, the sensitivity analyses provided adequate answers and it was not necessary to do additional research to obtain more precise estimates of the input variables. This was due to the consistency of the solution for varying sets of assumptions. Virtually all of the managers involved in the study found the results to be extremely helpful in arriving at a decision and expressed the opinion that this type of approach should be used in all future evaluations for facilities expansions. The use of the simulation model eliminated virtually all of the "emotional" types of arguments, since the implications of various assumptions could be shown quantitatively. The approach described proved to be instrumental in bringing together different viewpoints in obtaining an agreement among all persons involved, with the alternative of no major expansion of the forming facilities in the near future as the best solution.

QUESTIONS FOR REVIEW AND DISCUSSION

1. Explain the meaning of Exhibits 4 and 5 and relate what information can be derived from them in reaching the decision as to whether a foreign facility should be added.
2. What is your reaction to the use of an impartial coordinator in the total decision-making process? Justify your views.
3. In your own words, describe what information is conveyed by Exhibit 3.
4. Would you describe the decision-making technique used in this particular study as being essentially one using experience, mathematical models, simulation, linear programming, or what? Discuss.

part SIX

Planning

A fundamental function of management is planning. All management members plan, the degree depending upon the job requirements and the individual personality of the manager. Planning is the foundation of all management effort. It implements the opportunity to bring resources together and to influence what the members of an enterprise can achieve and can be, not simply accepting what is being achieved and what they are now. Several existing aspects of planning are included in Part VI.

Merritt L. Kastens, whose expertise in planning extends over 30 years, points out in his reading, "Who Does the Planning?" that the chief executive officer (CEO) should plan the long term directives of a company, decide on priorities among objectives, and the allocation of resources. Yet, a "Planning Director" or "Director of Planning" is justified on the basis that a qualified person is needed to coordinate the plans of the various managerial members of the enterprise, to structure the alternatives, and to determine sequences of decisions. The common problem of planning in many organizations is failure to distinguish between the directing function and the analytical or structuring function.

In the next reading, "Planning for Expansion," J. Phillip Golds emphasizes his viewpoint that planning for expansion exemplifies the essence of all planning. Certainly proper expansion of a given enterprise should be planned, and probably the fundamental concepts of planning can be visualized most readily by means of planning for growth. This reading serves as an excellent review of management planning in action.

"Out of Business" by William Wong presents planning being used effectively in terminating a business enterprise—in this case a refinery. The case history presented reveals the many ramifications which must be met in a plant closing. The reading explains how answers to these knotty questions were fitted into a neat comprehensive plan. The blueprint of the shutdown provides informative reading and demonstrates the wide scope of planning and the many considerations entering into its formulation.

177

21. Who Does the Planning?*

MERRITT L. KASTENS

There is pretty good agreement on just what an ideal planner should be, particularly among the people who write the copy for the personnel wanted ads in the Wall Street Journal. He should have a good solid grounding in finance and accounting as well as some considerable experience in some aspects of the marketing function. If he is to work in a technically based company, he should have some active experience in research or development. An engineering degree or an MBA—preferably both—is usually considered desirable. He should have some line experience in the industry with which he is involved but, in addition, should have a broad awareness of opportunities outside of that industry. Increasingly, he is expected to have some considerable skill in complex mathematical manipulations.

Furthermore, he is expected to have a fertile imagination, productive of many new ideas, and the courage of his convictions to present these ideas convincingly, both in writing and verbally. On the other hand he is expected to be a master conciliator and arbitrator, to reconcile conflicting views into a mutually acceptable concensus without imposing arbitrary decisions in his own right. Finally he is expected to have infinite patience and profound dedication, as a teacher and even evangelist, so that he can introduce his fellow managers to the value of a rational and orderly approach to their responsibilities.

This paragon should ideally be under 40 because if he is older than 40 he either (a) has too many fixed ideas, (b) is not sufficiently imaginative, or (c) costs too much money.

These specifications pretty much add up to the definition of an ideal president or at least an ideal general manager with the addition of a somewhat godlike objectivity and a superhuman tolerance for frustration. It is therefore not surprising that the same management periodical that would publish the qualifications for this super planner is very apt to have

* Source: Reprinted with permission of *Managerial Planning*, January-February 1972, pp. 1–3. Merritt L. Kastens is a counselor to business and universities and has an independent practice.

in the next article a strongly emphasized tract with the message, "The chief executive officer must be the chief planner."

There is obviously some confusion as to just what is a president and what is a planning officer. The confusion is undoubtedly grounded in ambiguities in the meaning of the words "plans" and "planning." This is not surprising in view of the great variety of meanings we all place on these words in both casual and technical discourse. However, if you mean by planning, the setting of the long term directions of the company, the deciding of priorities among objectives, and the relative allocation of resources, then this must be the senior executive's responsibility. Otherwise he is abdicating his position and not running the company.

The analysis of present situations, the structuring of alternatives, the sequencing of decisions, the coordination of the complex inputs both factual and judgmental available in an enterprise of any size, are certainly valuable functions and normally would be the responsibility of a staff officer whether he has "planning" in his title or not.

The attempt to differentiate these two kinds of functions is increasingly reflected in the appearance of titles like "Coordinator of Planning" or "Director of Plans" and similar modifications of the familiar "Planning Director" or "Vice President—Planning." This is all to the good. It is essential that there be this conscious differentiation of function if the power of formal planning to increase the validity of strategic decisions and accelerate corporate development is to be realized.

The most common cause of failure of the planning concept and the source of much of the disillusionment that planning has engendered in many organizations is the confusion between the decision making or directing function and the analytical and structuring function.

The program frequently arises because of a wishful hope on the part of the chief executive that some procedure, some "black box," or maybe some special breed of witch doctor can make his decisions for him or make his decisions automatic. If the president succumbs to this fallacy and the "planner" he hires is an aggressive sort, the planner may end up making the actual decisions from behind the throne and the CEO will find himself merely passing them on to the organization. The hazards of this Rasputin-type arrangement are quite obvious. The "planner" does not have the execution responsibility and has infinite avenues for evading the onus if the decision goes sour, whereas the man in the position of responsibility very seldom fully understands the rationale behind the decisions. The second phase of this situation is almost inevitable. The nature of the relationship cannot for long be hidden from the remainder of the executive structure of the organization and they may eventually mount a palace revolt which will either remove the planning officer physically or isolate him organizationally in such a way as to eliminate his influence.

The alternative, and it is not so infrequent as you might think, is for the planner to end up as CEO himself. Such a move of course has the effect of recombining the decision making authority with the responsibility. The prognosis in such a situation is not at all certain. In many instances it has worked out very well, in which case the so-called planner has merely taken a somewhat unconventional route to the top of the executive structure. However, very good planning technicians sometimes do not make good line executives or at least they have to undergo an additional learning period after they find themselves actually on the decision-making spot.

There is an alternative scenario for the president who decides to buy his company some planning "by the yard." He advertises for a planner, hires a well qualified man, tells him to set up a planning department, and says "OK, you make some plans for us," and the president goes back to his office to go "to work." In this case the planning department produces a lot of reports, which are more or less widely distributed and sometimes read. The department, or at least the director, from time to time gets a pat on the head, perhaps through a mention in the annual report, and the next time there is a cost reduction program the planning department gets eliminated. The magic "black box" that the president bought didn't work quite simply because it was never plugged into the circuit. The planner in this case is not really expected to make decisions. More critically the decision makers are not committed to employ any planning type thinking. As long as the management style of the company is not changed to provide for planned decision making by the responsible line executives, it is inevitable that the planning department will end up off in a back room somewhere, sometimes a rather lushly furnished back room, and ultimately fall victim to the valid criticism of being a bunch of ivory-towerites.

Incidentally, the planning professionals don't always resist this isolation as much as you might expect them to. It's rather fun to pursue the intellectual, analytical games of drawing up "credible scenarios" for the future of the company and then sort of sit back and say that if those dopes up in mahogany row were only smart enough to follow these schemes, what a terrific company this could be.

If we accept that the directing, decision-making, priority-setting aspects of planning can only be handled by the policy-making executives themselves, what does the "professional planner" contribute? Well, he is chief "whipper-in" to assure that the organization's planning cycle is completed and on schedule. He coordinates and integrates substituent plans. He is coach and critic to the responsible executives in matters of format and structural logic. He and his staff make special studies and analyses and in general provide the quantitative planning inputs. Very often he is the unofficial arbitrator between conflicting points of view.

But actually he can take a still more active role in the planning process and still not usurp the essential decision-making role of his senior colleagues. A planning office can provide a procedural site which can bring together various reactant ideas within the organization which might not otherwise have come into contact with one another and thus caused things to happen that would not otherwise have happened. The "planner," can be the site where new ideas and new opportunities first react with the existing business system. To do this he must be in broad contact with the existing enterprise so that once he has absorbed and reacted to a new idea he can bring about a secondary reaction with the appropriate unit of the existing structure much as an active catalyst does in a chemical reaction.

Furthermore, he can so conduct his analytical activities that his numbers speak for themselves so loudly and clearly that strategic cul-de-sacs are mercilessly exposed and developmental adventurism identified as the diversionary activity it often is.

But he can seldom do this except within a total management system that is attuned to rational processes and broad perspectives. If he deludes himself that he knows an incantation that will guarantee corporate growth and profits, he adds nothing to the intuitive, hunch-playing enterprenuer and invites his own eventual extrusion. If he tries to run the company from the backseat he is apt to demolish both planning and planner.

Given such a coherent environment, however, where the management recognizes the authority of well-organized facts and insists on rational structure in the consideration of strategic decisions, the skillful planning technician can make major contributions to the management process. He can maximize the probability of successful ventures and provide considerable protection against potentially catastrophic undertakings. He can facilitate the concentration of resources in high-yield operations and save immense amounts of management time which might otherwise be dissipated in interminable meetings with ambiguous agendas. He can promote timely response to changing circumstances, and provide insurance against complacency. The one thing he is least likely to do is "plan" the future of the company.

QUESTIONS FOR REVIEW AND DISCUSSION

1. Elaborate on the statement that confusion between the decision-making function and the analytical and structuring function has produced failure and disillusionment of the planning concept.
2. "Planning professionals don't always resist being managerially isolated and being 'ivory-tower' occupants." Why don't they?
3. By concentrating on the analytical and structuring function, what contributions can the management planner make?

22. Planning for Expansion*

J. PHILLIP GOLDS

Is planning for expansion really any different from any other *planning?* Surely every company that holds out the idea that it is planning is planning for expansion in one way or another. I don't think that we plan to contract or to stand still. So let's review first the planning procedure and then the ways in which a company can expand. Perhaps we can then concentrate on a few of those ways which are particularly pertinent to a company that is in the expansion game.

First a quick look at the steps in the planning process. I am sure these are well known to all of you but we don't want to miss any steps in talking about planning for expansion. These steps are:

1. Conceptual. This refers to setting the environment, hopefully making it challenging and imaginative, developing your company philosophy, and making an assessment of strengths and weaknesses.

2. Objectives. Long and short range, what kind of a company do you want to be, what are your profit and investment objectives, and what position in your industry are you striving for.

3. Goals and strategies. This involves looking at your markets, how are you going to expand (if that is your objective), considering economic and technical factors capitalizing on your strengths, doing something about your weaknesses if you can or if you can't what are you going to do to circumvent them?

4. Planning at the operating level. Consideration of sales, prices, volumes, production costs, services, manpower, and allocation or resources.

5. Financial planning. Developing capital budgets, sources of funds, the allocation of capital, putting the plan in dollar terms.

6. Evaluation, consideration, review. The examination of cost-volume relationships, breakeven points, capital limitations, and meeting corporate objectives.

---

* Source: Reprinted with permission of *Managerial Planning*, May-June 1971, pp. 28–32. J. Phillip Golds is controller and secretary-treasurer, Robin Hood Multifoods Limited, Montreal.

7. Implementation and commitment. The challenge of the participation of operating management.

8. Control. The measurement of results, use of alternative strategies.

Let us now look at the ways of achieving that expansion. Included here are market enlargement, integration, new products, new businesses, and acquisitions.

First, the idea of expanding the present business; selling more of the same or similar products to more of the same or similar customers. What kind of customers do you now sell to: supermarkets, department stores, manufacturers, service stations, farmers, hopsitals, or whatever? You already have these accounts. You know something about their needs and businesses, and they are used to doing business with you. What other products do they use that you could manufacture or buy and distribute to them, or what other services could you supply to those established accounts?

On the other hand, you have an existing line of products for which you presumably already have skills in manufacturing or distributing or servicing or whatever you do. What other industries or categories of consumers can you sell your products or services to?

Perhaps another way of expanding within the framework of a business you are already familiar with is to take some area where you are already a major consumer and get into that business yourself. If you incur a lot of transportation costs, should you be in the transportation business? If you use a lot of forms, should you be in the printing business? If you use large quantities of some particular raw or semifinished materials, should you become your own supplier? Do you do a lot of financing; should you have a financing division?

This of course is just integration, backwards or forwards. There are both opportunities and pitfalls in these areas, but wherever you are spending large amounts for someone else's goods and services you will probably find that your own organization has a lot of expertise on which you can capitalize.

Possibly the kinds of expansion I have just talked about have less to do with planning for expansion than seeking and finding opportunities, but sometimes these get overlooked because they are too close to home and the situations are too familiar.

Now let's look at some of the more organized and systematic ways of planning for expansion through new products, new businesses and acquisitions.

How does one go about planning for new products? Planning for this kind of activity is indeed difficult, and even more difficult is implementing such plans. This activity must be closely controlled and directed to produce commercially profitable results. How much time and money have we all seen go into new products that didn't even get off the ground, or perhaps after an initial burst of activity which we mistook for success fell off into just another slow moving item. Surely planning for new products has to follow, very closely and carefully, the steps in the planning process that we just looked at.

What about new businesses? Perhaps the new business route and the acquisition route to expansion are so much alike that we could deal with them together. I believe the thinking and planning process has to be the same for both. In the case of developing a new business you carry out the planned expansion by creating the new business yourself while if you choose to go the acquisition route you finish by seeking out and making a deal with the other company whose business you want to acquire. You have to decide whether you want to invest the resources and time yourself to develop a new business, and stand the risks of success or failure yourself, or pay a price to someone else for having done all those things for you.

Surely it is in these areas of expression, new businesses and acquisitions, that proper planning is most essential to success. It's been well said that if you don't know where you are going any road will get you there. So you must know where you are going.

Both the risks and the rewards are high. As the other kinds of expansion plans are being implemented, there are various opportunities along the way to change or redirect your efforts to meet changed circumstances. Both with new businesses or acquisitions there are only a few key decisions points along the way which once taken mean the commitment of resources on a major scale. Therefore, these have to be the best kinds of decisions that we can make. A new business or acquisition program can be meaningful and truly successful only if it is closely keyed to corporate motives, needs and objectives.

This takes us back to the very first steps in the planning process: consideration of the corporate environment, establishing the atmosphere of action and purpose, sorting out the corporate philosophy, and determining the direction to go in.

What are the corporate objectives? Usually, we hear the objective set in the simplest terms: to make a profit. Or in little more sophisticated terms to maximize the return on investment. Worthy objectives, indeed! But if that is the only objective—to make a dollar—it would follow that any new business or acquisition will do that has profit making potential, and if it is legal. But I suggest that you need much more in the way of objectives—some deep thinking to establish your corporate reasons for being and purpose.

Just to make the point I'd like to state some of the objectives that we in Robin Hood have developed and use. One of our objectives is, of course, to make a profit and we state it as follows:

Goal—to achieve long range profit growth equal to 10 percent annually, and a proper return on investment.

Coupled with this goal are the following objectives and philosophies:

To develop managers who can promote and manage growth.

We believe in building for lasting success.

We consider it more important to become better in any particular period than to become bigger.

We believe in solid growth and that solid growth can only come from excellence.

We have many established product lines and we will expand those lines that have good potential.

We will diversify into growth areas which complement our basic food and feed businesses.

We will develop, produce and market only those new products which offer a unique benefit or advantage to the consumer.

We establish high quality standards and we are determined to maintain a quality edge.

We strive to be technically competent and imaginative in all areas.

We devote our energies to building franchise businesses rather than spending time on one shot opportunities.

We believe in planning—long, medium and short-range, and once the short-range or annual plan is made we alter course only reluctantly.

We will not be so inflexible as to miss real opportunities, but we do not permit false opportunities to distract us from our real objectives.

These philosophies and objectives are in printed book form which is distributed to all of our management people. I don't suggest that these are the only ones or the best ones but only to make the point that a company should have this kind of a basis from which to develop its planning. The objectives should go much further than just planning to expand or planning to make a profit.

With a foundation of philosophies and objectives such as I have referred to for our own company, let us get on with the planning process relating to new businesses and acquisitions.

A very important point here is an evaluation of your own company's strengths and weaknesses. The new business or acquisition you are seeking should be one which reinforces and meshes with the strengths and weaknesses in your own company. I suggest that you go at this sort of analysis by preparing a profile chart of the strong and weak pieces on your corporate organization, and be honest about it. In Chart 1, I have illustrated a company that is stronger in technology than in management skills, that is strong financially but needs building in market resources, that is adequate in production capacity but has not kept up in research, that is long in engineering but is not too strong in product lines, and which has to sum itself up as being only average in growth potential.

What kind of a new business or acquisition should this company look for?

With its strengths in technology and finance, it should look for a company that is imaginative and has commercially good ideas but lacks the resources technically or financially to develop them.

It should look for a company that can add management and marketing strengths.

It should seek out new businesses or acquisitions that will open new doors in product lines.

It will have to do something about its research capabilities.

CHART 1. Profile of Strengths and Weaknesses

```
                    |        |        |        |        |
                    0                                    100
Management          _____
Technology          _____
Finance             _____
Marketing           _____
Production          _____
Research            _____
Engineering         _____
Products            _____
Growth Potential    _____
```

Then by putting together its own and some other company's strengths and weakness profiles it can produce a new chart where these various capabilities are balanced and will result in a new total organization that has improved potential for growth. This is the kind of new business or acquisition that our example company should concentrate on.

Having set out your own corporate objectives and purposes in some depth and made an analysis of your own strengths and weaknesses, what comes next in the process of planning for expansion? Let's refer back to the list of steps in the planning process.

We have covered the first two and have to get into the real practical working parts, i.e., working out the goals and strategies and making plans at the operating levels. To start setting these in the areas of new businesses and acquisitions, I believe you have to start with quantity and get to the quality later. You need ideas; dozens and dozens of them. You need to assemble all the ideas throughout your organization, from all levels of management. You need to marshal all your resources and opportunities for making contacts for possible new businesses. You need to get everyone involved.

I think you will find that the entire planning process is an excellent vehicle for communicating the corporate philosophies and objectives to all levels of your organization.

Gather together all the ideas for possible new businesses and acquisitions. Go outside to your marketing advisors, your financial contacts and enlist their help, or make use of outside consultants.

Next, analyze and check out the possibilities that you learn about. Each time you go through you will screen out a lot of candidates who do not fit in with your plans, or do not give you the opportunities for expansion that you want.

Finally, if you have done your homework well in analyzing yourself, your needs, your strong and weak points, etc., out of this process will come the few good candidates that show promise of being what you want and eventually you will get down to the one or two that are your targets. Actually, you are likely to find that you have a dozen or more "irons in the fire" at the same time at different stages of development. Some that you are looking at, some that you are analyzing, and some that you are getting serious about. I don't know what the ratio is but you may find yourself looking at a hundred possible new business or acquisitions for one that you succeed with.

Next, taking your present business and the new business you are going to acquire or develop, comes the problem of working out the operating plans: the sales volumes, the pricing policies, costs, resources, manpower planning, and so on. But with a new and enlarged field to work in this is a very demanding and exciting part of the process. Here is where you need the full participation of everyone in your organization.

After this step, planning at the operative level, comes the writing down and coordination of all these plans in terms of quantities, dollars, etc. These are the operating and capital budgets that we are familiar with. Then the final evaluation, consolidation and review; the testing against corporate objectives, capital limitations, etc.

In our organization we think of planning, including planning for expansion, as taking place in three major phases. First, the challenge from top management down through the organization to meet the corporate objectives. Second, the response from all levels of the organization to meet that challenge with the ideas, the checking and the development steps taking place up through the organizational levels as the planning develops. Finally, the approval of the plans by top management, and since all levels have participated in the development of those plans the acceptance by all and their commitment to achieve them.

The final steps in the planning process are pretty familiar to all of us but absolutely vital to the success of planning: the implementation, the commitment of all levels of management, and the procedures for regular control and review of achievement against plan.

I mentioned that getting into acquisitions or new businesses involved a few but major decisions where large commitments are made. These large commitments need to be closely controlled and managed. Special routines may be necessary to develop figures on the actual achievements. Where a new business is developed internally it may be necessary to set up special accounting procedures to identify the results. If an acquisition is made and the separate corporate identity is maintained, then normal accounting will produce the results of the enterprise; but as the operation becomes more and more integrated with your own operations some other procedures will be required to measure the results. These need to be created and established in advance.

Finally, I have to return to the point I made in opening. Very likely planning for expansion is no different from planning—period. Success in the expansion planning game will come from sound planning and accomplishment of plans, just as it will in any other area of business activity.

REFERENCES

1. Evans, Marshall K., "Profit Planning," *Harvard Business Review,* July-August 1959, p. 45.
2. *U.S. News & World Report,* November 16, 1970, "Who Are the Unemployed?" p. 54.
3. *Business Week,* September 5, 1970, "White Collars Are a Little Wilted," p. 15.
4. *Wall Street Journal,* Monday, June 27, 1970, (Eastern ed., p. 1).
5. *Wall Street Journal,* Thursday, June 18, 1970, (Eastern ed., p. 1).
6. *U.S. News & World Report,* November 23, 1970, "Aerospace Jobs: Still Dwindling," p. 89.
7. Ibid., p. 89.
8. *Advertising Age,* October 5, 1970, "Ad Agencies Don't Paint Rosy Picture for Final Quarter," p. 1.
9. *Wall Street Journal,* Thursday, November 12, 1970, (Eastern ed., p. 1).
10. Steiner, George A., "Rise of the Corporate Planner," *Harvard Business Review,* September-October 1970, p. 133.
11. *Wall Street Journal,* Friday, October 16, 1970, "Axman Cometh for White Collor Brigades as Mills Slash Payrolls in Austerity Drive."
12. *Industry Week,* November 2, 1970, "Cost Reduction, or Else," p. 23.

QUESTIONS FOR REVIEW AND DISCUSSION

1. Which step of the planning process included in this reading do you feel is most important for a business enterprise's expansion? Justify your answer.
2. Discuss reasons for the recommendation given of evaluating your own company's strengths and weaknesses when relating the planning process to new business and acquisitions.
3. According to writer Golds, planning for expansion takes place in three major phases. Name and discuss these phases.

23. Out of Business—A Plant Shutdown Is Always Painful, but It Need Not Be Merciless*

WILLIAM WONG

EL DORADO, Ark.—Everywhere one looks around American Oil Co.'s refinery here, workers are busy. Some are carting shiny new parts in and out of warehouses. Others are piling personnel records and old inventory and supply records into boxes and attending a seemingly endless round of meetings with management. Things, in short, are humming.

But the flurry of activity is deceptive. It's not aimed at keeping the refinery going full blast. Instead, it's intended to accomplish just the opposite—a total shutdown.

That's bad news for this peaceful southern Arkansas town of 26,000. For 50 years, the refinery has been one of El Dorado's economic mainstays. Employment at the refinery in recent years has averaged about 275, and property taxes paid by the facility have helped El Dorado achieve many a municipal improvement.

But as bad as the news is for El Dorado, it isn't as bad as it might be. The reason: American Oil is bending over backward to make the shutdown as painless as possible. From a public announcement nine full months before shutdown day to extensive efforts to relocate workers at other American Oil operations, the company has tried mightily to hurt as few people as possible.

"A Wholesome Approach"

This approach isn't unique to American. In fact, it has been taken with increasing frequency in recent times as the sluggish economy has resulted

---

* Source: Reprinted with permission of *The Wall Street Journal*, February 28, 1972, p. 1. William Wong is a staff reporter of *The Wall Street Journal*.

in scores of plant closings. "Most companies have gotten away from the abrupt and brutal closings of years past," says Alfred E. Cummins, a professor at Case Western Reserve University's School of Management. Adds Sidney Kriser, president of Industrial Plants Corp., a plant liquidating firm: "Management today in general has a wholesome, more humanitarian approach to what happens to employes after their separation. Most publicly held companies are trying to do the best possible thing for their employees."

A "wholesome" approach, however, is far from universal. In many instances, workers are still suddenly assembled and summarily fired. In other cases, work forces are methodically trimmed, creating an agonizing existence for those left on the job. They wonder when the ax with their name on it will fall. Plants involved in such gradual closedowns are usually allowed simply to die, with little or no explanation from management.

But on the whole, experts contend, companies these days are leveling more often with their employes, telling them the bad news as straight as it can be told. That's certainly the feeling among workers at the American Oil refinery here, as well as among civic leaders and townspeople in El Dorado. American Oil, they say, has gone to extreme lengths to make sure everyone involved knew in advance what was coming, how it would be handled and the reasons behind the action. As the refinery closing also illustrates, shutting down a plant can be a complex and exhausting process.

A Difficult Decision

From the outset, of course, the decision to close the refinery was anything but easy for American Oil. About three years before the final decision, officials say, long-range projections made an eventual shutdown a distinct possibility. Then, in late 1969, according to Frank K. Webb, American Oil's manager for refining coordination, it became clear that a decision had to be made.

"We got some of our economists together and got three or four different approaches to the problem," says Mr. Webb, who is in charge of the shutdown. In effect, he says, the economists tried to determine whether the company, looking five or ten years ahead, would still need the capacity of the old and relatively small El Dorado refinery. Some of the economists said the refinery, capable of turning 43,600 barrels of crude oil daily into gasoline, fuel oil and other petroleum products, should be closed; others disagreed. But finally, due to economic factors, the study group decided in early April that it would recommend a shutdown.

While the economists were debating, other members of the study group delved into other areas of consideration. One area, for example, was what to do with the refinery's crude oil supply, some of which was shipped from Texas and some obtained locally. Another was to investigate the company's projected manpower needs for the next five years to determine what could be done with the El Dorado employes.

"Nobody was happy or glad that we were closing El Dorado," Mr. Webb says, "but once the decision was made, everyone pitched in with great enthusiasm to do the best possible job of devising plans to close it down well."

A Precise Timetable

After the shutdown decision was made, the group began to devise detailed plans to handle each phase of the shutdown, including a precise timetable on how and when to announce the decision to employes, politicians and community leaders. The entire shutdown package was given final approval on May 6, 1971, by the directors of Standard Oil Co. of Indiana, American Oil's parent company.

All told, harsh economic realities forced the final shutdown decision. The refinery's main source of crude—from the El Dorado area—had dwindled to 52,000 barrels a day from 85,000 barrels a day in 1960. This supply in recent years has been shared by American Oil and a refinery operated by Lion Oil Co., a division of Monsanto Co. Thus, it was necessary for American Oil to make high-cost pipeline shipments of crude from Texas to El Dorado. In addition, officials say, the El Dorado refinery was "too small to meet the technological competition of larger refineries, which can operate more efficiently at lower per-barrel costs."

The announcement timetable was elaborate. The company set May 20, 1971—a full nine months before the scheduled shutdown date—as the day it would publicly announce its decision. Six days before the announcement, American Oil officials began hopscotching from Chicago (corporate headquarters) to Washington, D.C., to Little Rock to El Dorado. The purpose of all the travel was to explain to Arkansas' U.S. senators and representatives and key state and local officials why the company was closing the El Dorado facility. Moreover, American Oil sent out explanatory letters on May 18 to 150 top civic and business leaders of El Dorado.

These elaborate advance briefings illustrate a lesson well learned by American Oil. Back in 1958, it abruptly closed a refinery in Destrehan, La.—without first telling local, state or federal politicians, who later complained loudly about the company's action. "We simply misjudged the political aspects" of the Destrehan closing, a company official admits.

The timing of the El Dorado announcement was particularly sensitive. The town was busily preparing for a big week-long celebration in June to commemorate the 50th anniversary of the discovery of oil in the area. Despite the obvious dampening effect American Oil's shutdown announcement might have on the impending gaiety, the company decided it couldn't wait beyond May 20. "We were concerned about our obligation to the employes to let them know the decision as soon as we could so that they might plan accordingly," says Larry Durland, the plant manager.

"We really searched our souls on this decison," sighs Mr. Webb. "We anguished over it more than anything else. It was fully two weeks that we wrestled with it."

Surprisingly, local leaders say the announcement didn't deflate the good times of the celebration. "It wasn't a hindrance nor did it hurt the celebration one bit," declares William Alley, executive director of the El Dorado Chamber of Commerce. A possible reason: American Oil participated fully in the celebration, contributing manpower and equipment to help set up (and then clean up) the replica of a 1920s oil-boom town.

May 20 itself was a day full of meetings, all for the purpose of telling what the company was doing and why. First, corporate officials and Mr. Durland, the plant manager, broke the news to the salaried employees. Then they faced local union leaders and groups of hourly workers. A press conference and a luncheon for civic leaders followed.

Although rumors about the closing had been circulating for years, the actual announcement stung some like a slap on the face. Judge Carlton Jerry, the top county administrator, says the time of the announcement "certainly was a gloomy period for our people." John Phelps, chairman of the workmen's committee at the refinery, adds, "There were a lot of rumors, but still, when the announcement came, it was a shock to all of us."

Once the initial shock subsided, the company set about resolving its biggest question: what to do with the refinery's 275 employes. The study group discovered that the projected manpower needs of the company's 10 other U.S. manufacturing facilities and other units exceeded the total number of El Dorado employes affected by the shutdown. Mr. Webb therefore asked the other facilities to freeze outside hiring so that El Dorado employes could have first crack at job openings.

With that beginning, the job-placement program for El Dorado workers launched into a series of questionnaires and personal interviews aimed at giving employes one of three choices: to transfer to another company facility at company expense; to seek a job outside the company in the El Dorado area, again with company assistance; or to take early retirement.

The bulk of the placement program centered on job-transfer interviews, which stretched from early June to late November. Representatives from seven different American Oil facilities visited El Dorado and conducted a total of 862 interviews. According to Joseph Feeney, employe relations director at the El Dorado plant, 176 of El Dorado's 214 hourly employes and 31 of its 61 salaried workers received one or more job offers from other company plants.

When all is said and done, the company figures it will spend about $1 million for moving some 200 El Dorado employes to other company locations. Another $700,000, it estimates, will be spent on severance and early-retirement benefits. The money factor played virtually no part in the company's decision to transfer, rather than simply lay off, El Dorado workers, Mr. Webb maintains. He says the average costs of severance-retirement and moving expenses are about equal—$5,500 to $6,000 per employe. In transferring El Dorado workers, Mr. Webb adds, the company benefits by retaining experienced workers. However, he says there's also a disadvantage, since transferred workers are generally older than workers hired from outside the company.

American Oil's efforts in helping workers find jobs has understandably pleased employes. "The company has bent over backwards for me," declares John Osborn, a 42-year-old mechanic who's transferring to the company's Whiting, Ind., refinery. Mr. Osborn surmises that "99%" of his fellow workers feel as he does. (The company paid for a week-long house-hunting trip to the Whiting area for Mr. Osborn and his wife and will pay moving and temporary living expenses when they get there.)

On the less sticky, but no less massive question of what to do with the refinery property and machinery, American has made moves to benefit both the community and itself.

The refinery is located on about 440 acres of gently rolling hills. About 400 acres of the land will be donated to Union County. The company is currently negotiating to sell the other 40 acres to a pipeline company. The 400 acres to be given to the county adjoin a 600-acre industrial park, and Judge Jerry says the gift will be used for industrial purposes. The donation, valued by American Oil at $2.2 million, includes the company's water wells and a number of standing structures such as the single-story brick administration building, warehouse, several shacks and a boiler room.

According to Mr. Webb, selling the land would have netted the company 75% (or about $1.6 million at best) of the assessed valuation, after a 25% capital-gains tax, but would probably have required a long wait to find buyers. While donating, on the other hand, will net the company less money—a tax credit this year of about $1.1 million—the money in hand (through the tax credit) plus the positive impact on the community tipped the decision away from selling, Mr. Webb adds.

Of the millions of dollars worth of machinery at El Dorado, American Oil is seeking to sell some refining units and other equipment to outside sources; other American Oil plants will also have a chance at claiming idled machinery. Office fixtures, such as furniture and filing cabinets, are being given to local charitable organizations and churches. And one of two plant fire trucks is being given to the nearby town of Norphlet.

Throughout the entire closing operation, American Oil corporate officials in Chicago have kept in constant touch with plant administrators. A recent visit to El Dorado by Mr. Webb was typical of the kind of corporate-plant coordination that has occurred.

After hearing a report from Mr. Durland, the plant manager, and his staff, on the current status of the job-placement program, Mr. Webb commented: "Well, it looks like we're in pretty good shape as far as the people situation is concerned." On the issue of machinery disposal, he declared: "Here's what I propose—we turn our purchasing people loose to start soliciting bids from 'junkies' (scrap dealers). It'll take them quite awhile—maybe even a year—to come in here, inspect, then bid."

Plant closings are nothing new for 55-year-old Mr. Webb. He had a hand in supervising the much-criticized Destrehan refinery shutdown in 1958, and he coordinated the closing of the company's Neodesha, Kansas, refinery in 1970. In fact, he admits, he's occasionally, although jocularly, called "undertaker" or "the hatchet man."

American Oil's performance in El Dorado has won raves from local leaders and employes, despite the fact that the community is losing an employer that pays about $3 million in annual salaries and wages and contributes, for example, $162,000 a year to the local school district.

County Judge Jerry says, "We're grateful for their generosity" in donating the property. El Dorado Mayor I. L. Pesses declares, "American Oil has done a commendable and excellent job in the way it announced and is closing the refinery. We have no ill feelings toward them; they've acted in good faith." Union leader Phelps adds, "The company has taken a step forward in plant closings."

QUESTIONS FOR REVIEW AND DISCUSSION

1. What is your general reaction to the company's planning in closing the refinery?
2. Make several suggestions for improving the planning by the company for the plant's shutdown.
3. In your opinion were the decisions regarding the disposition of the company's land, machinery, and office fixtures, good decisions? Why?
4. What major alternatives were open to the company other than the decision to shut down the plant? Would selection of one of these alternatives have seriously affected the planning required? Discuss.

part SEVEN

Organizing

Organizing receives a great deal of attention by managers. History reveals that military and government leaders of the very first civilizations of mankind were vitally concerned about getting masses of people to work together effectively, to achieve common goals, and to obtain monolithic group effort instead of a host of individual efforts. Today, organizing is still a major focal point of a manager's efforts. For arising from organizing —the organization—is the nucleus about which internal activities of an enterprise revolve and the entity to which external forces direct their influence. Further, the behavior of persons both as members of a group and as individuals are conditioned by the existent organization. And whether managerial motivational efforts succeed or fail, depend in great measure upon the job make-up, the personnel relationships, and the work environmental conditions, all of which are greatly influenced by the organizing efforts.

Dr. Robert N. McMurry in his reading, "Avoiding Mistakes in Selecting Executives" emphasizes the importance of executive selection and placement. The best combination of qualities required for executive success varies according to the demands of the particular opening, the candidate's basic beliefs, the general nature of the enterprise activity, and the organizational philosophy and environment projected. Common mistakes made in selecting executives are listed and discussed. Also included is a valuable and comprehensive seven-step program to follow in executive selection.

The next reading is "Matrix Management Structures" by Dr. Robert E. Shannon. While the use of this type of structuring is increasing, the concept is not new; its roots and philosophy appear in Frederick W. Taylor's *Shop Management* of 1911. Dr. Shannon explains under what conditions matrix management is desirable and also discusses major advantages and disadvantages. In addition, tips on its implementation are given.

Richard S. Muti presents a concise history of the developments leading to the existence, recognition, and use of informal groups within formal organizations. In his "The Informal Group—What It Is and How It Can Be Controlled," Lt. Muti presents the characteristics of the informal group and suggests practical ways for a manager to work with such groups in order to gain mutual benefits.

24. Avoiding Mistakes in Selecting Executives[*]

ROBERT N. McMURRY

The viability of a business, that is, whether it will be a "thruster" or a "sleeper" (to use the interesting words of a British study[1]) is determined almost wholly by the competence, vision, and courage of a *small number of key executives*. A study conducted in Great Britain in 1966[1] embracing six quite disparate lines of business, makes an interesting distinction between the firms it designates as "thrusters" and those it characterizes as the "sleepers" in their industries. In all six of the areas researched, it found that one, two, or, at most, three producers dominated their markets, controlling in the aggregate from 60 to 80 percent of the total volume. These are the "thrusters." Supplementing these leaders, from 10 to 30 smaller, often marginal concerns, competed among each other for the remainder of their markets. These were designated as the "sleepers." Many parallels exist in the United States.

In many instances it is one man, the chief executive, operating at the apex of the business, and supplemented by a limited number of key subordinates, who is solely responsible for the status of the business. Actually, many of the greatest commercial successes in America can be attributed primarily to the genius of *one man*, e.g., General Motors to Alfred Sloane; Sears Roebuck to General Robert Wood; Pan American Airways to Juan Tripp, and the resurgence of Montgomery Ward to Robert Brooker. It is for this reason that the selection of the men to guide the destiny of an enterprise and administer its operation is of such critical importance.

[*] Source: Reprinted by permission from the July 1970 issue of the *Michigan Business Review* (pp. 7–14), published by the Graduate School of Business Administration, The University of Michigan. Dr. Robert N. McMurry owns The McMurry Company, a consulting firm, Chicago.

[1] A PEP Report, *Attitudes of British Management* (more popularly known as "Thrusters and Sleepers"). Baltimore, Md.: Penguin Books, 1966.

Qualities of a Top Executive

Competence for the top level executive is the product of a mix of both inherited and acquired qualities. However, given good health and adequate intelligence, most of the attributes which have led to his superior competence have been acquired in the course of his development, and reflect the influences to which he has been subjected and the mores and values of the culture of which he is a part. Thus, for example, *nearly all leading executives tend to subscribe to the values, principles, and goals characteristic of the Protestant or Puritan Ethic.* Nearly all of them believe in what are now disparagingly called by many the "bourgeois virtues" of hard work, perseverence, frugality, pride of craftsmanship, obedience to constituted authority, and loyalty to the employer. Their values are in marked contrast to those who hold the Mediterranean Ethic, i.e., a man should expend only enough effort to earn what he needs for enjoyment of the good life and such worldly pleasures as may appeal to him. Furthermore, most effective executives tend to be much more *inner* than *other* directed. They are more fixed in their conviction of the rightness of their beliefs; hence, less subject to influence by their peers. They have great confidence, albeit sometimes misplaced, in the essential rightness of what they are doing. They are also frequently men of unusual courage and self-assurance, who habitually exercise sound judgment, who ideally have an exceptional degree of creativity and imagination, and who are receptive to innovation and change. Since basic courage and decisiveness, coupled with imagination, a truly innovative spirit, and sound judgment, are very rarely encountered in the population as a whole, it is probable that not more than one person in 10,000 is qualified to head up an enterprise of any magnitude in today's demanding, highly technical, rapidly changing, and generally volatile milieu. (One of the major ironies of the world today is the fact that the leading Communist societies, Russia and China, are now the strongest advocates of their equivalents of the Protestant Ethic. It is the leaders of these societies who are now most vigorously attempting to remold their people's thinking in order to win their acceptance of the merits of industry, sobriety, pride of craftsmanship and a generally austere mode of life.)

Different Qualities Required in Different Positions

While certain attributes such as the foregoing are requisite for all executive positions, the specific combination of traits, attributes, etc., demanded by a particular opening in management will vary somewhat in terms of the level of the position and the nature of the industry to be served. For example, automobile manufacturing and chemicals tend to be much more volatile and demanding of top management than are utilities, banking, and insurance (as reflected in the differences in the compensation paid their key officers).

The degree to which the position is *structured,* i.e., the amount of control to which the incumbent is subjected, likewise plays an important role. An executive in a highly structured position is supported in his decision making by precedents, rules, regulations, manuals, and the presence of a superior who is available to answer his questions. If necessary, the latter will even make his more difficult decisions for him. A well structured job usually demands few risk-taking decisions of the incumbent.

The *unstructured* job, on the other hand, has few or none of the foregoing supportive and protective features; the incumbent is largely on his own; his personal competence and courage determine whether he will sink or swim. Generally, the higher the position is in the hierarchy of management, the less the structure. Thus in most companies the chief executive has the least structured job. On the other hand, nearly all positions below the vice president or general manager level are totally or at least extensively structured. Line administrative positions, because the occupant "decides and acts," tend to be less comprehensively structured than are staff positions where the incumbent merely "recommends." In general, the less the position is structured, the greater the demands which will be placed on the incumbent. (It is of interest to note that there is an almost perfect negative correlation between degree of structure and level of compensation, i.e., the more all-inclusive the structure, the lower the pay.) This, of course, reflects the working of the law of supply and demand: there is an ample supply of candidates for activities demanding little risk taking: few for those which call for hard decisions.

The Problems of the Chief Executive

The most demanding of all management positions is that of the chief executive. This is because, in the final analysis, *he* carries the ultimate responsibility for the growth, profit and future of his enterprise. Furthermore, all of these responsibilities are centralized in *him.* To quote Harry Truman, his is the desk at which "the buck stops." He has no superiors to share the risks of his position, i.e., there is no one else to blame if things go wrong. In this sense, his role can be compared to that of the captain of a ship: he must accept ultimate responsibility for trouble even though personally he may not have contributed to it.

Several features of the chief executive's position can make it excruciatingly demanding. There are:

1. Although he has many to whom he can turn for advice and counsel, he cannot evade the fact that when the crunch comes, the sole responsibility is *his.*

2. Most, perhaps as many as 80 percent of his decisions, relate *to the future*. Hence he can never have complete and reliable information on which to base them. (Who can anticipate exactly how conditions will be from five to ten years hence?) Yet he must often deliver his answer *today*. In consequence, most of his business decisions must be in the nature of calculated risks.

3. As head of his company, he will almost invariably be the least informed of what is going on in his enterprise (he is the ultimate victim of poor internal communications, is often the recipient of slanted or willfully inaccurate information, and, unfortunately, often has little control over any tendency on his part to be unreceptive to information which he does not wish to hear or believe). In view of this, even many of his day-to-day decisions must be based on incomplete or questionable information. In addition, many of them will be further contaminated by his biases, fears, and proneness to wishful thinking. In consequence, a number will be wrong. This will subject him to additional stresses.

4. While nominally he has total authority over his enterprise, he often discovers that his instructions are distorted or even blocked and that his ability effectively to influence his people is more theoretical than real. Few business organizations are genuinely well integrated and unified entities. Instead, many are highly pluralistic and rivaling congeries of disparate functions each with competing goals and interests and with strong centrifugal tendencies. It requires a strong, sometimes ruthless leader to hold such groups together. Often their only point of commonality is their hostility to top management. Hence, he can never expect to be universally loved.

5. If his organization is to grow, i.e., be a "thruster" and avoid obsolescence, he must constantly plan ahead and innovate. But, unfortunately, not all innovations prove successful. Actually only a small percentage of the new products or services placed on the market in any one year survive and far from all mergers and acquisitions prove to be satisfactory.

6. In addition, the professional executive is faced with the difficulty of coping with potentially or actually threatening conditions over which he has little or no control, e.g., changes in his company's ownership, economic declines, the disappearance of markets, threats of acquisition by raiders, war, political upheavels and conflicts with other major elites, such as big government and big labor.

Courage and Decisiveness, the Prime Requisites of an Executive

Taking all of the foregoing factors into account, the role of entrepreneur-manager in a business enterprise, despite the prestige and earnings associated with it, is frequently filled with frustration, harassment and anxiety. (As a rule, the least secure position in a company, unless he happens to own it, is that occupied by the president.) In consequence, it requires an unusual and uniquely well qualified individual to cope with its demands and problems. Hence, of all of the attributes demanded of the occupant of the top post in any undertaking, *courage, decisiveness, and self-confidence* are of the greatest importance. An executive can have every other qualification, but if he is lacking in these, he is almost certainly bound to fail. (This likewise applies in a lesser degree to all other major management positions.)

What It Takes to Be an Entrepreneur-Manager

Thus, using the position of chief executive as a prototype, the following personal attributes and qualifications, named roughly in descending order of their importance, are absolute prerequisites for success:

1. Courage, self-reliance, and freedom from dependence.

2. Sound judgment, i.e., common or "horse" sense, (a capacity for realistic thinking).

3. Creativity and constructive imagination, together with a receptivity to change and innovation.

4. Integrity (some executives have succeeded without it; nevertheless it is generally a valuable asset).

5. The ability to plan and organize and anticipate contingencies.

6. Energy and drive (the chief executive must often be the "spark plug" of his enterprise).

7. A fair but firm disciplinarian who does not fraternize with his subordinates and has no pets, favorites or strong biases.

8. A capacity to be ruthless when necessary (he may be called upon to close a plant, throwing 2500 people out of work).

9. He must, as noted, be essentially inner-directed and subscribe to the values characteristic of the Protestant Ethic, i.e., he must be convinced of the merits of industry, of frugality, of submission to constituted authority, of pride of craftsmanship, etc.

Ancillary qualifications for an entrepreneur-manager include a knowledge of finance, training and experience in business principles and methods, empathy, and hopefully some degree of personal charm and magnetism ("charisma"). Obviously, he must be above average in intelligence, but he does not need to be a genius. (Actually, it is probably better for him not to be too intellectually inclined, since some "profound thinkers" have a tendency to lose contact with reality. They confuse "What should be" for "What can actually be done.") Likewise, as captain of his undertaking, it is best that he *not* be a specialist or technician in any particular field. He is ideally a generalist. His primary function is innovation and long-range planning. (As Peter Drucker puts it, "The basic postulate to entrepreneurship is the assumption that whatever is now being done is probably already obsolete.") Hence the goal of the *thrusting* executive is not only to do it better, but to do it differently as well. He must also practice management by exception and leave the day-to-day administration of the business to his subordinates. Finally, he must be a skilled leader and be capable of *delegating authority as well as responsibility.*

The Role of the Vice Presidents

For positions below that of the chairman or president and perhaps the executive vice president, the primary function of the executive staff is to *administer* the policies set forth by the chief executive and to run the business on a day-to-day basis. They are the *functional* heads of the enterprise. Most of their activities are well structured. Hence, at these levels, the primary emphasis in selection must be placed on *technical expertise* (experience, training, administrative skill, creativity and imagination). This is particularly true of staff specialists, whose primary function is *advisory.* Few of these have any significant decision or policy making authority but simply make recommendations within the fields of their expertise. Included in this group are the president's legal and tax advisers, financial experts, engineers, research and development personnel, public relations technicians, accountants, purchasing agents, medical staff, and personnel and labor relations specialists. All of the attributes enumerated above as prerequisite for success as a chief executive are desirable for any and all executive positions, except that a demand for courage and decisiveness diminishes with increasing job structure.

In addition to the qualities enumerated above, it is, of course, obvious that every candidate for an executive position must possess certain elementary personal qualities. Among these are the *habits* (values in action) of vocational stability, industry, ability to get along with others, perseverance, and appropriate vocational goals, needs and motivations. In addition, he must enjoy reasonable mental health, i.e., be free from mental quirks, idiosyncrasies, or peculiarities which will interfere with his productivity or cause him to be disruptive or abrasive in his dealing with others. Likewise, he must have a reasonably tranquil home environment; be compatible with his wife; not suffer unduly from distracting off-the-job problems such as debts or ill health and not engage excessively in activities which will interfere with his carrying out of his work, such as drinking, gambling, or the pursuit of women.

Where Management Errs

Management's primary problems in the selection of executives lies in the fact that frequently *it neither understands the true nature of their jobs nor knows exactly what to look for in a candidate.* In consequence, it makes its most egregious blunders by overweighting such elements as the candidate's experience, schooling, and technical expertise. (This is also in part because these qualities are relatively obvious and easily measured.) Likewise they do play important roles in *middle management*. What few managements recognize is the fact that executives seldom fail because of any deficiency in their *technical skills and expertise*. The majority who experience trouble do so primarily because *they lack courage, self-confidence, and decisiveness*. While most are loathe to admit it, they are "running scared" in their jobs.

Such frightened executives tend to become reactionary and reluctant to innovate (because they fear change); to become hostile and defensive (to deny their insecurities); to become indecisive (because they fear to accept responsibility); and to become autocratic and punitive, i.e., bullies and tyrants in dealing with their subordinates (to conceal their own feelings of inadequacy). These are among the executives who have been so aptly described by Laurence Peter and Raymond Hall in their book, *The Peter Principle*.[2] They are the men who have been advanced to their first or second "levels of incompetence."

A second common management error in the selection of executives is a tendency to be overinfluenced by such superficial qualities as appearance, manner, and facility of verbal expression. Some men have been advanced into management primarily because they "look like executives." Sometimes they have also been qualified but not invariably so. Similar sources of error arise from an overevaluation of the school the individual has attended or his social status, e.g., WASPs often tend to be specially favored. It is rather probable that if such an ugly person and prickly personality as the late Alfred Steinmetz were to apply for a position today, he would be accepted by few employers.

A third almost universal error on the part of management is to assume that because a man is performing well or has had long experience at one level of responsibility (and structure) he is equally qualified to advance to a higher and often far less well structured position. An example is the case of the star salesman who is unwisely promoted to sales manager. This is because his superiors do not realize that *managing* is not only a significantly different activity from *selling* but that it requires a considerably greater degree of stamina because *it is generally a less well structured position*. In short, the work of manager is usually more complex, the responsibilities are greater, and his job security is markedly less.

Unfortunately, the assessment of a man's courage, self-confidence, and decisiveness is complicated by three facts: first, the man on the street has little or no awareness of the acuteness of his needs for security, structure,

---

[2] Laurence J. Peter and Raymond Hall, *The Peter Principle*. New York: Bantam Books, 1969, p. 8.

and supportive supervision. It would conflict too brutally with his self-image. Hence if asked directly about his willingness and ability to take risks, make decisions, etc., he will, of course, report that he "loves a challenge." Second, there is no relationship between these factors and intelligence and schooling. A person may be a genius intellectually, and still have an acute need for security and structure. Third, *there are no psychological tests or similar measurement devices available to determine objectively how much self-confidence the subject has.* Because of these factors, the nature and importance of this trait and knowledge of the techniques available for its assessment in a candidate are often inadequately understood by management.

The Seven Steps to Executive Selection

In view of the foregoing factors, if men are to be properly chosen for key executive positions, particularly those of a line, administrative character, it is essential that their qualifications be carefully matched against the requirements of the job they are to fill. The following program describes the seven steps that are necessary to do this.

The first step, of course, is the determination in precise detail of the nature of the position to be filled. This requires answers to the following six questions, which cover the basic parameters of every executive position:

1. What will be the nature of the incumbent's duties, responsibilities, scope of authority, and reporting relationships?

2. How much and how will he be compensated?

3. What are the *technical* requirements of the position?

4. To what extent is it *structured?* (How much real autonomy will the individual have?)

5. What is the leadership style and what are the performance expectations, values, and tolerance for competition from subordinates of the prospective superior (to insure at least reasonable compatibility with him?)

6. What are the opportunities for advancement offered by the position?

The second step is to ascertain the candidate's *values* by asking him a series of open-ended, "knock out" questions, designed to cover:

1. His life goals and aspirations.

2. His opinions concerning the business or industry for which he is being considered. (For example, some persons are biased against the liquor industry.)

3. His attitudes toward all significant aspects of the job, e.g., his prospective duties and possible needs to relocate or to travel.

4. His financial expectations.

5. His aims with respect to his future with the company.

6. His values as they relate to the legitimacy of profits, the role of industry in the economy, etc.

The third step is to obtain relevant personal data about him, his make-up and his background by means of:

1. A comprehensive application form.
2. Transcripts of his school records.
3. A test of intelligence.
4. Various personality tests, e.g., the TAT, a sentence completion test and the Cornell Index.

The fourth step is to confirm the accuracy of the data already obtained from the applicant through the use of telephone or personal contacts with previous superiors and, when necessary, with schools. In addition, an assessment of the quality of his leadership skills (including self-reliance, courage, and decisiveness) is obtained by ascertaining from previous superiors the extent to which:

1. He has exhibited authentic leadership skills on or off previous jobs.
2. He has been sure of himself and decisive on his previous jobs, i.e., has made his own decisions, handled his problems on his own and has acted independently of his superiors. (The man who "leans" on his superiors or is prone to "second guess" them is usually also weak, insecure, and indecisive.)
3. He has shown a particular style of leadership in dealing with his subordinates, e.g., laissez faire, democratic-participative, manipulative, benevolently autocratic, or absolutely and bureaucratically autocratic. (If he is an autocrat, bureaucrat, or a tyrant, he is probably weak.)
4. He can delegate *authority* (weak men rarely do so).
5. He habitually takes flight into detail. (Men who are running scared often seek refuge in a preoccupation with petty detail.)
6. He has developed strong, competent subordinates. (Weak men often fear subordinates who may be potential threats to their security.)
7. He has had pets and favorites or strong personal biases. (Weak men tend to look on their pets as sources of support for themselves.)
8. He has habitually accepted responsibility for his own and his subordinates' errors. (Frightened men are prone to alibi and blame others.)
9. He can take protracted pressure without panicking or becoming disorganized. (Weak men often crack under pressure.)
10. He reacts negatively to criticism. (The weak man resents criticism and becomes defensive under it.)

The fifth step is to ascertain the candidate's habits, character make-up, principal motivations, and the extent of his emotional maturity and mental health by a one to two hour structured or patterned personal interview conducted in depth. This interview covers his:

1. Work and service experience.
2. Schooling.
3. Early home environment.
4. Present marital, social and domestic situation.

5. Finances.
6. Health.

Finally, by combining all of the foregoing data, it becomes possible to form an overall estimate of the candidate's:

1. Principal attitudes and values.
2. Technical experience and fields of expertise.
3. Chief character traits as revealed by his "track record." i.e., it is indicative of his:
   a. Vocational stability.
   b. Industry.
   c. Ability to get along with others.
   d. Perseverance.
   e. Loyalty.
   f. Leadership.
4. Primary needs and motivations.
5. Intelligence and mental health.
6. Self-reliance and capacity to work under unstructured conditions.

This permits a measure of the extent to which he matches the requirements of the opening.

Sixth, he must be given a thorough physical examination.

Visiting the Candidate's Home

The seventh and final step is to visit the candidate's home and ascertain its probable influence, positive or negative, on his success. The object of this visit is to meet his family, to acquaint them with the nature of the position, to describe both its favorable and unfavorable aspects, and to determine:

1. Whether any special conditions exist, e.g., a retarded child, which might induce complications?
2. Who is dominant in the home, the candidate or someone else?
3. The nature of existing relationships within the home, i.e., the extent to which the wife and other family members are congenial and supportive or, in contrast, negative and a potential source of problems.
4. The family's attitudes toward:
   a) The nature of the activity, e.g., some families object to the liquor business or to insurance sales.
   b) The husband's travel schedules, the hours, etc.
   c) The amount and mode of compensation.
   d) The possibility of transfers or relocations.

With these data about the candidate, it becomes possible, with a surprising degree of effectiveness, to match his qualifications meaningfully against the opening for which he is being considered. To begin with, this procedure permits the ascertainment of his suitability in terms of each of the five parameters of the position. While the prediction of a candidate's *success* must, of necessity, be tentative because of contingencies which cannot always be anticipated, a prognosis of *failure* for him can be made with a high degree of assurance. This is because of a simple fact: *although it requires the combination of many skills, motivations and other attributes to insure success as an executive, a serious deficiency in any single trait or characteristic can almost invariably guarantee his failure.*

Effective steps for the evaluation of a candidate for an executive position, whether he be up-graded from within the company or recruited from outside, are inevitably involved, time-consuming and costly. Furthermore, many executives regard themselves as good judges of men. Hence, they can see little need for elaborate selection programs such as the foregoing for candidates for *management level positions*. (Paradoxically, they do accept "scientific selection procedures" for use in the hiring of factory, office and sales personnel and for members of middle management.) However, it is in the selection of senior managers and executives that the need for evaluation is greatest. This is because it is more difficult and the costs of an error are greater. Furthermore, these costs are not limited to those arising from the incumbent's outright failure. In some instances it may take from three to five years for an executive's inadequacies to become clearly manifest. Much damage can be done in the interim. Even lost time in finding a replacement can be expensive.

QUESTIONS FOR REVIEW AND DISCUSSION

1. List and discuss the types of information sought during the second step of the seven-step executive selection program, which second step is designed to ascertain the candidate's values.

2. Enumerate and discuss some of the different qualities required by executives in different positions.

3. Based on this article, what are the three major and common management errors in the selection of executives? Discuss fully one of these errors.

4. For what purposes is visiting the candidate's home recommended as a part of the executive selection program? Do you favor this practice? Why?

25. Matrix Management Structures*

ROBERT E. SHANNON

Since the advent of the space program there has been great interest in possible technological spinoffs and the application of the knowledge and experience gained to other sectors of national life. It may very well turn out that the most valuable spinoff will be our improved knowledge of how to plan, coordinate, monitor, and control multitudinous organizations working to accomplish complex undertakings.

At its peak, the Apollo/Saturn Program entailed the management and coordination of a government headquarters; several widely dispersed government laboratories and centers; some 20,000 industrial contractor, subcontractor and supplier organizations; faculty and students at 200 universities and colleges; and the efforts of almost 400,000 nongovernmental workers. In terms of technological and managerial complexity, it has certainly been a unique national experience from which much can hopefully be learned. The managerial problems of the large, multiplant, multiproduct industrial organization differ from the Apollo/Saturn management problems only in magnitude and scope, not in complexity. With this thought in mind, several studies of the Apollo/Saturn Program management system have been conducted. (1) and (2).†

Perhaps one of the most striking findings of these investigations was the discovery of the amazingly wide and extensive use of the so-called "Matrix Management Structure" throughout NASA and its major contractors. At the beginning of the space program the organization of the NASA Headquarters, field centers, and industrial contractors was pretty much along traditional hierarchial, line and staff concepts. Some were decentralized or organized along product or project lines, and others along functional lines. But as the program progressed, each of the NASA

---

* Source: Reprinted with permission of *Industrial Engineering*, March 1972, pp. 26–9. Dr. Robert E. Shannon is associate professor of industrial and systems engineering, University of Alabama, Huntsville.

† Numbers in parentheses refer to references at end of reading.

centers and major industrial contractors evolved into basically the same organizational pattern. It is important to note that this structure was not imposed upon them by higher authority or the government, but, rather, derived from their own experiences and internal needs. Since the evolution to the widespread use of the matrix structure was universal among the NASA agencies and major contractors, the questions naturally arise of why did they go that way, and would such an untraditional structure be beneficial to other organizations?

Description

The basic concept of matrix management is . . . illustrated in Figure 1. There is an old saying that there is nothing new under the sun, and this is true of the matrix organization concept. Its roots and philosophy go back at least as deep as Frederick W. Taylor's proposals for "functional management." (3) As early as 1911, Taylor presented the basic arguments for the matrix organization in his classic book, *Shop Management*. Although his proposal for "functional foremanship" was not widely accepted, and although he was dealing strictly with production shop management, the basic concept and philosophy are the same. He argued that in enterprises organized along military or hierarchial lines the duties required of the managers, "are so varied; and call for an amount of special information coupled with such a variety of natural ability, that only men of unusual qualities to start with, and who have had years of special training, can perform them in a satisfactory manner."

If this was true of industrial production shops in Taylor's days, it was magnified many times over in the space program of the sixties. There were no previous comparable programs to provide the years of special training and experience needed to develop the broad knowledge and capabilities required of the managers. Most of the managers in the aerospace industry were young and inexperienced, especially when compared with executives in more established industries. Thus, the matrix organization was a natural solution to the problem of the breadth and depth of knowledge required and the need for built-in checks and balances between young, inexperienced managers. It made it possible to train managers in a comparatively short time, who could readily and fully perform the functions demanded of them, even though they were called upon to deal with highly complex problems of a broad, interdisciplinary nature.

Obviously, the titles of the program managers and also the functional lines of responsibility will vary from organization to organization. Likewise, the determination of whether the program managers or the functional managers are the vertical (line) or horizontal (staff) segments varies with the internal organizational philosophy of each organization involved. The important aspect is the formal specialization of manage-

FIGURE 1. Matrix Management (establishes an interplay of checks and balances between a group of managers with specific product, program, or project responsibilities, and another managerial group with specific functional responsibilities)

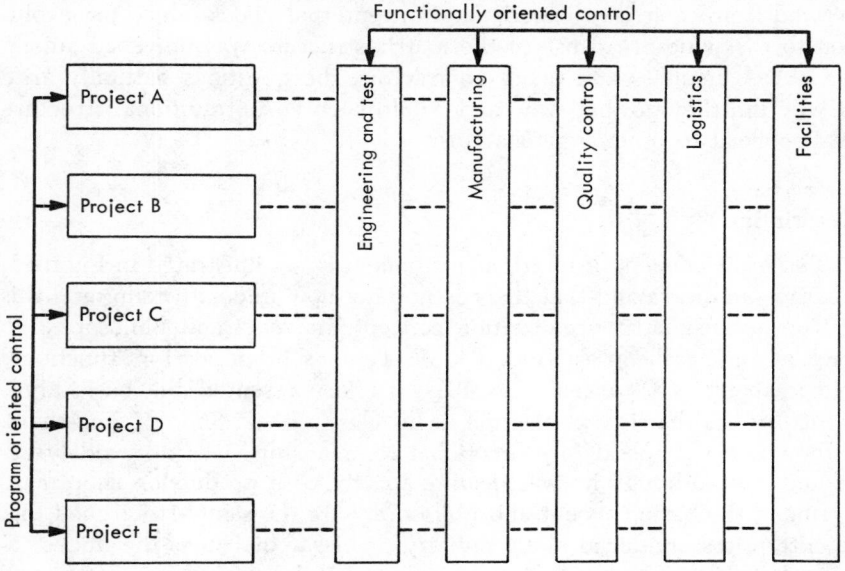

ment responsibilities from the two viewpoints (product and function) and the establishment of built-in checks and balances between the different responsibilities.

In a company with management basically decentralized and organized around product-line responsibilities, the functional executive provides a unifying force which crosses the boundaries of the various product-line organizations to establish and maintain high standards of technical performance; to transfer the latest techniques and practices throughout the company; to insure that certain important technical aspects are not being overlooked; and to assure that experienced personnel are retained and developed.

In the company that is organized primarily along functional lines, the program or project executives provide the unifying coordination to insure that their project or program is getting the appropriate attention and required level of effort from each of the functional areas. In addition, the project manager continuously monitors the status of costs, schedules, and performance; provides the technical integration; defines requirements; and provides the prime contact with the customer for program activities. Regardless of which was horizontal and which vertical, in the organizations studied, the program managers are clearly in charge of the programs. Functional executives have appeal channels, but they can neither ignore nor procrastinate on a decision by a program manager. While the functional executive implements the decisions of the program manager, he is in the position to, and expected to, re-raise or question any decision with new facts as often as he feels it necessary. The program and functional managers both report directly to top management. Conflicts which cannot be settled by the appropriate program and functional managers are referred to higher management for resolution.

When operating under a matrix management approach, it is obviously extremely important that the responsibilities and authority of each manager be clearly defined, understood, and accepted by both functional and program people. These relationships need to be spelled out in writing. It is essential that in the various operating policies, the specific authority of the program manager be clearly defined in terms of program direction, and that the authority of the functional executive be defined in terms of operational direction. A typical breakdown of the program and functional managers' responsibilities and authority is shown in Figure 2. This particular breakdown is the one used by the Rocketdyne Division of the North American-Rockwell Corporation. (2)

Closely tied into the matrix concept of organization, as applied in the space program, has been the use of the "work package" management control system. The underlying philosophy of the work package system is the concept of management by objectives and decentralization of accountability. Implementation of the system requires that a work package tree be constructed by breaking the overall task down by product components (hardware, software, and services) and then further breaking down these product oriented elements into functional work packages. Each work package is basically a performance control element. Each work package is negotiated with and assigned to a specific organizational manager. This work package manager agrees to a specific objective (which is measurable), detailed task descriptions, specifications, scheduled task milestones, and a time-phased budget in both dollars and manpower for his work package. He is then held fully and personally responsible for that work package in terms of technical, schedule, and cost performance by both the program and functional managers. All program tracking and accounting for control purposes is then done by work packages.

Implementation

The problems of acceptance of the matrix organizational structure have not changed much since Taylor's day. The popular conviction that the very foundation of good management rests upon the principle of unity of command (i.e., that no one can work under two bosses at the same time) is so deeply rooted that many managers cringe at the very thought of matrix organization. They fail to recognize that almost every organization today contains elements of the matrix philosophy although camouflaged under the mythology of line and staff. When the quality control

FIGURE 2. Typical Description of Program and Functional Manager's Responsibilities

Program Manager

Program Direction:

Directs and controls company program and functional organization and subcontractor activity to achieve program objectives

Develops master program plans

Determines and issues the work breakdown structure and related work statements, budgets, and schedules which define *what* effort will be accomplished, *when* it will be performed, and who will have accountability

Assures the attainment of the technical, schedule, and cost objectives of the program

Program Control:

Monitors cost, schedule, and technical results against master program plans

Replans and rebudgets as necessary to assure accomplishment of program objectives

Monitors contractual reporting

Configuration Management:

Controls changes and assures configuration accountability affecting the program

Customer Coordination:

Provides the prime contact with the customer for program activities

Administration:

Approves the assignment and concurs in merit increases of key functional personnel assigned to the program

Functional Manager

Operational Direction:

Determines *who* will perform detailed tasks, *where* they will be done, and how they will be accomplished

Provides a stable base for the development of talent and skills to assure maintenance of technical capability

Provides necessary facilities and services to support program requirements

Operational Control:

Responsible for the technical excellence and quality requirements of assigned tasks

Assures that all tasks are accomplished in accordance with technical specifications, on schedule, and within budget

Administration:

Performs administrative services in support of personnel assigned to a program

Initiates merit increases for all personnel within his organization

department can reject a batch of parts or shut down a production line; when the scheduling department tells the plant what to make and when to make it; when the engineering department tells the plant how to make something—you have functional management and the elements of the matrix organization. Traditionalists will argue that it is not so, but they are confusing semantics with reality.

It is probably not by accident that a new, young industry, pioneering on the frontiers of knowledge, was the first to give matrix organization widespread, formal acceptance. Old myths (the necessity of unity of command) and traditions (separation of line and staff) die hard. But the old organizational structures decentralized along either product or functional lines simply would not work in the Apollo/Saturn Program. Groups originally organized along both traditional lines evolved and merged into the matrix structure where they could have the best of both worlds.

The matrix structure is also being experimented with in universities, the bedrock of conservative traditionalism. Southern Methodist University and others have organized the management of their graduate and research programs in engineering in a matrix structure (Figure 3). The University of Alabama in Huntsville has likewise begun the direction of its undergraduate engineering program along similar lines. The primary motivation has been the necessity of providing a framework for interdisciplinary training in such fields as systems engineering, environmental engineering, bio-medical engineering, and computer sciences, which do not clearly or properly belong to one of the traditional departments. Again, the responsibilities and authority of the different directors must be clearly defined. Experience has shown that the establishment of new interdisciplinary programs under a matrix structure is much easier, and parochialism and interdepartment feuds are minimized.

Summary

We will probably see greatly increased acceptance and use of the matrix concept. However, it certainly is not a panacea for all organizational problems nor should it be used by everyone. It can be very useful with young, inexperienced managements or when dealing with complex, interdisciplinary tasks.

The purpose of organizational structure is to (1) Specialize executive activity (2) Simplify the tasks of management and (3) Group employees for the purpose of direction and control.

The matrix structure provides us with one more possible variation to consider when we are seeking (1) Specialization of management skills (2) Built-in checks and balances (3) Rapid transference of technical know-how between programs or projects (4) Greater flexibility of skilled manpower utilization and (5) Reduction of duplication of effort and thus reduced costs.

FIGURE 3. Southern Methodist University's Organization of Graduate and Research Programs in Engineering (a matrix structure)

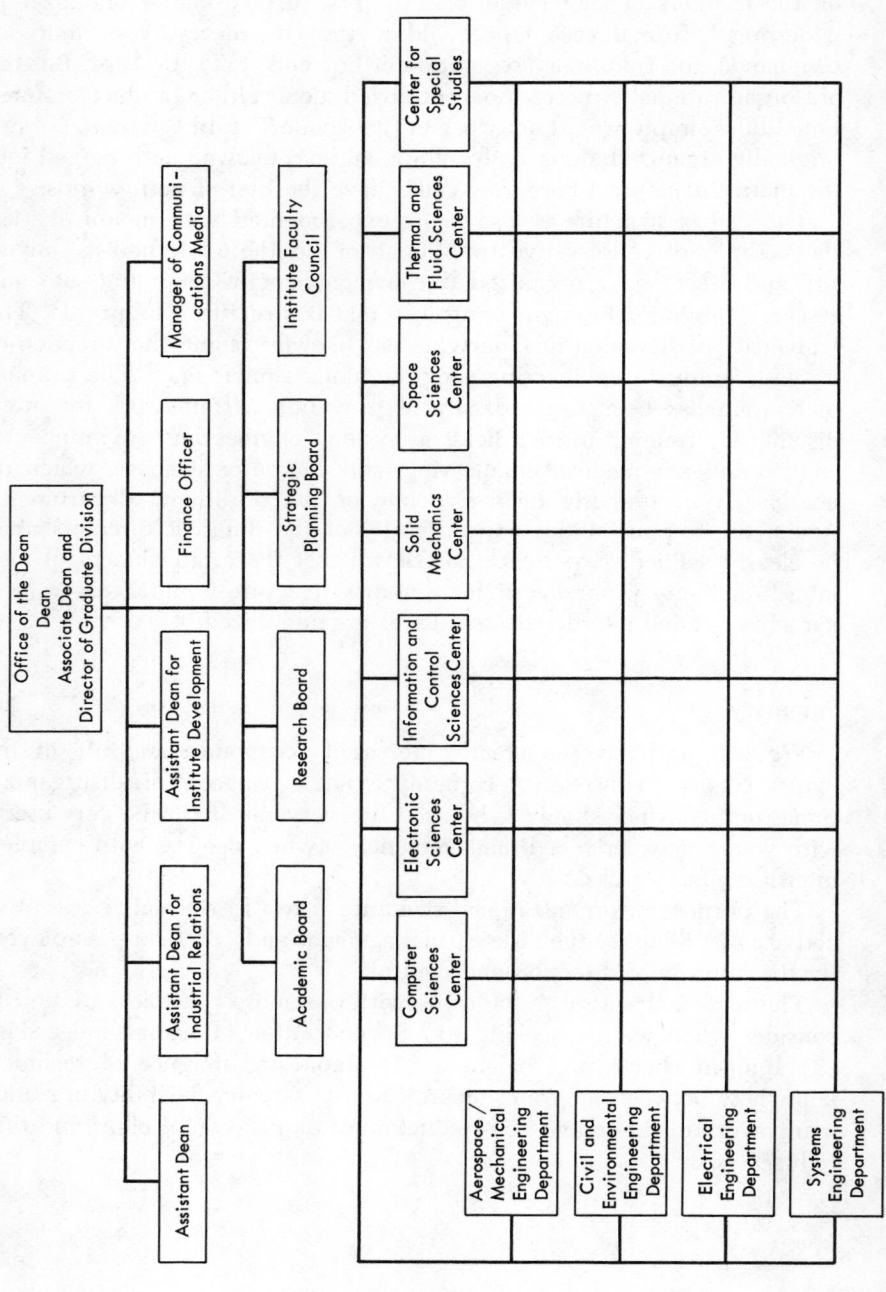

REFERENCES

1. Shannon, R. E. "Apollo/Saturn Program Management," chap. 3, *Sourcebook of Saturn Benefits, UARI Report,* University of Alabama in Huntsville, Research Institute, December 1970.
2. "Apollo Program Management," Staff Study for the Committee on Science and Astronautics, U.S. House of Representatives, U.S. Government Printing Office, Washington, D.C., July 1969.
3. Taylor, F. W., *Scientific Management,* Harper & Row, New York 1947.
4. Ignizio, J. P. and R. E. Shannon, "Organization Structures in the 1980's," *Industrial Engineering,* September 1971.

QUESTIONS FOR REVIEW AND DISCUSSION

1. Describe the "work package management control system" applied in the space program and closely related to the matrix concept of organization.
2. Comment on Figure 3 and note (a) possible advantages and (b) possible disadvantages of this type of organization.
3. Are you of the opinion that a matrix organization structure would be advantageous for your school, place of work, or a business with which you are familiar? Justify your answer.
4. Elaborate fully on the following quotation, "Thus, matrix organization was a natural solution to the problem of the breadth and depth of knowledge required and the need for built-in checks and balances between young, inexperienced managers."

26. The Informal Group— What It Is and How It Can Be Controlled *

RICHARD S. MUTI

When Joe Simpson reported for his first day of work at the Wilson plant, Harry Eaton, the shop supervisor, introduced him to the ten men he'd be working with in the die shop. After a brief tour of the shop, Simpson settled down at his machine, anxious to begin the day's work. By mid-morning, he had turned out half his day's quota of dies, and it seemed a cinch that he'd beat the standard output by at least a hundred. Not bad for the first day on the job, he thought. But he wondered why the standards were set so low. It didn't seem right that a new man should be able to step in on the first day and exceed the output that the company had set for its more seasoned workers. He shrugged it off, and continued to turn out the dies at an even pace.

Just before noon, Ed Morgan, one of his coworkers in the shop, stopped at Simpson's machine.

"Hey, Speedy Gonzales, you got a light," said Morgan, taking a cigarette and offering the pack to Simpson.

Simpson laughed. "Sure," he said. He stopped work and accepted one of the cigarettes, happy for the pause and grateful for Morgan's friendly gesture. After both cigarettes were lit, Morgan spoke first.

"What do you think of Eaton, the supervisor?" Morgan asked.

"He seems like a real nice guy," replied Simpson.

Morgan grunted. "It's all an act, believe me. He'd sooner turn you in than look at you. You've got to watch what you say around him. He's a 'company man' all the way."

"Oh," said Simpson.

"You know, I've been watching you all morning, Joe," said Morgan. "You're going to kill yourself the way you've been working. You ought to

* Source: Reprinted with permission of *Personnel Journal*, August 1968, pp. 563–71. Richard S. Muti is a Lieutenant, United States Navy, Norfolk, Virginia.

slow down and take it easy like the rest of us. Say, you don't own part of this company, do you?"

Simpson laughed. "No," he said, "but I could sure use some of that bonus money they pay for beating the standard."

"We all could use the money, Joe, but don't you see what'll happen? We all start turning in work over the standard and, sure, they'll pay us the bonus for a while, but then what happens. The first thing you know, they go and raise the standard on you. Then where are you—breaking your back, turning out more work for the same money you got in the first place. It doesn't make sense, does it?"

"You know," said Simpson, "I never thought of that before."

"Listen, kid," said Morgan, "You'll do alright around here. Stick with me and I'll teach you the ropes in no time. Say, why don't you come to lunch with me and the guys. We always go to this little place around the corner."

"Say, that'd be great," said Simpson.

"See you later," Morgan said as he walked off, "and remember—*slow down.*"

Simpson turned to his machine and began work again. That Morgan is quite a guy, he thought. He really knows what the score is. He unconsciously settled back into the same, efficient pace, punching out the dies with an easy economy of motion. But after a few minutes, he caught himself, and slowed his pace noticeably. He looked up from his machine at the faces of his coworkers. They were all smiling at him, nodding their heads in approval.

Joe Simpson has just been introduced to an informal group. He has met the group's leader, Ed Morgan, who set him straight on what the group thinks of Harry Eaton, the supervisor, what the group feels is a fair day's work, and where the group likes to eat lunch together. In time, Simpson will be taught all the group's norms and values. The pressures to conform will be great, probably too great for an average man like Simpson to resist.

The situation described above is fictional, of course. There is no "Wilson plant," as such. But the exchange between Simpson and Morgan, with only the names changed, probably takes place many times daily in the plants and factories across the country. A new man joining a small work force is taught the informal group's standards and norms, instructed in the proper attitude to have, and given time to conform, or else. It occurs at every level. Shop space or office space, blue collar or white collar, manager or operator—every echelon of American business is rife with informal groups.

Not every informal group is antagonistic toward management, as was the case in the die shop at the Wilson plant. Indeed, some groups can be extremely cooperative, policing their members with regard to tardiness or absenteeism, or even exceeding managerial demands for output. For example, a group of salesmen might have as its goal high sales, the higher the better. Management might do well to cultivate such a group, to encourage its growth and strength. An informal group can also be neutral, with goals purely social in nature. Caution is necessary in dealing with neutral informal groups. By restricting fulfillment of the group's social needs, management can easily turn a neutral group into an antagonistic group, at odds with the company at every ground.[1]

Origins of the Study of Informal Groups

Not until the early 1900's did management really begin to recognize the existence of informal groups. The problem of restricted output was perceived as early as 1911 by Frederick W. Taylor. He and other scientific managers felt that the problem could be solved by having management, rather than the workers, determine production rates.[2] Time-study men went to work to help management set production standards, but they probably only increased the workers' determination to regulate output, since retiming of a job almost always meant a cut in pay. Workers felt, especially during the depression, that by working slowly, they could make their job last longer. It was, for them, a defensive device to protect them from the whims of management. It indicated a basic distrust betweeen management and the workers.

Henri Fayol, one of the leading proponents of the Universalist school of management, felt that the interests of the company should prevail over the informal group. In 1916, he stated that combating the ignorance, ambition, selfishness, laziness, and weaknesses that cause the interests of the company to be lost sight of is "one of the great difficulties of management." He suggested three ways to effect this subordination of the individual to the company: firmness and good example on the part of superiors, agreements as fair as is possible, and constant supervision.[3]

Although Taylor and Fayol were among the first to identify informal groups, their studies contributed little to the understanding of group structure and behavior. There were still many unanswered questions. Why did informal groups exist? How were they formed? What factors affected group behavior? The first really definitive study of the informal group was the bank wiring room phase of the Hawthorne Experiments, which began in November 1931. This study stands today as one of the major accomplishments in this field. It exposed for the first time the inner work-

---

[1] Robert Dubin, *Human Relations in Administration* (Englewood Cliffs, N.J., 1961), pp. 84–85.

[2] Loren Baritz, *The Servants of Power* (Middleton, Conn., 1960), p. 96.

[3] Henri Fayol, "General Principles of Management—From Division of Work to Esprit de Corps," in *The World of Business,* ed. by Edward C. Bursk, Donald T. Clark, and Ralph W. Hidy (New York, 1962), p. 1691.

ings and hidden mechanisms of the informal group, and for this reason, it is dealt with in some detail here.

In this phase of the Hawthorne Experiments, fourteen male operators in the bank wiring room of the Western Electric Company were observed during the period November 1931, through May 1932. An observer, stationed with the group, followed certain rules to gain the group's acceptance. He assumed no formal authority, he tried to be noncommittal in any argument, he respected all confidence, he tried not to be overimposing in gathering information, and he became, through speech and behavior, as much a part of the group as possible.[4]

The observer found that the fourteen workers had an intricate, informal social organization of their own. There were subgroups, cliques, and isolated individuals. The personal relationships of each operator in this informal organization "determined to a large degree his status in the group, the expectations of the other members, and the kinds of satisfactions and expectations he had of himself."[5]

The group set standards of behavior for its members, and enforced its standards by using ridicule, sarcasm, or "binging"[6] to keep its members in the fold. They also set standards of production. By adjusting production reports, the group effectively circumvented the "bogey"[7] set by management. The workers liked to have some completed work saved up and ready to turn in on days when output was low. Consequently, they reported a consistent output that often differed from the actual output.

In an attempt to explain differences in output among individual operators, dexterity and intelligence tests were administered to the group. The lowest producer of the group ranked first in intelligence and third in dexterity. It was concluded that no direct relationship between performance and ability to perform as determined by dexterity or intelligence tests existed.

The sentiments of the group were: (a) don't be a "rate buster," (b) do your share of the work, don't be a "chiseler," (c) don't be a "squealer," and (d) don't put on airs (i.e., if you are an inspector, don't act like

---

[4] F. J. Roethlisberger and William J. Dickson, *Management and the Worker* (Cambridge, Mass., 1956), pp. 388–389.

[5] Baritz, pp. 92–93.

[6] Roethlisberger, p. 421. "Binging" is a physical attempt to control workers who deviated. It was used to regulate the output of the faster workers. The observer in the wire bank room remarked, "one of them walked up to another man and hit him as hard as he could on the upper arm. The one hit made no protest, and it seems that it was his privilege to 'bing' the one who hit him. He was free to retaliate with one blow. One of the objects of the game is to see who can hit the hardest. But it is also used as a penalty."

[7] Ibid., p. 418. "Bogey" is the standard output as determined by management. Wire bank workers feared that if they consistently met the bogey or exceeded it, management would raise the bogey or cut the piece rate, causing an operator to work harder to make the same pay.

one). At first glance, it would seem that the group was antagonistic toward management. But the researchers point out that, in fact, there was no conscious effort on the part of the workers to oppose management.[11] The workers were not hostile toward management; the Western Electric Company had a reputation of being very fair with its employees. The restriction of output in the bank wiring room could not be blamed on poor management or inefficiency, either. Actually, the bank wiring group's output compared most favorably with similar work of other companies. What, then, caused the regulation of output? The researchers concluded that "noneconomic motives, interests, and processes, as well as economic, are fundamental in behavior in business."[8]

The findings of the bank wiring room phase of the Hawthorne Experiments created great interest in human relations in industry. It seemed that management had two alternatives—either change the informal group's thinking so that it paralleled management's or neutralize the group's power to control standards. Perhaps a better understanding between management and workers could more closely align the logic and sentiments of the informal organization to the formal organization. By asking for suggestions and criticisms, the workers could have had a more active role in the decisions concerning them. The Hawthorne experimenters, more closely attuned to management policies, failed to adequately explain the informal organization, merely terming the workers' behavior as irrational.

The work of many early human relations experimenters is suspect. Many of them believed that industrial cooperation meant that labor should do as management said. Elton Mayo, the head researcher at Hawthorne, failed to recognize that the informal organizations of workers may have been necessary antidotes to an overbearing management. In fact, the Mayo school barely touched on the idea that management, itself, was filled with informal organizations, that managers, just like workers, could act "emotionally and irrationally." This antilabor, promanagement attitude of Mayo and his colleagues has caused much of their work to be severely criticized by some social scientists.

Management's reaction to the informal group at odds with formal policy was limited. Either the group had to be destroyed or its thinking changed. The bank wiring experiment showed that the group's power exceeded management's. It seemed that the second alternative—promoting friendly informal groups—would more likely meet with success. Amid cries of manipulation, management sought to encourage groups to think constructively along managerial lines.

Sociometry, the study of personal likes and dislikes, provided a technique for greater understanding of informal associations. In 1934, Jacob L. Moreno introduced this technique of learning about the group through

---

[8] Ibid., p. 557.

study of its individuals. Using this approach, it became possible to "speak of the degree of cohesiveness of a specific group and to make comparisons between one group and another."[9] Sociometry asked questions of individuals such as: who do you like best, least in your shop? who do you like to work with best, least? A sociometric map or sociogram provided a means of displaying these social choices of the shop workers.

In a further attempt to understand group behavior, several men tried to classify the informal work group. Elton Mayo and George F. Lombard formed three classifications. The "natural" group, composed of six or seven members, functioned automatically, unguided by supervision. The "family" group, about thirty members, had a core of regulars that provided an example for the other members. The "organized" group was large and had a direct relationship with management (e.g., the "whole factory" concept).[10]

Leonard R. Sayles probably came closest to a realistic classification of informal work groups. He placed the groups into four basic categories. The *"apathetic"* groups are those least likely to make complaints or to join together to pressure management. They are characterized by a dispersed leadership, not clearly identified or accepted, internal frictions that cause low cohesion, and undercurrent of discontent, but little action to change things. Their jobs are usually in a noisy environment, with little interaction between members.

The *"erratic"* groups are easily incensed over minor, insignificant issues, or can remain inactive when confronted with more important grievances. When they do take action, they are poorly controlled and inconsistent. This type of work group is most susceptible to conversion to good relations with management. They have a strong, independent leadership, but high turnover lessens their cohesiveness. Their jobs consist mainly of crew operations or groups performing similar tasks.

The *"strategic"* groups are the shrewd instigators, searching for loopholes, comparing economic benefits, reacting to unfavorable management decisions. They are highly cohesive groups with a strong leadership that uses group pressure tactics to best advantage. Men in the strategic groups are the most active union participators. They maintain high work standards in their jobs, which usually consist of crew or assembly type operations.

The *"conservative"* groups are composed of highly skilled workers with high status, engaged in individual operations throughout the plant. They are the most stable, most likely to give warning before taking any action. They are least likely to be union participators. Members of the conservative groups are characterized by self-assurance, success, and patience.[11]

---

[9] Baritz, *The Servants of Power*, p. 177.
[10] Dubin, *Human Relations in Administration*, pp. 88–89.
[11] Ibid., pp. 90–95.

Characteristics of the Informal Group

A small group can be defined as two or more people who interact with one another in face-to-face relations over an extended period of time, who differentiate themselves in some way from others around them, who are conscious of belonging to the group, and whose relations with one another are taken as an end in itself. It's impossible to set an upper limit on group membership. The only limiting factor is that all members must have direct personal contact with one another. This would probably necessitate a group no larger than fifteen or twenty members.

Informal groups are formed because they satisfy human needs. Every human being has a need for companionship, for identification. This need to belong is most easily satisfied at one's own level. One needs understanding from one's friends to combat life's frustrations and tensions. The informal group provides answers for its members; it serves as a "guide to correct behavior." It helps solve work problems. Teamwork can get the job done more easily and enjoyably, and can promote either efficiency or work restriction. Protection for its membership is another function of the informal group. There is strength in numbers—strength to resist changes, or to fight managerial demands for greater production. The methods the group uses to oppose management can vary from merely cutting down on the work pace to outright sabotage of the work.[12]

Satisfying these individual needs of belonging, prestige, recognition, etc., is the primary function of the informal group. The informal group is a natural unit in which work decisions and judgments are reached. It provides an atmosphere for testing new procedures, and creates standards of conduct for its members.

Group standards of behavior pervade the informal social organization. They can take many forms—eating lunch together, following certain customs to make the job easier, and regulating production, to name a few. Management may either benefit or suffer from the group's standards and group pressure to conform. It depends on how close the goals of the group are to the goals of management.

"There are also group standards of attitude—or norms."[13] "This job is great," or, "that foreman should be fired," are examples of what group norms might be. These attitudes could be completely unfounded, but to the group they are real, and management must recognize they exist.

The group member experiences certain pressures to conform to group standards and norms. The individual point of view becomes aligned with the group's point of view, and since the group satisfies the member's social needs, he accepts the group's goals. He wants to be "well regarded" by the other members. A member who exceeds the group's accepted level

---

[12] Leonard R. Sayles and George Strauss, *Personnel* (Englewood Cliffs, N.J., 1960),
[13] Ibid., 65.

of output may find himself ostracized. Any deviation from group standards may cause the member to be isolated, given the "silent treatment." He may be left out of group activities. More direct methods of pressuring the individual to conform include letting management know of the deviant's "mistakes," flooding his desk with work, or even sabotaging his equipment.

The enforcement of group standards and norms is a four phased operation. First the new man is educated. He learns what the group expects of him. Then he is watched by all the group members to see if he conforms. He is bound to make mistakes, and for any deviation, a warning is given, and surveillance continued. Finally, disciplinary or rewarding actions ensue.

The sum total of forces acting on group members, causing them to remain a part of the group, is called group cohesiveness. As cohesiveness increases, so does the power of the group over the individual increase. There is more pressure to conform. Many factors affect group cohesion. Size is one factor. The smaller the group, usually, the more cohesive it will be. Lack of homogeneity will decrease cohesion. There will be a tendency for subgroups and cliques to form, made up of members with like interests and backgrounds. Easy communications between the members and physical isolation of the group from other groups will both increase cohesion.

Supervisory practices can influence cohesion. For example, if management promotes competition between group members, there will be a lessening of cohesion. Likewise, rewarding teamwork builds cohesion. Outside pressure is a factor. Threats from outsiders result in increased cohesiveness that tends to remain, even after the danger or inequity is removed. Successful group ventures, which cause the group's status as a unit to increase, also build cohesiveness. Other contributing factors are a high degree of dependency upon the group, stability of the group, the presence of ritual in the daily contacts of the members, and strong leadership.

The group's leader tends to be the member who most closely conforms to the group's standards and norms, or the one who has the most information and skill related to the group's activities. The leader must enable the members to achieve their private goals as well as the group's goals. Consequently, leadership must simultaneously satisfy two conflicting needs of the group—that for initiative and guidance, and that for harmony and mutual acceptance. Often, a leader may begin by satisfying both these needs, but before long, he can effectively assume only one of these roles. "As a result, there are often two leaders: a task or work leader and a social-emotional specialist."[14] When given the choice, most leaders prefer the popular role. The controlling role loses its player popularity.

---

[14] Joseph A. Litterer, *The Analysis of Organization*, (New York: John Wiley & Sons, Inc., 1965); p. 116.

The informal leader can sometimes mold and change the group's goals and norms. When he speaks, the group listens, and is influenced. But if he tries to change things too fast, he can lose his leadership role.

Informal groups overlap. People belong to a number of informal groups, a fact which sometimes causes conflicts and stress. When an individual is a member of two conflicting groups, he will experience emotional strain, which he will attempt to reduce by resolving the conflict in favor of the group to which he is most closely tied.

Managing the Informal Group

The first step in any scientific method is defining the problem. Managing the informal group begins just as basically. Management must first recognize that informal groups exist. Once this is acknowledged, management should gather as much information as possible about the existing groups. Who belongs to which informal groups? What are the goals of the different groups? Are they opposed to the company's goals? What are the operating techniques of the groups? How cohesive are they? On-the-spot managers are probably in the best position to find out this information. They should be trained in group behavior and human relations so they may deal more effectively with the informal groups they supervise.[15] The supervisor is the key to good management–informal group relations.

The supervisor can gain cooperation only by respecting the group's standards and norms. Supervisors have been characterized as the "men in the middle." They are formal leaders, but must rely on more than the authority of the formal organization to get successful results. They must build acceptance of themselves by the informal group, and, in effect, attain some portion of the role of informal leader. Formal authority alone will not be enough to give the formal leader sufficient influence.

A good supervisor knows what the group expects of him, and adjusts his behavior accordingly. He makes *fair* demands of the group. He must emphasize "getting the job done," rather than use authority for its own sake. Rules imposed on the group should be reasonable. Time honored customs should be respected whenever possible, although there are times when such customs are in direct conflict with managerial desires. At such times, action should be taken to thwart the custom, but perhaps not by frontal assault. Management must weigh the implications carefully before taking a position at odds with the accepted practices of the group.

More positive action would be to give the informal group an opportunity to participate in decision making. Group discussion of problems can gain acceptance for decisions. Management seems least willing to give the

---

[15] George S. Odiorne, "Put Cliques to Work for You," *Nation's Business* (August 1958), pp. 50–53.

group decision making powers in production areas: output standards, production planning, use of equipment, changes in technology. It seems more willing to let the group handle areas like absenteeism, tardiness, health, and discipline. It is most willing to let the group decide in areas where there is a common goal, like accident prevention.

"Letting the group decide on its own production goals is the most certain way of getting the group to accept them."[16] Of course, management cannot be certain the group will make the right decision. Whether the decision is left to the group depends on what management knows about the group. Are they hostile to the company? If this were the case, they certainly wouldn't be given decision-making powers in an area as vital as production. But if the group is not openly antagonistic, management would be wise to let the group take an active role in decision making. If management does give some decision-making powers to the informal group, it is most important that the gesture be sincere. The group can readily detect insincerity. Nothing could be more detrimental to promoting good relations with the group than taking a patronizing attitude.

Encouraging group discussion and decision making will help to develop group responsibility. Unimportant and trivial jobs increase the group's feeling of irresponsibility. Management must build group responsibility by making the job more important, or at least, by making the people in the job feel more important. Allocating work assignments at the group level, decentralization, and decreasing specialization will result in added group responsibility, and utimately increase the effectiveness of a co-operative group.

Management should give informal leaders a chance to gain recognition by working with rather than against management. Build good relations with the informal leader—pass information to him, ask his advice, have him train others. But beware of the dangers. It is sometimes hard to identify the group leader. The group spokesman is not necessarily the leader. There may be different leaders for different group functions. A close management-leader relationship may cause the leader to lose status (and eventually, his leadership role) in the group. He could get the reputation of being a "company man." This could happen if the leader were asked to deviate from the group's norms. It is important not to build cooperation so far that it becomes favoritism.

Should management try to build cohesiveness? There is no clear answer to this question. Cohesive groups display teamwork, higher morale, lower turnover and absenteeism, and are easier to supervise. But high cohesive groups may not readily accept new employees. They may not cooperate well with outsiders. Consequently, competition and hard feelings between rival groups can develop. Does high cohesiveness increase

---

[16] Henry Clay Smith, *Psychology of Industrial Behavior* (New York, 1964), p. 155.

productivity? Studies show that a highly cohesive group produces either somewhat higher than the average or somewhat lower, depending on the attitudes of the group. Cohesiveness means that the group members will follow more closely the group's norms, be they beneficial or not to the company.

If the group is cooperative, or even neutral, management should obviously try to encourage cohesion. The use of sociometrics to avoid the formation of subgroups and cliques is one tactic. Helping to bring isolated individuals into the group will increase each employee's identification with the group. Stability promotes cohesion, so management might cut down on transfers in and out of the group. When new workers are assigned to the group, a "big brother" type system to help them gain acceptance more quickly would contribute to cohesion. Group piece rates rather than individual piece rates develop teamwork and cohesion.

If management feels that compatibility between informal and formal goals is not possible, it should work toward weakening or destroying the group. This could be accomplished by moving personnel about, particularly the informal leaders. Stressing dealing with individuals rather than the group will lessen cohesiveness. Since group standards will be strengthened in areas where external standards are weak, beefing up company policies and standards may be necessary in some areas.

Resistance to change by the informal group can be disastrous to a company in an industry where change is imperative. "But we've always done it this way," is the cry most often heard. This resistance is natural. We all fear the unknown, and that is basically what change is. Therefore, if it wants to get a change accepted, management must furnish accurate and meaningful information about company plans through either formal or informal channels. The group should be informed why management made a decision that concerns them. Any objections from the group should be cleared up as quickly as possible. A trivial matter unattended to could lead to more deep-seated problems.[17] It is usually more effective to try to influence people as group members rather than as individuals. Even so, it is still difficult to change the group, because of the support members receive from each other.

Conclusions

The existence of informal groups within formal organizations can no longer be ignored. They must be dealt with effectively—on friendly, cooperative terms, if possible, or on decisive, not-so-friendly terms, if necessary. Cooperation between formal and informal organization is desirable.

---

[17] John T. Doutt, "Management Must Manage the Informal Group Too," *Advanced Management* (May 1959), pp. 26–28.

Lower turnover and absenteeism, higher morale, higher production—these are the rewards when a strong, highly cohesive group's goals are closely attuned to managerial goals. If this is the case, management should do all it can to create a permissive atmosphere for the formation of informal groups. If an informal group is antagonistic to the company, management should try its best to change the group's attitude. But failing in that, it should attempt to weaken or destroy the power of the group.

Effective action is impossible without a thorough knowledge and understanding of informal groups at all managerial levels. Managers should be trained in group behavior and human relations. This is especially important at the supervisory level, where day to day encounters take place.

Above all, it is important that management, itself, maintain an open-minded realistic attitude about informal groups, and not be led into the trap of thinking that management is always right, the group always wrong. If there is a better way to do something, the group will probably be the first to find it. Informal groups perform necessary functions—they satisfy human needs. Management should help satisfy these human needs whenever possible, thereby encouraging group goals and company goals to coincide. Of course, there will always be a gap between manager and worker. Understanding is the only power that can fill that gap.

QUESTIONS FOR REVIEW AND DISCUSSION

1. Why are informal groups formed? Discuss in some detail.
2. Explain how supervisory practices can influence group cohesion.
3. List the major suggestions for managing the informal group as given by writer Muti.
4. In working with groups at school, work, church, or other organizations, relate an experience you have had in dealing with informal groups.

part EIGHT

Management and Human Behavior

Knowledge of human behavior is essential in management. It filters into every aspect of management because what human beings think, what they do, and how they do it are conditioned by their behavior. Typically, a manager has problems of adjustment to other managers and to his subordinates and likewise they, in turn, have similar problems. A great deal of energy is spent in these adjusting efforts and in trying to minimize the almost perpetual conflicts.

A person adjusts to the values, norms, and patterns of behavior of a group he joins. This is no small task. At our present developmental stage of management, we do not have definitive, precise, and totally reliable answers about human behavior. But neither are we in total darkness. Much attention and effort are being directed to this area and as a result, our knowledge and understanding are steadily increasing. The readings selected for Part Eight reflect the current status and accomplishment in advancing both the art and the science of human behavior.

"New Approaches to Working with People" by Duane E. Thompson points out the human want to experience satisfaction of needs through human relationships. A brief history of man's views about superior-subordinate relationship is provided leading up to recent studies pertaining to interpersonal relations. Identified is a "managerial style" that helps create a working environment in which human beings may experience high levels of satisfaction. Such a style features three kinds of interrelated behavior: (1) interpersonal support, (2) participation in decision making, and (3) high-performance expectations.

Robert H. Schaffer in his reading, "The Psychological Barriers to Management Effectiveness," describes how managers escape situations that provoke anxiety, are threatening, or are depressing to them. These escapes are commonly brought about by use of subtle and frequently unconscious stratagems. For example, the denial of certain facts or always appearing

too busy are among the common means employed. Much managerial behavior is justified for what appears to be rational and goal-oriented reasons, but actually it is to satisfy the psychological needs of the manager.
An understanding of these invisible mechanisms used to avoid unpleasant
managerial situations can assist management. Pertinent ways of doing this
are suggested in the reading.

In the next reading, "A Positive Approach to Women in Management,"
M. Jane Kay admirably sets forth the thesis that women should be management members because of their qualifications enabling them to contribute to the organization's success. This positive viewpoint is essential.
Having women in management should not be looked upon as fulfilling an
obligation or legal requirement. What constitutes a positive approach is
spelled out in the reading as are also the topics of the treatment of women
in management and the attitudes toward women managers.

Next and last is "Six Propositions for Managerial Leadership" by Norman George and Thomas J. Von der Embse. Based on research including
the authors' study of attitudinal orientations of some 650 managers and
administrators from a variety of organizations, six diagnostic tools are presented for purposes of definition of the elements of the problem and also
of focus on the critical issues of leadership. In this scholarly and stimulating paper, the belief is expressed that a dynamic model of leadership is
evolving. How a leader behaves depends upon many dynamic factors
which act in a somewhat complex manner. Although a theory of leadership
supplying discrete and valid answers to specific situations is not yet developed, the six propositions presented in this article contribute significantly to man's knowledge and understanding of managerial leadership.

27. New Approaches to Working with People*

DUANE E. THOMPSON

As we all witnessed, man's final few steps to the moon were directed by another man. Throughout the mission, a series of highly effective interpersonal relationships were critical to the achievement of that "one small step for man, one giant leap for mankind." Our steps into outer space will continue to be guided and controlled not only by technology, but by the effectiveness of interpersonal relations—the ability to cooperate with and to motivate others.

Although we may not be directly involved in our nation's space program, although our lives may never be so inextricably interwoven with those of our fellow human beings, it behooves us, nonetheless, to give careful consideration to the improvement of our own interpersonal effectiveness. I will consider first just what creates effective relationships between two human beings. Interpersonal relations are most effective when each participant has an equal opportunity to enhance the fulfillment of his needs.

For example, in space, the crew members are totally dependent upon each other, not only for the success of the mission, but also for their very lives. Under these conditions highly effective interpersonal relations emerge. This is not to say that there are no tensions. There may be considerable stress between members, but the job gets done. Isn't this what counts? Consider also the college marriage that goes sour when the young law graduate suddenly finds success. What made the marriage effective before graduation, yet a failure a short time later? Why do some bridge clubs stay together year after year? What is the basis for effective superior-subordinate relationships? In each case aren't those involved experiencing satisfaction of their needs through the relationship? These examples cover a wide range of settings, hence there is a wide range of specific kinds of appropriate behavior. The terse orders of a spacecraft would be out of place at the bridge table; family intimacies have no place in the office.

* Source: Reprinted with permission of *Credit and Financial Management,* May 1970, pp. 20–21, 34. Dr. Duane E. Thompson is program director, Center for Labor and Management, University of Iowa.

Unfortunately, there are no handy rules of thumb that can be prescribed. I do believe, however, that to be effective in our dealings with one another we must know and be sensitive to the needs of others whether they be wife, bridge partner, customer, client, subordinate or boss.

A Changing View of Man's Needs

Although I realize that not all members of organizations supervise others, I will nonetheless comment in terms of the superior-subordinate relationship. For years we have stumbled about with the problem of finding a workable base for the relationship of subordinate to his boss and the total organization. At one time our nation's economy was young and industry had an insatiable need for muscle, so we took an economic view of man. From about 1900–1920, when this view was most prevalent, it was assumed that man would be willing to sell his time, talents, energy and muscle in exchange for money. It was further assumed that if we could show this man an economic advantage to working harder that he would become more productive and that by his earnings he would find work to be worthwhile.

In the years since 1920 we have seen several revisions of this view. The view prevalent from 1920 to 1940 was that of a psychological man. This period corresponds with a time of initial emphasis and growth of psychological testing in business and industry. It was assumed that if we could capitalize on the employee's individual differences and assist each individual to gain recognition, he would not only be productive, but his work itself would be a worthwhile experience.

As was the case with the earlier view of economic man, the view of psychological man was soon modified. One of the major sources of modification was the Hawthorne Experiments conducted by Western Electric Company in conjunction with Harvard University. Out of these years of experimentation in an industrial setting came the view of man as a social being. Here it was assumed that no motivation was stronger than a desire for group association and that if we could provide meaningful social relationships at work, productivity and morale would be increased. As with the earlier view, this has also come to be regarded as an inadequate explanation for the behavior of man at work or to provide the basis for meaningful interpersonal relations.

Satisfiers and Dissatisfiers

A major breakthrough in the search for a theory to explain man's motivation was made in 1959 by Frederick Herzberg.[1] The first step, involving

---

[1] Frederick Herzberg, *Work and the Nature of Man,* World Publishing Company, Cleveland, 1966.

200 accountants and engineers, has since been repeated with a wide variety of groups. These studies are based on the simple request to think of a time when you felt exceptionally good or exceptionally bad about any job you have had. This could be either a long range or a short range situation. If the person started out telling a favorable aspect, he was asked to tell an unfavorable aspect, thus each person was led to not only tell the good times but also the bad times. Literally hundreds of such statements have been collected and analyzed. The bad experiences, referred to as dissatisfiers or hygiene factors, may be categorized as company policy and administration, competency of supervision, pay and fringe benefits, interpersonal relationships and working conditions. The good experiences have been called satisfiers by some, motivators by others, and include such things as achievement, earned recognition, work itself, responsibility and advancement.

Examining the two types of experience, we find that they are caused by different factors. The dissatisfiers are those situations extrinsic to the job itself. They form the environment within which work is performed. On the other hand, the satisfiers are intrinsically related to the work. It is relatively easy to alter the dissatisfiers. One can change the organizational policy and the way it is administered. One can give pay raises and increases in fringe benefits without too much difficulty. Working conditions can be changed. Competency of supervisors can be increased. It's quite another story however, when one looks at the satisfiers. How can we give another person a sense of achievement? This is a personal experience as is the feeling of earned recognition. Every manager knows from bitter experience the frustration of attempting to force someone to accept responsibility against his will.

Since we can't give the satisfiers directly, perhaps the only thing that we can do is to provide an opportunity for the individual to experience achievement, recognition and responsibility for himself. The real question remains then, "What can we do through our interpersonal relations to provide this opportunity?"

Interpersonal Style

Through recent behavioral science research, several related approaches to more effective interpersonal relations have been suggested. As one part of this research, analysis of managerial behavior in several dissimilar organizations has enabled behavioral scientists to identify a managerial style that tends to create the kind of a climate within which employees may experience high levels of satisfaction. As an aid to understanding, the style may be divided into three kinds of interrelated behavior.

Interpersonal Support. Those managers who are most successful at stimulating greater satisfaction among their subordinates are viewed as providers of high level interpersonal support. Specifically, successful managers encourage those reporting to them to reach out in new directions rather than protecting them from taking too big a risk. This is done by taking the errors of subordinates in stride, as long as they learn by the mistakes, and trying to find out what went wrong rather than who caused the problem. In addition, managers can give support by being approachable and easy to talk to.

We must bear in mind, however, that support is defined by others. It is not how we *believe* we behave; rather, it is how others—in the light of their background, personality, and expectation—*perceive* our behavior. For this reason there are no "rules of thumb" that can be set out for us to follow. If we want to be supportive, we must actively seek feedback from others to help us assess the effects of our behavior, and we must be willing to change our behavior in the light of the feedback.

Unfortunately, those managers least likely to be supportive are those most unlikely to know the effect of their behavior on other people. Few managers, for instance, in terms of ability to stimulate high levels of motivation, have little if any conception of how they affect their subordinates.

Participation in Decision Making.   A second general characteristic of successful managers is their willingness to share information and involve their subordinates in decision making. These executives will try to get their subordinates' ideas before making decisions and can see merit in these ideas even if they conflict with their own. So that their subordinates can contribute effectively, successful managers make a special effort to help their people understand the objectives of the organization. In addition, they are willing to give subordinates all the information they want as opposed to giving only as much information as is needed to do the immediate job.

Participation in decision making is simply any effort on the part of the manager to gather and give real consideration to the ideas of his subordinates on matters that concern them. The manager must make the final decision, and he is responsible for the results. This form of participative decision making is not restricted to groups. It is equally applicable on an individual basis where perhaps the manager and one subordinate discuss a problem. It does, however, demand good faith—the manager must be able and willing to accept and implement the ideas of the subordinate with regard to important aspects of the job.

High-Performance Expectations.   Finally, the managers most successful at stimulating satisfaction demonstrate high performance expectations of their subordinates. In addition to high expectations, two features stand out. The expectations must be consistent from day to day, and there must be accurate feedback of results, and generous amount of credit for superior performance.

In many respects we become what we think others believe us to be. So it is with the manager-employee relationship. If the manager has confidence in his employees and conveys his expectation of superior performance to subordinates, the tendency is to perform in a superior manner and experience the satisfaction of a job well done. If, on the other hand, the manager lacks confidence in the ability of his subordinates and conveys this feeling to them through close supervision, frequent controls, and pressure for performance quotas, the subordinates tend to behave in a manner which fulfills the manager's prophecy. The manager, therefore, is faced with a two-fold task. On the one hand he must find ways to actively demonstrate his confidence and high expectations to his subordinates, and at the same time change those conditions that unintentionally reflect a lack of confidence and the expectation of poor performance. Words alone are not sufficient. Actions (in the form of controls, reports and the like) must be considered, for if the language of words and the language of action do not agree, actions will prevail.

To put this on a broader social base, what about our interpersonal relations with others—with our customers, clients, and others in the office?

Can't we show them interpersonal support by regarding them as worthwhile human beings who would also like to experience achievement, earn recognition and grow psychologically? Must we hold to our positions so tenaciously that we will not be influenced by the ideas of others, and thereby rule out any joint or participatory decision making? Finally, why not run the risk of expecting the best of people? Perhaps we will be disappointed from time to time, but more often than not we will be pleasantly surprised.

Am I an unrealistic idealist? If not, perhaps we can find ways of becoming more supportive and accepting other ideas. We can look for the best in others and thus help them to enrich not only their jobs but their lives.

QUESTIONS FOR REVIEW AND DISCUSSION

1. Discuss "interpersonal support" by a manager as an aid in creating an environment within which an employee may experience high levels of satisfaction.

2. It is pointed out in the above article that when a manager uses high-performance expectations of his subordinates, he must also make sure that he uses two additional features. What are these features? Give illustrations to demonstrate your answer.

3. Identify satisfiers as explained by Frederick Herzberg and give examples of satisfiers. For the most part, what is the major source or what type of experience causes satisfiers to be present? Discuss.

28. The Psychological Barriers to Management Effectiveness*

ROBERT H. SCHAFFER

The body of literature on the relationship between psychological factors and the achievement of organization results is large and still growing; a minimum, however, has been written about the issue that is probably the most pervasive and most expensive and holds the greatest potential for change. The reason so little has been written about it is that, like the atmosphere, it is all around us yet invisible to the unaided eye.

"It," in this case, refers to the countless ways all of us subtly mold our jobs and our behavior on the job for what we believe to be rational, goal-oriented reasons, when actually we are being impelled by the pressure to satisfy psychological needs of which we are largely unaware. Sometimes these invisible or camouflaged mechanisms actually help the business, but often they drain energy from the enterprise or interfere seriously with its work. This reading will try to make this ubiquitous phenomenon more visible and to suggest its far-reaching implications for strategies of management.

THE DUALITY OF BEHAVIOR

All human behavior is a fascinating blend of the rational and the irrational, the conscious and the unconscious. On the one hand, people are logical machines that perceive reality, make measured evaluations and judgments, and then respond with behavior calculated to achieve explicit objectives. At the same time, we attempt to satisfy psychological needs and minimize anxiety by methods of which we are largely unaware. This is an unending 24-hour-a-day job to avoid situations in which we feel anxious, threatened, or depressed, or appear to be incompetent, foolish, weak, and

* Source: Copyright 1972 by the Foundation for the School of Business at Indiana University. Reprinted with permission. Robert H. Schaffer heads Robert H. Schaffer & Associates, Stamford, Connecticut.

so forth. We steer toward situations (and try to manipulate the situations we are in) so that we feel accepted, respected, productive, and safe. The subtle (and usually unconscious) strategems that we employ to succeed in this endeavor, are known by the familiar term "defense mechanisms."

Rational goal-oriented behavior and unconscious defenses do not operate as two independent mechanisms. During a lifetime, the defensive reactions become built into everything we do. Yet we tend to see our behavior as logical and rational, and thus have difficulty in distinguishing that part which is shaped by our needs to minimize anxiety.

We are much more aware of the defense behavior of other people, though we may not diagnose it as such or understand what causes it. We are all well aware of the buck-passer, the responsibility escaper, and the corporate underachiever, the man with ability who somehow always seems unable or unwilling to deliver. We know there is nothing rational behind examples of behavior like these that we see every day of our working lives:

A bright and able vice president of R & D has an assistant director who is regarded generally as rather incompetent. Yet, for some reason, the boss is quite pleased with his assistant and has just given him a raise.

This president, whenever a crisis looms or a severe problem arises, calls a series of meetings involving everybody who might have something to contribute, and many who do not. These meetings are animated and lengthy. Rarely do they result in clear agreement on actions to be taken. Often the crises are settled in ways completely unrelated to the meetings. Nevertheless, whenever an emergency arises, all the officers prepare for meetings that last well into the night.

Mr. X is a prototype "authoritarian" manager. He never invites his people to participate in decisions; he always issues orders; and he often addresses his people in a tough tone of voice. An acute observer would see that, despite his manner, he rarely is explicit and clear-cut in his demands. Thus, for all his toughness, they have a million ways to not do what he wants them to do.

Although written as humor, Parkinson's books come closer than much of the academic literature to capturing the mysterious ways in which men's hidden motivations lead organizations down pathways that are quite unrelated to where everyone says he wants to go.[1] But the fact is that so far most of what has been perceived and written about is the noticeable, or even the off beat and bizarre.

Before focusing on the interference between rational and defensive behavior in management, the point should be made that defense mechanisms often produce considerable successful managerial behavior. The forces that drive the most successful, able, and hard-working managers ahead, that encourage them to take risks, that inspire them to innovate and per-

---

[1] See, for example, C. Northcote Parkinson, *Parkinson's Law* (Boston: Houghton Mifflin, 1957).

form in many other unusual ways often stem from deeds of which they are unaware. This positive side contains many clues for management strategy, once we better understand the other side of the picture, the rich variety of disguised behavior that managers use to satisfy their own psychological needs which are nonproductive for the enterprise.

The phenomena described here do not represent any psychological breakthrough by the author; rather, the effects of some well-known and thoroughly described psychological principles will be illuminated, effects which (like the missing "Emperor's New Clothes" in the children's story) are obvious but unrecognized.[2]

DEFEAT WITHOUT TRYING: THE INVISIBLE BARRIERS

People try to minimize anxiety first by perceiving and interpreting the events around them, and then by acting in response to those perceptions, in ways that are most ego protective and reassuring. And both these mechanisms, perceptual and behavioral, can permit managers to achieve anxiety reducing results at the great expense of organization achievement results.

Distortions in Managerial Perception

Everybody wears colored glasses in order to see things in terms that are most fitting to our particular psychological needs and readiness. Thus while we share the same reality with others, we each tend to see that reality in our own terms.

For example, imagine that we are going to interview all the managers in a company, asking each two questions: "What is it that keeps your enterprise from achieving much more than it is currently achieving?" and "What will it take to get this enterprise moving more effectively?" Although responses will vary a great deal from person to person, we can predict one result with considerable certainty. Virtually no one will attribute the shortcomings of the enterprise to shortcomings in his own managerial competence or behavior. Similarly, few will suggest that improvement in his own effectiveness might be a key to accelerating the organization's performance.

This predictable finding (test it if you doubt it) illustrates one of the most common and most limiting perceptive defense mechanisms of managers—the *"doing all I can in these circumstances"* illusion. Most managers

---

[2] For more detail concerning these principles, see Chris Argyris, *Interpersonal Competence and Organizational Effectiveness* (Homewood, Ill.: Richard D. Irwin, Inc., 1962); Alan N. Schoonmaker, *Anxiety and the Executive* (New York American Management Association, 1969), pp. 138–50; or the master himself, Sigmund Freud, "The Psychopathology of Everyday Life" in *The Basic Writings of Sigmund Freud* (New York: Random House, Inc., 1938).

place a definite boundary around their own scope for initiative. Within that boundary they see themselves as doing all they possibly can. When the boss is stuck he can blame it on unmotivated, unqualified, or disloyal people; the people can blame it on their boss or various circumstances beyond their control. Needed improvements are always somebody else's job.

During the 1970–1971 recession many managers have been heard to rationalize almost every kind of disappointing performance in terms of the "state of the economy."

A team of managers in a large company was confronted with a demand for reduced costs. Although statistical evidence indicated that comparable companies were indeed performing at higher levels, most of these managers asserted that "their conditions were quite different," and that only by sacrificing quality or cutting maintenance could costs be reduced.

Thus, step by step, each manager whittles away huge areas of opportunity for initiative. We simply take them out of our line of vision. If they remain in sight, we have to confront each pathway of unexploited opportunity, and this could give rise to anxiety about our inability to respond. It is simpler to live in an environment that has been circumscribed so that it is controllable. Imagine how an enterprise would change if each of its managers perceived his current level of performance as not the ultimate of what could be achieved, but as the mere beginning of a constantly expanding level of achievement. But this will not happen easily. These distortions in perception are extremely important to the people who hold them and, moreover, are completely believable to them and to almost everybody else.

Another form of defense by perception is *denial*. In the film "Never on Sunday" the heroine, Ilya, perceives the Greek tragedies as syrupy soap opera. While murder and mayhem occur before her eyes, she sees only love and happiness. This was a joke in the film, but similar behavior on the part of management is not uncommon. If the problem is too difficult to cope with, we may solve it by not seeing it.

Even though a possibly superior competitive product was already being market tested, managers of one company convinced themselves that their key customers, many of years' standing, would never be so disloyal as to leave them.

One company enjoyed an unusual spurt of growth and profits because of certain market conditions that were temporary in nature. In the resulting euphoria, however, all of its top management acted as if *they* had found the secret to a perpetual Christmas.

The head of a newly created, highly sophisticated central staff group assured his boss and his colleagues that the new function had been very well received throughout the organization. In fact he had aroused considerable suspicion and hostility and few people would trust him with sensitive information.

Xenophobia describes a third form of defense by perceptive distortion. Man has a general tendency to differentiate between the good guys (with whom he identifies) and the bad guys. Thus the world is divided into heroes and villains, our team and their team, the "free" world versus the Communists, and so on. There is this same tendency in enterprise to see our team—the idealized heroes—lined up against the villains. It takes many forms; production versus sales, headquarters vs. the field, line versus staff, one product line versus another, and so forth.

During a major operations improvement effort in a large multiplant company, headquarters staff people complained that the managers in operations resisted new approaches to their jobs. Field people maintained, with equal vigor, that headquarters was presenting them with "academic" and impractical recommendations. These fervent accusations spared each group from focusing on its own need to change and improve.

In another company the president told a consultant, "We're just not getting enough good new products from R & D." The head of R & D told the consultant, "I can't set any directions for either our basic research or our product development because top management simply won't tell us where this company is supposed to be heading."

In a fast-moving, highly competitive industry, one company's marketers were convinced that their manufacturing division was incompetent because of increasing costs, poor quality, and poor service. The manufacturing people were equally convinced that unnecessary "catering to customer whims," and excessively large variety of sizes and custom options, and too many changes in instructions from production planning were undermining their ability to even hold their own, to say nothing of improve.

Of course, there is almost always some truth—often plenty of truth—to these allegations, which only makes it more difficult to see the psychological defense mechanisms at play. So long as one sees the major responsibility for change as resting with the other fellow, he need not feel a sense of responsibility for taking initiative. Thus management can blame the union and the union can blame management; planners can blame the operators for being "too focused on today" and the operators can blame the planners for being "too academic." This sort of distortion permits us to free ourselves, to a certain extent, of self-doubt. The nagging anxiety that might be aroused is masked as we get increasingly agitated about what the other fellow is not doing.

When Don Quixote dreams the impossible dream, it is romantic, even inspiring. But when managers *dream the impossible dream* (another form of perceptual distortion) rather than come to grips with possible solutions, the enterprise suffers. This happens when a manager, to relieve his anxiety about a very tough goal, convinces himself that it is really beyond achievement. Once convinced, what more need he do? A variant of the impossible dream defense is to believe that the only way to reach an important goal is through some prior accomplishment which, at the moment, looks impossible. This too will relieve the manager of the pain and struggle of searching for approaches that might be within his power.

For years this consumer products company suffered from impossibly difficult relationships. Plant productivity, abysmally low, reflected this state of affairs. Management felt that improvement depended on a shift in relations between management and the union, and a thaw on the part of the union with regard to work restrictions. Such a thaw would undoubtedly have opened the pathway to greater productivity, but it was highly unlikely to occur. Since the managers firmly believed, however, that this was *the* key to performance improvement, they were free to overlook many programs of action that were feasible even in their current situation.

The preceding examples illustrate how we organize our perceptions of the world to reassure ourselves and minimize personal anxiety and uneasiness. While this may be useful to us in one way, it often closes off the great number of alternatives and possibilities for realistic action that are open to us.

Behavioral Escapes

There are many different ways in which managers, by their actions as well as their perceptions, can unwittingly minimize their anxiety at the price of accomplishing the very goals they seek. Probably the most common escape is through *busyness*—the manager's "Linus blanket." Almost all managers complain that they are too busy. They wish they had more time to think, to plan, and to view their jobs from a broader perspective. The assumption is that their busyness is a result of real job demands. The fact is, however, that many managers keep themselves comfortable by keeping busy. Quiet, unplanned time, empty desk tops, and silent telephones can provoke tremendous anxiety. Such pauses give them time to recognize many of their doubts about how things are going.

The large enterprise provides limitless opportunities for managers to keep busy. There are countless documents to be read and responses to be written (which will in turn generate new papers to be read); there are frequent meetings; telephone calls come in a random pattern. Any number of problems, emergencies, and crises cry out for management time. There are dependent subordinates who are happy to take up as much time as the executive cares to give, and company showmen who enjoy putting on presentations or meetings for anyone who will take the time to listen.

One of the greatest rationalizations of management is: "We've simply got to figure out how to get some time around here to do some thinking and planning." Considerable effort has been wasted in trying to redesign executive jobs, delegate routine tasks, shift the flow of paperwork, and so forth, in the hope that these steps will free the managers for the planning and thinking. The fact is that, for most managers, this "freedom" is often very uncomfortable.

One director of a large manufacturing operation reorganized his job and his relationships with his associates so that they would carry more responsibility. Shortly thereafter, he went on a two-week vacation. When he returned, his in-basket contained only five or six items. In the past, there would have been enough material upon his return to fill two brief cases and an entire week end at home. "To tell you the truth," he confided, "even though I designed this result myself, I can tell you that I feel very uncomfortable and out of touch with things."

Managers are also able to keep themselves psychologically comfortable by *escapes into structure and system.* In order for large enterprises to work, human endeavor must be organized and institutionalized; there must be regular, understood procedures and routines. Thus every enterprise builds up its own pattern of operation at every level, which makes it possible for everybody to understand how things should be done. At the same time, in order to survive and thrive, the enterprise must be able to change directions and policies; a balance is needed between routine and change. The problem here is that familiar routines are comforting and reassuring, while abandoning or restructuring institutionalized behavior can be disquieting. Thus, particularly in relatively stable organizations, it becomes increasingly difficult to distinguish clearly between those institutionalized practices that serve a real function and those that are merely vestigial.

Certain regular meetings are held, not necessarily because there are purposes to be served but because that is when that committee has always met. Reports are produced, not because somebody needs information but because somebody else has the responsibility of producing those reports. The executive committee meets every Monday morning, and its agenda tends to be made up in the same way each week. The methods of running the meeting—including what people feel free to bring up—tend to remain the same. But what is it that the committee is trying to accomplish? What do they want to do over the next six months or a year? Could they best accomplish these results by meeting five times a week? Or once a month? What are the means by which they should attack their most important objectives? These are tough questions, and frequently it is more reassuring to simply carry on with the regular meetings in the regular way with the same faces.

Even those who protest most loudly about "too many meetings in this place" are often co-conspirators in maintaining the schedule. Why? Frequently because a three-hour meeting on the schedule "takes care of" that chunk of time. The manager no longer has to consider how best to use these hours in the face of competing possibilities.

Management literature universally stresses the need to "manage by objectives," to have clear, well-defined goals and a method for measuring progress towards them. Most managers, however, are very skillful at *escaping from commitment*, avoiding unequivocal acceptance of exceptionally difficult goals. All sorts of escape hatches are built into the establishment of goals to allow for "conditions beyond control" in case of short-falls (although most managers will not hesitate to take credit for achievement).

Financial vice president: "Sure we can go for a new issue now, but if you think we can get $25 a share in this market you're crazy."

Manufacturing manager: "Sure you can cut our maintenance budget, but you'll just pay for it in down time and off-spec product."

School superintendent: "I agree it is important to measure and evaluate the results of educational programs. But the measures have to take into account some of the problems we have in this district that you don't find elsewhere."

How many progress reports have we read that say something like this: "While our achievements are up from last year, we feel that this is only a small fraction of what we should have been able to accomplish. We have therefore set our sights on . . . ."

Our observations suggest that many managers become quite uncomfortable when they discover that their subordinates' view of a reasonable goal is significantly lower than their own. While the human relations literature, focusing on theories X and Y stresses the inhibiting effect of the boss on the subordinate,[3] the fact is that anticipation of a direct confrontation on the question of appropriate goals with one's subordinates can be traumatic to the boss. The manager wonders whether his people will rebel or, by one means or another, refuse to do the job or sabotage the goals. Will they be able to prove somehow that his goals are outrageous? Or might they quit?

To avoid these awful possibilities, managers frequently scale down the goal to a level that will be acceptable. They do not do this consciously, of course, and there are always enough "facts" to explain such a de-escalation even to themselves. Sometimes a manager who has been forced to give ground will harbor an underlying sense of irritation. He may react by becoming overtly aggressive, hostile, or authoritarian, or engaging in other histrionics that reassure him as to his toughness.

The insidious nature of all these unconscious barriers to management effectiveness is best perhaps illustrated by cases in which managers, seek-

---

[3] See, for example, Douglas McGregor, *The Human Side of Enterprises* (New York: McGraw-Hill, 1960).

ing to upgrade the effectiveness of the organization or overcome its problems, *adopt programs which are in themselves forms of escape*. When confronted with the consequences of inadequate performance, managers often prefer to see the fault clearly directed away from themselves. They also like to be able to look elsewhere for solutions, and are all to ready to believe that problems arise from faulty organization arrangements, the wrong management "style," inadequate information systems, lack of motivation on the part of others, or poor human relations or communications in the enterprise. They will carry out—or engage staff groups or consultants to carry out—all sorts of programs that are supposed to solve the problems. New management information systems will be installed. The enterprise will be reorganized. Managers will go off to examine their human relations.

These programs are often demanding, difficult, and time consuming. A manager deeply engrossed in them enjoys a number of self-defeating "benefits." He can comfort himself with the thought that he is vigorously attacking the issues. If he has brought in staff or consulting help, he can assure himself that experts are studying the situation. This permits him to overlook the things that *he* might be able to do differently to achieve better performance.

The president of one company could not bring himself to look his associates in the eye and reach agreement and commitment on some necessary tough performance goals. Instead, he went off with them to a human relations "confrontation" session in which many of his methods were subject to attack. After much open give-and-take, a variety of new ways of working were agreed upon. None of the discomfort of that meeting and the consequent shufflings around in company relationships and procedures, however, was as upsetting to him as forcing the issue on performance achievement would have been.

Another company whose profits were slipping downward went through a whole series of company reorganizations, each one designed to produce the "right" structure to manage the company effectively.

THE UBIQUITOUS FORCES

The illustrations in this article suggest the profound and pervasive ways by which anxiety-minimizing behavior becomes imperceptibly blended into the life of the enterprise through either unconscious or partly conscious means. These illustrations are merely samplings from a catalog that could easily outweigh Sears Roebuck's. We have focused on the "problem" side, but we must not forget that unconscious anxiety-reducing drives also impel us to behavior which can be highly productive.

How can a grasp of these ubiquitous forces help the leaders of enterprise? Four important principles underlie three strategic concepts which I believe are of universal importance to everybody concerned with establishing appropriate goals for an enterprise and mobilizing resources to achieve them.

The Principles

Universality. Every human being, by one means or another, employs unconscious or partly conscious devices to keep from feeling uncomfortable. Some of these devices may help us achieve goals that we and our associates say we want to achieve. Others, as we have seen, are obstacles. Some may have no effect whatever on the achievement of goals.

Necessity. These forces are universal because they are essential to the maintenance of equilibrium. If one considers all of the real and imagined dangers to which man is exposed—including the fact that life is a temporary condition—it is obvious that worries and fears could easily overwhelm us. These defense mechanisms permit us to put worries out of our minds.

Individuality. Early in life we begin developing ways of dealing with difficult and trying events. These early patterns affect later ones, and gradually each person develops his own unique pattern of responses and defenses. This pattern of defensive reactions is built into all our behavior and becomes a major part of what we think of as each person's personality.

Stability. These patterns of reaction, gradually developing over a lifetime deep within the personality, tend to become fairly fixed in people by the time they reach adult life.

Any strategy of management based on ignoring or thwarting the reality of these defense mechanisms is bound to fail as is any based on the illusion that these fundamental patterns can be readily changed in an individual or a group. It seems to me that the major weakness of even the most creative work in human relations is its failure to come to terms with these facts. There seems to be a persistent belief that some universal ideal style for management can be defined (for example, Theory Y). But the facts suggest that while Theory Y may be great for some managers, others perform at their worst in ambiguous situations and at their best when they are told what to do.[4] Similarly, the belief that a brief human relations training program can produce insights that permit people to successfully change their fundamental work patterns flies in the face of too much data.

Similar weaknesses underlie many other one-variable attacks on management effectiveness.[5] When management tries to upgrade performance by reorganizing the company or a department, by introducing new man-

---

[4] For one good study on this subject, see John J. Morse and Jay W. Lorsch, "Beyond Theory Y," *Harvard Business Review* (May-June 1970).

[5] For a cogent attack on "simplistic" models of organization change, see Leonard Sayles, "Whatever Happened to Management?" *Business Horizons* (April 1970), pp. 25–34.

agement sciences approaches, or by increasing an R & D budget, it may be dealing with the manifest aspects of a problem while failing to come to grips with the latent aspects. Thus, hidden barriers continue to undermine the new system or the new organization as effectively as the old.

The Strategies

This leads to what I believe to be the three most important strategic implications for making the most of managerial potential and minimizing the inhibiting effect of the escape mechanisms. These are the use of multivariate strategies for change, the imposition of work disciplines on the job of management, and the maintenance of tough achievement goals.

Multivariate Strategy of Change. Any major effort to change the productivity or effectiveness of an enterprise must be designed so that, as new managerial methods, systems, and approaches are introduced, there are simultaneous efforts to help managers develop, grow, and become confident in operating in new ways. In considering any major change, it is important to discover not only what the objective facts suggest, but also to determine the readiness for changes in the enterprise. To design a change that goes beyond what people are able to deal with is to invite the mobilization of defenses against success of the new organization, method, or approach.

If change projects are designed to match both what is objectively needed and what people are ready to do, the project can not only accomplish its immediate purpose, but also provide managers with new skills as well as the reassurance and positive reinforcement necessary to create readiness for more ambitious steps. In this kind of framework, major change, instead of becoming a series of disruptive crises and battles, becomes an accelerating, self-sustaining process involving many aspects of the organization's performance. Success at each level provides the foundation for next steps. As the enterprise changes, its managers grow, and as they grow they can handle more change.

Imposing Work Disciplines on Management. The production worker's job, the clerical job, and the first-line supervisory job can be defined in terms of specific behavior and specific results. The further up the line, the more difficult it becomes to describe precisely the goals and the steps to achieve them. Thus the more responsible the job, the greater the opportunities for managers to confuse their escape and defensive behavior with their result-producing behavior. To minimize this possibility, it is necessary for managers to attempt to capture in writing as much of their jobs as possible in terms of commitment to definable (and quantifiable) goals, the strategies and work plans to be employed in achieving them, the timing of various steps, and the measures of progress along the way.

Each new decision area that management considers begins as ill-defined ideas. Only as management strives to shift more and more of the ambiguous and ill-defined into the orbit of specific control—where its work is defined, measured, and recorded in writing—can management protect itself from its own subtle and insidious escape mechanisms.

Maintaining Tough Goals. As the real demands for achievement in an organization diminish, the degree to which escape mechanisms dissipate energy increases geometrically. The organizations in which people seem to have the greatest morale and human relations problems, which have too many meetings, and whose executives are unavailable because they are so busy, are those organizations whose members have the lowest achievement goals (or, if their goals are high, the easiest means of escaping from failure to achieve the goals).

One of the classic errors of modern organization theory is the belief that in such cases the morale and human relations problems must be solved as a prerequisite to improving productivity. This view confuses cause and effect. Where the real demands for management performance are high, where tremendous energy and concentration are required, and where there may not be enough people to get the job done, the least energy is dissipated on off-target escapes. High standards and high productivity may be the key variable here.

In trying to employ these three strategies, of course, the manager must battle with his own escape desires, since each of the three strategies requires him to move into possibly uncomfortable and anxiety provoking areas. But it can be done on a gradual step-by-step basis—if not alone, then with the help of staff or outside consultants—and the results are worth the fight.

QUESTIONS FOR REVIEW AND DISCUSSION

1. Name and discuss two common counterproductive behaviors used by a manager to escape anxiety provoking situations.

2. From your experience or that of a friend, give an example of the defense behavior of other people.

3. What are the three strategic implications for maximizing potential and minimizing the use of escape mechanisms by a manager, as presented in the above article? Discuss briefly.

4. Describe the principle of individuality and also the principle of stability that underlie the three strategic concepts which are presented in the above article.

29. A Positive Approach to Women in Management*

M. JANE KAY

A woman in the space program? Ridiculous!! That was the sentiment ten years ago. Today Astronaut Alan Sheperd says, "It's inevitable." Hopefully, what he means is that in a program so important to the nation, all available resources must be utilized. Those best qualified to perform the necessary functions cannot be excluded if the program is to be of optimum effectiveness.

How does management's attitude toward women in top level positions compare with the above? Some executives are still saying, "Ridiculous!"; the more enlightened ones are saying, "It's inevitable"; while the progressive ones are welcoming the opportunity to have a broader base from which to fill higher level positions. The latter realize that maximum results are achieved by effectively utilizing the abilities of *all* people.

Through the years women have experienced difficulty in moving up the managerial hierarchy. Admittedly, part of the reason is their reluctance to prepare for executive level positions and to assume the responsibility that top jobs require. More insidious however, is the resistance of many of the present occupants of such positions to make them available without regard to race, religion, sex, color, or national origin. While civil rights legislation and federal contract compliance guidelines have forced managements to examine their actions regarding the advancement of women, changes in their attitudes are more difficult to influence. Including a woman in their ranks, regardless of her qualifications, is still looked upon as fulfilling an obligation rather than a positive action that will contribute to the organization's success in more than an "image-making" way. Certainly women must welcome any opportunity for promotion, regardless of the reason. It would be nice, however, to have a more realistic response to the recognition of ability as the criterion for advancement.

---

* Source: Reprinted with permission of *Personnel Journal*, January 1972, pp. 38–41. M. Jane Kay is director of personnel services, The Detroit Edison Company.

250

Comparison with Racial Minorities

Even the most unsophisticated executive is aware that the movement to provide opportunities for women to advance to higher level jobs is here to stay. Although much is being said and written about affirmative action for minorities, women are still at the equality seeking stage. Undoubtedly, as racial minorities have progressed to the affirmative action stage, so will women—perhaps at an accelerated pace based on their observations of the former group. It is estimated that progress toward equality of opportunity for women is three to five years behind that of racial equality.

If there is anything positive about such a lag, it is the opportunity that it provides business, industry, government, and education to take voluntary action to provide women with greater opportunities. Certainly such efforts would be preferable to being forced by outside agencies to instigate affirmative action programs. It would indicate that management has learned something from its experience with racial minorities and is sincere in its avowals to provide equal opportunity for all.

A Positive Approach

What are some of the things that managements can do?

Instigate an open promotion policy

1. make promotional opportunities known to employees
2. follow objective selection procedures
   —state the job requirements
   —make a written evaluation of each candidate's qualifications
   —give specific reasons to substantiate selection

Inventory present women employees with professional training

1. assure that they are on jobs where their training is appropriately utilized
2. explore their progress in comparison to men with similar training
   —examine pay relationships
3. consider action to equalize their status
4. check the proportion of women at various job levels
   —project the picture five or ten years in the future

Provide developmental opportunities for women

1. rotate them to jobs in various areas of the organization
2. encourage their participation in professional organizations
3. include them in management training programs and seminars
4. reimburse tuition for outside courses

Actively recruit women for professional level jobs

1. contact women's professional organizations for assistance
2. Attract them away from organizations that have limited opportunity
3. create a job when it finds a particularly well qualified woman
4. send recruiters to women's colleges

State publicly the organization's policy of nondiscrimination on the basis of sex

1. publish such a statement by the top officer
2. make all management representatives (officers, managers, and supervisors) aware of it
3. assure that its intent is being implemented
4. reward supervisors who are taking a positive approach

Examine personnel policies for possible discriminatory practices

1. eliminate sex requirements from job specifications and ads for job openings
2. discourage arbitrary physical requirements that preclude selecting women
3. include a nondiscrimination clause regarding sex in union contracts
4. offer maternity leaves
5. equalize fringe benefits
6. don't hide under state "protective" laws

Keep informed on the status of such things as

1. the Equal Rights Amendment and other pending legislation, both federal and state.
2. Equal Employment Opportunity Commission rulings
3. Office of Federal Contract Compliance guidelines
4. decisions in Equal Pay Act cases
5. objectives of women's rights organizations
6. day care center needs
7. part-time job opportunities for professionally trained women

Realize that facts counteract the myths about women workers.

1. a woman's place is not necessarily in the home
2. the majority of women are working for more than extra money
3. attendance records and turnover rates for men and women on similar level jobs do not vary
4. the quality of a mother's care is more significant than the quantity
5. given the opportunity, women can handle responsibility equal to men
6. those who complain most about women supervisors have never worked for one

Treatment of Women in Management

Just as important as moving women into management positions is how they are treated when they have "arrived." A good rule of thumb is to treat them as equals, giving them the same responsibility and authority and having the same confidence in their decisions as men in similar positions. A woman's performance should be judged on the same criteria as her male peers and there should be no difference in the dedication expected. Women cannot expect favored treatment if they want true equality. When earned, however, the form of recognition and rewards should not differ or be less than those of men.

It should also be recognized that men may accord women different treatment in a business and in a social situation. For instance, in the former it is unnecessary to observe such amenities as standing when a woman enters the room, lighting her cigarettes, opening doors, and paying for her lunch. The "ladies first" concept need not be as evident. The question of a first or last name basis with other executives is sometimes difficult for a woman in management to resolve. Generally, it is advisable to do what male peers do in a similar situation. If they normally call the president by his first name, so should a woman on a comparable level job.

Attitudes toward Women Managers

It is especially important that all management representatives reflect a positive attitude regarding women in management. Certainly some may resent having them there and personally have negative feelings. They should be cautioned not to express these prejudices in public. Many organizations publicly proclaim they are equal opportunity employers while their officers and managers privately (and sometimes not so privately) decry or scoff at women's efforts toward equality. Such expressions can be damaging to public relations.

Simple Justice

Personnel practitioners will recognize that most of the above suggestions are simply good personnel practices. They are essentially what human relations is all about. It would seem that the desperate need for talented people to lead our institutions would preclude discriminatory practices.

In the last analysis, it is undeniable that an individual woman successfully performing on a job can do more good and change more attitudes than all the other efforts for equality combined. In order to prove her worth, however, a woman must be provided with the opportunity to achieve such a position. While some decry the angry rhetoric and hostile voices heard in women's attempt to gain equality of opportunity, unfortunately, these sorts of things seem to be necessary to bring the problem to management's attention. Hopefully, we will be able to cut through the confusion and get to the core issue, namely, whether women will be given the opportunity to utilize their abilities in open and forthright ways as men are permitted to do, or whether they will be forced to continue to fight the battle of negativism.

The title of the report of the President's Commission on Women's Rights and Responsibility is the best answer to the question. It is "A Matter of Simple Justice." To fulfill their responsibility to strive for the maximum productivity for their organizations, managers can do no less. As they fulfill their role as good citizens, they must do more. As astute businessmen, they will do more. The mutual advantages of a positive approach to women in management may well be the determining factor in the future progress of society.

QUESTIONS FOR REVIEW AND DISCUSSION

1. To achieve a positive approach to inclusion of women in management, writer M. Jane Kay outlines eight major actions. What are these actions?
2. Elaborate and comment on the quotation, "Moving women into management is important, but equally as important is how they are treated when they have 'arrived'."
3. As you see it, in the management field will women ever attain true equality with men? Justify your answer.

30. Six Propositions for Managerial Leadership*

NORMAN GEORGE and THOMAS J. VON DER EMBSE

What is the state of the art of managerial leadership research and theory? Progressing quite well, we suggest, and promising to be useful to management—*provided* we are careful and realistic in suggesting how the research results are to be used.

This reading will set forth six propositions which, it is hoped, will add to the growing body of leadership research. These propositions have emerged from research, including our own study of attitudinal orientations of over 650 managers and administrators from a variety of organizations, including nonindustrial institutions. The six propositions focus on the relationships between managers' attitudes and behavior and several other dimensions, including organizational structure, operating systems, environmental conditions, and demographic factors. The relationships are selective. They do not purport to deal with all the ramifications of leadership behavior and organizational effectiveness, but they are sufficiently inclusive to be useful in analyzing conditions and forces in effect within an organization.

Overview of Leadership Research

Three decades ago, management literature abounded with the traitist approach to leadership analysis. The practice was usually to postulate a profile of the effective leader in terms of personality characteristics. But while the emphasis was on personal traits, the profiles usually included some factors that are better classified as skills rather than traits in the psychological sense. Thus the "good leader" was not only "decisive" and

---

* Source: Copyright, 1972 by the Foundation for the School of Business at Indiana University. Reprinted with permission. Dr. Norman George is professor of management, University of Dayton, and an attorney. Dr. Thomas J. Von der Embse is professor of management, Wright State University, Dayton.

255

possessed "good judgment," but he was also "able to communicate and could project an air of confidence."

This exclusive emphasis on the make-up and abilities of the individual executive was replaced by the situational approach, which viewed leadership as a process that, in turn, was a function of the interactions among the manager, the work group, and the organizational environment. The manager himself was still a central focus of study, but the emphasis was upon observation of more discrete behavior in the context of the organizational setting.

The polarization of the styles-of-leadership concept in recent years seems, oddly enough, a throwback to the traitist approach. It is perhaps fair to say that McGregor's "X" and "Y" theory of management was the stimulus for the spate of "models" of leadership styles.[1] But before accusing McGregor of resurrecting a kind of traitist approach to leadership, it is important to note that McGregor's approach was essentially cultural rather than psychological. He was still "situational" in the sense that emergent leadership styles, according to his theory, resulted from prevalent cultural values and thus took into account more than the behavior of the individual manager. When he talked about the underlying attitudes of the "X" manager and the "Y" manager, he was discussing not any particular manager but the widely prevalent cultural values of managers in general.

The most recent treatments of leadership theory and research still look carefully at the behavior of the manager, but they relate this behavior more directly to other organizational dimensions. The Woodward studies placed great emphasis on the nature of the production technology. Lorsch, Lawrence, and Morse related competitive conditions to the organization's operating system and the interaction of both of these factors to the resultant behavior within the organization. Fiedler's contingency theory attempts to elaborate a model of managerial leadership in which leadership style becomes a function of managerial and work group attitudes and behavior and organizational conditions, such as task structure and modes of interaction.[2]

Uses of Leadership Research

Ideally, the end result of research should be to prescribe or suggest to managers what ought to be done in a given situation. But at this point we

---

[1] Douglas V. McGregor, *The Human Side of Enterprise* (New York: McGraw-Hill, 1960).

[2] See, for example, Joan Woodward, *Industrial Organization* (New York: Oxford University Press, 1965); John Morse and Jay Lorsch, "Beyond Theory Y," *Harvard Business Review* (May-June 1970), pp. 61–68; and Fred E. Fiedler, *A Theory of Leadership Effectiveness* (New York: McGraw-Hill, 1966).

urge caution. The nature of the management process and the web of inter-relating factors in any given situation are complex, much too complex to permit many, if any, prescriptive statements that are generally applicable. Such statements would almost always have to be qualified by such conditions as "all other factors being equal." But all others factors are seldom equal; each organization has its own unique set of conditions and circumstances. Some recent research, for example, suggests a certain fit between leadership behavior patterns and organization structure, calling for adaptation of one or the other. But any number of factors, in a particular situation, could mitigate against the prescribed fit.

It is much more prudent and realistic, therefore, to regard the relationships that emerge from the research as diagnostic tools of organization analysis, rather than precise guidelines as to what ought to be done. Managers are action and decision oriented. They must decide what needs to be done and act accordingly. But before management can decide where it wants to go and how to get there, it needs to diagnose where it is now. With this knowledge base, it can better determine likely obstacles and conditions that may require change or adaptation. Management-by-objectives programs, for example, require a degree of consultative goal setting. A diagnosis of existing leadership patterns and organizational factors might point to the need for some preconditioning to increase the likelihood of effective implementation.

It seems accurate to say that a dynamic model of leadership is now evolving. Some refer to this as a contingency model or theory. It is in the context of such a model that the six propositions discussed below should be viewed. They should not be regarded as standing alone; rather, they are intended to be used as related units of analysis.

How an effective manager behaves, whether consultatively or directively, depends upon several factors: the kind of production or operating system; whether a company's production, engineering, and marketing are characterized by rapid changes or relative stability; the level and types of skill and education of the work group; and the degree of structure that emerges as a result of these factors. Not only will these factors vary among organizations, but also within the same organization over a span of time.

The promise of this trend of research and theory building is that the kind of studies evolving, because they constitute a departure from traditional static approaches, can provide useful conceptual tools of analysis. With these tools, a manager has available a framework for determining why certain leadership patterns are present in the organization and what to expect from them, and whether a dominant pattern of directive or consultative management for an organization unit is desirable and appropriate to the present set of conditions, including the operating system, production, marketing and engineering system stability, and personnel characteristics. Finally, if change is desirable, the insight from the newer research approach assists the manager in deciding where to begin and what to expect as a result of the change.

The analysis of our study data did not rely solely on "hard criteria," that is, the quantitative measurements of the scales and bio-organizational information. Through group discussions and individual interviews with a sizable portion of our statistical sample, we were able to add considerably to our understanding and interpretation of the results. This kind of information not only added detail, but often provided key factors and insights that explained relationships in some areas and the lack of relationships in others (see Figure 1).

The Six Propositions

Our six propositions are intended as diagnostic tools of analysis, rather than prescriptions for specific action. They are, in a sense, precedents to decision and action. They point to relationships that the manager should use, along with other considerations, in analyzing the situation as it exists now, anticipating possible obstacles to desired end results, and assessing conditions for success.

The propositions are based upon a combination—a synthesis—of reported research and observations, including our own study and observations. The authors' research, which is now progressing into a new phase, deals with attitudinal factors related to leadership behavior and selected organizational and demographic characteristics. It was designed to complement, build upon, and elaborate other research already reported and referred to.

The propositions themselves are stated in rather broad terms. If they appear to be somewhat general or oversimplified, it is merely because we have chosen to limit the number to six, leaving it for later to elaborate points and delve into some of the ramifications in greater detail.

Proposition 1: Flexibility in leadership style is both desirable and feasible.

Probably few will disagree that flexibility in style is desirable. More recent research, such as that of Lorsch and Lawrence, Woodward, and others, serves to negate what now certainly appears to have been a tendency of some earlier studies to suggest that consultative management was preferred in nearly all instances. Studies have shown clearly that this is not the case.

Even though some of the research (such as that of Lorsch and Lawrence, and Woodward) approached the problem from the point of view of which styles actually emerge under different organizational and technological settings, there is a strong implication that the desired style differs with the situation. The realities of the situation, including the fact that under certain conditions organizational units that were generally characterized by the directive mode of management were evaluated highly effective, are taken into account. The work structure often simply does not permit much latitude for consultative management, at least not to any great extent.

What may be more controversial is the question of whether or not a manager *can* be flexible. To some behaviorists, this is questionable because, they say, leadership style reflects one's basic personality, which changes little after the early years in life. But this view, it is suggested, has sometimes tended to confuse the issue. The question is not necessarily how much one can change, but how much flexibility in behavior an indi-

FIGURE 1. Differentiation in Leadership Orientations along Six Dimensions (N = 650)

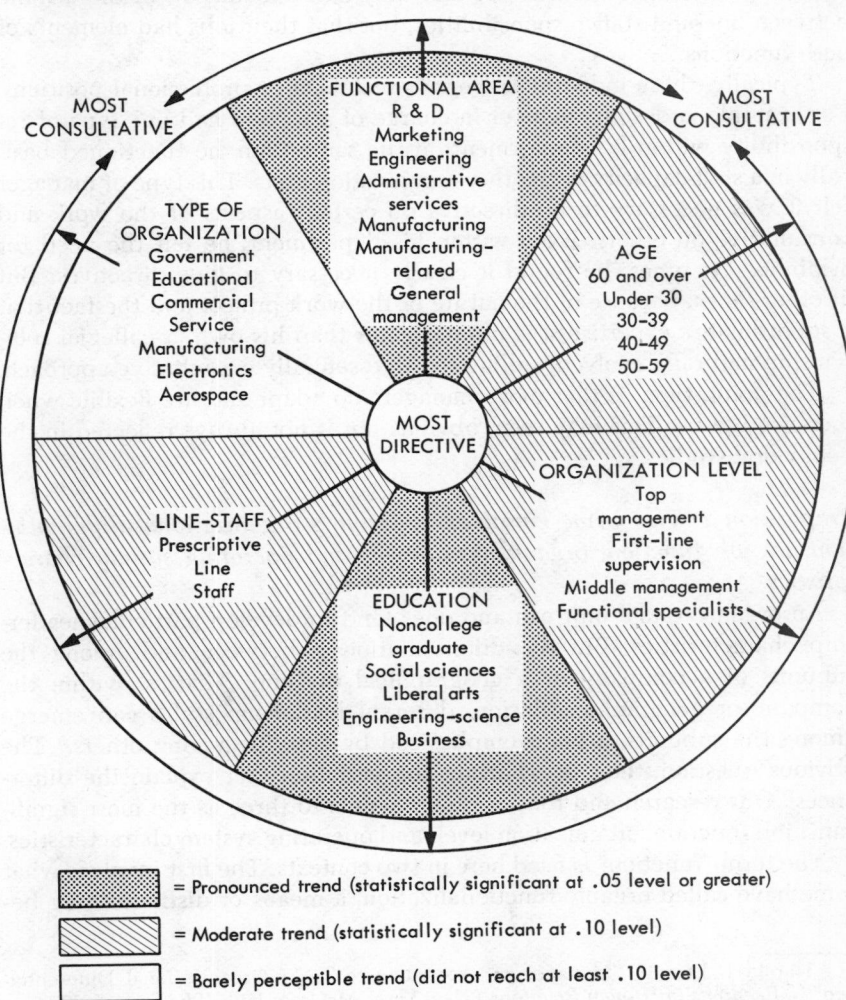

vidual's basic personality permits. This range of behavior is, for the typi-cal manager, not necessarily narrow.

A good deal of the research points out that there is considerable adap-tation by managers. When the prevailing organizational structure and management practices influence and even dictate a mode of leadership behavior, many managers obviously have adapted. One facet of our own study throws light on flexibility and adaptation in still another context. Most of the subjects were not extremely oriented in either direction, that is, directive or consultative. A revealing insight emerged from a pursuit of this point with those who were closest to the mid-point of the scale. A large number of these individuals had difficulty classifying their positions as either line or staff. It was not that they had difficulty in distinguishing between line-and-staff responsibilities, but that their jobs had elements of both functions.

Typically, these individuals were in technical or professional positions. For example, a design engineer in charge of a section had line type of re-sponsibility within his department; at the same time, he functioned basi-cally in a staff capacity with other organization units. This type of manager felt it was necessary to be directive on certain aspects of the work and consultative on others. Even within his department, he felt the need for flexibility. At times, he found it clearly necessary to give directives. But at other times, because of the nature of the work project and the fact that a subordinate's expertise was often greater than his own, a collegial rela-tionship naturally evolved, calling for an essentially consultative approach.

The point, then, is that most managers do adapt and are flexible when they need to be. This may seem obvious but is not always reflected in the behavioral studies.

Proposition 2: The prime variables underlying organizational differentia-tion are job function, organization levels, and operating system charac-teristics.

An organizational unit can and does tend to develop particular leader-ship characteristics. But the differentiation is between and among the subunits of a company or a geographical division. That is, within the company or geographic division, different leadership styles can emerge among the subunits, a point emphasized by Leavitt, among others.[3] The obvious question, then, is what are the variables that explain the differ-ences? Our research and that of others points to three as the most signifi-cant: job function, organization level, and operating system characteristics.

The term "function" is used here in two contexts. The first involves what some have called organic functionalization, a means of distinguishing be-

---

[3] Harold J. Leavitt, "Management According to Task: Organizational Differentia-tion" in *Readings in Human Relations* (New York: McGraw-Hill, 1964), pp. 3–15.

tween basic business functions. Thus, there is the marketing function, the manufacturing function, the production function, the finance function, and so on. These may be further subdivided. For example, we have found it significant to distinguish between manufacturing and manufacturing-related functions, the former consisting of work activities more directly related to production than the latter. Production planning and control, for example, would usually be defined as manufacturing-related in our context.

The second context in which the term function is used relates to the line-staff concept. Both of these functional differentiations serve to explain differences in leadership modes within a company organization. Marketing managers, as a unit within our total sample, were found to be significantly more consultatively oriented than manufacturing managers, for example. While one must be careful not to generalize too broadly from the functional distinction alone, it is apparent that the greater and more explicit the constraints involved in the function itself, the more likely the manager in that position will be directively, rather than consultatively, oriented. This conclusion is further reinforced by the fact that differences among organizations were not as prominent in our study as were differences among functions. In other words, when comparing manufacturing, aerospace, educational, commercial, service, governmental, and even religious organizations, managers in similar positions do not differ as markedly in leadership orientation as do managers in different positions in a single organization.

The explanation is found by combining with the functional factor the variable often referred to as "operating system characteristics." This factor is similar to the concept used in the Woodward and Lorsch, Lawrence and Morse studies in defining differences in technological systems. The present authors' point of departure from the earlier research, however, lies in the delineation of operating systems within an organization. Thus, it is valid to suggest the existence of various operating systems, each relating to particular functional areas but broader in scope than the duties implied and/or described for the function.

The marketing area is a good example. In explaining leadership orientation, it is far more appropriate to examine the technology and operation of the marketing system—in contrast with, for instance, the production system. Marketing systems tend to be more ambient than production systems. Marketing organizational relationships tend toward lower job structure, more positive change orientation, greater diffusion of authority, less fragmentation of work activities, and greater autonomy of individual movement.

The point is that these same considerations carry over into other functional areas. Even more important, these two variables, functional differentiation and operating systems, combine to produce a need for certain leadership orientations. Both are, however, horizontally distinguished from other areas. Organizational differentiation implies both vertical *and* horizontal perspectives.

The vertical factor emerging as most important is organization level. Of the three management groups—supervisory, middle, and top—middle managers tend to be most consultative. The implications of this finding extend beyond internal factors and into certain universal considerations regarding the middle management role.

Greenidge and Steinmetz, in a recent article, reported a management syndrome characterized by a highly consultative and participative orientation.[4] The authors related this, in turn, to the current evangelism of the management and organization development profession. While the authors associated this syndrome with top managers, the point is that the conditioning effect of management training helps also to explain the middle management trend toward high consultation. Middle managers have, in recent years, frequented seminars of all sorts, especially grid training, management by objectives, laboratory "t" group sessions, and similar programs in which the developmental criteria are almost singularly based on democratic, participative management.

Evidence from our research clearly supports this observation. Of all samples in the study, those drawn from practitioners after taking an MBA human relations course were significantly more consultative. While a certain amount of self-selection bias was undoubtedly involved, it is apparent that conditioning through training and education can and does encourage certain leadership models which, in turn, will tend to condition the attitudes of managers on the job.

Another more speculative consideration in the case of middle management relates to the status of the position itself. Various popular conceptions of the middle management position view it as any or all of the following: a paper-shuffling function, a buffer or pressure point between top management and first-line supervision, a proving ground for top management prospects, a repository for "retreads" and organizational deadwood, and/or a junior executive level with certain important responsibilities but with limited decision authority. Still others view the position as the focal point for decentralized authority.

It is not our purpose to evaluate the merits of these various conceptions of middle management, but rather to underscore the distinctive orientations of middle, first, and top level managers. At the risk of some generalization, the highly consultative attitude of middle managers suggests that, at this organization level, factors such as perceived uncertainty regarding organizational role, limited authority in making decisions, and, more im-

---

[4] Charles D. Greenidge and Lawrence L. Steinmetz, "Realities That Shape Managerial Style," *Business Horizons* (October 1970), pp. 23–32.

portant, getting top management support for those decisions produce the kind of atmosphere in which consultation regarding decision matters will tend to prevail.

Proposition 3: Differences in leadership style orientation derive from cultural factors and are in a state of transition.

Bennis has postulated that "democracy is inevitable" in organizations.[5] It would not be taking undue liberty to suggest that, in our context, he predicts that the consultative mode of leadership will ulimately prevail. The prediction itself is virtually impossible to dispute, since inevitability suggests no finite time dimension. In a relative sense, however, it seems clear that the over-all trend in leadership attitudes is toward the consultation end of the continuum. However, the matter of emergent leadership behavior is much more complex, as shown in the preceding discussion regarding organizational differentiation. Nevertheless, it is apparent that cultural factors do have an important impact on leadership style orientation.

Two factors stand out: age and education. The findings showed a consistent pattern of leadership orientation based on the age factor. Simply stated, younger managers tend to be more consultatively oriented than older managers. Furthermore, this pattern is fairly consistent as the age brackets are broken out. Age does correlate inversely with the consultative-directive scale, that is (except for the over 60 group), the higher the age, the more directive the manager.

The correlation also holds up with the education factor, although it must be pointed out that the data relative to education are largely confined to formal education. Thus, we found college graduates more consultatively oriented than noncollege managers. The differences are, moreover, quite large from a statistical viewpoint.

Because of the myriad factors that should be considered in assessing the impact of cultural factors, one should not generalize too broadly. On the one hand, as suggested earlier, the quantity and orientation of management training are bound to have some long-range effect on leadership orientation. On the other hand, one might point to competitive conditions and changing technology as among the factors that cannot be overlooked as influences that could shape attitudes in different directions. Nevertheless, we have found considerable evidence in the nature of hard criteria on age and education that do suggest a long-range trend toward more consultative leadership.

Proposition 4: Differences in leadership modes exist between line-and-staff managers.

[5] Warren G. Bennis and Philip E. Slater, "Democracy is Inevitable," *Harvard Business Review* (March-April 1964), pp. 51–59.

The intensive technological base of the newer industries, such as aerospace and electronics, has led several observers to suggest that traditional line-and-staff distinctions will eventually fade and that the deployment of highly trained individuals in project teamwork situations will diffuse decision authority among various organization roles. As indicated earlier, the perceived differences between line and staff are often quite ambiguous. But, considering the difficulties in classification, one cannot dismiss the fact that differences can and do emerge.

The classical line-and-staff distinction focused on different kinds of authority. Thus, staff authority is largely advisory, and line authority is the right to command or issue directives. In the context of leadership styles, staff would find it necessary to rely on its ability to influence line managers, while line could rely to an extent on the weight of its formal authority. Staff, therefore, would be expected to operate in a more consultative mode.

The authors' study lends some support to the classical view, in that staff managers and specialists as a group and across varying types of organizations were more consultative than line managers. It was necessary, however, to include a third category—prescriptive—to distinguish those personnel whose functions may be formally defined as staff, but in practice normally exercise considerable authority regarding organizational decisions related to their specialties, for example, production control, purchasing, quality control, and budget analysis. Separating this group increased the differentiation of the functions. This, in turn, tells the manager that the line-staff distinction is insufficient and that a third group exists, which is neither line nor staff but which tends to be directive in attitude. Awareness of this third dimension could help to prevent line-staff conflict, particularly when viewed as a difference in role behavior and expectations.

Proposition 5: External forces can modify leadership modes; changing competitive conditions are a prime example.

Leadership patterns are products of a number of interrelating factors. Most of the ones we have discussed so far are internal to the organization in a sense, although new managers in the organization might be viewed as an external influence, at least in the initial phases of their performance. But external factors do have an effect which is sometimes quite discernible. Particularly significant may be the effect of changing competitive conditions.

It should be noted first, as researchers such as Lorsch, Morse, Lawrence, and Woodward have documented in references noted earlier, competitive conditions are significant elements in the system of factors that explain the emergence of differing modes of organizational leadership styles. Although these researchers focused on the internal operating system, it is clear that competitive forces were among the controlling factors. A stable market, for example, will be reflected in the manufacturing technology. The rate of change demanded by the market will also influence directly the general thrust of R & D and design engineering work. And these factors, as has been noted, are related to the kind of leadership that emerges.

But this proposition emphasizes that changes in competitive conditions can and do produce changes in leadership patterns, often with dramatic promptness. While these changes may eventually turn out to be temporary, under certain circumstances, which we will discuss, the change can prove to be relatively permanent.

It is reasonable to expect a general increase in the directive mode of managing internally because of more severe competitive conditions; however, these conditions can produce or influence behavior in the opposite direction for those members of the organization who have regular contact with people outside the organization. The marketing group almost immediately comes to mind. Our study included data on a marketing association group in a specific geographical area. A large percentage of its members represented companies that had been unusually affected by the business downturn in 1970. As a group, this sample was more consultative on the average than the rest of our marketing manager sample and was also less risk oriented.

Even lacking highly rigorous controls in our research design to validate the presumption generated by this finding, it seems reasonable to say that, during times of more intensive competition, marketing personnel in the field are likely to continue their basically more consultative attitude orientation. In view of the likelihood that they must woo the customer even harder, some small shift toward an even greater consultative orientation is at least possible, if not likely.

One might also conjecture that during times of increased competition even the marketing group would generally be subject to directive approaches; marketing managers might begin to breathe more heavily down the necks of their district managers. But the evidence supports the generalization that attitudes of marketing people are strongly influenced by the nature of customer relations. This is not confined to the salesmen themselves, but is also reflected by sales and marketing managers.

A study by Tosi and Carroll, although focusing on objective setting in connection with management by objectives, is consistent in a general way with our results and earlier comments.[6] They found that marketing personnel perceived themselves as having considerably more voice in setting their objectives than did most other classes of managers. Tosi and Carroll explained this by pointing out that salesmen and sales managers almost always have the best and the most information when it comes to the sales

---

[6] Henry L. Tosi, Jr., and Stephen J. Carroll, "Some Structural Factors Related to Goal Influence in the Management by Objectives Process," *MSU Business Topics* (Spring 1969).

outlook in their specific areas. While Tosi and Carroll were looking at marketing personnel's perceptions of the degree of influence and power they had in setting objectives, we would put it in terms of the degree of consultation in this decision area.

In summary, external forces can modify leadership modes. The external forces operate directly upon some segments of the organization, such as marketing and those groups which regularly meet customers (field services, for example), and less directly for other groups. The impact depends on how sensitive various operations must be to customer or client.

While we have discussed only the force of competition, this is not the only external factor that can change or modify leadership patterns. We might have pointed to such other factors as government regulation, especially in cases when a company might come under investigation with respect to antitrust laws or the Federal Trade Commission, for example. A change in the local union's international affiliation is another example. But most of the evidence so far indicates that competition is the external factor of prime importance affecting leadership patterns.

Proposition 6: Institutional effects are not as important as the previously mentioned variables as determinants of emergent leadership patterns.

Our study included groups of administrators in secondary education and in religious organizations. These groups, as distinct entities in our study, did not differ greatly from industrial and business groups in attitudinal orientation. Neither the educational nor the religious administrators, as a group, were significantly more consultative, for example, than groups of industrial managers. The differences in orientation within these groups were related basically to the same factors as within manufacturing and industrial groups: the function performed, the nature of the operating system, organization level, the line-staff differentiation, education, and age.

Perhaps a caveat is in order here. Longitudinal studies may very well show some changes in view of the well-known forces at play in these institutions. These two types of organizations (educational and religious) are experiencing demands for greater participation in decision making, not only by components of the internal system, but external societal elements as well. Perhaps these groups will become more consultative and group oriented on the average. But there is nothing to indicate that differentiation *within* a particular educational or religious organization will decrease. Furthermore, we indicated earlier evidence of long-range trends in average orientations in industrial organizations resulting both from cultural factors and structural considerations (relatively more technical and professional personnel in the firm).

Another way of putting it is this. What is important is that within these types of organizations operating systems may be changing and new functions may be displacing old ones. In addition, a new breed of administrators is coming into the picture. Influence from forces external to the organization unit should also be "plugged in." These are the important units of analysis, the same units applicable to other institutions, including business and industrial.

The Propositions as Tools

We have suggested six propositions for managerial leadership. These propositions, like all the emerging leadership concepts founded on research evidence, should be regarded as diagnostic tools. Their use can be explained by suggesting as strongly as possible how *not* to use these concepts. They should not be used as static descriptions that serve to classify organizations. Instead, the approach here has been to concentrate on relationships.

Furthermore, these relationships can change, and continuous research is necessary to identify the changes. But these relationships, if they are relatively fundamental, should not change too rapidly. If that occurs, we have obviously not yet found the first order or first level of relationships. It is necessary to work from these most basic relationships to use these concepts in a practical sense.

The primary uses of these propositions, then, are as diagnostic tools. Ideally, such tools can be used at any point in time to describe the mix of leadership elements in an organization; predict changes in leadership mode by analyzing and forecasting changes in the mix; and help an individual manager to adapt his behavior or leadership style through analytical assessment of the mix of forces and conditions.

What does it mean—particularly to the manager who looks for something useful? One use is suggested by the postulations of some researchers. They have suggested that, given a certain mix of the elements, certain practices, structures, and policies are predictably dysfunctional. Consequently, they are in conflict with what the mix of elements tends to "force." To this, one should add an elaboration in terms of the time dimension. A manager could make a calculated estimate of the probabilities of correcting the dysfunction within a reasonable and acceptable period of time by viewing the mix as dynamic (that is, subject to change), and by injecting into the system analysis the degree of permanency of certain underlying elements, such as attitude orientation, plus the potency of modifying influences, such as competitive forces and the resultant immediate changes.

Thus, a manager can assess and roughly measure a system's capacity for adaptability. Suppose, for example, that a company or one of its divisions is pondering the advisability and feasibility of going into a line of business that calls for producing a highly standardized product; success will depend upon cost and service efficiency. Described another way, a high technology company seeking to diversify contemplates development of a segment of business that is less technology-intensive and is much more competitive on cost and service efficiency. It proposes to develop this business internally. One question it must ask in determining strategy is whether or not its personnel can adapt to what would essentially be a different operating system. An analytical study of the mix of forces and factors discussed in this reading should, it is suggested, enable the company to better assess the chances of successful adaptation.

Obviously, according to recent experiences of some of the defense-related industries, this probability has not always been correctly calculated. We can reasonably surmise that the failures could be explained, partly at least, in terms of the need for quicker decisions, more immediately responsive control, and other factors, all of which point toward a more directive rather than consultative mode of managing.

To have determined accurately the probabilities of successful adaptation to the new leadership mode would have entailed finding out not only the nature of behavior or leadership patterns that had existed, but also the degree and permanency of, for example, a consultative orientation. It may have also entailed pinpointing where and in which particular parts of the organization a rather high degree of directive managing would be required. Conceivably, this could have been a crucial factor in deciding position assignments and over-all criteria for staffing.

It is not suggested that the use of these analytical tools will provide precise or discrete answers. The tools themselves are not that exact, the variables are numerous, and the interrelations highly dynamic. But it is suggested that the analysis can be useful to management in identifying what to look for, what to expect, and what hurdles will need to be overcome, and in developing a framework for applying managerial judgment and knowledge. In short, it could help management focus on the critical problems with which they should be concerned.

This may be all that leadership research and the development of theory and principles can ever do—help managers to define the elements of the problem and focus on the critical issues. But this is no small contribution.

QUESTIONS FOR REVIEW AND DISCUSSION

1. Relate your understanding of the statement that the six propositions for managerial leadership should be regarded as being diagnostic tools rather than precise guidelines.
2. Can external forces modify leadership modes? Include illustrations in justifying your answer.
3. Explain the meaning of Figure 1 in the above reading.
4. Discuss the three prime variables underlying organizational differentiation that appear to affect managerial leadership.

part NINE

Actuating

Much of the current managerial literature deals with working effectively with people. The influence of people upon the functioning of management cannot be denied. Indeed a large number feel it is the essence of management. Individual motivation, personnel interactions, and informal social relationships are being examined closely. The emphasis centers on the role of work in relation to the needs and the capabilities of the human being. Commonly the hierarchy-of-needs framework is followed.

It is contended that in many cases there is underutilization of human potential and a severe lack of genuine job enthusiasm. As a result a person becomes alienated from his job, frustrated, and "boxed in" an unhappy situation. To minimize these undesirable results, but more important to give positive stimulation and job satisfaction to work efforts, modern management is vitally interested and active in improving the social, psychological, and physical motivational climate of the work situation. To this end, these practices are followed: keeping personnel fully informed; improving the contents, methods, and relationships of jobs; and encouraging development and growth by each individual employee.

"Managing Upward Communication" by Gary Gemmill poses some of the major difficulties in getting communication to flow adequately from the bottom to the top of an organization. Important reasons why these communication hurdles exist and suggestions for attaining good upward communication are pointed out.

Equally as important as effective upward communication is downward communication which is expertly handled by Andrew B. Chase, Jr., in his reading, "How to Make Downward Communication Work." The importance, types, and appraisal of downward communication along with recommendations for management members including a specific program to follow are included in this informative paper.

Baruch Lev and Aba Schwartz in their reading, "On the Use of the Economic Concept of Human Capital in Financial Statements," discuss the interesting and increasingly important concept of determining the

269

economic worth of an employee considered as an asset of an organization. Rarely is human capital included in the financial statements, yet the belief is common that the human being represents the most valuable asset of an organization. What is the dollar value of an executive, a skilled operative employee, an outstanding professional athlete? Authors Lev and Schwartz stimulate questions of far reaching influence.

A common problem dealt with in the next reading, "New Life for Dead Enders" asks what a manager should do to motivate an employee on a dead-end job. A straightforward discussion is given and includes specific suggestions to follow. This is a practical paper of much interest to the manager of today.

A short, but highly provocative reading is Vermont Royster's "Education for What." Some of the very basics of our current higher educational system are challenged. The controversial issues raised are certain to elicit active discussion among readers of this reading.

The next and last reading is "Learning Curves that Work" by Surender N. Goel and Robert H. Becknell. The variables of starting efficiency, learning rate, and operation time standards are related in a model. From this model it is demonstrated how a learning curve for a specific operation is determined. The mathematical values are computer processed and can be used to express the number of days required for a normal operator to reach an acceptable level of performance. Such information is used to give the trainee a practical goal toward which to strive and likewise the manager is informed of the time required to acquire the needed skill for the particular operative task.

31. Managing Upward Communication *

GARY GEMMILL

The problem of upward communication appears to be endemic to superior-subordinate relationships. It is a common observation that subordinates in their relationship with superiors often conceal and distort their real feelings, problems, opinions, and beliefs because they fear disclosure may lead superiors to punish them in some way. Decisions by subordinates not to disclose such information results in a superior being unaware of how his actions affect them. This lack of feedback may prevent him from changing his managerial style or from correcting misperceptions on their part. Similarly, he is put in a position where he is unable to share knowledge with them that might lead to improvements in their performance. Perhaps most important, however, from a manager's perspective, is that this lack of communication may cut him off from some essential information.

Given that concealment and distortion by subordinates can be costly, is there anything a superior can do to lessen it? Is it possible for him to lower the probability that subordinates will conceal or distort their communication with him? If it is possible, what must he do in his relationship with subordinates? How can he manage their upward communication?

Why Subordinates Distort Their Upward Communication

An understanding of the factors that lead subordinates to distort upward communications is a prerequisite for managing it. One frequently cited reason for such concealment and distortion is that subordinates believe their superior may penalize them in some way for disclosing their real opinions, feelings and difficulties. Stated in a propositional form:

* Source: Reprinted with permission of *Personnel Journal*, February 1970, pp. 107–10. Gary Gemmill is assistant professor, Syracuse University.

271

If a subordinate believes that disclosure of his feelings, opinions, or difficulties may lead a superior to block or hinder the attainment of a personal goal, he will conceal or distort them.

According to this proposition, a subordinate enters an organization with such personal goals as moving upward as fast as possible achieving stable or increasingly higher earnings, or doing work that leads to growth in his abilities. In pursuit of these goals, he evaluates contemplated actions in terms of how he believes they will facilitate their attainment, attempting to avoid actions he believes may hinder. At various levels of personal awareness, he may conceal or distort his opinions, difficulties, or feelings when he believes disclosure may lead a superior to do something to block or hinder attainment of his goals.

For example, if he receives a salary increase he considers unfair, he tells his superior it is more than fair because he is afraid that by expressing disappointment he may injure his promotion prospects. He may believe the superior would consider him an ingrate or interpret his remark as an insult to his managerial proficiency and hold it against him when his name comes up for promotion. This belief, however, may not be grounded in reality since the superior may not actually attach a penalty to the expression of disappointment. But if the subordinate believes there may be one, it is sufficient for him to distort his feelings to avoid the possibility that the superior might react to disclosure by blocking or hindering the attainment of his personal goal of upward mobility. This may be done consciously. In some situations, however, the subordinate may not be fully aware that he is distorting the feedback to his boss.

The Origins of Disclosure Beliefs

Subordinates acquire beliefs about the types of information to avoid disclosing to superiors from many sources. For example, subordinates who have worked for a superior for a number of years may instruct new subordinates that careerwise, it is unwise to express ideas for improvements to him. They may even cite a case where a subordinate was purportedly penalized by him for rocking the boat. While the belief may lack an objective basis, if the new subordinates accept it, the probability that they will disclose ideas for improvement is reduced.

Some beliefs are undoubtedly founded in general social norms or corporate "folklore." For example, "subordinates should not display emotions in the presence of superiors" or "subordinates should never question the decisions of superiors." If subordinates have internalized such a norm, the probability is great that they will make decisions not to disclose their feelings or criticisms of decisions handed down to them. Indeed, they may even consider it legitimate for a superior to reprimand them if they make such disclosures.

Some beliefs originate in a subordinate's direct observation of types of disclosures that he perceives his superior dislikes. For example, when he disagrees with a superior who becomes emotionally upset and defensive he may say to himself: "I shouldn't have disagreed with him even though he told me he wanted me to feel free to do so. It's obvious he is upset by it. He may hold it against me when my name comes up for promotion or a new assignment. I'd better play it safe in the future and refrain from voicing my opinions." Rightly or wrongly, he considers the superior's reaction to disagreement to be a threat. He perceives the superior as being capable of blocking attainment of his personal goals and acts in a way to avoid it.

Where subordinates have not directly or indirectly acquired beliefs about the types of disclosures that may be penalized, they frequently operate on an uncertainty principle. When they are unable to predict if a superior will reward or penalize disclosure, to avoid the risk of a penalty they make a decision not to disclose. When in doubt, they say nothing.

Empirical Studies of Upward Communication

There are a number of empirical studies that offer support for the proposition that subordinates makes decisions not to disclose their feelings, opinions, and difficulties because they are afraid that their superior may punish them in some way for doing so. Vogel, in a study of approximately 2,000 employees in 8 companies, found that almost a majority of them believed that if a subordinate told his immediate superior everything he felt about the company, he would probably get into a "lot of trouble," and that the best way to gain promotion was not to disagree very much with a superior.[1] This study, however, identifies only the prevalence of these beliefs and not how or where they were acquired.

Read, in a study of fifty-two superior-subordinate pairs in three companies, found that the accuracy with which subordinates disclosed their difficulties to superiors was negatively related to their desire for upward mobility.[2] The greater the desire of subordinates for upward mobility, the less likely they were to accurately disclose their difficulties to their superiors. The amount of inaccuracy in the upward communication, however, was affected by the perceived influence of the superior over their careers and how much they trusted him not to hold disclosures against them in considering promotion. The greater his perceived influence over their careers and the lower their trust in him, the more inaccurate their upward communication of difficulties. Read points out, however, that even

---

[1] A. Vogel, "Why Don't Employees Speak Up?" *Personnel Administration*, May-June 1967.

[2] W. Read, "Upward Communication in Industrial Hierarchies," *Human Relations*, vol. 15, 1962, pp. 3–15.

when subordinates trust their superiors not to hold disclosures against them or block mobility, high mobility aspirations militate against disclosure.

Blau and Scott in a study of agents in a federal law enforcement agency found that the agents were reluctant to take their work-related problems to superiors even though they were officially expected to do so.[3] They believed that exposure of problems might be interpreted by superiors as a lack of independence, resulting in a low rating. Perceiving the possibility of a goal block by superiors, they decided not to disclose their difficulties in order to avoid it.

Argyris has also found that subordinates often conceal their feelings, opinions, and difficulties from superiors because they are fearful that they may be penalized in some way for such disclosure.[4] He suggests that one of the primary reasons for lack of disclosure is that many organizations place a high reward value on rational-technical aspects of behavior and discourage or penalize emotionally based behavior. When, for example, a subordinate expresses feelings in a discussion, the superior tells him to keep his feelings out of it. The subordinate thus learns not to disclose his feelings to avoid a career penalty of being labeled as too "emotional."

Managing Upward Communication

The important question remains: What, if anything, can a superior do to lessen the probability that subordinates will conceal or distort their real feelings, opinions, and difficulties when communicating with him? Unfortunately, there has been little if any research directed to this question. Thus, the intent here is to conceptually examine factors that would appear to have a significant role in managing upward communication.

It seems clear that an awareness that subordinates tend to filter upward communication is a necessary condition for lessening it. Given awareness diminishing the probability would seem to require a change in their perception of penalties for disclosure. The crux of the problem is establishing a relationship where they feel they will not be penalized by the superior for disclosure. It is possible for a superior to create such a climate? If so, how can he do it?

Changing the Basis of Perceived Penalties

If the superior's control over the personal goals of subordinates were decreased, their fear of receiving a penalty for disclosure would un-

---

[3] P. M. Blau and W. R. Scott, *Formal Organizations*, San Francisco: Chandler, 1962, pp. 128–134.

[4] C. Argyris, "Interpersonal Barriers to Decision Making." *Harvard Business Review*, Vol. 44, March-April, 1966, pp. 84–97.

doubtedly decrease. It is perhaps unrealistic, however, to expect this to be a feasible alternative, given the type of organizational structure prevalent in our society. It is a fact of organizational life that a superior has a fairly high degree of control over the means of satisfying the personal goals of subordinates. He can often, for example: fire, layoff, block promotion, block salary increase, or hold back developmental assignments if he doesn't like what he hears from a subordinate. Even though he may claim there is no penalty for disclosure, and, in fact, can refrain from applying one, as long as the subordinate believes there may be one, or believes he can't hold back a penalty even though he wants to, he in all probability will refrain from disclosure.

Eliciting Disclosure Decisions through Rewards

While it may not be feasible to create a situation in which a superior lacks control over the personal goals of subordinates, it may be possible for a superior to improve the chances of openness by rewarding incidences of disclosure. Stated in a propositional form:

The more a superior rewards disclosure of feelings, opinions and difficulties by subordinates, the more likely they will be to disclose them.

To create a relationship in which subordinates perceive disclosure as rewarding or not threatening, a superior can begin by telling them he expects them to have problems and disagreements and that he would like them to disclose them.

Obviously, simply telling them that they should feel free to discuss their feelings, opinions, and difficulties is not enough. They want to know if such actions on their part will, in fact, be rewarded or punished. Here, again, words by the superior to the effect that there will be no penalty are not sufficient to bring about a decision to disclose. Subordinates realize there is often a difference between what a superior says he wants to hear and what he actually wants to hear. The problem from their viewpoint is one of determining if he means what he says. How would he really react to disclosure? What types of disclosure can he tolerate? If he didn't like what I said, would he hold it against me?

These questions deal with the subordinate's perception of the consistency between the superior's words and actions. Are his actions consistent with his statement? It is a common belief in our culture that actions speak louder than words. Thus, it is perhaps not surprising that subordinates test out the consistency of a superior's words and actions by observing how he actually reacts to disagreements, expression of emotions, or reports of difficulties. If his response is a hostile or a demeaning one, they may conclude that there is a penalty for disclosure, even though he tells them there is not. In short, they may feel that his actions contradict his statements of the behavior he says he really wants, and they give priority to his actions. Because of the perceived penalty for disclosure, they learn to conceal their problems and disagreements from him.

At a minimum then, managing upward communication requires a superior to reinforce verbally stated expectations of leveling with actions that lead subordinates to view disclosure as a rewarded response or, at least, a response that does not result in a perceived penalty or threat. When subordinates made decisions to disclose, the superior must act in such a way that they will find the situation rewarding or at a minimum nonthreatening. Sometimes this means that he must act contrary to his natural inclinations. Any expression of hostility or impatience will be perceived by subordinates as a threat or a perceived penalty which will seal off disclosure in the future. To increase the probability of future disclosure, he must reward instances of disclosure, since rewarded responses tend to be repeated while unrewarded ones tend to be eliminated.

To further increase the probability of disclosure by subordinates, a superior may use himself as a disclosure model in his relationship with them or his own superior. When talking with them, he makes a practice of disclosing his feelings, opinions, and difficulties, demonstrating that he practices what he preaches. Stated in a propositional form:

The more a superior discloses his own feelings, opinions and difficulties to subordinates and his superior, the more likely subordinates will be to disclose theirs.

Such modeling would tend to reinforce his verbally stated desire for disclosure, thereby increasing the probability of disclosure.

To sum up, managing upward communication involves building a relationship with subordinates in which disclosure is encouraged and rewarded. It must be supported by the superior. Subordinates must know that they can express their feelings, difficulties, and opinions without fear of reprisal. They must look upon the superior as a source of help rather than as an all powerful judge.

QUESTIONS FOR REVIEW AND DISCUSSION

1. Discuss some important reasons why subordinates may not disclose full information to their superiors.
2. Comment fully on this statement, "The best practical way to decrease subordinates' fear of receiving a penalty for disclosure is to decrease the superior's control over the personal goals of the subordinate."
3. What are the recommendations presented in this article to elicit full disclosure by subordinates to their superior? Elaborate on your answer.

32. How to Make Downward Communication Work*

ANDREW B. CHASE, JR.

Company executives agree that there is an increasing need for effective employee communications systems if the company is to achieve "success." They also agree that employee information systems have as a starting point: objectives.[1] Management is realizing that in order to maintain closely knit ties with employees and to insure maximum output for the firm, the communication channels in a company must be modern, effective and as humanly personal as possible.[2]

Causes of Ineffective Downward Communications

At one time companies were small enough so that management was able to devote some of its time to face-to-face contact with its employees. Today, however, many companies have expanded to the point where such contact with employees is all but impossible. As a result,

1. The superior may fail to explain the subordinate's duties or fail to give the subordinate an accurate "picture" as to where he stands in the organization;
2. The subordinate may fail to understand an explanation and may not be in the position to question it; and
3. The management and subordinate may have a conflict of values. (Non-management personnel have a different value system. Consequently, management must orient the communications to the existing worker goals.)

---

* Source: Reprinted with permission of *Personnel Journal,* June 1970, pp. 478–83. Andrew B. Chase, Jr., is computer systems design engineer, E. I. Du Pont de Nemours and Company, Wilmington.

[1] Robert Heady, "What Is the Best Method of Employee Communications?" *Industrial Marketing* (April 1966), p. 31.
[2] C. J. Dover, *Management Communication on Controversial Issues* (Washington, D.C., BNA Incorporated, 1965), p. 24.

Major problems which can arise as a result of inadequate management of a company in attempting to communicate with employees include:

1. Getting the right information at the right time to the man who needs that information.
2. Getting messages accepted, understood, and acted upon. Part of the cause of this problem lies in the manner or technique used to channel the information. Many supervisors and managers can be good decision makers, but poor communicators.
3. Failure of the originator to formulate a clear objective before communicating.
4. The size of business and the magnitude of communication are problems in themselves.

Robert N. McMurry, Professor of Management at the Harvard School of Business, states that to keep communication failures at a minimum, personal contacts are necessary between top management and low level nonmanagement personnel. He also points out that by permitting personal discussions between the two parties with a direct "Feedback" from the workers, there could be a great elimination of misunderstandings.[3]

Regardless of the cause, the degree of communication failure between managers points to a defect which may be magnified in the behavior of people at lower organizational levels. Because of the great variety of causes, the problem of obtaining adequate communication and understanding between management and the workers is a complex one that defies any single solution.

Types of Downward Communication

There are four media of superior-subordinate communications in the business world; oral, written, both oral and written and visual communication. The oral and written mediums of communication have also been divided into the formal and the informal types.[4]

Oral communications involve person-to-person contact. It offers a man-to-man personal approach for a two-way discussion. It has the advantage of being rapid and can be quickly changed to meet the listener's mood and temperament. But at the same time, it has the disadvantage of being costly and it is prone to error in transmitting information.

Written communications provide recorded information and data which can be referred to at a moment's notice. This method of communication is best utilized in dealing with special situations and problems or events

---

[3] Robert N. McMurry, "Conflicts in Human Values," *Harvard Business Review* (May-June 1963), Vol. 41, No. 3, p. 139.

[4] William Scholz, *Communication in the Business Organization*, (Englewood Cliffs, New Jersey: Prentice-Hall, Inc., 1962), p. 87.

of general interest. For example, if a new plant is in the process of construction and top management wants to inform all of its employees about it at the same time, the company's house organ would probably be used to transmit the message.

The oral-written type of communication involves the person-to-person contact plus an exchange of information using written data. An example of this would be a situation where a superior presents certain project reports to his subordinates.

Finally, the visual method of communication is used in cases where instructions are given to a group. For example, a sales manager presenting new selling techniques to his salesmen might use charts or slides as part of the group training program.

Table 1 illustrates the most common type of superior-subordinate communication media.

TABLE 1. Methods of Communications Matrix

	Informal	*Formal*
Oral	Personal contacts	
	Interviews and Counseling	Staff Meetings
	Telecomm	Public Address System
	Employee Plant Tours (Orientation)	Conferences
		Order-giving and Instructions
Written	Company Magazines	Company Policies
	Bulletin Boards	Management Newsletters
	Daily News Digests	Company Reports
Both Oral and Written	Face-to-Face contact between superior and subordinate where written information is exchanged.	Company meetings where reports and data are presented.
Visual	Sound-Action Exhibits	Motion Pictures
	Closed-Circuit T.V.	Slides
		Chart Talks

Definition of the Problem

In a recent study conducted by the writer, the managements of over 150 firms, large, medium and small, old and new, union and nonunionized, indicated that ineffective downward communications existed because of:

1. The lack of clearly defined objectives.
2. The lack of proper understanding by management from top to bottom regarding responsibility for downward communications. Respondents holding top management positions felt that first-line supervisors should

be the ones to communicate to nonmanagement personnel, while respondents holding supervisory positions felt that it is top management's responsibility to communicate downward to all of its employees.
3. Management's failure to take time to see whether or not their present communication techniques are effective. While the majority of respondents ranked face-to-face contact as the most effective communication technique, many stated that because of the lack of time, formal written communiques have to be substituted for personal contact with subordinates.
4. Management's nonresponsiveness to holding regular meetings between supervisory and nonsupervisory personnel, to discuss current business and working conditions.
5. Finally, the lack of an established communications training program to teach management personnel the art of understanding role-playing, together with employee goal and value system differences. The management respondents felt that such a program would increase the effectiveness of communication events but at the same time would be very costly.[5]

Appraisal of Specific Downward Communication Methods

To have good communications between the superior and his subordinate, a number of physical and psychological elements must be present. First, there must be an objective for communicating. The executive who claims to have good communications but at the same time, is unable to specifically state certain objectives, is only deceiving himself in thinking that he will get his message across.

A second element of good downward communications is the content. The message to be transmitted must possess the following qualities:

1. It must be accurate. That is, the message must be a true report, be it good or bad, concerning information about the company. If, for example, management decides to report only a half truth concerning the company's financial position, and purposely tries to cover up certain important facts, this can do real harm since it gives official status to an error or worse yet, to a lie. When employees realize that the information management gives them is only partly accurate, they will pay little attention to what is transmitted to them in the future.
2. It must be both definite and specific in meaning. Management must state clearly the reasons why it has taken a specific stand. It must define not only certain actions taken, but must also demonstrate to the employees how all of the members of the company will be affected by these decisions.

[5] Andrew B. Chase, *A Survey of Downward Communication Problems.* MBA Thesis, (Drexel Institute of Technology, Philadelphia, June 1967).

3. It must be forceful, i.e., the message must be stated in a way to show that management carries a firm conviction for any actions taken which may affect the company. A manager who does not really believe in a decision which has been made, cannot honestly expect his employees to believe in its validity.
4. It must suit the occasion and must be receiver-oriented. The message must be stated in such a way that subordinates will have no trouble understanding how it directly affects them. For example, a message announcing a piece rate wage plan should say that it was designed to reward good workers.
5. It should not contain complexities, but be stated as simply as possible. The contents of the message should be transmitted in such a way that the recipient will understand and be able to grasp it quickly. The more complex the explanation, the harder it will be to get the point across to the subordinates. People will invest time and effort in understanding a message only in proportion to the importance of the message to them. An employee may spend two hours computing the number of vacation days to which he is entitled, but won't give even five minutes trying to understand a management directive concerned with reducing waste. To get and hold employee interest, the superior must discuss one point of the message at a time, and state the message in such a way that the employee will feel that he is an integral part of the operation.
6. Finally, it should contain no hidden meaning. A message may have one meaning under certain circumstances and another under different circumstances. To avoid misunderstanding, it is advisable to explain briefly the developments leading up to the message.

The third element of downward communications to be considered is that of the communication technique which should be employed to effectively get the message across to the recipient. The supervisor's daily face-to-face contact with his employee is the mainstay of all management communication.[6] In a survey conducted by Harold P. Zelko in regard to various forms of downward communications, it was found that aside from individual face-to-face contact, the most effective media were small employee meetings and management letters sent directly to employees' homes. Media considered least effective were morale posters, pamphlets on special subjects, pay inserts, and reading racks.[7]

Equally important is the need for certain psychological elements. The first of these is management's responsibility to recognize and understand the differences which exist between their own value system and that of the employees. Robert McMurry feels that before management can have a good communications system with its employees, it must first compare,

---

[6] Harold P. Zelko. "Downward Communications: A Survey of Company Practices," *Management Review* (May 1956), p. 344.
[7] Ibid.

as objectively as possible, its values with those of its employees, within the broad frame of reference of conditions which prevail within the company, the industry and the economy.[8] The aim of this comparison is for management to attempt to integrate conflicting desires of its employees, once it realizes their existence. If management decides to ignore the fact that these value differences exist, it will only be strengthening the barriers to good downward communications. Of course, as Mr. McMurry points out, it will never be possible to integrate the employees ideologies, completely. "Management must accept the fact that since most worker values cannot be significantly modified, the only thing left for it to do is to accept them as unchangeable facts of life and plan its communications program accordingly."[9]

Second, because management understands that many company goals are not in agreement with employee personal goals, management must see to it that the goals of the company are presented to the employee with the purpose of showing him how many of the company's goals coincide with his own. (See Figure 1.) In 1960, when Texas Instruments growth began to slow, the company decided to adopt a philosophy built on informal communication, company identification, and dedicated effort at all levels. The upshot was that it brought about closer informal communication ties between management and nonmanagement personnel, together with increased employee performance.[10]

Recommendations for Executives

Downward communications may be improved by the adoption of the following steps:

1. A communication training program for all management personnel should be initiated.
2. Top management should go out into the plant and offices regularly to talk to employees about their problems.
3. There should be regular and frequent meetings between supervisory and nonsupervisory personnel. All employees should be given a chance to participate.

The communications training program should be structured in such a way as to first introduce management personnel to the various formal and informal network overlays which exist within a typical company.

It should be explained by the professional trainers that the use of communication overlays emphasizes the inevitability of significant relation-

---

[8] Robert McMurry, "Conflicts in Human Values," *Harvard Business Review* (May-June 1963), p. 135.

[9] *Ibid.*

[10] Scott Myers, "Who are Your Motivated Workers?" *Harvard Business Review* (January-February 1964), Vol. 42, No. 1, pp. 73–76.

FIGURE 1. Theoretical Closed Communication Flow Plan

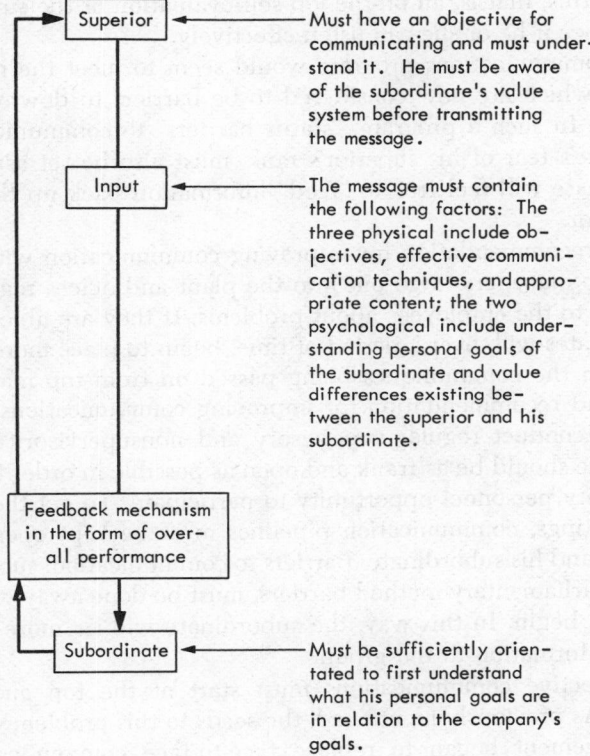

Superior ◄————— Must have an objective for communicating and must understand it. He must be aware of the subordinate's value system before transmitting the message.

Input ◄————— The message must contain the following factors: The three physical include objectives, effective communication techniques, and appropriate content; the two psychological include understanding personal goals of the subordinate and value differences existing between the superior and his subordinate.

Feedback mechanism in the form of overall performance

Subordinate ◄————— Must be sufficiently orientated to first understand what his personal goals are in relation to the company's goals.

ships other than the formal and, therefore, is very difficult to comprehend.[11] A discussion concerning the understanding of cultural differences which lead to goal and value system variations should be conducted.

The next phase of the program should include discussion of:

1. Objectives for communicating;
2. Effective methods or techniques used to communicate to a particular audience;
3. Whose responsibility it is to communicate downward; and
4. What should be contained within the message proper. The trainer should explain the importance of orienting messages toward employees' interests, such as, their own accomplishments, the true performance of the business relative to the entire industry, and operating problems within the company, as opposed to policies and procedures and day-to-day operating methods.

---

[11] Edwin B. Flippo. *Management: A Behavioral Approach,* (Allyn and Bacon, Boston, 1966) p. 470–71.

A final phase of such a program should include periodic in-the-field "listening" drills, that is, an on-the-job self-evaluation of the supervisor or manager to see if he or she can listen effectively.

Such a communications program would seem to meet the majority of deficiencies which are now considered to be barriers to downward communications. In such a program, "status barriers" to communication, i.e., a subordinate's fear of his superior's rank, must also be set aside so that the subordinate will feel free to "feed" information back up the channel to his superior.

The first recommendation for improving communication within a firm is for the top managers to go out into the plant and offices regularly and often to talk to the employees about problems. If they are able to do this the subordinates will, over a period of time, begin to place more trust and confidence in the communiques being passed on from top management.

The second recommendation for improving communications is for the company to conduct regular supervisory and nonsupervisory discussion groups. These should be as frank and open as possible in order to give the nonsupervisory personnel opportunity to participate. To get the most out of such meetings, communication pipelines must be kept open between the superior and his subordinate. Barriers to communication, such as status barriers or parliamentary method barriers, must be done away with before the meetings begin. In this way, the subordinate will be more willing to contribute information to the group.

Good, effective communications must start at the top and proceed downward. As previously mentioned, the seeds to this problem were sown when management began to replace face-to-face communication with more formalized, impersonal techniques. Although management has the primary responsibility of communicating pertinent matters to its employees, often the employees receive the information that they want to hear from either the grapevine or the union via union leaders or union newspapers.

There is no set formula which unconditionally guarantees successful communication between a supervisor and his subordinate. But by understanding all of the aforementioned variables, the success can be maximized.

In the final analysis, personal contact between superior and subordinate can lead to successful communication only when the superior realizes and understands that his subordinate's value system and goals may be completely opposed to his own. However, it must also be remembered that the enormous size and complexity of many businesses today, form a barrier which prevents face-to-face superior-subordinate communication.

QUESTIONS FOR REVIEW AND DISCUSSION

1. Relate the five reasons given in this article for the existence of ineffective downward communication in an enterprise.

2. What should be the contents of a communication training program as pointed out by writer Andrew B. Chase, Jr.?

3. Why is it deemed desirable for a manager to recognize and understand the differences which exist between his own value system and that of his subordinate?

4. For greater effectiveness the content of downward communication has certain characteristics. What are these characteristics? Discuss briefly.

33. On the Use of the Economic Concept of Human Capital in Financial Statements[*]

BARUCH LEV and ABA SCHWARTZ

> *"The most valuable of all capital is that invested in human beings."*
>
> Alfred Marshall, *Principles of Economics*

INTRODUCTION

The dichotomy in accounting between human and nonhuman capital is fundamental; the latter is recognized as an asset and therefore is recorded in the books and reported in the financial statement, whereas the former is totally ignored by accountants. Most economists, on the other hand, have a different view on this issue. Milton Friedman, for example, states:

> From the broadest and most general point of view, total wealth includes all sources of "income" or consumable services. One such source is the productive capacity of human beings, and accordingly this is one form in which wealth can be held. [8, p. 4][†]

The definition of wealth as a source of income inevitably leads to the recognition of human capital as one of several forms of holding wealth, such as money, securities, and physical (nonhuman) capital. This attitude toward human capital has a broad range of applications in economics. For example, the value of human capital appears in some demand functions for money (of business enterprises as well as households) as an argu-

---

[*] Source: Reprinted with permission of *Accounting Review*, January 1971, pp. 103–12. Baruch Lev is chairman of the department of business administration, The Hebrew University of Jerusalem. Aba Schwartz is lecturer in economics, The University of Tel-Aviv, Israel.

The authors are deeply indebted to Professor Sidney Davidson, Dean of the Graduate School of Business, University of Chicago, for helpful comments.

† Numbers in brackets refer to reference at the end of the chapter.

ment along with other forms of nonhuman wealth [8, pp. 9, 13], human capital is recognized as an important factor in explaining and predicting economic growth [2], etc. Human capital is thus treated in modern economic theory on a par with other forms of earning assets.

On the other hand, the different attitude of accountants toward human capital was succinctly expressed as follows:

A favorite cliché for the president's letter in corporate reports is "our employees are our most important—our most valuable—asset." Turning from the president's letter and looking to the remainder of the report, one might ask, "where is this human asset on these statements which serve as reports of the firm's resources and earnings? What is the value of this most important or most valuable asset? Is it increasing, decreasing, or remaining unchanged?" [4, p. 217]

The objective of this article is to provide a practical measurement procedure by which some of the questions raised in the preceding quotation can be answered. Specifically, the possibility of using the economic concept and measurement of human capital in financial statements is explored. It is shown that the suggested method provides decision makers with information about organizational matters hitherto not reported by accountants. The order of discussion is as follows: Section II provides a discussion of the concept of human capital and its measurement. Section III extends this concept to the firm's level. Section IV elaborates on implications for decision makers from human capital reporting. Section V discusses some conceptual accounting problems involved in incorporating human capital values in the financial statements. Finally, Section VI provides some concluding remarks. The Appendix presents a hypothetical example demonstrating the measurement of a firm's human capital.

THE CONCEPT OF HUMAN CAPITAL

Irving Fisher, one of the originators of human capital theory, notes:

Capital in the sense of capital value is simply future income discounted, in other words, capitalized. . . . But the basic problem of time valuation which nature sets us is that of translating the future into the present, that is, the problem of ascertaining the capital value of future income. *The value of capital must be computed from the value of its estimated future net income, not vice versa.* [7, pp. 12–14, emphasis supplied.]

Capital is thus defined as a source of income stream and its worth is the present value of future income discounted by a rate specific to the owner of the source (or to the potential buyer).

Fisher's definition does not distinguish between human capital, which is a source of income embodied in a person (in the form of his brute force and his natural and acquired skills), and nonhuman capital. There is, however, an important distinction: the ownership of human capital is nontransferable (in a nonslave society) while nonhuman capital can be traded in the market. In a world of certainty this distinction is of no consequence for the determination of capital values since certainty implies a perfect knowledge of future income streams associated with the source and of future discount rates. Given this knowledge, the present value (i.e., worth) of human as well as nonhuman capital can be uniquely determined. In a world of uncertainty, however, future income streams and discount rates are not perfectly known and consequently the present value of the source cannot be uniquely (objectively) determined. Nevertheless, in the case of nonhuman capital we can still infer its value from observed market prices which reflect the present value of future earnings to the traders. Such a derivation of value from market prices cannot be made in the case of human capital since it is not traded. Thus, in a world of uncertainty an important distinction exists between human and nonhuman capital.

The difficulty in determining the value of human capital under uncertainty is responsible for the initial lack of systematic treatment of the subject in economics. However, during the last two decades economists have become aware of the grave consequences of this omission, as Gary Becker notes:

Recent years have witnessed intensive concern with and research on investment in human capital, much of it contributed or stimulated by T. W. Schultz. The main motivating factor has probably been a realization that the growth of physical capital, at least as conventionally measured explained a relatively small part of the growth of income in most countries. The search for better explanation has led to improved measures of physical and to an interest in less tangible entities, such as technological change and human capital. [2, p. 1.]

Consequently, a theory of human capital measurement has been developed and its impact on macroeconomic problems investigated [2, 3, 9, 11, 12, 14, 15, 16, 17, 18]. An extension of this approach to the firm's level, as advanced in this paper, seems natural.

The Earnings Profile

An earnings profile is a graphic or mathematical presentation of the income stream generated by a person (i.e., by his human capital), see Fig. 1. A typical earnings profile first increases with age, reflecting the capability of human beings to earn (on the job or elsewhere) and thus increase their productivity. As the person ages, productivity declines because of technological obsolescence and health deterioration, a fact expressed by a decrease in the annual earnings. Since the profile reflects only earnings from employment and not from capital assets it terminates at retirement or on death if that occurs earlier.

FIGURE 1. Earnings Profiles of U.S. Males, 1949

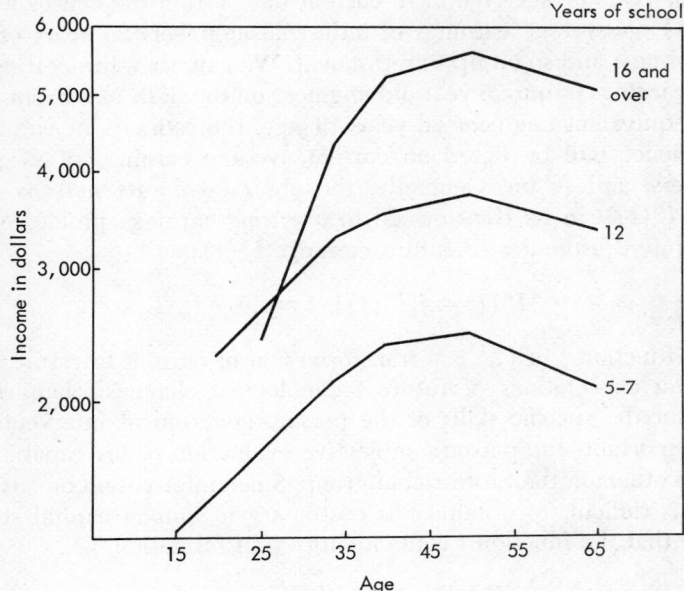

Source: U.S. Census of Population (1950), Ser. P-E, No. 5-B: Education, Tables 12, 13.

Measurement of Human Capital

The value of human capital embodied in a person of age τ is the present value of his remaining future earnings from employment. This value for a discrete income stream is:

$$V_\tau = \sum_{t=\tau}^{T} \frac{I(t)}{(1+r)^{t-\tau}} \tag{1}$$

where:

V_τ = the human capital value of a person τ years old.
$I(t)$ = the person's annual earnings up to retirement. This series is graphically represented by the earnings profile.
r = a discount rate specific to the person.
T = retirement age.

Strictly speaking, expression (1) is an *ex post* computation of human capital value at any age of the person, since only after retirement is the series $I(t)$ known. This is of little use in our case where we need the *ex ante* values of human capital. Hence, the observed values of $I(t)$ in (1) should be replaced by estimates $I^*(t)$ of future annual earnings. The best source of information for these estimates is current data on earnings distribution classified by age, education, skill, etc. Consider, for example, the problem of estimating the future earnings series of an industrial engineer, 25 years of age. We have current data (from the census and other sources) on average earnings of industrial engineers 25 years of age, 26 years of age, and so on up to retirement. We can, therefore, estimate next year's earnings of our 25 year old engineer on the basis of current earnings of an equivalent engineer 26 years of age, the estimate of earnings two years hence will be based on current average earnings of 27 year old engineers, and so on. Generally, the observed *across persons* earnings profile $I°(t)$ can be transformed to *overtime* earnings profile, providing the required estimates of future earnings $I^*(t)$:

$$I^*(t) = f[I°(t)], \ t = \tau, \cdot \cdot \cdot, T. \tag{2}$$

The function f in (2) is a transformation of current to future earnings reflecting expectations of future technological changes, changes in demand for the specific skills of the person, government intervention, and most important—the person's subjective evaluation of his capabilities relative to others in the professional group. Since information on such future events is difficult to obtain, it is customary in human capital studies to assume that the function f is the identity transformation, i.e.,

$$I^*(t) = I°(t), \ t = \tau, \cdot \cdot \cdot, T \tag{3}$$

Thus, the prediction of next year's earnings of the 25 year old engineer will be equal to (not just based on) current earnings of a 26 year old equivalent engineer.[1] The estimated human capital value of a person τ years old is thus:

$$V_\tau^* = \sum_{t=\tau}^{T} \frac{I^*(t)}{(1+r)^{t-\tau}} \tag{4}$$

where $I^*(t)$ is determined by (3).

Expression (4) ignores the possibility of death occurring prior to retirement age. This can be incorporated into the model by the use of mortality tables which provide the death probabilities. Specifically, the probability of a person dying at age t is presented by the long-run mortality rates of persons with the same characteristics (race, sex, education, etc.). When this probability is $P_\tau(t)$, the *expected value* of the person's human capital is:[2]

$$E(V_\tau^*) = \sum_{t=\tau}^{T} P_\tau(t+1) \sum_{i=\tau}^{t} \frac{I_i^*}{(1+r)^{t-\tau}} \tag{5}$$

---

[1] In cases where price level changes are significant, an adjustment for these changes can be made. Specifically, $I^*(t)$ will equal $I°(t)$ adjusted for expected price level changes.

[2] $P_\tau(t)$ is the conditional probability of a person of age τ dying in year t.

Statistical Sources

Since our main purpose is to advance a *practical* application of human capital concepts in accounting we briefly discuss some sources of data.

Practically all empirical studies concerned with human capital measurements in the U.S. are based on the 1960 census data published by the Bureau of the Census [19]. This census provides cross-sectional data on earnings classified by age, race, sex, education, geographic area of employment, etc., and most useful for our application—by profession or skill. Average earnings profiles of professional groups of employees (e.g., unskilled employees in the meat packing industry) can be determined from these data. The earnings profiles can be refined by keeping constant several personal characteristics. For example, if an average earnings profile for electrical engineers is too crude (i.e., the group of electrical engineers in the U.S. is too heterogeneous), the earnings profile of white, male electrical engineers, employed in the automobile industry, can be determined, thereby making the group for which an earnings profile is determined more homogeneous.[3]

Of special importance for practical use is a condensed version of the 1960 census available on magnetic tape. This is a 0.1 percent random sample of the total U.S. population included in the census. Since a complete census is taken every 10 years, current data will soon be available.

Mortality tables, needed for formula (5), are available for every country and region. Such tables are extensively used by life insurance companies in determining their premium scale and reserves.

HUMAN CAPITAL VALUE ASSOCIATED WITH THE FIRM

We have discussed thus far the conceptual and practical problems involved in measuring the capital value of a person or a homogeneous group of persons. The determination of the total value of a firm's labor force is a straightforward extension. The firm's labor force will be divided into homogeneous groups of employees such as unskilled employees, semiskilled, skilled, engineers of different kinds, salesmen, managerial staff, etc. Average earnings profiles, based on census data, will be constructed for each group and the present value of human capital calculated. The sum of present values over the various employee groups will provide the total human capital value associated with the firm. A simple hypothetical example of such a computation is provided in the Appendix.

The firm's value of human capital thus measured is based on average earnings data of homogeneous groups of employees in the U.S. A given firm, however, may employ persons of higher or lower quality than the

---

[3] For the practical construction of such refined profiles, see [9].

average and accordingly pay different wages and salaries than those indicated by the census-based data. If the firm employs a large number of employees of different kinds it will be possible to determine earnings profiles based on the firm's own wage scale. Specifically, cross-sectional data on wages currently paid to groups of employees will be substituted for the census data to determine the earnings profiles. We can thus compute for a firm's labor force a *general* value of human capital and a *specific* value, the former based on overall census data and the latter on the specific wage scale of the firm. It should be emphasized again that the specific value of human capital can be computed only if the firm's labor force is large, i.e., when there is an ample amount of cross-sectional data to form the earnings profiles. The appropriate discount rate for determining the firm's human capital value seems to be the cost of capital. This is the rate used in capital budgeting decisions and also the opportunity cost of the firm's resources.

IMPLICATIONS OF HUMAN CAPITAL REPORTING

Disclosure of human capital values by business enterprises will provide financial statement users with valuable information. The relevance of this information lies in the fact that it concerns organizational changes in the firm's labor force hitherto not reported by accountants. Following are some inferences for decision makers (investors as well as management) that could be drawn from reported values of human capital.

(a) The determination of human capital values suggests a new set of financial ratios. For example:

The ratio of human to nonhuman capital indicates the degree of labor intensiveness in the firm. The extent of labor intensity is believed to have widespread implications for the firm's operations. For example, economists, especially in the area of industrial organization, investigate the effect of labor (or capital) intensity on inter- and intra-industry variations in rates of return. The relative degrees of labor and capital intensity within countries are believed to affect world trade.[4] Lacking direct measures for labor intensity, economists use indirect ones such as value added per employee, or sales per employee. Such measures are crude since they treat all employees as equal; a highly skilled engineer and a janitor are given the same weight in the measure. The suggested ratio of human to nonhuman capital assigns different weights to different employees according to their earning power. Labor intensity thus measured reflects the quality as well as the quantity of the labor force.

---

[4] This is the well known Heckscher-Ohlin factor proportions theory which asserts that each country exports that commodity which is most intensive in the country's abundant factor.

The firm's total value of human capital can be disaggregated according to subgroups of the labor force (see example in the Appendix of this reading). Several ratios are suggested by such a disaggregation; for example, the ratio of the value of scientific staff to the total value of human capital. This ratio indicates the extent of "skill (scientific) intensity" in the firm. Skill intensive industries are those with a relatively large scientific and research staff, e.g., chemical products, electronics, pharmaceuticals, etc. The effect of skill intensity on rate of return and growth is a currently debated issue. Here again researchers use extremely crude measures to detect the effect of skill intensity such as R & D expenses, number of college graduates as a percentage of the total number of employees, etc. Such measures are not sensitive to variations within the scientific employee group, whereas the suggested measure reflects such variations.

(b) Reported human capital values will provide information about changes in the structure of the labor force. For example, differences over time in the values of a firm's human capital may result from changes in the age distribution (i.e., "vintage") of employees. Recall that human capital values are determined by capitalizing earnings over the expected useful life (to the enterprise) of employees. Therefore, a change in the age distribution of the labor force would obviously affect the firm's human capital values. Suppose, for example, that no change has taken place in the structure of the labor force during 1969 (i.e., no employees were hired or laid off). In this case, the value of the firm's human capital at the end of 1969 would be smaller than that of the previous year (assuming, of course, no changes in the earnings profiles). The firm's time series of human capital value thus contains information about changes in the structure of the labor force. The phenomenon of an "aging firm" often discussed in organization theory will be indicated by such a time series when other factors (e.g., number of employees) are held constant. It has been suggested that the aging of the firm's labor force affects its rate of growth and relative share in the industry vis-à-vis the "younger" and more aggressive firm's labor force. Such hypotheses can be tested by using the reported values of human capital.

(c) The difference between the general and specific values of human capital (discussed in the preceding section) is another source of valuable information for management and the analyst. The specific value of human capital is based on the firm's actual wage scale while the general value is based on industry-wide wage averages. The difference between the two therefore indicates the level of the firm's wage scale relative to the industry average. Specifically, if the industry-wide wage averages are taken as a standard, this difference indicates to what extent the firm's wage scale is above, on a par with or below the standard. Such information which is not currently communicated to users, may explain the observed phenomenon of firms which consistently pay higher wages than the industry averages. It is sometimes argued that such firms employ the professional elite and hence experience a higher rate of return or growth than their competitors. Others are skeptical about such a hiring policy claiming that when wages are equal to employees' marginal productivity[5] then no extra returns can result from employing superior employees. Reporting the general and specific values of human capital will thus enable users to investigate the effects of specific wage and hiring policies.

Management might try to increase profits in the short run by hiring low quality employees. Such a policy can produce damaging effects which will be realized only in the long run. However, if human capital values are reported they will currently reflect the change in hiring policy and thereby deter management.

CONCEPTUAL ISSUES IN REPORTING HUMAN CAPITAL VALUES

The problem of reporting human capital values in financial statements has two distinct aspects: (a) the measurement of the value of the firm's work force which is the subject of this article, and (b) measurement and amortization of the firm's *investment* in human resources. The few articles concerning human capital reporting in financial statements [4, 5, 6, 13] deal exclusively with the second aspect.[6]

It is often assumed that the objective of human resource accounting is to determine the net worth, or dollar value of an individual employee to a firm. This is not the case. Rather, we are trying to develop concepts and techniques for measuring a firm's investment in its human organization, the rate at which those investments are being consumed, and which investments are more productive than others. This is not the same as measuring the value of individuals and surely raises *fewer objections*. [13, p. 46, emphasis supplied]

What are the objections that can be raised against the incorporation of human capital values in accounting reports?

(a) It can be argued that human capital (excluding a slave society) cannot be purchased or owned by the firm and therefore would not be

---

[5] This will be the case when the firm's production function is homogeneous to the first degree.

[6] Most of the research on the subject has been conducted by R. Lee Brummet, Willard Graham Professor of Business Administration at the University of North Carolina, and William J. Pyle of the Institute for Social Research at the University of Michigan. Preliminary results of this research are reflected in the 1969 financial reports of R. G. Barry Corporation which was the first to report investment in human resources. For a description of this case, see [13].

recognized as an asset in accounting. This is obviously true with respect to individual employees who can usually resign at will[7]; however, it is not so obvious with respect to the firm's *labor force* as a whole. As long as employees can be replaced it does not matter for our purpose whether the labor force always contains the same persons or is a rapidly changing group. The labor force as a whole is constantly associated with the firm and it can be constructively regarded as being "owned" by it.

Moreover, in modern economies where firms are usually purchased as going concerns (e.g., merger), payment is often made for intangible assets such as a stable and high quality labor force.[8] For example, it is customary in the insurance industry to determine the value of the sales force at the time of acquisition or sale. This is usually done by forecasting the firm's future earnings, determining its present value, and then allocating a portion of the present value to the human resources. A firm's human capital can thus be purchased and in a sense "owned" by it.

(b) It can be argued that the labor force is not an asset since it does not have a "service potential" extending beyond the current period. Specifically, employees are paid for rendering *current* services and no asset is formed by these payments. If this were true then no firm would invest in (as opposed to maintain) human capital. However, the prevalence of programs such as orientation courses for new employees, executive programs, employees' training programs, facilities for improving employees' morale, etc., is evidence to the contrary. Such expenditures are made with the expectation of future returns, i.e., they increase the service potential embodied in human capital and this creates an asset.

The problem of reporting human capital values is closely related to the issue of long-term leases and other executory contracts. In both cases the firm rents the services of capital (human in the former, physical in the latter) owned by others. Those who favor the presentation of leased assets on the balance sheet would similarly endorse the reporting of human capital.

Accounting at present recognizes most market transactions involving goods, services or money as one of the elements of the transaction. Present accounting also generally ignores, except in special circumstances, transactions involving an exchange of a promise for a promise. Leases, purchase commitments, executive and other labor contracts are generally denied recognition until the services or goods specified in the contract are either used, delivered, or paid for. Many of these contracts meet the standards of verifiability, freedom from bias, and quantifiability at least as well as other reported events. [1, p. 32]

---

[7] This statement ignores long-term employment contracts whose importance in the U.S. is declining.

[8] All payments for intangible assets are aggregated by accountants in the goodwill resulting from acquisition.

In accordance with the suggested presentation of long-term leases, human capital values may be presented on the assets side of the balance sheet and the present value of the firm's liability to pay wages and salaries on the liabilities side. The two values are equal by definition: Changes in the values of human capital from period to period would not be recognized as income but would merely be matched by changes in the liability.

(c) Some accountants might accept the notion of human capital being an asset yet object to reporting it on the grounds that it cannot be "objectively" measured. We feel, however, that the preceding sections demonstrated that the degree of objectivity in human capital measurements, which are usually based on census data, is not lower than that of many conventional valuations in accounting. For example, depreciation charges are often estimated from industry-wide equipment mortality data,[9] the determination of reserves by life insurance companies is based on general mortality tables, pension liabilities and product guarantees are also statistically estimated.

The above arguments suggest that human capital values may be an integral part of financial statements. This conclusion is consistent with the recommendations of the AAA committee in *A Statement of Basic Accounting Theory*

External users may wish to know degrees of employee morale, customer satisfaction, product quality, and reputation of a given entity. If quantification of these were possible, a substantial amount of additional relevant information could be provided the external users. The accountant must constantly be alert to the possible applications of new measurement methods to develop additional quantifiable information for external users. [1, p. 29]

CONCLUDING REMARKS

The value of the human capital associated with a business enterprise is not reflected in its financial reports. While some initial strides have been made toward measuring and amortizing the investment in human resources, the determination of human capital values is still an unsolved (and untouched) problem. The economic theory of human capital provides the basis for a practical solution to this problem.

The major limitation in the concept and measurement procedures advanced above is that the firm's value of human capital is not necessarily equal to the portion of the firm's income contributed by the labor force. Specifically, labor is one of several inputs in the production process; its value therefore, should be determined on the basis of that portion of total income contributed by it. Such a determination of value accords

---

[9] See in this context a recent suggestion for using the life expectancy of physical assets for estimating depreciation [10].

with the well-known accounting concept of "service potential." However, in real life, input factors are interdependent and there is probably no practical way of dividing the total contribution among them. Consequently, accounting values of physical assets are determined by their market prices and not by their relative contribution to the firm. Therefore it seems reasonable that values of human capital may also be similarly determined. In the absence of market prices for human capital, the best approximation to its value is the measurement procedure based on census or firm earnings data.

TABLE 1. Distribution of Employees by Age and Skill

Age	Unskilled	Semi-skilled	Skilled	Profes-sionals	Total
25–34	700	–	10	40	750
35–44	300	40	10	30	380
45–54	–	10	20	20	50
55–64	–	–	–	10	10
Total	1,000	50	40	100	1,190

APPENDIX

The computation of the firms value of human capital is demonstrated in the following hypothetical example. Table 1 shows the decomposition of employees in the firm by age groups and degrees of skill. Table 2

TABLE 2. Average Annual Earnings (Dollars) Classified by Age and Skill

Age	Unskilled	Semi-skilled	Skilled	Profes-sionals
25–34	5,000	6,000	7,500	10,000
35–44	5,500	7,000	8,000	12,000
45–54	6,000	7,500	9,000	13,000
55–64	5,500	7,000	9,000	15,000

TABLE 3. Total Values of Human Capital (Dollars) by Age and Skill (capitalization rate = 10 percent)

Age	Unskilled	Semi-skilled	Skilled	Profes-sionals	Total
25–34	35,822,500	–	764,310	4,281,760	40,868,570
35–44	15,908,400	2,686,880	786,990	3,546,990	22,929,260
45–54	–	626,670	1,529,540	2,308,440	4,464,650
55–64	–	–	–	921,600	921,600
Total ..	51,730,900	3,313,550	3,080,840	11,058,790	69,184,080

shows average annual earnings for each age and skill group. These data can be obtained from the census or from the firm's own current wages. The data in Tables 1 and 2 are sufficient for calculating the present values of future earnings for each group of employees, i.e., the values of human capital. These values (assuming a capitalization rate of 10 percent) are presented in Table 3. For example, the total human capital value of the 700 unskilled employees in the age group 25–34 is $35,822,500.[10] The total human capital value associated with the firm is $69,184,080. The degree of skill intensity in the firm is measured by the ratio of professionals to total human capital value:

$$\frac{11,058,790}{69,184,080} = 0.16.$$

REFERENCES

1. AAA, *A Standard of Basic Accounting Theory* (American Accounting Association, 1966).
2. G. S. Becker, *Human Capital* (Columbia University Press, National Bureau of Economic Research No. 80, 1964).
3. M. J. Bowman, and R. G. Meyers, "Schooling, Experience, and Gains and Losses in Human Capital Through Migration," *Journal of the American Statistical Association,* 62 (September 1967) pp. 875–98.
4. R. L. Brummet, E. G. Flamholtz, and W. C. Pyle, "Human Resource Measurement—A Challenge for Accountants," *The Accounting Review,* 43 (April 1968), pp. 217–30.
5. ——, ——, and ——, (Editors), *Human Resource Accounting: Development and Implementation in Industry* (Ann Arbor, Michigan: Foundation for Research on Human Behavior, 1969).
6. J. Douthat, "Accounting for Personnel Training and Development Costs," *Training and Development Journal,* 24 (June 1970), pp. 2–6.
7. I. Fisher, *The Theory of Interest* (A. M. Kelley, Reprint of Economic Classics, 1961).
8. M. Friedman, "The Quantity Theory of Money—A Restatement," in *Studies in the Quantity Theory of Money* (The University of Chicago Press, 1956).
9. G. Hanoch, "Personal Earning and Investment in Schooling," unpublished Ph.D. dissertation, University of Chicago, 1965.

---

[10] This value is obtained by the following calculation. Assume, for simplicity, that all the 700 employees are 25 years old. The future earnings stream (based on Table 2) for each employee is:

$5,000 a year for the next 10 years,
$5,500 a year for 11 to 20,
$6,000 a year for years 21 to 30, and
$5,500 a year for years 31 to 40.

The present value of this series of 40 numbers multiplied by 700 (the number of employees in the group) is equal to $35,822,500. The discount rate is 10 percent. All other values in Table 3 were similarly calculated.

10. Y. Ijiri, and R. S. Kaplan, "Probabilistic Depreciation and Its Implications for Group Depreciation," *The Accounting Review*, 44 (October 1969), pp. 743–56.

11. J. Mincer, "Investment in Human Capital and Personal Income Distributions," *The Journal of Political Economy*, 66 (August 1958), pp. 281–302.

12. ——, "On-the-Job Training: Costs, Returns, and Some Implications," *The Journal of Political Economy*, 70 (October 1962), pp. 50–79.

13. W. Pyle, "Accounting for Your People," *Innovation*, 10 (1970), pp. 46–55.

14. A. Schwartz, "Migration and Earnings in the U.S.," unpublished Ph.D. dissertation, University of Chicago, 1968.

15. T. W. Schultz, "Investment in Human Capital," *American Economic Review*, 51 (March 1961), pp. 1–17.

16. ——, "Reflections on Investment in Men," *The Journal of Political Economy*, Supplement, 70 (October 1962), pp. 1–8.

17. ——, *The Economic Value of Education* (Columbia University Press, 1963).

18. L. Sjaasted, "The Costs and Returns of Human Migration," *The Journal of Political Economy*, 70 (October 1962), pp. 80–93.

19. U.S. Bureau of the Census, *U.S. Census of the Population:* 1960. Vol. I. Characteristics of the Population, Parts 1–50. (Washington, D.C.: U.S. Government Printing Office, 1963). See especially, Subject Reports: Education Attainment, Final Report PC(2)5B. (U.S. Government Printing Office, 1963).

QUESTIONS FOR REVIEW AND DISCUSSION

1. Comment fully on this quotation, "Some accountants might accept the notion of human capital being an asset yet object to reporting it on the grounds that it cannot be 'objectively' measured."

2. Do you feel the means for measuring human capital presented in this article would be helpful to a business such as a professional football team in determining the worth of a player bought or sold? Discuss.

3. Discuss some important implications of human capital reporting brought out by this article.

4. Referring to the appendix of this reading, in Table 1, the ratio of professionals to total work force is 100 to 1190, or .084, whereas the degree of skill intensity is shown as .016. How do you account for this difference?

34. New Life for Dead Enders*

On the surface, Ammazz Paper Products Co. appeared to be extremely fortunate. When its sales manager retired, Ammazz had two assistant sales managers, both apparently capable of stepping smoothly into the top job and both 55 years old.

After a thorough study of their qualifications, Bill Johnson was rated slightly more capable and was given the sales manager job instead of John Brown. So Ammazz seemed to be set for the next ten years with a sales manager who almost certainly would be effective, and with a proven assistant.

However, that rosy situation never materialized. Mr. Brown's bitterness about not getting the promotion disappeared quickly, but something else stepped in and severely damaged his performance.

Mr. Brown realized that the sales manager position probably would not be open again until about the time he would retire. So, he faced the prospect of spending the rest of his career doing the same thing he already had done for a number of years, even though he was capable of doing more. He had reached a dead end. He had no motivation to continue to excel.

Ammazz Paper Products Co. wasn't so fortunate after all. It had a big problem.

On the other hand, Bemuzz Tool Co. apparently had no such problem with Joe Smith. He was a first-class engineer, in fact, one of the best anywhere at transforming an industrial need into an efficient machine tool. Mr. Smith was 45 years old, and so Bemuzz was counting on another two decades of engineering excellence from him.

Bemuzz executives also were familiar with Dr. Laurence J. Peter's principle, and they believed they knew enough about Joe Smith to be fairly certain that the next logical step for him in the hierarchy—to engineering management—would be a disastrous promotion to his level of incompetence.

Mr. Smith preferred to handle his projects all alone as much as possible, taking care of even the most minute details himself rather than letting

* Source: Reprinted with permission from *Industry Week*, August 16, 1971, pp. 36–42. Copyright, Penton Publishing Co., Cleveland, Ohio.

some of the willing and able younger engineers help out. This may be a great quality in an engineer (which he would continue to be), but it certainly is a poor one in a manager (which his superiors would not let him become).

A perfect situation? Only on the surface. After several years of watching less capable engineers promoted to management, Mr. Smith concluded he was in the same boat with Mr. Brown, our would-be sales manager. Although his company would have occasional vacancies above him which Mr. Brown's would not, Mr. Smith also had reached a dead end. His motivation disintegrated, and his performance declined.

Bemuzz, like Ammazz, had a problem.

"You run into it frequently," says Byron Hoyt, contracts administrator, Rocker Industries, Harbor City, Calif.

And it's a bewildering problem. While he can point to the example of an ex-foreman at Rocker who returned to a partsmaking job and found happiness as a dead-ender, Mr. Hoyt admits: "To be quite honest, we've never found a really good answer. Frequently there seems to be nothing to motivate that individual—other than that little carrot which still is hanging out in front of him which he is never going to reach."

Some "Candidates" Nominated

So the search for the answer goes on.

Some believe it lies in the area of job enrichment, the specialty of Roy W. Walters, president, Roy W. Walters & Associates, Ridgewood, N.J. His approach is to motivate an employee in a dead-end job by "continually redesigning that job."

Another approach uses a format of alternative career paths, switching a dead-ender to another of the company's job hierarchies where the possibility of advancement exists. One variation of this is the flexible hierarchy philosophy practiced by Douglas N. Jones, corporate director of employee relations, International Business Machines Corp. (IBM), Armonk, N.Y.

In some cases, such as Joe Smith's, a "dual ladder" system allows motivation through money and status without promotion to the employee's level of incompetence. Dow Chemical Co., Midland, Mich., has used such a system for nearly two decades to prevent the creation of that type of dead end.

And motivating employees in dead-end jobs is only one of the payoffs derived from twice-a-year conversations each manager at Universal Foods Corp., Milwaukee, has with each of his subordinates. Universal's president, Robert T. Foote, believes that "the best way to motivate persons for whom promotion is unlikely is to make their personal objectives and the company's objectives compatible," with the manager-subordinate talks as the vehicle for achieving this compatibility.

Dead-End Jobs Can Be Richer

Job enrichment can be an effective tool for motivating dead-enders, Mr. Walters says, because his concept of enrichment challenges the validity of the traditional business hierarchy and its symbol, the organization chart.

"Most people, when they think of job design, think of little boxes," he continues, "and they even try to define particular jobs with little descriptions, which I think are useless and meaningless pieces of paper. I'm trying to get people to see that, if they want people to continue to grow and develop, that box really ought to be conically shaped, getting larger and larger and probably having a dotted line across the top."

As an example of "box" jobs, he cites a major company in heavy industry which is now attempting to enrich its sales jobs. The salesmen "are guys who make from $25,000 to $60,000 a year, and they are willing to say that really their jobs haven't changed in 20 years," Mr. Walters explains. "And I say, 'How dull!' If I'm a salesman, even though I'm making good money, and my job's the same as it was 20 years ago, I'm probably bored out of my tree. So the problem becomes: how do you redesign that work so that the guy continues to get excitement out of his job?"

Such an employee's manager must "add requirements for new learning and add new responsibilities, even though they may be very minor in nature. In other words, his superior must try to coax new growth out of him," he says, claiming such efforts are beginning to pay off, as indicated by the following exclamation from a dead-ender in the 55- to 60-age bracket:

"You know, for the first time I'm beginning to get excited about my work. Now, when I come home at night, I don't say, 'Do you know what those guys swindled me out of today?' I say, 'Look what they let me do today!'"

Mr. Walters challenges those managers who believe a subordinate has reached his highest level of competency. "I think there are areas in which they don't know much about a man's competency," he argues. "Most people have capabilities that we're not aware of, because the circumstances of their jobs never caused them to be demonstrated. I think management's job is to cause those capabilities to be shown."

As an alternative to the hierarchy which produces dead-end jobs simply because there are no openings at a higher level, he suggests "a fluid and dynamic concept of jobs. I don't think they can be allowed to 'run out.' They must constantly be looked at for change."

Referring to this "John Brown" variety of dead-ender, Mr. Walters says: "If I'm his boss, he's not going to knock me off, because I have a seat higher than his, and there's only one. So I have to keep him growing. Really what I must do is to start shoving him some of the things I'm doing.

"Now that comes as a little bit of a threat to some bosses, but we can overcome that by saying, 'You've given more responsibility to that subordinate you thought was dead-ended, and that frees you up for maybe 8 hours a week. Now what are you going to do with that time? What you must do is reach up to the boss above you and ask what he's going to give you.'

"Once you start that process, you have a very healthy, growing, fighting, dynamic, aggressive organization."

Sounds good, but does it work? Definitely, says Jewell Westerman, secretary, Travelers Insurance Co., Hartford, Conn. The enrichment program at Travelers was applied at the entry level—keypunch operators—but the program could apply at any level, and in fact this one had an impact on higher levels. And the enriched jobs weren't dead-ended in the John Brown or Joe Smith sense, but the size of the operators-to-supervisor ratio minimized the motivational value of potential promotion.

Specifically, Travelers made these changes:

"First of all, we made people responsible for their own unit of work," Mr. Westerman says. Included was responsibility for scheduling—and for meeting those schedules.

"Now they can correct obvious coding errors. Before, they were told to punch it as they saw it. They know coding as well as anybody, and it was frustrating for them to punch in the wrong code."

They took over responsibility from supervisors for keeping records on how they spent their time and on quality and quantity—and are doing it more accurately.

Each operator now corrects her own errors. "Before, the errors came back from the computer and were given to any operator." The new system provides feedback and aids training.

"They deal directly with clients. Before, work was given to them in one-hour batches with no identification. Now an operator has her own customer (such as the payroll department) with full responsibility for that client's jobs. If there is a problem, the operator, not the supervisor, discusses it with the client, so there is a little entrepreneurship built in."

As a result, there have been increases in productivity and quality (30%), and improvement has been noted in the absentee and turnover rates and attitude.

However, the changes "created a vacuum in the supervisors' jobs," Mr. Westerman adds. "Whereas supervisors had been just sophisticated keypunch operators, we now have forced a behavior change on them by taking their work away. They were forced into different kinds of duties which they structured themselves and took from their bosses. This gave them a higher order of tasks to perform, a more important job.

"This same thing happened to the manager of the unit. We created a vacuum in his job by moving work back down the organization. As people get promoted, they tend to take their work with them. So what this does is to change that flow and start pulling the work back down. Now the manager is doing the budgeting, planning, leading, and controlling that he was not doing before."

Guide Him toward Another Path

Probably no organization is so rigidly structured—and thus prone to the development of dead-end situations—as the military. However, the U.S. Air Force has added an equally comprehensive system for combating dead ends to its rigid hierarchy. The concept has been labeled the "career progression ladder" and includes the idea of alternative career paths.

Adopted in varying degrees by a number of companies, the plan at these companies is as follows:

When an employee is hired, he is told what the progression of responsibilities is, the requirements for each step, the probable length of time for each step, and the consequences of reaching a step where he must be passed over. At each step, an out is provided, usually in the form of training possibilities which will allow the employee to move to another ladder or to a higher rung on the same ladder.

IBM's Mr. Jones uses the same basic idea, but within a framework he hopes has little resemblance to the military hierarchy. "We don't have formalized structures for personnel, and we try not to have rigid progression systems," he explains.

"It depends pretty much on the circumstances of the individual. In career planning, we work fundamentally with the concept of the man and the manager. The manager, looking at the man's individual capabilities and desires, tries to determine with him what his next logical step is and the type of background and training he needs to get there. We don't want our people to feel that they're victims of the system."

Emphasis is on building on strengths, rather than criticizing weaknesses, and quite often the strengths suggest a switch to another career path. Mr. Jones cites a number of examples of employees who reached a dead end on one path, switched, and then rose significantly higher on another path. Among them is the case of an engineer who had reached a dead end fairly low on the engineering scale, but demonstrated qualities that would be strengths in production management. After changing paths, he worked his way up to a plant manager's job.

Reward Talent without Moving It

Dow's dual ladder system equates managerial and professional positions, both in salary and status. "Probably our system was created after recognition of the problem of what might be called dead-enders," says Dr. John L. Aitken, manager of organization and management development at Dow's Human Resources Center.

However, because of the dual ladder, the Joe Smith type of dead-ender no longer exists, so "the whole thrust of our program is only to move up the professional ladder people who are unusually competent," Dr. Aitken says. Probable competence or incompetence as a manager no longer is a consideration. Competent professionals who prefer to stay in their specialties are simply rewarded for what they have done, rather than being forced into an area in which they might not do as well in order to gain rewards.

For a company such as Bemuzz Tool which has no dual ladder system, adoption of this type of program would seem to be the perfect method of revitalizing Joe Smith. He was a highly competent engineer who needed no job enrichment to make his work meaningful and fulfilling. He simply believed his efforts were going unrewarded. With a dual ladder, he might have been given the title of "chief engineer"—equal in salary and status to engineering manager—while remaining in his area of competence.

"I don't know that we've been 100% successful," Dr. Aitken comments, "but I would say that we have avoided it [the Joe Smith type of situation] in large measure." Probably because managerial progression is faster, he believes there still may be more prestige associated with the managerial ladder than with the professional ladder in some functions. However, the system does provide the opportunity for an employee whose talents and/or goals are nonmanagerial to gain rewards many companies reserve for managers.

American Dream Challenged

Universal's Mr. Foote apparently isn't one to back away from a mighty adversary. In motivating his employees, he battles "the Great American Dream that everybody has to climb to the top of the heap. I think one of the problems is that we're all taught in school that the only way to become successful is to become the top dog. That isn't necessarily the proper definition of success or happiness. If it were, the only successful and happy guy in the company would be the president or the chief executive officer, but we know that isn't true."

This top-dog complex is one of the targets of the manager-subordinate conversations, and Mr. Foote believes it is slowly overcome as the employee's objectives and those of the company become increasingly compatible. "If you can achieve this compatibility over a period of time, you can help people understand that they're very worthwhile and successful even though they may not become vice president, or may not get that next job up, and that all these jobs are important to the company."

Maybe if he were working for Universal Foods instead of Ammazz Paper Products, even John Brown could find happiness as he spends the next ten years working for his former equal Bill Johnson.

QUESTIONS FOR REVIEW AND DISCUSSION

1. What are the major alternatives available in efforts to motivate the employee for whom no more promotions are likely? Which alternative do you favor? Why?
2. Comment fully on this statement: "Capabilities of many executives are unknown because their past assignments and jobs have never caused their total capabilities to be demonstrated."
3. As a manager would you favor formalized structures for personnel and follow well-publicized clearly described rigid progression systems? Why?
4. Describe the "dual ladder" approach presented in this article. Do you favor its use? Why?

35. Education for What?*

VERMONT ROYSTER

One of the American articles of faith has long been that since education is good for you then the more the better, and that the best of all is massive doses for everybody.

We began with compulsory education for the very young, on the reasonable theory that illiterates are handicapped in life, even though a good many of the good men who made America were uneducated and some of them actually illiterate, at least in the language of their new country.

From this worthy beginning we moved on, about a generation or so ago, to a compulsion toward universal college education. A college education became not only every man's birthright but one that he had to exercise or somehow be found wanting. A young man without one was marked as a person either deprived by society or deficient in himself.

This attitude has had several effects. One was a proliferation of degrees, until somewhere some college offered a degree in just about everything. Another was a sort of down-grading of all degrees. Since every man was supposedly entitled to an A.B. and required one as a credential, the pressure was on to get one for just about everybody, lowering standards if necessary, with the consequential devaluation of the bachelor's degree.

This moved the pressure up to higher degrees, the master's and above. But, perhaps paradoxically, rigidification set in on the requirements for many advanced degrees. In many fields the Ph.D. has become the necessary credential but the curriculum for it, essentially research oriented, has often borne little relationship to what the holder needs or what he will do thereafter.

Another consequence, and no small one, has been a financial crisis for the nation's colleges, public or private. From an educational standpoint they have been overwhelmed by numbers, from a financial standpoint overwhelmed by deficits.

---

* Source: Reprinted with permission of *The Wall Street Journal*, December 10, 1970, p. 12. Vermont Royster is a staff writer of *The Wall Street Journal*.

Naturally all this has brewed a counter movement. The young dropouts are in effect denying this article of faith; that is, that a college education is a must for everybody. And lately even older voices have been raised questioning the present state of higher education and the public's attitude toward it.

In that sense the Carnegie Commission on Higher Education is really revolutionary. What it has done in its recent report is challenge the very basics of our higher educational system, including also that assumption that everybody ought to have massive doses of it.

And these are, remember, quite respectable voices. The chairman of the commission study is Clark Kerr, formerly chancellor at Berkeley, and its members include university presidents of wide viewpoints (David Henry of Illinois, Theodore Hesburgh of Notre Dame) and "hard-headed" industrialists such as Norton Simon and Ralph Besse. No avant-garde dreamers, these.

One of their proposals is to reduce the "credential society's" 1,600 different degrees to 160. Another is to reduce the time—the time-wasting?—required to obtain them. They recommend that able students begin to take college-level courses in high school, and that college curricula be so arranged that energetic, full-time students can get their degrees quicker.

On the graduate level, their proposals aim at cutting a full year off the time required for an M.D. or a Ph.D. Moreover, in the case of the Ph.D. they recommend it be used as a research degree only, and that a new advanced degree—they would call it doctor of arts—be substituted for those who wish to concentrate in a special field but are not research minded.

But this only begins the icon-breaking. The commission takes the view that high school graduates should not feel compelled to go to college, at least not immediately or at least not to embark on the standard four-year college curriculum.

Some high school graduates might not go on at all. Some might profit from a few years in the "real world" and then, being older and more strongly motivated, return to college later. Some might be better served by a half-way house, taking a two-year college course and then deciding whether that is enough or whether they want to go further.

To meet the credentials gap for these two-year students, the commission endorses the A.A. (associate of arts) degree to be offered primarily by two-year community colleges. The advantages are two-fold. For those impatient for immediate jobs, the two-year course would give them a degree as a handle and sufficiently equip them for many jobs. For the four-year colleges, the advantage would be a weeding out of the many who now spend a few college years in aimless experimentation and then drop out anyway.

The advantages of something like this seem to me manifest. For one, and one not to be lightly dismissed, it would reduce the financial load on the educational system which society must pay for one way or another. The commission estimates that by 1980 the savings would run somewhere between $3 billion and $5 billion.

But the biggest advantage would come from a change in attitude. For the essence of the commission's view is that "education" is not some single product which can be packaged the same way for everybody and is good for everybody in the same quantities.

This attitude, once accepted, leads to some re-thinking on many things, regardless of the merits of the specific commission proposals. Take the controversy over open-admission policies. No one needs to demand it of Harvard, for example, even while recognizing that it might be socially useful for community colleges or other public institutions.

In short, education does not have to be an everything or nothing process. Not everybody wants, or needs, the same kind of education or in the same quantity; moreover, people's educational needs change as they change. Nor does every educational institution of "higher learning" have to be cut from the same pattern.

A rather obvious thought, perhaps. But since we have so long accepted it as obvious that everybody ought to have a college education, and the more massive the dose the better, it's refreshing to hear voices saying it ain't necessarily so.

QUESTIONS FOR REVIEW AND DISCUSSION

1. Do you agree or disagree with the general content of this article? Elaborate on your answer.
2. Offer your suggestions to improve education offered by universities.
3. What effect do you envision a reformed education system might have upon management? Discuss.

36. Learning Curves that Work*

SURENDER N. GOEL and ROBERT H. BECKNELL

Most manufacturing companies today are faced with labor unions demanding that a consistent approach be undertaken for determining the length of time necessary to learn a manufacturing operation. Many publications have dealt with learning time based on the number of pieces produced cumulatively to reach an objective level of performance. However, labor unions have requested that learning be expressed in the number of days or weeks required to reach an acceptable level of performance.

In response, the managements of many companies have arbitrarily assigned a number of days or weeks to learn various manufacturing operations. This solution results in learning schedules that are highly inconsistent from one operation to another. For example, employees might be required to fully learn punch press or electronic assembly operations in six weeks. The average employee can easily learn to operate a punch press in six weeks. However, it is considerably more difficult for an employee to learn to assemble complex electronic components in this same period of time.

At NCR, we undertook the project of determining a consistent scientific approach to arrive at a solution to this problem. The objective of this project was to find the daily efficiency for consecutive days when an incentive employee is learning a given manufacturing operation.

An average operator working at an incentive pace in this plant maintains an average efficiency of 125 percent. The efficiencies of all incentive employees are normally distributed around the mean of 125 percent, with a standard deviation of approximately 10 percent. Then, based on a two-

* Source: Reprinted with permission of *Industrial Engineering*, May 1972, pp. 28–31. Surender N. Goel is systems analyst, manufacturing standards department, NCR, Dayton, Ohio and Robert H. Becknell is administrative assistant, manufacturing standards department, NCR, Dayton, Ohio. The authors greatly appreciate the help they received from Dr. L. S. Gephart and Professor V. Balachandran, University of Dayton, and Mr. V. T. D. Balaraman, Manufacturing Operations Analyst, NCR, who made completion of this project possible.

FIGURE 1   **FIGURE 2**   **FIGURE 3**

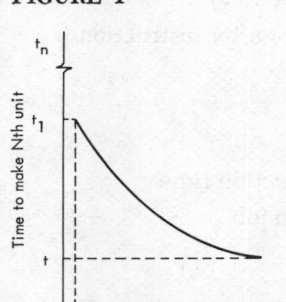 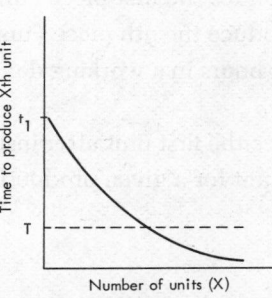

Wrong Model I produced a negative exponential curve that did not correlate with the facts of learning in the plant.

Wrong Model II curve indicated operator efficiency is unlimited, which just isn't so.

Right Model III is same as II except that maximum operator efficiency is practically 145 percent.

sigma limit (95 percent of employees) the maximum efficiency will be 145 percent.

Two Wrongs . . .

During the research of this project, three mathematical models were considered. The first two were proven to be unsatisfactory for application to our operations.

Model I. On first examining learning curves, they appear to be exponentially distributed. Therefore, we started our research with a negative exponential curve to represent the learning rate of an incentive employee, Figure 1. The equation for this curve is:

$$t_n = t_1 + (t_1 - t)e^{-RN}$$

where:

t_n: time to produce the nth unit.

t_1: time to produce the first unit after instruction time.

t: minimum time in which a unit can be produced by an operator working at his maximum pace (definitely faster than the average incentive pace)

e: exponential constant, equal to 2.718

R: learning rate

Without detailing the calculations here, we found that the slope of the learning curve was a very large number that did not correlate with historical data for learning in this plant.

Model II. After determining that an exponential curve does not represent a learning curve, we resorted to the following model, in which:

T = the standard time to produce one piece (unit)

t_1 = the time to produce the first piece (unit) after instruction

t_n = the time to produce the nth piece (unit)

P = the number of hours in a working day

R = learning rate

t_1 = time to produce the first unit after instruction time

$A = t_1/T$ = a constant for a given production job

FIGURE 4

Learning Rate = 70.0%   A = 5.0

Days	0.05 Pcs.	0.05 Eff.	0.10 Pcs.	0.10 Eff.	0.15 Pcs.	0.15 Eff.	0.20 Pcs.	0.20 Eff.	Std. Time In 0.25 Pcs.	0.25 Eff.
1	114	71	45	56	25	46	17	42	13	40
2	163	101	69	86	41	76	28	69	20	62
3	178	111	79	98	48	89	33	82	24	74
4	186	116	84	104	52	97	36	89	28	87
5	192	119	87	108	54	101	38	94	29	90
6	196	122	91	113	57	106	41	102	30	93
7	198	123	92	114	58	108	41	102	32	99
8	201	125	94	117	59	110	43	107	33	103
9	203	126	96	119	61	114	43	107	34	106
10	205	128	96	119	61	114	44	109	34	106
11	206	128	98	122	62	116	45	112	34	106
12	207	129	98	122	63	118	46	114	36	112

Hrs./Unit

0.30 Pcs.	0.30 Eff.	0.35 Pcs.	0.35 Eff.	0.40 Pcs.	0.40 Eff.	0.45 Pcs.	0.45 Eff.	Pcs.	Eff.
10	37	8	34	7	34	6	33	5	31
15	56	12	52	10	49	8	44	8	49
20	74	16	69	13	64	11	61	9	56
21	78	18	78	15	74	13	73	11	68
23	86	19	83	16	79	14	78	12	74
25	93	20	87	17	84	14	78	12	74
25	93	21	91	17	84	15	84	14	87
27	101	22	96	19	94	16	89	14	87
27	101	22	96	19	94	17	95	14	87
27	101	23	100	19	94	17	95	15	93
28	104	23	100	20	99	17	95	15	93
29	108	24	104	21	104	18	101	15	93

Sample set of learning curves. Learning rate (70 percent) and starting efficiency (20 percent) are constants for this set. The 10 time standards (20 percent) are constants for this set. The 10 time standards (0.05 to 0.50 standard hours per unit) provide 10 different curves. Example: On the 7th day, the normal learner will produce 32 pieces at an efficiency of 99% if the standard time to produce one unit (T) is 0.25 hours, the learning rate (R) is 70 percent, and the starting efficiency on the first piece (1/A) is 20 percent.

This model is based on the assumption that the time to produce the *nth* unit is reduced by R each time the number of pieces is doubled. The time taken by an operator to produce the *nth* piece $= ATR_n$. The results obtained by applying this model indicated that the efficiency of operators was unlimited. Obviously this is not practical. The curve given by this model is shown in Figure 2.

Make a Right

The assumptions and nomenclature used in Model III are the same as those used in Model II except that the daily efficiency of an operator was restricted to 145 percent. The curve for this model is shown in Figure 3.

Using the same procedure as in Model II, following are the calculations of time taken by an operator to produce the units specified:

$$1\text{st} = A \cdot T$$
$$2\text{nd} = (A \cdot T - T/1.45)R + T/1.45$$
$$(2)^2\text{th} = (A \cdot T - T/1.45)R^2 + T/1.45$$
$$(2)^n\text{th} = (A \cdot T - T/1.45)R^n + T/1.45$$

$$\text{Let } (2)^n = X \text{ or } n = \frac{\log X}{\log 2}$$

FIGURE 5

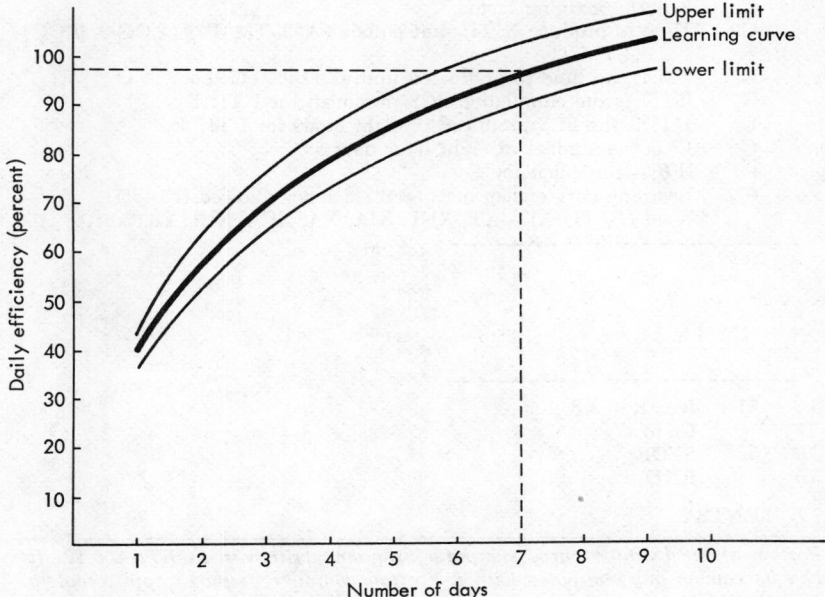

Illustration of the Figure 4 learning curve (middle) curve for the 0.25 time standard. Upper and lower tolerance limits may be added.

Therefore, time to produce the Xth unit,

$$t_x = (A \cdot T - T/1.45)R\frac{\log X}{\log 2} + T/1.45$$

Then the number of units m_j produced in a day is given by the following equation.

$$P = \sum_{x=M_{j-1}+1}^{M_j} t_x$$

$m_j = M_j - M_{j-1}$ and m_j is the number of units produced on the *j*th day.

The equations for t_x and P above, were input in the computer and the data obtained were very practical when compared with historical samples.

FIGURE 6

1		Dimension sum (4000), J(10), JS(10), IFF(10), JD(10)
	C	T is the standard time / unit in hours
	C	XIT is the initial value of T
	C	XT is the increment of T
	C	XFT is the final value of T
	C	XIA is the initial value of A
	C	XA is the increment of A
	C	XFA is the final value of A
	C	XIR is the initial value of R
	C	XR is the increment of R
	C	XFR is the final value of R
	C	A is the equal to the inverse of the starting efficiency
	C	R is the learning factor
	C	Time to produce X TH unit equals (A*T-TM)R**(LOG X/LOG 2) +TM
	C	TM is the time to produce a unit at 145% efficiency
	C	JS(I) is the cumulative PCS produced for I TH I
	C	J(I) is the PCS produced in eight hours for I TH T
	C	IP is the number of eight hour days
	C	IFF is the efficiency
	C	Learning curve when maximum efficiency allowed is 145%
2		Read (5, 95) XIT, XT, XFT, XIA, XA, XFA, XIR, XR, XFR

- -

- -

76	51	R = R + XR
77		Go to 47
78	52	STOP
79		END
	SENTRY	

Portion of the learning curve computer program, written in FORTRAN IV. It can be run on any computer with a Fortran compiler, requires approximately 20K. Different values of R, A, and T can be input into the program at the same time. This program is capable of calculating the learning data for a maximum of ten different T's in one run, but any number of different values of R and A.

FIGURE 7

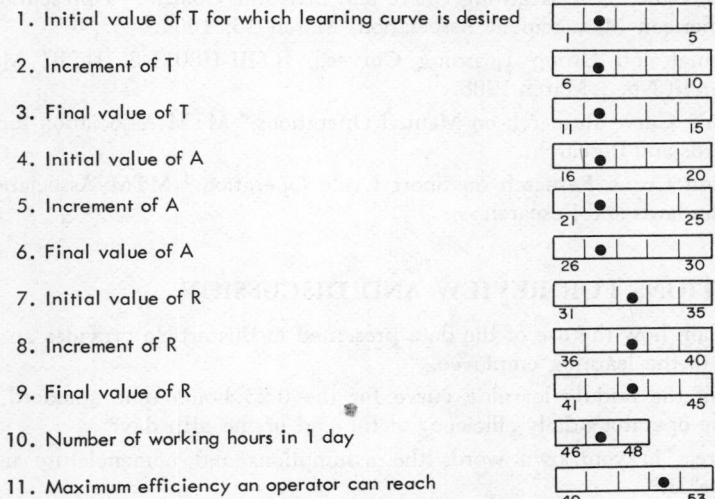

1. Initial value of T for which learning curve is desired

2. Increment of T

3. Final value of T

4. Initial value of A

5. Increment of A

6. Final value of A

7. Initial value of R

8. Increment of R

9. Final value of R

10. Number of working hours in 1 day

11. Maximum efficiency an operator can reach

Data form is used to prepare data card for the computer program, Figure 6. The "increment of T," item 2, is the interval between consecutive T's. For example, if you want learning curves for T from 0.10 to 0.50 standard hours per unit in steps of 0.05 standard hours (0.10, 0.15, 0.20, etc.), then the "initial value of T" is 0.10, the "increment of T" is 0.50, and the "final value of T" is 0.50.

These data have now been used and validated for jobs where historical data was not previously available.[1]

Application

Sample results are shown in Figures 4 and 5. A portion of the learning curve computer program and the data form used to prepare the data card are shown in Figures 6 and 7.

Another application of these data which is used at NCR is in the payroll department. New employees are compensated for the time they spend learning as given by the learning data. For example, if an employee is put on a learning curve where $T = .40$ hrs., $R = 70\%$ and $(1/A) = 20\%$, then on the 7th day he will be paid $(100\% - 84\%) \times 8$ hours above his earned production hours unless the total of these hours is less than 8 hours in which case he is paid for 8 hours. This provides an incentive to employees who are learning.

---

[1] The complete Fortran Program is not included in this article. Those who are interested in obtaining the program should write to Mr. R. A. Meyer, Manager, Manufacturing Standards Department, National Cash Register Company, Main and K Streets, Dayton, Ohio 45409.

BIBLIOGRAPHY

Liekhus, Gene, "The Learning Curve and Schedule Control," a presentation to American Management Association, March 15, 1964.

"Individual and Group Learning Curves," IITRI-H8011-3, IITRI Monthly Report No. 3, March 1968.

"Learning Curve Research on Manual Operations," MTM Association for Standards and Research.

"Learning Curve Research on Short Cycle Operation," MTM Association for Standards and Research .

QUESTIONS FOR REVIEW AND DISCUSSION

1. Explain how the use of the data presented in this article provides an incentive to the learning employee.
2. Using the middle learning curve for the 0.25 hours time standard, what is the operator's daily efficiency at the end of the fifth day?
3. Express in your own words the assumptions and nomenclature used in model II.
4. Operation HW has a learning rate of 70 percent, starting efficiency of 20 percent, and standard time to produce one unit of 0.40 hours. How long, according to the above article, should it take for a normal learner to produce at an efficiency rate of 100 percent? Justify your answer.

part TEN

Controlling

Controlling, a key function of management, is the managerial effort taken to adapt actual activity to planned activity. It is in the nature of a follow-up to ensure attainment of stated goals. This examination of results can be applied to any sized entity desired—from the one extreme of an entire economy to the opposite extreme of the accomplishment of an individual worker. Controlling always consists of these three steps: (1) measurement of the performance, (2) comparison of performance with a standard or expected performance, and (3) correction of any deviation between actual and expected performance.

In "Cost-Volume-Profit Analysis" David O. Jenkins presents a simplified and easy-to-understand interpretation of what is frequently referred to as break-even point problems. The basic equation offered facilitates the use of a computer for solving cost-volume-profit problems. The handling of the analysis, interpretation of the results, and the possible applications are clearly presented.

In the next reading, William L. Campfield's "Auditing Management Performance," controlling is discussed from the viewpoint of evaluating a firm's total activities from the management perspective. This reading provides a picture of what a modern management auditor does both in private and public sectors. The author stresses ways in which the management auditor is being influenced by the new challenges and responsibilities brought about mainly by the dynamics of management. For example, there is great need for reliable standards against which total managerial performance may be measured. Also, answers are needed to difficult questions, such as, "Within an enterprise, what can be predicted about the total net effect arising from many scattered but related control points?" Also, "What effect will the use of newer techniques and management facilities have upon overall controlling efforts?"

Dr. Richard A. Elnicki's reading, "ROI Simulations for Investment Decisions" is thought provoking and well written. He contends that uncertainty considerations make the common discounting methods unreliable. It is recommended that distributions of return on investment (ROI) are closer to reality than a single estimate. By having such information available, the manager can consider ROI's and risk attitudes toward outcomes that are possible, not toward outcomes that are not certain.

37. Cost-Volume-Profit Analysis*

DAVID O. JENKINS

A generalized formula approach to cost-volume-profit analysis can serve as a foundation on which to build a systematic pattern of data gathering and can be applied to companies of varying sizes in various industries. Such a formula can be derived from the behavior of a few basic variables and can be applied by computer.

Cost-volume-profit analysis is, of course, relevant to many questions that management must answer. What volume and mix of products or services constitute the optimum profit plan? What prices must be charged to provide a sufficient contribution toward coverage of fixed costs and generation of adequate net income? What is the maximum cost that could be paid to an outside manufacturer in lieu of internal production? What ceiling must be placed on discretionary expenditures that are nonvariable in relation to volume? What profit will result from a specified combination of quantities, prices, and costs?

A systematic data gathering approach is needed to provide answers to questions such as these, but is often absent in practice. A research monograph recently published by the National Association of Accountants suggests that executives in small and meduim-size manufacturing firms "could attempt to become more orderly in their general decision-making activities" and "could begin to use more of the concept, theory, and techniques (such as contribution margin analysis) of managerial accounting in their decision activities."[1] Replies to a questionnaire indicate the following average order of importance of various operating decisions (1) cost-volume-profit analysis, (2) product pricing, (3) financial budgeting, (4) capital

* Source: Reprinted with permission of *Management Services*, March-April 1970, pp. 55–57. Copyright 1970 by the American Institute of CPAs. Dr. David O. Jenkins is associate professor of accounting, University of Southern California.

[1] Gary A. Luoma, *Accounting Information in Managerial Decision-Making for Small and Medium Manufacturers*, Research Monograph No. 2, National Association of Accountants, New York, December, 1967, p. 69.

equipment analysis, (5) inventory control, (6) make-or-buy products or components.[2]

However, "research indicated that in the areas of cost-volume-profit analysis, inventory control, and make or buy, no set procedures are followed by decision makers," whereas in the other areas "evidence indicates some pattern *in the* gathering of data and the rendering of a decision."[3]

The Basic Formula

Careful consideration reveals that, among all of the seemingly diverse questions requiring cost-volume-profit analysis, there are only five basic variables, and that a generalized formula involving these variables can provide a framework for the systematic gathering of relevant data, regardless of the nature or size of the business involved. The basic equation is:

$$Q\,(P - V) = F + I$$

where:

Q is quantity or volume in units
P is selling price per unit
V is variable cost per unit
F is fixed cost in total
I is income or profit

Multiple sources of income can be represented by:

$$Q_1(P_1 - V_1) + Q_2(P_2 - V_2) + \ldots Q_n(P_n - V_n) = F + I.$$

"F" is placed on the right side of the basic equation because it is a non-variable sum unaffected by the mix of revenue sources. Any attempt to reduce it to per unit terms is artificial and may be misleading.

The general formula can be applied to various types of businesses. The multiple sources of revenue on the left side of the equation could represent various products, services, rental units, admission prices, or whatever is involved in the business under consideration.

The use of a formula must not be allowed to convey the impression that specific solutions can be determined with absolute precision. Most costs are mixed costs which include both fixed and variable elements. Even purely fixed or variable costs may be subject to random variations. The relation between selling price and volume is seldom known more than roughly, and demand is generally unpredictable. Cost-volume-profit analysis must be preceded by and supplemented by other techniques such as market surveys to help forecast sales and regression analysis to identify when and how costs vary. However, despite its admitted limitations, cost-

---

[2] Ibid., p. 57.
[3] Luoma, *Accounting Information in Managerial Decision-Making*, p. iv.

volume-profit analysis is still deemed to be very useful, as evidenced by its number one ranking in the survey mentioned earlier. Furthermore, there does not appear to be any limitation involved in a formula approach which is not inherent in the very nature of cost-volume-profit analysis itself.

Care must be taken to identify properly the pattern of cost or revenue behavior. For example, it would *not* be appropriate to include in "V" sales commissions based on a percentage of dollar sales, because such commissions would vary with selling prices as well as with units sold—with "P" as well as "Q"—whereas "V" is defined as cost which varies only with units —only with "Q." Commissions should be treated as a reduction of "P."

Occasionally certain data may not seem to fit anywhere in the suggested equation. For example, lease revenue may consist of a fixed minimum amount plus an additional amount varying with sales of the lessee. Where does the basic formula provide for "fixed revenue"? The answer is to treat such revenue as an offset to fixed costs. Thus, "F" is to be thought of as a net fixed dollar outlay.

Once problem data are identified in terms of the generalized formula, it is a relatively simple matter to rearrange the terms to solve for any unknown. Thus the equation for required quantity in units can be expressed as

$$Q = (F + I) / (P - V)$$

and the formula for the breakeven point $(I = \$0)$ is simply

$$Q = F / (P - V).$$

The breakeven point in dollars of revenue would be

$$QP = F / \frac{(P - V)}{P}.$$

Note that the breakeven formula is just one of several possible variations of the basic equation and that the formula can be varied in other ways to assist in solving problems in which a target volume has been established and some other variable must be computed.

For example, the income that will result from a specified combination of volume, price, and cost factors can be determined as

$$I = [Q (P - V)] - F.$$

Given cost data plus a target volume and profit, the formula for required selling price is

$$P = V + [(F + I) / Q].$$

The formula for maximum allowable variable cost per unit is

$$V = P - [F + I) / Q].$$

Note the similarity of the two preceding equations, each of which requires computing a required contribution margin per unit. If a limit on fixed costs is to be determined the following equation is appropriate:

$$F = [Q\,(P-V)] - I.$$

If a company previously offering a single product wishes to determine a selling price for a second product consistent with cost data, expected volume, and target profit, the problem can be expressed as follows:

$$P_2 = \frac{(F+I) - [Q_1(P_1 - V_1)]}{Q_2} + V_2$$

where P_2 is the required selling price of the second product.

Other examples could be given, of course, but the foregoing should be sufficient to illustrate the flexibility and applicability of the generalized formula. Although the last example was stated in terms of multiple products, it could just as well have been applied to multiple services or other sources of income as noted previously.

The use of a basic equation also facilitates the preparation of a computer program for solving cost-volume-profit problems. A more realistic situation involving many products or services would not increase the number of basic variables or the relationships among them and a computer simulation should be quite feasible.

Cost-volume-profit analysis is useful in helping management deal with a wide range of questions, but a systematic data gathering approach is needed to facilitate such analysis. Since there are a limited number of basic variables involved, explicit recognition of these in the form of a generalized equation may help management establish a system that will provide relevant data in a form suitable for use in cost-volume-profit analysis for any size of organization. The larger the organization, the more effective the use that may be made of a computer.

QUESTIONS FOR REVIEW AND DISCUSSION

1. Express in words the basic equation of cost-volume-profit analysis.
2. What types of managerial questions does cost-volume-price analysis answer?
3. Assume company A has a single product which is sold for $5.00. The company management wishes to realize $30,000 profit before taxes. Plant, equipment, and administrative staff (classified as fixed cost) amount to $42,000. The variable cost per unit is $2.60. How many units must the company sell to realize its profit objective? What is the company's break-even point?

38. Auditing Management Performance*

WILLIAM L. CAMPFIELD

Management auditing—variously termed operational auditing, performance auditing, or just simply internal auditing—has evolved over the past two decades as a professional review and evaluation of an organization's total activities from the perspective of management. In this context, the management auditor's principal value to management is two-fold: (1) through test and evaluation of management's prescribed decision making and performance machinery, he assures management that its decisions are derived soundly and that allocation and use of organization resources are likely to conform continuously to management's plans and objectives, and (2) by concerted test and analysis in major program and responsibility areas, he alerts management to potential major deviations from plans or potential uneconomical use of resources.

Management auditing has evolved in a constantly changing environment. It may be useful for our discussion to examine the broad changing social and economic environment in which managers and their advisors, auditors included, must operate.

Changing Environment

There have been countless descriptions and explanations of the ideological and technological changes that have been occurring at accelerating rates. Some of the more significant happenings are summarized below.

We are a nation of about 200 million people—highly mobile and domiciled predominantly in large urban areas. At the present rate of growth, there will be about 350 million of us in the year 2000.

* Source: Reprinted with permission of *Financial Executive*, January 1971, pp. 24–28, 32, 34. William L. Campfield is assistant director, Office of Policy and Special Studies, U.S. General Accounting Office. The views expressed in this article are the sole responsibility of the author and are not intended to state policy of the U.S. General Accounting Office or other organizations.

We are increasingly knowledgeable and technically oriented people with rising expectations of places to apply our skills and talents, and also with rising expectations for higher standards of living.

We are experiencing a phenomenal growth in the productive and service capacity of the private sector and comparable growth in the service capacity of the public sector—with a need for policies and mechanisms to keep both sectors operating and interacting in some kind of agreed-upon balance.

We are engaged as a nation in a highly intensified struggle to preserve the country's natural environment and natural resources, thus calling forth increased research for development of alternative resources and requiring added restraints on the use and exploitation of the country's environment and resources.

We are a nation of incredible technological know-how with a capacity to build highly sophisticated spacecraft; to control walks in space; to construct third-generation computers with large memories and to make use of random access, real time, and time sharing; and, through use of exotic mathematics, we can simulate all kinds of life circumstances before they happen.

The explosive increase in our ability as a nation to create wealth (in the form of things with a market value) presently far outdistances our ability to distribute this wealth in a way which provides the greatest benefits to the greatest number of people.

Underlying all, we are economically affluent, but we are faced with a gap between the expectations of a large segment of society and the reality of poverty, discrimination, and ill health in the world's richest and most powerful nation.

Now, what does all of this mean? In respect to management, it probably means that managers will need a better understanding of the total world in which we live—social, political, economical, technological, and moral; self-renewal and commitment to meet the legitimate demands and unsatisfied wants of the populace; and the ability to meet the ultimate challenge, as Peter Drucker states in his article "Integration of People and Planning," (*Harvard Business Review,* December 1955) of integrating their individual intellectual, or social, or moral skills into one balanced and organized practice of management based on the long view and the bold imagination. Duane Wilson, in "Dynamic Auditing in a Changing World," (*The Internal Auditor,* Sep/Oct 1969), has noted that the successful manager of today and tomorrow will be the one who can reconcile skillfully the diverse and often times conflicting social, economic, and political considerations of the external world with the internal goals, plans, and operations of the organization he manages. Just as the era of change has challenged managements, so too have management auditors been challenged to respond to the increasing need to assist managers over a wide range of organizational and societal circumstances.

Let us now turn to some evidences of the ways in which the management auditor is viewing his new challenges and responsibilities.

Broadened Audit Scope and Purview

The management auditor is concerned, as indicated earlier in this article, with the substance of management planning and control. This means that he must be concerned with helping management spot potential trouble spots, for example, identifying and reporting operations where units costs are increasing; poor communications between responsibility centers; breakdowns in programming and scheduling, etc. But, most importantly, the ultimate responsibility of the management auditor is to evaluate the over-all efficiency and economy of the entity which he examines.

In his article "Management Auditing," (*The Journal of Accountancy*, May 1968), John Burton expresses the belief that it will not be long before shareholders and investment analysts start requesting that a management, and the external and internal auditors servicing that management, furnish adequate information about the quality of management's performance.

He further delineates an approach to develop standards of managerial performance, a summary of which is useful to our discussion of management auditing challenges and opportunities. Here are some of the significant ways in which standards of managerial performance might be constructed:

1. Assigning relative "quality points" to the various areas of management control within a firm, and from this developing an over-all index of the quality of control procedures which might serve as a basis for comparison among firms. Some of the broad control areas to which the "quality point" system might be applied are organization control (e.g., procedures manuals, stated corporate objectives); planning and information systems (e.g., operational budgets, cost controls, long-range planning); asset management (e.g., inventory control, capital budgeting); marketing system (e.g., market research, sales analysis); and production system (e.g., production planning, labor relations, purchasing, and procurement).

2. Developing standards for financial performance supplemental to the conventional net income figure. Examples of the new success indicators might be ratio of operating return on sales earned by the firm compared to the average return on sales earned by the industry, and ratio of operating return on long-term capital earned by the firm compared to the return earned by the industry.

3. Comparing results of performance by the firm on major projects with forecasted results on a project basis.

Let us examine some ways for management auditors to break further frontiers of services to management by taking two examples from industry, one from the findings and implications of a management audit report of labor control reported by Joseph W. Dodwell in "Operational Auditing: A Part of the Basic Audit" (*Journal of Accountancy* June 1966), and the other a hypothetical case involving the review of a capital budgeting decision.

Labor Control Audit

Examination of several plants of a company showed that the entire plant labor force, including direct and indirect workers were workers by the day. This meant that these people were paid for time rather than for production in accordance with some accepted productivity measurement standards. In addition, although production levels varied substantially from month to month, there were no variations in direct labor levels during the year, and indirect labor had become frozen at a relatively high level. Further, a tour of selected plant sites showed large groups of employees milling about waiting for materials, machines, operating instructions, etc. Many excessively long coffee breaks were observed, and many of the direct-labor employees stopped their machines about an hour before quitting time to prepare for leaving the plant. And, in some plants, it was a frequent practice to schedule "fill in" work near the end of each day in order to permit direct-labor workers to complete a full day of apparent work.

All of the foregoing circumstances cried out for the auditor to recommend that the client firm include in the production control system which already had been recommended a system of engineered labor productivity measurement standards, the general model for which was drawn in broad outline by the auditor.

Capital Budgeting Decision

Suppose, for example, a company is considering investing $20 million in plant expansion. It would be naive to believe that the auditor can ensure that the decision will be a profitable one. What he can do, however, is develop criteria for judging the decision. The auditor could, for example, use a series of questions, such as the following, in order to pass judgment on whether a capital budgeting decision was procedurally good or bad.

1. Did the company have a system for developing detailed alternative plant expansion plans and programs?

2. Does the company have a prescribed evaluation procedure for selecting among plant investment alternatives? For example, is the decision based on a payout comparison, and is the decision based on a discounted cash flow computation?

Professor Williard Stone ("Auditing Management Efficiency," *The Aus-*

tralian Accountant, March 1967), in suggesting expanded ways to audit management efficiency, has proposed that standards be established to appraise a firm's achievement of its public responsibilities. Here is a summary of key standards and measurement factors suggested by Professor Stone:

1. Response to national and state citizenship obligations. Measured by such things as the extent of the firm's compliance with antitrust laws, antidiscrimination laws, and other general welfare laws.
2. Contribution to the gross national product. Measured by the assistance which the firm's product gives to the United States in maintaining a favorable balance of trade; i.e., how important to the national economy is the firm's product?
3. Response to local community citizenship. Measured by compliance with local laws, and the extent of action taken to help control threats to the health of the community; e.g., participation in pollution control programs.
4. Contribution to community progress. Measured by the amount of taxes paid by the firm, employment furnished, and the firms's direct contributions to civic projects; e.g., contributions and assistance to junior achievement clubs.

There are, of course, many other areas of management's responsibility to which the techniques and insights of management auditing can be applied. It can be said that the future of management auditors in the modern social and economic environment is limited only by the kind and extent of services they are prepared to provide.

We would be remiss indeed if we did not have a few words to say about the new quantitative techniques and management sciences, and the need of management auditors to ensure that they will have continuous competence in all areas in which they offer services.

It takes little skill to predict that the future will witness increasing use of the theorems and techniques of management sciences to deal with information systems design and information flows for management planning and control. Already management science techniques are being used extensively in procurement management and inventory control, in capital budgeting decisions, in determining plant locations, in scheduling equipment usage and production runs, and a number of other routine operations.

The problem at hand is for the management auditor to keep abreast of new techniques and knowledge in the evolving management sciences to the extent necessary to maintain his competence in whatever areas he offers services. I will not even attempt here to recite how this continuing education should be undertaken. There are innumerable guides in the professional literature and in the in-house instructions and programs of most auditing organizations. Suffice it to remind ourselves that the future will belong to those auditors who have both the foresight and the will to keep prepared for whatever profitable services are suggested by the turn of events.

328   *Management: Selected Readings*

Management Auditing in the Federal Government

Our discussion thus far has pointed exclusively to illustrations about the practice of management auditing in the private sector. Although the basic concepts and approaches of management auditing are universal, it is useful to examine some instances of the practice of the art in the public sector.

The manner in which the federal government collects and spends money is of at least passing interest to most citizens. To the U.S. General Accounting Office (GAO), which has a statutory responsibility to assist Congress in its overview of federal revenues and expenditures, the interest is one of constantly looking at a broad spectrum of federal activities in the interest of helping federal managers achieve the three "E's"—economy, efficiency, effectiveness.

The United States government, probably the largest and most diverse single complex of activities and operations in the world, much like other organizations in the public sector, does not have the built-in profit and loss yardstick and control that is available to managements in the private sectors. Consequently, the GAO, in carrying out its overview responsibilities, examines, reviews, and evaluates federal programs and activities and the use of public funds in terms of how effectively, efficiently, and economically planned programs and activities have been accomplished.

During a typical year, the GAO will send about 150 audit reports to Congress. These reports are available to the public. In addition, it makes many more reports—upwards of a thousand—to committees or members of Congress and to heads of executive departments and agencies. Some of these reports contain privileged information and accordingly are not made public.

In the course of a year, GAO will make public audit reports on management planning and operations over a wide range of endeavor. Presented below are capsule descriptions of the range of GAO audits during recent months.

1. An examination of the development and procurement by the Army of the Sheridan tank-weapons system, which showed a lack of effectiveness and control by the Army. GAO recommended changes in the Army's procedures for development of a weapons system.

2. A study of Project Mohole, the National Science Foundation project to extend man's knowledge of the planet by drilling through about 25 miles through the earth's outermost crust. The program was terminated because its costs ran out of control. GAO found out why and so advised Congress.

3. A report showing a need to strengthen controls by the Agricultural Research Service over the public sale of pesticides resulting in strong corrective action by the Department of Agriculture.

4. An examination of costs accruing to the government when companies with defense contracts lease rather than purchase land and buildings needed for the completion of their work. GAO found it would be cheaper to purchase land and buildings than to lease them and so advised Congress.

5. A study to determine whether the Department of Defense could achieve economies through consolidation of its maintenance of property operations. DOD maintains 29.5 million acres of land, buildings, streets, etc. GAO concluded that in areas of large military concentrations, such as Norfolk, Va., and Hawaii, consolidations could mean savings to the government.

6. Disclosure by a GAO audit that the government of Vietnam denied certain U. S. contractors permission to operate airlift services required by the contractor to fulfill the assignments which he had contracted to carry out for that country.

7. A recommendation that the Department of Interior improve its procedures for acquiring wetlands—marshes, bogs, swamps—for purposes of conservation of waterfowl.

8. An assessment of the Army's management of its supply system in support of its combat needs in Vietnam. GAO found that while a high level of support was achieved, this was not accomplished without costly and inefficient procedures, a basic cause being a lack of a logistics organization capable of rapid and large-scale expansion at the time needed.

9. A recommendation based upon a broad and careful review that a thorough Presidential study be made of the role of nonprofit organizations having research and development contracts with the government.

10. A report showing that with the cost of maintaining automatic data processing equipment used by the government now amounting to $50 million annually, departments and agencies could achieve economies and also operating advantages by maintaining the computers themselves instead of having maintenance performed by outside contractors.

The foregoing list gives a pretty good picture of the ways in which management auditors can help government managers search for and control impediments to effective, efficient, and economical use of public resources.

Now let us turn to a broader example of the way in which GAO has exemplified the expanding horizons of management auditing. Pursuant to the Economic Opportunity Act Amendments of December 1967 the GAO was directed to determine the efficiency of the administration of programs conducted under the Act and the extent to which these programs achieve the objectives of the Act.

The Economic Opportunity Act of 1964, commonly termed "the war on poverty" act, together with amendments enacted in 1965, 1966, and 1967, was designed to strengthen, supplement, and coordinate efforts of the United States to eliminate poverty by opening to everyone the opportunity for education and training, the opportunity to work, and the opportunity to live in decency and dignity. The actual operation of the "war on poverty" has been carried out by several departments and agencies besides the Office of Economic Opportunity (OEO). Programs were delegated to the Departments of Labor; Health, Education and Welfare; and Agriculture. The Small Business Administration also played a part.

GAO made a nationwide review of all the major OEO programs such as Community Action, manpower, health services, education programs, legal services, VISTA and so on. This was one of the largest audits that GAO has ever been called upon to make. Over the 15 months of the review, not only were the resources of the GAO audit staff in Washington used, but the staffs of its 16 regional offices throughout the country were also used. At times there were as many as 250 auditors at work on this assignment.

This massive and difficult audit review and evaluation cannot be summarized too easily in a short article such as this. The report of review was issued to the Congress in March 1969.*

It is relevant to note some of the major difficulties in trying to evaluate the efficiency and effectiveness with which OEO administered the poverty program. These included the urgency of getting programs underway as quickly as possible; problems in the development of a new organization and in obtaining experienced personnel; problems involved in establishing new or modified organizational arrangements at the local level; the delays and uncertainties in obtaining congressional authorizations and appropriations; the problems of working out relationships with other agencies and with state and local governments; and lack of consensus as to the meaning of poverty.

The GAO review and evaluation problem was further complicated by the absence of objective bases and measurements for making assessments and judgments. This dilemma occurs in any situation where programs are completely new and innovative, deal with intangibles such as improving the well-being of disadvantaged people, and are established with expected outputs and services not amenable to reliable, quantitative measurement. More specifically, the GAO or any other management review would encounter major impediments whenever any of the following situations existed:

1. Criteria are lacking by which to determine at what level of accomplishment a program is to be considered successful.

2. The methods for determining program accomplishments have not been developed to the point of assured reliability.

3. The large volume and variety of pertinent data necessary to ascertain program results have been and still are either not available or not reliable.

---

* For the reader interested in the detail, copies are available from the GPO. *Review of Economic Opportunity Programs* (B-130515)—Report to the Congress by the Comptroller General of the United States, The Government Printing Office, Washington, D.C., March 18, 1969, p. 228.

4. Program results may not be fully perceptible for many programs within a relatively short time frame.

5. Other programs—federal, state, local, and private—aimed at helping the poor, as well as changes in local conditions—employment, wage scales, local attitudes—have their effect upon the same people who receive assistance under the programs authorized by the act.

6. Amendment to the act and revisions in agency guidelines at various times have necessitated redirection of programs and other changes, which have affected the progress of programs in the short run.

As might be expected, the GAO report disclosed varying degrees of accomplishment by OEO in the five broad program categories it administered; viz: community action, manpower, health, education, and other. The principal recommendations can be summarized as follows:

Programs. Eighteen recommendations broken down by the five broad program categories cover a range of suggestions pertaining to program planning, improving criteria for selecting program participants, establishing standards of performance, and evaluating program accomplishments.

Coordination and Organization. Five recommendations were made, including one suggesting the creation of a new office in the Executive Office of the President to perform the planning, coordination, and evaluation functions now vested in the Economic Opportunity Council and the Office of Economic Opportunity.

Evaluation. One recommendation was made that the suggested new office of the Executive Office of the President develop the evaluation function applicable to antipoverty programs.

Audits. One recommendation was made that responsible federal agencies should provide for more frequent and comprehensive audits of all antipoverty programs.

Perhaps the strongest conclusion drawn by GAO from the study was the demonstrated need for a central staff agency to carry out overall planning, coordination, and evaluation responsibilities with respect to antipoverty efforts. This agency, to be effective, would require the full support of the President. The report urged Congress to create such an agency.

Conclusion

Most knowledgeable students of economic organizations will agree that management auditing is becoming an important factor in helping an organization, whether private or public, achieve effective planning and control.

The basic purpose of management auditing is to help managements to find the best way to manage their organizations. Consequently, the well-informed and alert management auditor tries to render useful services over a broad range of today's operations, but he keeps a weather eye on tomorrow.

We have tried in this article to give a representative picture of what the service-oriented management auditor is doing in the private sector as well as in the public domain to help managements at every level achieve optimal results.

There is every indication that, in the future, the various publics—investors, taxpayers, creditors, labor unions, etc.—will be clamoring for more and more "independent" evaluation of managers' performances. Obviously, the wide-awake and motivated management auditors will be the avant garde of the professional corps which will render these much-needed objective evaluations of management's efficiency.

QUESTIONS FOR REVIEW AND DISCUSSION

1. What are some specific ways in which standards of managerial performance might be constructed?
2. Do you feel that appraisal of a firm's achievement of its public responsibilities is feasible and desirable? Why?
3. Of what significance to auditing management performance is the statement, "The United States Government does not have the built-in profit-and-loss yardstick and control that is available to managements in the private sectors?"
4. What are some major conditions or circumstances that impede management auditing efforts, especially in the case of governmental programs?

39. ROI Simulations for Investment Decisions[*]

RICHARD A. ELNICKI

Return on investment (ROI) measures based on discounted cash flows are generally recognized as being theoretically superior to accounting rate of return and payoff period for making investment decisions. However, the first-look and frequently the most important ranking index for many firms is the payoff period. This may be attributable to the lack of exposure to the discounting methods and the basic simplicity of the payoff period calculation. But these reasons beg the actual question. It is the *uncertainty* in real-world investment decisions that is primarily responsible for the relegation of the discounting methods to classroom or secondary status.

Uncertainty

Uncertainty considerations led to the conclusion that the discounting methods impute spurious or false accuracy to the indexes of preference generated by the internal rate or profitability index. The usual applications of the discounting methods do not reflect the uncertainty inherent in the predictions of cash flows.

Requiring a high internal rate or using high costs of capital for profitability indexes to reflect uncertainty further imputes false accuracy. Hence, it is to be expected that firms are reluctant to spend the time and effort necessary to use the discounted methods; the accuracy of the ranking indexes does not merit the cost.

Uncertainty can be taken into consideration directly via an analysis method that reflects the risk attitudes inherent in the "high liquidity" investment preferences held by most managements. The theoretical analysis of uncertainty can quickly become very complex and buried in mathematical notation. This discussion will avoid the complexities when possible.

[*] Source: Reprinted with permission of *Management Accounting*, February 1970, pp 37–41. Dr. Richard A. Elnicki is assistant professor of economics, Yale University.

Possible Outcomes

Given certainty, an alternative will be rejected if the outcome is undesirable according to some objective. Given uncertainty, an alternative will be rejected if the chances of undesirable outcomes outweigh the chances of desirable outcomes where an objective defines desirable and undesirable and an attitude toward risk gives weights to the outcomes. Hence, if return is the organization objective, the decision maker will reflect ROI's and risk attitudes toward *possible outcomes.*

The decision maker must have some idea of the sequences of events that will lead to possible undesirable outcomes. This assertion presumes that the decision maker is in his position because he has some knowledge of the interrelationships of events related to his position in the firm.

It follows that the decision maker can: (1) give estimates of events and sequences that will lead to outcomes and (2) specify most likely, optimistic and pessimistic amounts on events and sequences of events. The most likely, optimistic, and pessimistic events can be assigned chances of occurring as is done with PERT (Program Evaluation and Review Technique). The events can then be combined to show possible outcomes and the chances of the possible outcomes.

Assume a decision maker estimates that Alternative A will require a cash investment at time zero of $95, $100 or $105, with the chances of occurrence being 10 percent, 80 percent and 10 percent, respectively. He estimates that he will receive $105, $110 or $115 at the end of one year with the chances of occurrence being 20 percent, 70 percent and 10 percent, respectively.

The most pessimistic *outcome* is a combination of the two most pessimistic events:

$$\begin{array}{ll} \text{Investment:} & \$105 \\ \text{Receipts:} & \$105 \\ \text{Outcome:} & \$105/\$105 = 1.00 \\ & \text{or 0 percent} \end{array}$$

The most optimistic outcome is 21.0 percent, a combination of the two most optimistic events: Investment $95, Receipts $115 ($115/$95 = 1.2105 or 21.0 percent).

The pessimistic outcome, 0 percent, will occur if both pessimistic events occur; the chances of both occurring is the chance of the investment, .10 times the change of the receipts, .20, or .10(.20) which equals .02. Hence, assuming the investment and receipts amounts do not affect one another, the 0 percent ROI has only a .02 chance of occurring.

All possible outcomes and the chances of all possible outcomes are shown in Tables 1 and 2.

TABLE 1. Investment A: Possible ROI Outcomes

Investments	Receipts		
	$105	$110	$115
$95	10.5%	15.8%	21.0%
$100	5.0%	10.0%*	15.0%
$105	.0%	4.8%	9.5%

   * 10.0% = $110/$100 = 1.10 or 10%

If the decision maker wants to make money (the objective), he should consider all the alternatives available. Assume he can earn 6 percent on a one-year savings account he considers *risk free*, i.e., 6 percent is a certainty for all practical purposes. There is a .25 chance he will do better with the savings account than with A since the outcomes of 0 percent, 4.8 percent, and 5.0 percent have a total chance of occurring equal to .02 plus .07 plus .16 or .25. If he chooses the savings account over A because there is a .25 chance he will earn less than 6 percent ROI, he is *risk averse* by definition.

Real-world business investments, however, have many relevant decision factors and they will be in a time sequence. Given estimates of events under each relevant decision factor, the tables of possible outcomes and chances of possible outcomes can quickly approach the capacity of a large computer. Further, if continuous distributions are abstracted from the most likely, optimistic and pessimistic events on each relevant factor, as with PERT methods, it is frequently impossible to combine them mathematically. But, the desired information is a distribution of possible outcomes. The distribution of possible outcomes can be estimated by the numeric analysis method known as simulation. There is nothing profound or complicated about simulating ROI distributions; it is simply a work saver.

TABLE 2. Investment A: Chances of Possible Outcomes

Investments	Receipts		
	.20	.70	.10
.10	.02	.07	.01
.80	.16	.56*	.08
.10	.02	.07	.01

   * .56 = .70(.80)

ROI Simulation

The objective of simulation in this case is to get an estimate of the chances various ROI's will occur. Therefore, the method should give a distribution "close" to the actual distribution.

TABLE 3. Investment A: ROI Distribution

Array Order		Interval Order	
ROI	P(ROI)	ROI	P(ROI)
0.0%	.02	−2.5% − −2.4%	.02
4.8%	.07	2.5% − 7.4%	.23
5.0%	.16		
9.5%	.01		
10.0%	.56	7.5% − 12.4%	.59
10.5%	.02		
15.0%	.08	12.5% − 17.4%	.15
15.8%	.07		
21.0%	.01	17.5% − 22.4%	.01
Total	1.00	Total	1.00

Investment A, discussed above, had nine possible outcomes. Table 3 shows the ROI's, and the chances of the ROI's, P(ROI), in an array and an interval order; the array observations correspond to the entries in Tables 1 and 2.

To estimate the distribution of ROI's for Investment A, the initial estimates are assigned numbers, RN Slot, from 00 to 99, corresponding to the chances of the events. In Table 4, for example, the event receipts of $105 had a .20 chance of occurring and this event is assigned a twenty-number interval, 00 to 19.

TABLE 4. Investment A: Simulation Format

Investment			Receipts		
Event	Chances	RN Slot	Event	Chances	RN Slot
$ 95	.10	00—09	$105	.20	00—19
$100	.80	10—89	$110	.70	20—99
$105	.10	90—99	$115	.10	90—99

A table to two-place random numbers is then used to get "trial" outcomes. Pairs of random numbers will, over many trials, fall into the RN "slots" in Table 4 in proportion to the chances of the events on relevant decision factors.

The simulation of Investment A's ROI distribution was started by the random numbers 54 and 77. The 54 falls in the $100 investment slot and the 77 falls in the $110 receipt slot. Thus the first "trial" outcome was 10 percent ($100/$100 = 1.10). The first five trials had the outcomes shown on Table 5.

Fifty trials were performed in this manner. They are shown in Table 6 by proportions for comparison with the actual distribution of returns.

The simulation proportions are an estimate of the distribution of returns under Investment A; as the number of trials increases, the simulation dis-

TABLE 5. Investment A: Simulation Trials

	Random Number for:		Event		Trial Outcome
Trial	Investment	Receipts	Investments	Receipts	ROI
1	54	77	$100	$110	10%
2	96	02	$105	$105	0%
3	73	76	$100	$110	10%
4	56	98	$100	$115	15%
5	68	05	$100	$105	5%

tribution will get closer to the actual distribution. The trials are stopped when the proportions stop shifting between class intervals; pragmatically, this means when the proportions change by one percent or less after rounding.

Realistic investments will have sequences of events through time where the event in a year is in part dependent on the event of the previous year. This is demonstrated by the following simulation. Assume the decision maker can take Contract B for 5 years. He analyzes all available data on the relevant factors—price, market share, size of market, growth in market, labor rates, productivity, raw material prices and requirements, investment requirements, etc.—and concludes that net positive cash flows will be $24, $25 or $26 during the first year and $2 more, the same or $2 less *any* following year. The investment is to be made at time zero. No event affects other events except as stated for cash-flow changes. The relevant decision factors and events are shown in Table 7.

TABLE 6. Investment A: Actual and Simulated ROI Distributions

ROI	Actual P(ROI)	Simulation Proportions
−2.5% − −2.4%	.02	.04
2.5% − 7.4%	.23	.26
7.5% − 12.4%	.59	.56
12.5% − 17.4%	.15	.14
17.5% − 22.4%	.01	.00
	1.00	1.00

TABLE 7. Contract B: Decision Factors

Investment		Cash Flow Year 1		Annual Cash Flow Change	
Event	Chances	Event	Chances	Event	Chances
$ 90	.10	$24	.30	−$2	.30
$100	.70	$25	.40	-0-	.40
$115	.20	$26	.30	+$2	.30

The most pessimistic outcome is a return of −5% investment, $115; cash flow sequence, $24, $22, $20, $18, $16. The most optimistic outcome is a return of 19%: investment $90; cash flow sequence, $26, $28, $30, $32, $34. The most likely outcome (modal) is a return of 8%: investment, $100; cash flow sequence, $25 each year for 5 years. These sequences are shown in Exhibit 1.

All outcomes will be between those shown for the optimistic and pessimistic flow sequences plotted in Exhibit 1. The fan pattern reflects normal expectations on future events, viz., as predictions are made for more distant time periods, the range of possible outcomes increases.

Finding the actual distribution of returns for Contract B would be cumbersome. Tables similar to 1 and 2 above would be made but each would have 3 columns and 243 rows. If the decision maker gave 2-year estimates for each of the nine factors listed above, with only 3 events for each factor, the tables would have 3 columns and 59,049 rows. And, if continuous distributions were abstracted from the three events, it might be impossible to find the actual distribution of outcomes mathematically. On the other hand, simulation is almost trivial on a computer.

EXHIBIT 1. Contract B: Cash Flow Sequences

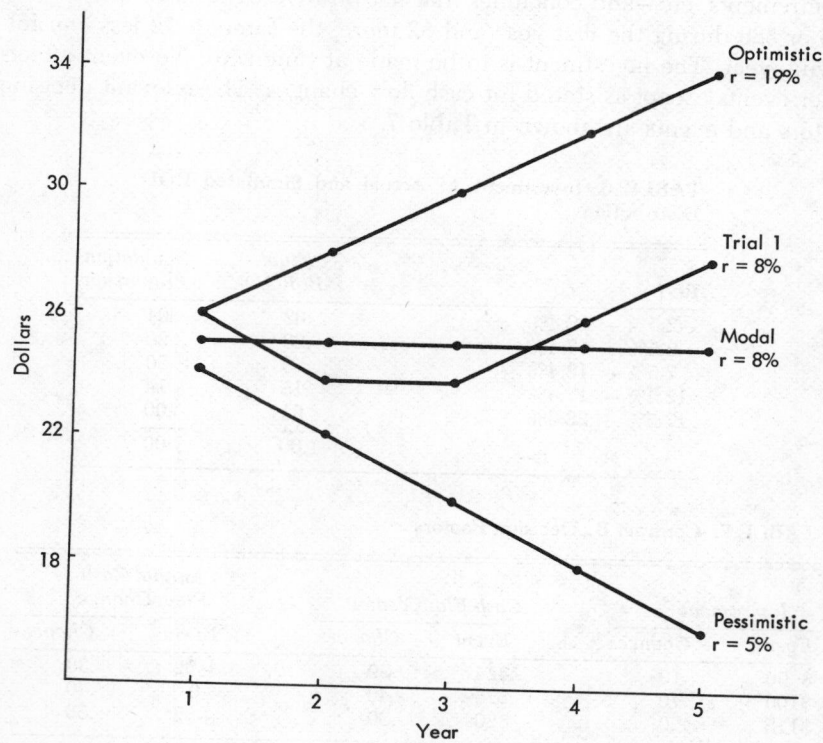

EXHIBIT 2. Contract B: Estimated ROI Distribution

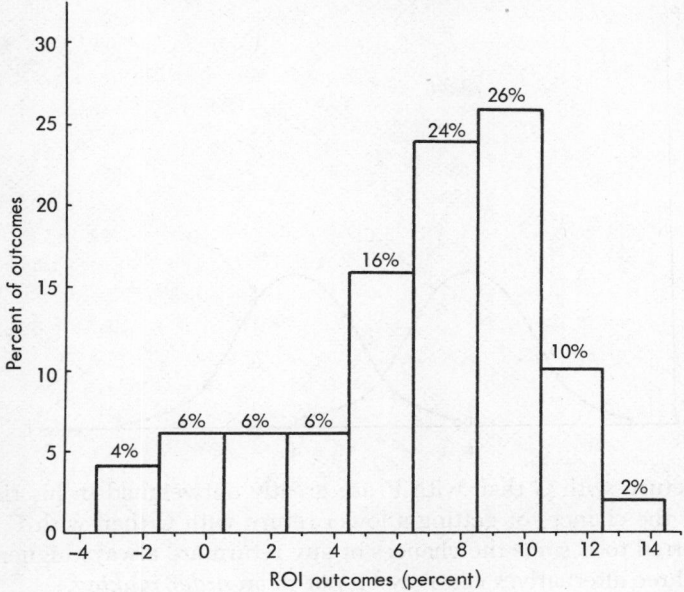

The actual distribution of Contract B ROI's was estimated by the simulation method described above. However, each trial required six two-place random numbers: one for the investment event, one for the cash-flow event in Year 1, and one each for the cash-flow change event the following four years. The 50-trial estimated distribution of Contract B is shown in Exhibit 2. The optimistic and pessimistic outcomes are not shown, since they have only a .00000243 and .00000486 chance, respectively, of occurring.

Alternative Choices

It is assumed that the decision makers make logical choices given their attitudes toward risk. This assumption *provides* the basis for using ROI distributions for decisions.

Assume two alternatives involving investments of similar magnitudes are available and only one can be taken: C or D. The ROI distributions are as shown on Exhibit 3; r_c and d_d are the respective average returns:

In Case 1, the risk averse decision maker will prefer D to C. For, the chances of getting an ROI equal to *any amount or more* are always greater with D than with C.

In Case 2, the choice is between C, E and F as shown on Exhibit 4. The risk averse decision maker will prefer C to E: the chances of getting an ROI equal to any amount or more are always greater with C than with E. And, he will always prefer F to C because the small chances of getting a

EXHIBIT 3. Case 1: Alternatives C and D

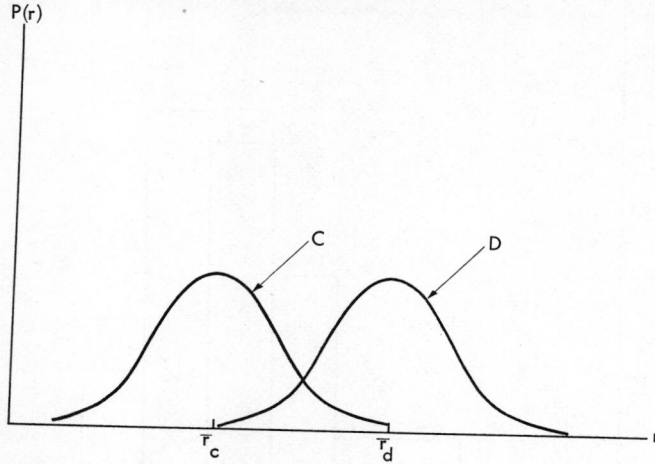

higher return with C than with F are greatly outweighed in his risk attitudes by the chances of getting a lower return with C than with F. F will
be preferred to E since the chances of any return are always higher under
F. The three alternatives can now be put in an *order ranking*.

Preference Ranking	*Alternative*
1	F
2	C
3	E

EXHIBIT 4. Case 2: Alternatives C, E, and F

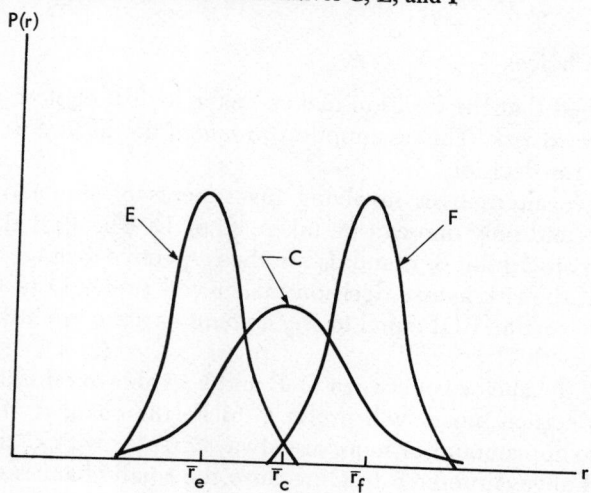

In case 3 we assume that the risk averse decision maker must choose between C and G as shown in Exhibit 5. In this case, the average returns are the same: $r_c = r_g$.

The risk averse decision maker will prefer G to C: the chances of lower returns under C as compared to G receive more weight in his risk attitudes than the chances of higher returns under C as compared to G. G is less risky to him. The spread of chances in the distributions can be measured by s, where s increases as the distribution becomes flatter.[1]

Note that the distribution of C is flatter than that of G. It follows that the s of C will be greater than the s of G, and since C is more risky because of the spread *s can be used as a measure of riskiness*.[2] Using s as a measure, it can be asserted that the risk averse decision maker will always prefer the alternative with the lowest s given that the average returns are equal.

Assume that the spread on G is equal to the spread on E. The risk averse decision maker will prefer G to C when their average returns are equal, but if G slides down to E keeping its spread, as shown on Exhibit 6, he will prefer C to G when G is on top of E.

Why the change? The chances of C giving a better return becomes greater as G approaches E. At some point as G is approaching E, the deci-

EXHIBIT 5. Case 3: Alternatives C and G

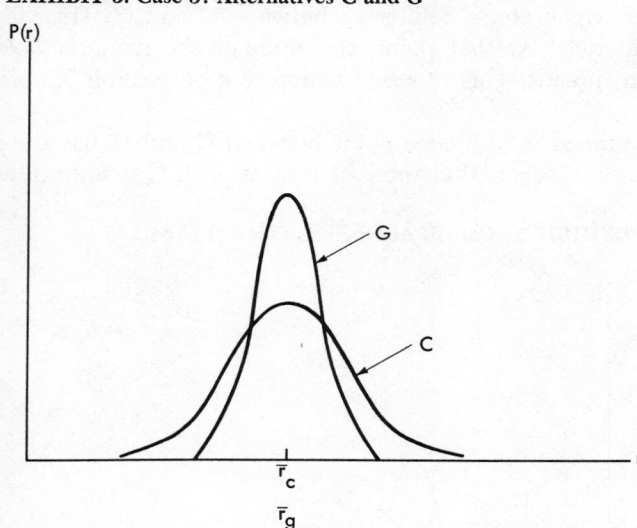

---

[1] The s in these cases is the standard deviation. If the distributions are skewed a third measure is needed. Skewed distributions are not discussed here because they only complicate the discussion of the trade-offs involved in choices.

[2] The analysis here is quite similar to the portfolio risk analysis model where investors specify security combinations with estimated variances, s^2's. However, this analysis is not attempting to define a risk minimizing frontier line.

EXHIBIT 6. Case 4: Alternative G becomes E

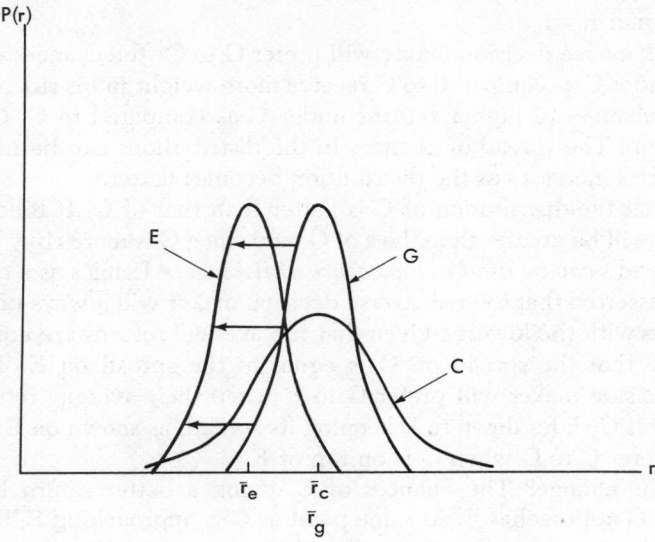

sion maker will become indifferent between G and C: He will consider them equal bets! At that point, the trade-off in averages *balances* the trade-off in spreads. This situation is depicted on Exhibit 7, comparing C and H:

The presumed indifference point between C and H has the following characteristic: The small chances of returns with C being under H's (on

EXHIBIT 7. Case 5: Alternatives C and H

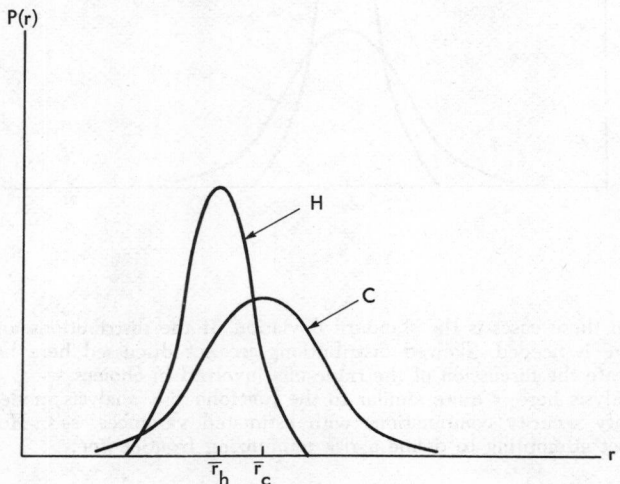

C's left tail) are exactly offset by the larger chances of returns with C being greater than H's (on C's right tail).

In those cases where the alternative with the lower mean also has the lower spread measure, the decision maker must consider how important the tails are in stating his preferences, i.e., he must focus on the issue at question—risk. It is not necessary to determine one indifference point as a benchmark, e.g., a given ratio of s to r. In fact, it may be incorrect to do so. Attitudes toward risk change through time and as a result of previous actual outcomes. Hence, the indifference point will change.

Risk attitudes also vary with the amount of money at risk. The president of a large corporation is likely to take a .25 chance of losing $5,000 to have a .25 chance of making an ROI of 30 percent or more. The effect of a $5,000 loss will be negligible. On the other hand, he is not likely to take a .25 chance of bankruptcy to have a .25 chance of earning an ROI of 30 percent or more.

Internal Rates versus Profitability Indexes

The internal rate of return vs. profitability index question on ranking loses meaning with the analysis method described above. Given *single estimates* of cash flows for each year, if he expected lives of two alternatives differ, the internal rate of return criteria can lead to one choice while the profitability index criteria can lead to the other. However, since the range of possible events increases as the time perspective increases, the distribution of outcomes becomes flatter (s becomes larger) whether the outcomes are in terms of internal rates or profitability indexes.

It is as easy to estimate a distribution of profitability indexes as it is to estimate a distribution of internal rates! If alternatives with different lives are being compared, the distribution of internal rates or profitability indexes on the alternative with the greater life will have the greater spread —risk measure—under normal expectations of future events.

Therefore, reflecting possible outcomes makes the two decision bases have the same effect on decisions. This leads to the conclusion that the internal rate of return vs. profitability index question on rankings is moot— it is raised by the completely unrealistic implicit assumption that single estimates for each year are accurate!

Conclusion

The use of ROI distributions is superior to the usual discounting methods and payoff: It eliminates the spurious accuracy inherent in single estimates since it forces the decision maker to consider possible outcomes. It reflects the attitudes toward risk held by most managements while remaining in return-on-investment terminology. And, it gives order rankings for investment alternatives of similar magnitudes.

Simulating ROI outcome distributions is easy. The hard part is on the tasks for which the decision maker in business earns his salary, viz., analyzing historical data, thinking through relationships on the myriad past and future investment factors and making best judgments of future events.

QUESTIONS FOR REVIEW AND DISCUSSION

1. Do you agree with the statement that return-on-investment distributions are closer to reality than single estimates? Why?
2. Explain how the numbers in the first two columns of Table 3 were obtained from Tables 1 and 2.
3. In your own words, tell what the chart in Exhibit 2 shows. What the chart in Exhibit 4 shows.
4. What qualifications must be kept in mind to use s, spread, as a measure of riskiness?

part ELEVEN

The Future and Management

People are always interested in what the future will bring and managers are no exception. While the future cannot be determined by projection of familiar patterns, it would appear reasonably certain that future developments in management will include broad changes and many new concepts. Undoubtedly the techniques used and the frameworks followed will be far different from those of today. Also, the effect of the external environment upon management will be wide and deep. Technology, government, and social forces appear destined to shape further the format of management to an extent that defies accurate description.

In "Toward a Social-Industrial Complex," Dr. Simon Ramo prognosticates about the decades, 1970–90. He envisions great progress in technology, but warns that what happens will be determined mainly by social, economic, and political aspects. Our part free-enterprise and part governmental-controlled economy will make up a social-industrial complex. As he sees it, government leadership is mandatory for effective environmental control to exist.

Emphasizing important issues to which future managers must address themselves rather than reviewing the forces that are producing change is the theme of John Diebold's "New Rules and Opportunities for Business." He discusses nine major issues and observes that two general characteristics underlie all these issues including (1) the interface between private and public enterprise, and (2) the significant changes that will affect the entire decision making process. For example, managers of the future will have to reach decisions in fields in which they have had no experience. Advances in technology and growth in government will challenge the best of managerial thinking. How to apply them for maximum human benefit will be the big problem.

The last reading is "The Pharmacist as Futurist" by Edward S. Cornish. Here the reader becomes aware of the existence of the World Future Society and other organizations engaged in the study of the future. An insight is gained concerning the work these organizations engage in, their connection with efforts to identify changes of the future, and the impact of their work upon society and management. An interesting table of future developments is also included in the article.

40. Toward a Social-Industrial Complex*

SIMON RAMO

The world between now and 1990 will have its fill of technology and resources issues—problems, opportunities, breakthroughs, controversies—a widening gap between developed and underdeveloped nations in consumption of increasingly scarce materials, growing pollution, failure to adjust to rapid technological change. And alongside these negatives, the promise of vastly improved communication and transportation, plentiful energy by nuclear techniques and fresh water by desalting the seas, weather control, new means for tapping the earth's hidden resources, and even, perhaps, control of aging.

Pessimists say civilization is doomed already by our greedy consumption of the earth's resources and the attendant impact on the environment. Optimists picture a fantastically better world based on technological development. But not everything that can happen will happen. Social-economic-political aspects, not technological ones, will determine what actually does occur. Our habits and priorities will select how we allocate our resources.

Looking to 1990

So for useful anticipation we are forced to consider the interface of technology with society. Let us look to 1990 through specific examples. First, however, let us disclose what these examples will suggest:

1. For real progress a systems approach will be needed, emphasizing interactions amongst numerous technological and social-economic parameters.

* Source: Reprinted with permission of *The Wall Street Journal*, February 16, 1972, p. 10. Dr. Simon Ramo is Vice Chairman of the Board and Chairman of the Executive Committee of TRW, Inc., Redondo Beach, Calif. This paper is adapted from an address delivered at The White House Conference on The Industrial World Ahead, February 7, 1972.

2. Great economic and social return will result from intelligent investment in advanced technology with increased productivity alone compen-
sating for the cost.

3. Insistent public demand to solve "social-engineering" problems—
urban development, pollution control, improved health care, poverty elimination—will exert a powerful effect on the allocations of resources.

4. Our hybrid economy, part free enterprise and part governmentally
controlled, will constitute a virtual Social-Industrial Complex by 1990, this
developing government-business teaming greatly influenced by technology.

5. From today's apparent surplus of engineers and scientists will emerge
a severe shortage with a need particularly for interdisciplinary "socio-
technologists."

As a first example, consider the new technology many see as the most
important of all because it amounts to the creation of synthetic electronic
brainpower. Since information makes the world go 'round, this development will impact on every activity of man. Applied to business and industry, fast and powerful man-machine information systems will enable managers to operate closer to total awareness and control, with optimum
scheduling and on-line measurement of labor, materials, cash flow and
product distribution. A logical step by 1990 is interconnection of information flow among industrial entities whose harmoniously interlocked operations will respond to market actions in real time with payment for services
and materials flowing electronically.

Now, is not such a superior handling of information the greatest boon
that technology could give to society? With enormous brainpower, the
machine partner would take on the more mundane tasks, the high-capacity
handling of information, the human partner rising to higher plateaus of
judgment, creativity and decision making. Greater productivity would
ensue.

But, there are some difficulties. The modifications of the structure of
operations needed to exploit the new technology will involve massive
start-up costs. These systems become economical only when there are millions of user terminals (even as with telephony or TV). Required are billions of dollars in operating losses, with more billions at risk for years before turnaround into a profit period. The pioneering capital needs are
beyond what even the largest corporations are likely to consider. Despite
the economic gain inherent in the productivity increase, the speed with
which this technology can come into being is contingent on teaming of
corporations and government. The government may need to sponsor large-
scale experiments and encourage joint ventures of private industry to
share risk.

Some identify information systems with a computerized, regimented,
planned economy. But recall that the foundation of free enterprise is the
free market. The more all goods can be offered for sale in a free market,

the closer we come to approaching full free enterprise. With information reaching every nook and cranny of the economy, a proposal to produce something could be considered immediately by potential purchasers everywhere. In 1990, with substantial discounts for commitments made early, we could deplete our bank accounts electronically by pushing the right button to commit for cars, air-conditioners, vacations, furniture, clothes, frozen foods and educational courses. Such direct communications could be used to schedule manufacturing and distribution. The profit-to-risk ratio would rise dramatically as the entrepreneur and the consumer communicate in an "on-line" market.

Advancing technology in this instance as in every other merely offers us choices. It does not determine the direction in which our society must go.

If scientific knowledge were used to the fullest world-wide in a match with social and economic factors, the problem of pollution would become tolerable. But such wise use of technology by all nations with agreed-upon criteria is an unrealistic ideal for attainment by 1990.

Unfortunately, private industry alone cannot assemble a market in which to sell depollution services. Without organized citizen action—meaning government—no meaningful customer-supplier relationship exists. To emphasize this, consider a very large project. A decade ago the then President announced that we would land a man on the moon "within the decade." Imagine that the present President announces a similarly bold program: "Before the '70s are over we shall depollute the Great Lakes."

He assigns an agency to direct the job and contracts go out to find out how to depollute the Great Lakes with the least cost and to meet specific economic and social criteria. But a great deal more than the basic science of environmental control emerges. Deep confrontations occur on how much we are willing to pay to protect the environment. Limiting growth of some industry around the lakes implies population shift. The project influences the pattern of society elsewhere in the U.S. and other parts of the world.

Thus, environmental control without government leadership is unlikely by 1990 or later. Once criteria, goals, trade-offs and basic research and development are handled strongly by government, private capital will be invested seeking profits on hardware and installation services.

Rapid Transit Problems

Urban problems will deserve a high priority in the '70s and '80s, urban rapid transit being typical.

An employe in a large city may live 10 miles from his work with no real choice, in view of the city's "design," to live closer. He drives this 10 miles in one hour at 10 miles an hour, polluting the air as he goes and using up his nervous energy in the traffic. He leaves his investment to stand all day in the parking lot. Tired before he even starts, his 40-hour work week accomplishes 30 hours worth but it takes him 60 hours portal to portal.

The productivity improvement, and economic payoff potential, is sinful to ignore.

However, the only transit systems that will constitute good return on investment will be those designed taking account of the entire life of the community. The federal government needs to launch substantial programs for system design of urban transit, done concurrently with system studies of broader urban requirements. With this effort disclosing the system fundamentals to ensure economic design and the common hardware elements required, private investment to develop specifics will follow.

More examples would merely strengthen the conclusion that almost every priority need involves technology, and that applying our know-how will yield economic returns and social benefits. However, we possess great organizational inadequacies and a lack of means to set goals, compare alternatives, and put together private and government entities into a Social-Industrial Complex to get on with what we want to accomplish.

Some of us must get over the hangup that insists government should leave everything to the private sector. Others must abandon the thought that private action means only "selfish interest" so we should become a totally government-directed nation.

Knowledge that we are actually a hybrid society, part free enterprise and part government controlled, doesn't prevent us from espousing simplistic views and avoiding discussion of innovative, cooperative organizational schemes.

Long before 1990 it will become apparent that we have a shortage of properly trained people, particularly the interdisciplinary, practical intellectual. Because it will be the only way to get started to get the job done, we shall create "social technologists" (perhaps we should say "poly-socio-econo-politico-technologists") in the school of hard knocks. They will become expert at applying science and technology fully to the needs of our society by pragmatic, day-to-day synthesizing of arts, disciplines, experience, motivations and human ingenuity, and will be invaluable components of the Social-Industrial Complex.

Some Predictions

Do these thoughts lead to reasonable 1990 predictions?

Before 1990 it may become apparent that it is wrong to countenance an antitechnology wave, confusing this tool of man, technology, with its misuse by man himself; to go on without setting goals, without planning, with priorities set by crisis. In contrast, we may come to act on the belief that the whole world will suffer from pollution unless there is world cooperation on goals and controls; that pollution will be minimized by wise technological development and ample energy supply; that we should use technology to the fullest to increase our resources whether it be more brainpower or more electrical power.

By 1990 we may have created new patterns for government-industry-science cooperation, the Social-Industrial Complex. We may have abandoned the idea that to articulate goals and objectives and study alternative plans is to embark on a one-way road to a complete state control of the economy and the life pattern. Instead we may see that to have freedom will require planning for it.

QUESTIONS FOR REVIEW AND DISCUSSION

1. Comment fully on this quotation, "Environmental control without government leadership is unlikely by the year 2000 or later."

2. Describe your comprehension of a "Social-Industrial Complex" that would assist us to get on with what we want to accomplish.

3. As you see it, does advancing technology determine the direction in which our society goes or do forces of societal, government, or consumers guide or select the direction given technological improvements? Discuss.

41. New Rules and Opportunities for Business*

JOHN DIEBOLD

Charles Dickens began *A Tale of Two Cities* with the lines, "It was the best of times, it was the worst of times." The same lines are appropriate as a commentary on today's world.

The insights of science, applied through the management of technology, have produced a society in which for the first time in human history wealth is not confined to a few. In doing so, science and technology have unleashed a worldwide social revolution the dimensions of which have hardly yet been suggested even by today's tumult.

While no man knows the future, we are beginning to recognize that we are at this moment living through a major disjunction in history and that we can no longer conceive the future, as we once could, as an extrapolation of familiar patterns.

Many phrases are used to describe this phenomenon. To cite four commentators: Zbigniew Brzezinski says that we are living *Between Two Ages*, entering a "technotronic era"; Peter Drucker feels we are in an *Age of Discontinuity;* Daniel Bell that we are entering the post-industrial era; and Alvin Toffler that we are suffering from *Future Shock.*

To reflect for a moment on Peter Drucker's analysis, he points out that the world between the two wars and up until today is remarkable not so much for its change as for its consistency with the patterns already discernible at the beginning of the century.

His point is that there is much to indicate that this era is now ending, and that we are living through the birth pains of quite a new period in history in which the change from our immediate past will be remarkable for its dimensions and extraordinary in its character.

* Source: Reprinted with permission of *Financial Executive,* December 1971, pp. 18–25. John Diebold is president, The Diebold Group, Inc.

Major Disjunction in History

Other observers, such as Dean William Haber of the University of Michigan, forecast a change from now to the end of this century greater than we have experienced since the year 1500 even though the years remaining in this century are fewer than those between the outbreak of World War II and the present.

The signal fact of our times is that we are living through a period of great social change, which colors everything that one can say about the form and the role of management in the immediate future. It is a singularly appropriate, and at the same time difficult, moment in which to address the question of what management's role will be in the future and how management will perform that role.

Management the Determinant

In a period such as this, can any of us doubt that the attention of managers must be not only on mastering the proliferation of new techniques but also on understanding that the environment in which management manages is in total change? A fundamental fact of this new era is that management—management of our infinitely complex network of public and private organizations—will above all else determine the character and the success of our future society, and the quality of human life within that society.

I should like to tackle the task of looking at management in the future, not by presenting once again a review of the forces that are producing change nor by painting a panorama of the world of management in the year 2000 or even in 1984. Both exercises are readily available. Rather, I should like to identify a few issues that seem to me important in considering management in the future. I have identified nine. One could make the list shorter; one could make the list longer.

There are two general characteristics underlying these nine points: (1) it is at the interface between private and public enterprise that I see the most interesting and the most important events relating to management in the next decade; (2) in the interface, and within both private and public management themselves, it is the decision process that will experience the most interesting changes. What stage could be more central to the process of management?

Management in the Public Sector

My first observation concerning management in the future is directly concerned with the interface between the world of public management and the world of private management. It is the changing character of managment in the political and public sphere.

Vastly more attention must be given to the identification of the goals and the consequences of alternative courses of public policy. Several phenomena are involved.

We have in the political process itself a major asset when we need to choose among alternatives appropriate to society. The problem is that we have not done a good job of defining the alternatives and their consequences in a way that will give focus to the political process. Without defined alternatives, decisions tend to be made by default or inadvertence or with insufficient attention to secondary consequences. When the alternatives are defined, we can trust the political process to give order to our priorities and to give direction to society.

All too often we focus on the short range and the expedient. We react to the needs of the moment and do not think of the long-term consequences of our actions. In the world we are entering, we must do more to identify the consequences of alternative actions. This means a number of things in the public sphere.

Today we are ruled by a tyranny of small decisions. We make decisions which seem of modest significance, but without fully understanding their implications. After a series of these "small decisions," we find we are locked into disastrous patterns that defy our capacity to break.

All about us are examples of major problems resulting from such a cumulation of small decisions that now require solution: the problems of the cities; of transportation; of the distribution of medical services; of education.

At the interface between the public and the private sectors are major examples of how many small decisions lead to severe problems. New approaches to management can play an important role in solving this kind of problem. Innovative management can provide the analytical acumen to give the public sector a better idea of alternatives and of the consequences of alternatives. Management can do a great deal with systems analysis, program planning, and budgeting and other new analytical techniques of modern management not only to help solve the same kind of problems faced in the past—and to clear up some of our most pressing public problems which were created by this "tyranny of past decisions"—but to insure a public decision-making process that avoids in the future the mishandling of the even more complex problems we shall face. A major element in a proper process is the establishment at each level of public management—legislative as well as executive—of an analytical group to identify the consequences of alternative choices.

Charles Schultze, a former director of the United States Budget Bureau and now at the Brookings Institution, wrote recently: "Not only do our social ends or values conflict, but being quite subtle and complex, they are exceedingly difficult to specify. We simply cannot determine in the abstract our ends or values and the intensity with which we hold them. We discover our objectives and the intensity that we assign to them only in the process of considering particular programs or policies. We articulate 'ends' as we evaluate 'means'." (*The Politics and Economics of Public Spending*, Brookings Institution, 1968)

We cannot go about choosing objectives for society in the abstract; it is only by continuous, rigorous analysis of alternative consequences and costs to society of alternative routes that we can make decisions. And it is here one finds the most important role of management in the future.

We have major problems of time frame with many implications. In politics we focus on short time scales. We put people into the legislature for brief periods and expect them to make decisions which may be politically unpopular today, yet of major benefit—or essential—a few years hence. Our society has a very short attention and interest span. We are concerned with immediate events. We must find a way which allows a man elected for two or four years to make decisions which are of consequence to society six, eight, fifteen, or twenty years, or even further ahead, although his decisions may be very unpopular only one year later when he must run again for office.

This entire article, and much more, could well be devoted to commenting upon other problems that will be encountered in applying more rational management to society's delineation and choice among alternatives. Thus, it is for more than one reason I have begun my list with this phenomenon.

Public Services Operated by Private Sector

I suggested earlier that it is in the public/private interface that we shall see the most important management developments in the next decade. Perhaps the most interesting of these is the prospect of operation by the private sector of many activities traditionally characterized as public services. Once we have identified objectives and assigned priority through political choice based on better understanding of alternatives, we must concern ourselves with operations.

Here lies one of the great and interesting opportunities and challenges: how to make fuller use of the most notably suucessful institution which we have in the West—private enterprise. What particularly distinguishes the private sector is its unequalled efficiency as resource allocator, the most efficient man has ever invented.

The challenge is whether we can apply this instrument to the operation of such activities as the distribution of medical services, to education, to the great public service areas. In these areas we have extremely low productivity, and in many of them productivity is declining. Yet our societies demand enormous increases in precisely these public services.

Here is one of the most interesting and exciting opportunities of our times: an opportunity for private business to participate in the largest growth sector of society and an opportunity for society to fulfill its aspirations—perhaps the only one! Once objectives are decided politically, we must apply the resource allocator and leave operation to the private sector.

In the United States, for example, 170 school districts in different parts of the country contracted last autumn with private companies to teach reading and mathematics. Many cities are beginning to contract out large areas of operations in which performance has been poor.

The attempts to simulate market conditions—to leave operations to the private sector—will be difficult but among the most interesting and exciting problems faced by management. We can unquestionably continue to provide many public services without going to the private sector by following old patterns. But as I have noted, the low productivity which characterizes many of these service areas severely limits society's ability to fulfill all that we have come to expect. We already have a level of expectation which is beyond our ability to deliver. I believe that institutional changes, among them the harnessing of operational efficiencies achieved when market forces are at play, are essential if society is to achieve the quality of life we all desire.

We must break old patterns that have not worked. The task of finding new approaches is the second opportunity I have singled out for emphasis in regard to management's changing role in the future. It is of very great consequence.

Again, this problem, like the analytical support necessary to setting public goals, has many implications. For example, we know very little about measuring productivity or, for that matter, about measuring performance in many of the most critical public service areas—education, for example.

Whether we do or do not involve the private sector in operations, we are still faced with the problem of how to measure, for example, effectiveness in education. It is a paradox that many countries allocate vast parts of their gross national products to education, health care, and other essential services. And yet they have virtually no operationally useful measures of performance. We need new ways to gauge effectiveness; we need quality controls of a kind that have not yet been invented.

Whether operation is allocated totally to the public sector, or whether we are able to involve the private sector, the development of such performance and productivity measures becomes one of the most interesting and challenging tasks of management in the future.

Multinational Corporation

As I said at the opening of this article most of my nine observations are related to the decision process and many to the interface between the public and private sectors; the third area I have identified has both characteristics. It is the role of the multinational corporation.

The problem of the multinational corporation is not political but a decision problem which produces political issues. Quite understandably, sovereign states do not want to have large parts of their economy impacted by decisions made outside their countries. This is at the heart of the criticism currently being leveled at multinational corporations. On the other hand, the multinational corporation also encompasses the other aspect of the public/private interface that I have discussed—it is a superb resource allocator and a superb transfer agent of management and technology.

Peter Drucker recently wrote in the journal *The Public Interest:* "The multinational corporation is by far our most effective economic instrument today, and probably the one organ of economic development that actually develops. It is the one nonnationalist institution in a world shaken by nationalist delirium. It is not a political institution itself and must not be allowed to become one. Yet it puts economic decisions beyond the effective reach of the political process and its decision-makers, the national governments. The problem of how we accommodate this tension between economic rationality and political sovereignty in the next few years will have a tremendous impact on both the economy and the working of government." ("The New Markets and the New Capitalism," *The Public Interest,* Fall 1970).

I think this problem has within it the greatest interest for management. It offers a real hope for economic development and an opportunity for all the world to benefit.

Once we recognize that the locus and nature of decision making is at the heart of the problem, we can begin to devote to its solution the effort and attention which it deserves. It is important to both society and to business; it is interesting; and it is my choice of the third area of importance to management in the future.

Integrated Decision Systems

The fourth area that I have identified is the need within private firms and public organizations for integrated decision systems.

A quotation that sums up my own reaction to the use of computers thus far is as follows: "The modern age has a false sense of superiority because of the great mass of data at its disposal, but the valid criterion of distinction is rather the extent to which man knows how to form and master the material at his command."

The fact that this passage was written by Johann Wolfgang von Goethe in 1810 detracts not one whit from its appropriateness and timeliness! I think it sums up today's problems. We have vast quantities of data; we have enormously effective means of manipulating it; and we have given too little attention to the heart of the problem. We make use of these technologies but devote little attention to the critical factor of decision making —of the intelligent use of the data.

We need to give much more formal attention to the design of decision systems and to information flows. This is a big area in which there has been far too little real effort by management despite the many times its desirability is noted. The use of information technology is simply too important to leave to the technicians. Yet, with notable exceptions, that is precisely what has been done.

There are many interesting and important facets to this process. One problem management faces is to understand how to test the validity of the data it receives. The problem that middle management faces is building systems which incorporate far more political, social, economic, and environmental information in order to be able to have genuinely useful decision systems.

Top management must have decision systems concerned with the environment within which business operates. I don't mean environment in just its ecological sense. Management more and more will be addressing itself to problems of the social, the political, and the economic environment in which it lives. Yet our decision systems today are very inadequate in this regard.

In the past, this inadequacy could be tolerated. Yet today we live in a world of lightning change. We have the means to create workable decision systems, but we have much pioneering and inventing of new concepts to do to achieve the goal.

This seems to me to be the fourth area of consequence to management in the future. A great deal more attention on the part of management must be given continuously to the design of the decision systems. Managers must involve themselves much less with the one level of operations and much more with the design of the decision-making system and with its continuous modification.

These systems will represent major commitments of manpower and money. They will require input from many disciplines, but far more from the social sciences generally.

We lack almost entirely a proper methodology for the design of information systems. We have many tools and techniques, but the great task of synthesis of these into a formal discipline has hardly begun. It will be one of the central activities of the next period of development of management.

Strategy Formulation

The fifth area is concerned with what one does with information. It is the problem of strategy.

Management will have to pay much more attention to the problem of formulating strategy; of definition of the enterprise; of looking at the consequences of alternative roles; of identifying the strategy of the business or of the organization if it is an enterprise in the public sector.

Long-range planning is not the only factor here; in addition there is planning for change and its counterpart, planning necessitated by change. Product life has been shortened, as have the lives of industrial and business processes; the reaction time of management today is too long. Too many managements today consist of people who wait and watch what happens and either follow the leader or let others make mistakes that they can avoid. But there are more and more situations for which there has never been a precedent. More and more the world of the future is one in which management must make decisions without having a historical precedent.

Much more attention must be given to the problem of decision making in unique situations. This again implies a whole area of theory, not only mathematical, but organizational and inventional.

The problem of making decisions in unique situations will be much more typical in the future than it has been in the past. Formerly, we had a variety of yardsticks as well as adequate reaction times; we don't any more. We know how to react rapidly on a tactical level, but we don't know how to alter strategies quickly. We don't know how to react to radically changing situations affecting the environment in which business operates.

In addition to those that I have identified so far, there is a wide range of possible choices of areas for management in the future. Attitudes toward return on investment are going to change in terms of both the time frames and the level of return required. In the States we have what has been called a performance syndrome, and attention to it has dominated business thought for the last five years. Attention to performance is focused on a six-month, one-year or two-year period, and yet we now live in a world where one must take a very much longer view. But we don't. Our financial decisions are made on short-term considerations.

Another problem is the concept of overhead and labor productivity. When you have no direct workers, you have a very interesting problem in defining overhead. We are rapidly arriving at that point.

Our concepts of productivity are old. Productivity measurements often are based upon assumptions that had their origins in another world; we must reconsider them in terms of our new world. In many cases the productivity of labor performing service functions is measured by salary. You thus can come up with nonsense figures. You end by calling an increase in expenditure for the same or poorer or less service an increase in productivity!

The traditional distinction between office workers and factory workers is another interesting area in which many of our theoretical concepts must change. It is already very hard to differentiate between the two groups of workers and will become more so.

In economic theory, we are faced with the most interesting gap between the world as it has become and the very much simpler and less dynamic world our theories would like us to assume exists. I think it is a fascinating phenomenon that the only economist in the last hundred years who has given attention to technological change as a central element in his system has been Joseph Schumpeter. Schumpeter's system of economic theory is the only one in which technological change and invention play a large part in the dynamics of the system—as they do in the real world. All other economists ignored technological change or relegated it to minor positions. Yet monumental technological change—changing our society and everything we do (except the way we approach economic theory) is a fact of our times.

Building with New Technologies

My sixth point is the very tough problem and opportunity for management in building stable, profitable businesses around many of the new technologies. This is a task that gets right to the heart of the ability of a business to survive in this new era. It involves basics: the kind of men and management attitudes we build into key positions; the way we organize; the financial and marketing concepts we apply. Most of all it involves an ability to examine with fresh eyes what it is that makes for success in these new fields; to understand the extent to which institutional changes may be necessary; and to understand just what scale of resources applied over what period of time by what kind of managers is necessary for success. Considerably more agility and entrepreneurial outlook are necessary to make successes of many of these new businesses.

One example is educational technology. Programmed learning and computer-based systems are two very strong and interesting tools. Many business firms saw that these developments would revolutionize education, and they rushed into the new field.

A completely new type of business could and, I believe, will result. Yet old concepts were applied to the planning, staffing, and financing of these businesses. Major firms found that they had run against stone walls. All had tried to build businesses in an area to which they rightly foresaw a growing proportion of gross national product would be devoted. Yet considerable institutional change was and is needed before the promise can be turned into a profitable business

Again and again we encounter this phenomenon—innovations with great promise for important segments of our future, applied with enthusiasm by talented people, turning into business disasters! I have come to believe that this is not a series of chance mishaps, confined to education or computers or other advanced technologies in isolation. Rather it is a basic problem growing more common as, in the tasks we undertake, we encounter the realities of our age: rapid technological change acting as an agent for major social change, which in turn demands widespread institutional change for business success.

Consider the other half of the educational example: the problem of how to build businesses which are mixtures of very advanced technologies and of services, and how stable businesses can be built for the long term with these elements.

In the past we were able to look to equipment manufacturers for ideas on how to sell the product. We learned to give away large amounts of engineering work as part of the equipment sale. Suddenly we find we are in businesses in which the engineering work is crucial and the equipment is incidental. It is in part the effort to apply to these situations the older "new" concepts of giving service that lead to trouble. The instincts and behavior of the entrepreneur are the key to management in this area. A way must be found to incorporate these qualities in large-scale businesses that are more typically characterized by organization men.

We have looked at two worlds: the world of business and the businessman, and the world of managers. The bridge between them is flimsy. Attention should be paid to the more interesting work going on at the frontiers of management training and research; in a half dozen or so establishments we are considering the problem of how to inject the entrepreneur's outlook into the building of an organization. This is essential to management in rapidly changing situations, where new factors are the determinants of success.

Managing Creative and Service Personnel

My seventh observation on the role of management in the future is the need for innovation in our concepts of effective management of creative people and of service personnel.

For many years our approach to labor-management relations has been an admirable concern with "justice." This has led us to the concept which today in effect guarantees equal treatment and expectation for average performance. This is appropriate to a blue-collar world, where large numbers of people perform routine tasks, but it is totally inappropriate to knowledge industries, where the creativity of the worker can determine the success or failure of the enterprise.

Concepts of personnel classification also are the same—inappropriate to a world in which the productivity of creative people is vital; in which talent is, in effect, capital.

We don't view talent as capital, but it is. Talent is the capital of many of the new enterprises that are being formed and which will dominate the future. Talent is the capital, yet not one of our theories accepts this; and none of our compensation factors recognizes it. The results are aberrations in our system, with splinter groups continually breaking off from larger organizations and disparate efforts at equity participation for talent, inevitably leading to friction in large organizations and further splintering. We try to respond to reality but rarely at this point are the attempts successful. The problem is that we don't yet have a conceptually sound basis for recognizing talent as capital and for designing compensation systems accordingly.

This area seems to me to be one of the interesting battlegrounds for advanced management in the future. Again, it is an area where management's approach will determine the success of many enterprises. Where the product is ideas, the people producing the ideas have a sense of values and a set of loyalties that differ from those our present personnel theories tend to assume. The problem lies in trying to interpret the work of many creative people and of learning how to measure their performance.

Finding ways to accommodate and put to work the energy and talents of creative people is a tough and increasingly central problem for management in the future.

Training for the Future

My eighth point is concerned with the process of developing managers. The process of training managers must change substantially.

It is no longer possible for top management to have had first-hand experience and knowledge of every aspect of the enterprise. This will be even more true in the future. Managers are going to have to be able to make decisions in many fields in which they have had no experience. They must make judgments in scientific and technical matters without having background or experience in those areas. This applies not only to business, but perhaps even more to government. We have not yet coped very well with this requirement.

As we encounter more and more situations in which science and technology hold the keys to success or failure, we face increasingly difficult problems in the selection and development of managers. We need managers who manage but who understand technology. The problem is that we shall also need scientists who are scientists; we can't continually drain off the best ones as managers. The managers will have to make more decisions previously made by the scientists. This is a subject I consider to be central to the problem of management in the future.

Many fascinating questions must be faced. For example, a characteristic which today makes management successful is the ability to make the right decision on little data. As we enter a world in which we can increasingly have all the data we want, the premium is on an ability to ask the right questions and interpret properly the results. Will a different kind of a man then rise to the top? What will be his characteristics? What kind of training and development will be need?

New Structures

My ninth point concerns structural change within the organization. It will be an interesting and an important area.

Our organization theory comes straight out of the first industrial revolution; it is farther and farther removed from reality. Very little interesting work is going on in this area except possibly in training techniques, and like so many of my other points, progress requires new concepts and new approaches to theory.

Organization theory comes from a world in which work was broken down by functional specialization, the heritage of the first industrial revolution—of Adam Smith and his pin factory. As we mechanized, we mechanized around these functional specializations in the interest of higher productivity. We built our machines accordingly. It is only in comparatively recent times that we began to concentrate on progress.

In today's world, technology allows us to do many things. The main problem we have had in using information technology properly is our inherited attitude toward organization structure. Today we have a technology that allows us to build machine systems which cut across departmental structures and more nearly parallel the real organic enterprise, but we are blocked from the effective use of this technology by our often unconscious organizational blinders. Here is an area in which there will be very exciting and important changes.

I have made this my last point. It is basic and important, yet will be slow to develop. Much of management will go right on as it has in the past, embracing what was appropriate in another world. The major activities and the major successes are going to be those which consider quite different approaches in theory, not only organization theory, but as I have already indicated in so many of my observations, new approaches in many areas that we have up to now been able to take for granted as basic and fixed.

What is needed very badly in nearly all these areas is a small amount of very creative work responding to the reality of a totally changed management environment. This is the essence and the main point of this article.

In all our concern with the social consequences of technical change, we take the technical change for granted, and we often come to feel it is going too fast. But as the distinguished economist, Kenneth Boulding, has pointed out, the greatest problem now is how to advance technology, not how to deal with technology that is advancing too rapidly.

The need for technology is still there. Most of the world's population is on the edge of starvation despite today's science and technology. These human problems must be faced. The problem for management is how to advance science and technology, how to apply them, and how to apply them with compassion and attention to the human consequences.

A quotation of the philosopher Alfred North Whitehead seems to me to best state the note on which I would like to close: "It is the business of the future to be dangerous; and it is among the merits of science that it equip the future for its duties. . . . In the immediate future there will be less security than in the immediate past, less stability. It must be admitted

364   *Management: Selected Readings*

that there is a degree of instability which is inconsistent with civilization. But on the whole, the great ages have been unstable ages." (*Science and the Modern World,* New American Library, 1944).

QUESTIONS FOR REVIEW AND DISCUSSION

1. List the nine points that author Diebold considers important in considering management in the future. Select one of these points and discuss it fully.
2. Whose responsibility is it to improve our intelligent use of data so that effective integrated decision systems are employed? How do you surmise this accomplishment will be won?
3. What changes in the development of managers do you feel will be necessary as the present situation of managers with little data making the right decisions becomes one of having all the data, asking the right questions, deciding, and interpreting the results? Discuss.

42. The Pharmacist as Futurist*

EDWARD S. CORNISH

Tomorrow began yesterday. In laboratories around the world new discoveries made possible the drugs that are being developed today and will be on your pharmacy shelf tomorrow.

The field of pharmacology is changing rapidly. Indications are that the changes may be even more rapid tomorrow. Thus pharmacists have special reason to be aware of the future and the changes to come.

Many may not be aware, however, that a whole new field of study has sprung up in response to man's increasing need to know more about the world into which he is being rushed by technological and social progress. The new field is variously called *futuristics, prognostics, prospection,* and *conjecture.* Some scholars refer to the discipline-in-formation as *futures studies,* with *futures* pluralized to emphasize that many possible future developments are being studied.

There is nothing mysterious about the methods of the new futurists. Admittedly there is much uncertainty and guesswork in their methods. Their forecasts currently are based mainly on studies of technological and social trends and the opinions of experts in given fields. Increasingly however, they are using such sophisticated techniques as mathematical models and simulation by computers.

The general view of the futurists may be summarized as follows:

Human life changes in important ways from year to year and decade to decade. For example, people today enjoy a far higher average standard of living than did people 50 years ago, and this affects the way their lives are led.

It is possible to identify many important changes as they are occurring, and, therefore, to make forecasts of likely future developments. One may note, for example, that transportation methods have been improving stead-

* Source: Reprinted with permission of *American Druggist,* July 13, 1970, pp. 30, 57, 87. Edward S. Cornish, World Future Society, Washington, D.C.

ily, and therefore anticipate that transportation 20 years from now will be considerably faster than it is today. One may also try to imagine the various consequences that will flow from such an improvement in transportation.

The future's not fixed, but can be deliberately shaped by human efforts. Science and technology are continuously enlarging man's control over the world; hence the future will increasingly be what man chooses to make it. When people become aware that the burning of coal and gasoline means an increase in the pollution of the atmosphere, they can act to prevent the realization of the future that they have foreseen.

In recent years, a number of respected organizations have become engaged in the study of the future. The Ford Foundation sponsored Resources for the Future, Inc., a research institute in Washington, D.C. The American Academy of Arts and Sciences in Boston has created a Commission on the Year 2000, headed by Columbia University sociologist Daniel Bell. An Institute for the future has been set up in Middletown, Connecticut.

The World Future Society, a nonprofit association serving people interested in the future, was organized in Washington, D.C., in 1966, and now has 11,000 members throughout the world. The Society's bimonthly publication, *The Futurist,* reports the forecasts that scientists and others are making for the coming decade. . . . The society's founders recognized that people of every profession and nationality have a legitimate interest in the future, and therefore anyone interested in the future is welcome to membership. A person may join the Society by sending his name, address and occupation, plus $10 for his first year's dues to: World Future Society, P.O. Box 30369, Bethesda Station, Washington, D.C. 20014.

Futurists believe that the study of the future will give mankind increasing power to make the future what it wants rather than see it become something it does not want. We have, curiously, little power over the present, for we cannot quickly change either our environment or ourselves. With enough time, however, we can change things quite dramatically.

Those who have worked in government report that programs, policies, and doctrines often change very slowly in response to current decisions—even when made by the President—but at the same time things may be changing very rapidly as a result of decisions made in the past. The reason is simple: it takes time to implement a decision. That means that the earlier a decision is made, the more potent it can ultimately be.

Even when we seem unable to change the future in ways that we would like, we can at least accommodate to future developments, if we anticipate them in time. This accommodation, which goes on for the most part at an unconscious level, is more important than we realize.

Accommodation is important because the rapid rate of social change has people reeling. The world is changing faster and faster. At the same time, people are living longer. In 1900, Americans could expect to live only about 45 years; now they survive more than 70. This means more and more people are spending their mature years in a world that is very different from the one they grew up in.

Anyone over 40," management consultant Peter Drucker points out, "lives in a different world from that in which he came to manhood. He lives as if he had migrated, full grown, to a new and strange country."

Today many of us are like buggywhip makers as we stare blankly at the rocket gantries and computer consoles of a civilization that has no use for our product. We have begun to experience "future shock"—the disorientation that occurs when too many changes take place too fast. We simply withdraw from a world that has become alien and incomprehensible.

Even pharmacists, who surely have grown accustomed to the appearance of new drugs, may be surprised at a few of the things that the experts foresee in the medicine of the coming decades. One recent study was made by Smith, Kline and French (SK&F) Laboratories in Philadelphia. Dr. A. Douglas Bender and his collegues reported on the study last year in a volume entitled "A Delphic Study of the Future of Medicine."

Delphic refers to the special technique used by SK&F researchers to ask questions of a number of experts. This technique, originally developed at the RAND Corporation in Santa Monica, California, has become one of the best established methods of getting a consensus of expert opinion concerning a possible future development. The experts are questioned individually and do not know what their fellow respondents have said or even

FIGURE 1. Comparison of Estimates from Three Delphic Studies

Statement	*SK&F Extramural*	*Rand*	*SK&F Intramural*
	Median Date of the Achievement		
Implanted artificial organs made of plastic and/or electronic components ..	1983	1982	1985
Chemical alleviation of serious mental disorders such as schizophrenia	1993	1992	1985
Chemical control over hereditary defects	1998	2000	2009
Chemical synthesis of protein for food .	1978	1990	1985
Use of personality control drugs	1983	1983	1995
Worldwide immunization against bacterial and viral diseases	1993	1994	2009
Stimulation of new organ growth	1988	2007	after 2017
Ability to control the aging process permitting significant extension of life span	1993	2023	after 2017
Use of drugs to raise intelligence level .	1978	2012	1985
Creation of primitive life form	1978	1989	after 2017
Use of telepathy and SP in communication	Never	Never	after 2017

who they are. On a second round of questioning, results of the first round are given, along with reasons given by each of the experts for the choice he made. The experts are still not identified, however, to avoid a follow-the-leader effect. The questioning is repeated several times, with respondents given reasons from their fellow panel members each time, so that they can weigh these in their own speculations.

SK&F queried experts both inside and outside the company and, interestingly enough, many of the questions were the same as those asked during a pioneering RAND Corp. study several years earlier. Thus it was possible to make a comparison between the experts inside the company, those outside, and the other experts earlier interviewed by RAND. The results were remarkably similar, as the compilation shown by Figure 1.

Another study of the future of medicine was made in 1969 by the Office of Health Economics in London. The 40 specialists participating in the study foresaw the greatest progress during the next two decades coming in organ transplants, prevention of coronary and vascular diseases, effective medicine for both viral and bacterial infections, and many mental disorders.

Problems they anticipated would be harder to solve include cancers, arthritis and those related to drug addiction.

QUESTIONS FOR REVIEW AND DISCUSSION

1. Comment on the data shown in Figure 1 of the above article.
2. Do you agree with the statement: "The future is not fixed, it can be deliberately shaped by human effort." Why?
3. Explain what is meant by Delphic Study Technique used by researchers.
4. Identify and relate the objective of the World Future Society.